Also by David A. Nichols

Lincoln and the Indians: Civil War Policy and Politics

A Matter OF Justice

Eisenhower and the Beginning of the Civil Rights Revolution

DAVID A. NICHOLS

SIMON & SCHUSTER

New York   London   Toronto   Sydney

SIMON & SCHUSTER
1230 Avenue of the Americas
New York, NY 10020

First Simon & Schuster hardcover edition September 2007

For information about special discounts for bulk purchases,
please contact Simon & Schuster Special Sales at
1-800-456-6798 or business@simonandschuster.com

Designed by Jaime Putorti

Manufactured in the United States of America

10 9 8 7 6 5 4 3 2 1

Library of Congress Cataloging-in-Publication Data

Nichols, David A. (David Allen), date.
    A matter of justice: Eisenhower and the beginning of the civil rights
revolution / David A. Nichols—1st Simon & Schuster hardcover ed.
        p.   cm.
    Includes bibliographical references and index.
    1. Eisenhower, Dwight D. (Dwight David), 1890–1969—Political and social
views. 2. Eisenhower, Dwight D. (Dwight David), 1890–1969—Relations with
African Americans. 3. African Americans—Civil rights—History—20th century.
4. Civil rights movements—United States—History—20th century. 5. African
Americans—Legal status, laws, etc.—History—20th century. 6. Civil rights—
United States—History—20th century. 7. School integration—United States—
History—20th century. 8. United States—Race relations—History—20th century.
9. United States—Politics and government—1953–1961. 10. Presidents—United
States—Biography. I. Title.
    E836.N53 2007
    973.921092—dc22   2007016867
ISBN-13: 978-1-4165-4150-9
ISBN-10:   1-4165-4150-0

To Grace, whose love, support, and wonderful assistance
made this book possible.

Contents

A Matter of Justice

Introduction

We have been pursuing this quietly, not tub-thumping, and we have not tried to claim political credit. This is a matter of justice, not of anything else.
—EISENHOWER ON HIS CIVIL RIGHTS POLICIES, OCTOBER 12, 1956

Fifty years ago, President Dwight D. Eisenhower ordered troops into Little Rock, Arkansas, to enforce a federal court order for school desegregation. That was an extraordinary action under any circumstances, but especially in a former Confederate state. A half century later, a president sending the army into an American city to enforce a court order would still generate huge controversy.

Little Rock was the tip of the civil rights iceberg for Eisenhower. As I will show in the following pages, during his presidency Eisenhower desegregated the District of Columbia (including its schools), completed desegregation of the armed forces, appointed progressive federal judges at all levels (including Earl Warren and four other Supreme Court justices), proposed and secured passage of the first civil rights legislation in over eighty years, and took steps to enforce the Supreme Court's school desegregation decision in *Brown v. Board of Education*, most dramatically by his military intervention in Little Rock.

Yet the myth persists that Eisenhower was, as even Stephen E. Ambrose, an admiring biographer, put it, "no leader at all" in civil rights and that his "refusal to lead was almost criminal." In 1991, Ambrose endorsed what he called "the best single volume now available on the Eisenhower presidency," in which Chester Pach, Jr., and Elmo Richardson asserted that Eisenhower's sympathies "clearly lay with southern whites, who he patiently said needed time to adjust, not with southern blacks, whom he impatiently criticized for wanting basic rights too soon." Arthur Schlesinger, Jr., in *The Cycles of American History,* called racial justice and McCarthyism "the great moral issues of the Eisenhower years" but concluded that "Eisenhower evaded them both." Tom Wicker, in a recent book in Schlesinger's *The American Presidents* series, contends that, given Eisenhower's popularity, he "might well have swung most of the nation in acceptance, however reluctant, of the Supreme Court's interpretation of the Constitution." Instead he was guilty of "a moral failing and a lack of vision."[1]

Why did the myth arise? First, Eisenhower was a unique and complex president; study of his leadership requires a multifaceted approach. He was not a professional politician, yet he was politically successful. He was a military leader, yet he was suspicious of reliance on military power. He detested political demagoguery, but he was frequently deceptive about his plans and objectives. In public he often projected a smiling, amiable, grandfatherly image, but in private he was intellectually sharp, sometimes profane, prudently decisive, and a skilled manager of men.

Above all, as a soldier Ike was a man of deeds rather than words. But historians and journalists love words; the least arduous way to study a president is to focus on his public utterances. Now, more than ever, politicians are judged by their "sound bites," and Eisenhower was not a sound bite politician. While presidential rhetoric is important, a myopic preoccupation with public statements produces a distorted picture of Eisenhower's leadership. We must look closely at what he did, not just what he said, or we will miss much of what Eisenhower was about in civil rights.[2]

Second, many documents revealing Eisenhower's leadership have either been unavailable or neglected. In the past generation, additional records on the Eisenhower presidency and civil rights have become available; in 2006, thousands of pages of documents on civil rights were released from the papers of Max Rabb, Eisenhower's chief White House aide on civil rights. But scholars have also neglected the documents that were already available, relying on public statements rather than the diaries, the minutes of meetings, the notes on telephone conversations, and the private correspondence, that illuminate Eisenhower's private intent. Careful attention to these documents casts Eisenhower's civil rights leadership in a new light.

Third, there is the issue of bias. Significant numbers of academics (myself included) have traditionally allied themselves with a particular political perspective. But a partisan explanation is too simplistic. Once an interpretation of a president's record, or a theory of presidential leadership, becomes conventional wisdom, historians and political scientists tend to treat it like holy writ, propagating the argument in articles and books and teaching it to undergraduate and graduate students. Political scientist Richard Neustadt and his followers defined successful presidential leadership for a generation of scholars and journalists, basing their model on Franklin D. Roosevelt and John F. Kennedy, and denigrating Eisenhower's allegedly indecisive style of governance.[3]

Finally, neglect of the Eisenhower record is rooted in its historic context. Ike was a nineteenth-century man, raised in an era of blatant white supremacy in American life. Despite losing the Civil War, the South eventually won the peace. By the time Eisenhower was born in 1890, slavery had been supplanted by a system of racial segregation, enshrined in law in the South and in practice in the North. "Jim Crow" society was characterized by segregated restaurants, restrooms, athletic events, water fountains, parks, swimming pools, entertainment, and schools. By the beginning of the twentieth century, nothing less than a social revolution could overturn this system of institutionalized racism sanctioned by an 1896 decision of the Supreme Court, *Plessy v. Ferguson*, that maintained that "separate but equal" facilities and accommodations for blacks were legal.

It was Dwight Eisenhower's lot to serve as president when frustration with this situation boiled over. The new climate was driven by the increasing importance of black votes in northern cities, more aggressive and sophisticated civil rights organizations, and soldiers, returning from World War II and the Korean War, who increasingly resisted the contradiction of fighting for freedom abroad while being denied it at home. This context is critical for understanding the Eisenhower era. The progressive racial standards of later times, so ingrained in our minds, should not be indiscriminately applied to the '50s. We must try to see the world as the men and women of the early 1950s saw it. Then we can appropriately assess their efforts, including Dwight Eisenhower's, toward achieving equality.

Invoking context does not mean we excuse the sins of a past generation. Otherwise, we could explain away the institution of slavery by invoking the mores of its time. This volume is not intended to minimize the incredible hardships that Jim Crow imposed on African-American citizens. Neither does it pretend to do justice to the real heroes of the civil rights movement, the African-American men, women, and even the children (as in Little Rock) who risked their lives to change America's racial climate. Likewise, the book does not analyze the impact of Eisenhower's racial policies on America's role in the world; others have addressed that issue.

I will not attempt to make Ike into a civil rights saint. My purpose here, rather, is to look over his shoulder to see what he saw, confront what he confronted, and help us discern, as best we can, his intent and accomplishments in domestic racial politics. Once that is done, we can better assess Eisenhower's place in the pantheon of American presidents.

CHAPTER ONE

The Candidate

I believe we should eliminate every vestige of segregation in the District of Columbia.
—PRESIDENTIAL CANDIDATE DWIGHT D. EISENHOWER,
SEPTEMBER 8, 1952

General Eisenhower was ready to run for president. Over the years, he had seamlessly cloaked his personal ambitions in a call to duty. Ike wanted the Republican Party to summon him to serve his country once more, so he purposely delayed a formal announcement of his candidacy. Eisenhower had learned long ago "to retain as long as possible a position of flexibility—that is, to wait until the last possible moment before announcing any positive decision."[1]

Herbert Brownell, Jr. was tired of losing. The New York attorney had managed Republican Governor Thomas E. Dewey's unsuccessful presidential campaigns in 1944 and 1948. Despite voters' support for Eisenhower in the early primaries, Brownell knew that Ohio Senator Robert A. Taft's candidacy made a draft impossible. Mutual friends had urged Eisenhower to consult with Brownell and, on March 18, 1952, the general wrote a confidential letter inviting him to Paris, where Eisenhower was serving as Supreme Allied Commander of the North Atlantic Treaty Organization (NATO). Brownell grabbed the next available plane and crossed the Atlantic under an assumed name. The moment was at hand for the general to end his silence.

Brownell spent March 24 at General Eisenhower's headquarters. Brownell later called the conversation "the experience of a life-time." He found Eisenhower "plainspoken and warm," ready to apply his experience to solving the nation's problems. Brownell probed the candidate's convictions on the Constitution and civil rights. The general recounted his efforts to abolish racial barriers in the army and, as Brownell recalled, stated "flatly" that if elected, his "first order of business" would be "to eliminate discrimination against black citizens in every area under the jurisdiction of the fed-eral government."[2]

Prepared for Leadership

Eisenhower had traveled a long road to this moment. He was born into a segregated society in 1890—six years before the Supreme Court ruled, in *Plessy v. Ferguson,* that "separate but equal" facilities were constitutional. His home town of Abilene, Kansas, numbered about a hundred blacks among the city's three-thousand-plus resi-dents. Segregation existed there but was not as rigid as in the Deep South; blacks had their own baseball team, churches, and social ac-tivities but attended some events with whites.[3] In that environment, Ike routinely learned to address Negroes as individuals, not as a race.

Eisenhower attended the U.S. Military Academy at West Point, which, despite a sprinkling of black cadets through the years, was a white establishment. His first assignments after graduation included posts in Texas, Maryland, and Georgia, where both the military and civilian society were segregated. Until World War II, even his north-ern assignments exposed him to blacks serving primarily in subordi-nate positions.

Despite his limited exposure to Negro issues, Eisenhower came to embrace a set of egalitarian principles. The probable sources for these ideals included his mother's teaching, his religious heritage in the River Brethren Mennonite sect, his study at West Point, and, in particular, a stimulating three-year assignment in the early 1920s with General Fox Conner in Panama. Conner, the owner of a huge library, had taken a special interest in Ike's intellectual development. Eisenhower's Panama duties left him with abundant time for study, and he later termed his service with Conner "a graduate school in military affairs and the humanities." It was in Panama that the young officer developed an unshakable reverence for the Constitution and the courts.[4] Eisenhower came to believe that the stability of the country depended on the American people supporting the law of the land, as interpreted by the Supreme Court.

The heartland culture that nurtured Eisenhower had also molded Herbert Brownell. His hometown was Peru, Nebraska, two hundred miles north of Abilene. Brownell possessed a large Lincoln library and was a sophisticated scholar of the Fourteenth and Fifteenth Amendments to the Constitution—the post–Civil War amendments that had granted citizenship rights to former slaves.[5]

Brownell's associates admired him to the point of adoration. A former law partner recalls that Brownell "combined seriousness with a generosity of spirit and an unfailing (often self-deprecating) humor that made him seem serene no matter how stressful the circumstances." Brownell spoke with "enormous knowledge and experience" and "listeners, no matter how notable and official, hung on his words as if they were hearing the voice of the law or history itself." Tom Stephens, appointments secretary in the Eisenhower White House, revered "the quiet, dignified manner" in which Brownell handled difficult problems, and observed that nothing intimidated him. Warren Olney III, an associate of California's governor Earl Warren, insisted after the 1952 election that he "did not want to go to Washington under any circumstances or for any position." But one interview with Herbert Brownell changed his mind, and Olney signed on to head the criminal division in the Justice Department. Olney warned a colleague preparing to meet with Brownell: "I think you will find that Mr. Brownell is a very persuasive man."[6]

This was the man to whom General Eisenhower, on March 24, pledged to invoke federal authority to combat discrimination. At this point in life, Eisenhower was not easily impressed; he had dealt with the giants of world affairs—Franklin Delano Roosevelt, Winston Churchill, Charles De Gaulle, and Josef Stalin. But the general was intrigued with Herbert Brownell. This was a man who could guide the inexperienced general through the minefield of presidential politics, and mentor him in the politics of civil rights. A year later, Eisenhower expressed awe in his diary that Brownell, for all his political experience, had not become "hardboiled." "The contrary seems to be true," Eisenhower wrote. "Certainly he has never suggested to me any action which could be considered in slightest degree dishonest or unethical. His reputation with others seems to match my own high opinion of his capabilities as a lawyer, his qualities as a leader, and his character as a man. I am devoted to him and am perfectly confident that he would make an outstanding President of the United States."[7]

Brownell, that "persuasive man," convinced Eisenhower that he should return to the United States and fight for the nomination of his party. A week later, Ike wrote to President Truman, asking for release from his command. By June 1, the general was back in Washington; he announced his candidacy on June 4 in Abilene.[8]

Eisenhower and Black Soldiers

Civil rights would not be a major issue in the 1952 presidential election. A cluster of cases—subsequently known as *Brown v. Board of Education*—challenging *Plessy v. Ferguson* was scheduled for review by the Supreme Court, but no ruling was imminent. Eisenhower's commitment to Brownell to invoke federal authority against discrimination was not a political strategy aimed at garnering votes; it was, as he stated years later, "a matter of justice."[9]

World War II had profoundly affected Eisenhower's perception of blacks and discrimination. In the segregated army, black soldiers were often detailed to serve the needs of top officers. In August 1942, not long after he was appointed Commanding General, European Theater of Operations, Ike was assigned a black valet, Sergeant John A. Moaney. Their relationship mirrored the contradictions of race relations in Eisenhower's America. Moaney's position as the subordinate of a white man echoed the inequalities of slavery and the Jim Crow system, but the two men became devoted to each other. Moaney served Eisenhower from 1942 until Ike's death in 1969. Eisenhower declared that he and the sergeant were "inseparable" and that "in my daily life, he is about the irreplaceable man."[10]

Men such as Moaney lacked opportunity for advancement in the armed forces; this reality clashed with Eisenhower's egalitarian values. Although he was obligated to comply with government policy requiring segregation in the armed forces, Ike sought ways to mitigate the impact of discrimination. In March 1942, the year Sergeant Moaney joined him, Eisenhower, acting in his capacity as chief of the army's operations division, communicated to the army's chief of staff, General George C. Marshall, his concerns for "the colored troop problem." Eisenhower had confronted tensions over black troop deployments everywhere from Australia to Alaska to South America. At one point, the Allies feared losing Australia to the Axis powers; so Eisenhower assigned black divisions to the country. When the Australian ambassador informed him that Australian law forbade bringing Negroes into the country, Ike recalled, he was "very firm—said all right—no troops." Frightened Australian leaders responded the next morning with a flood of cables reversing their position but insisting that the troops be withdrawn when the emergency was over. Eisenhower told his chief of staff, General Alfred M. Gruenther, "to stand his ground and make no differential between blood."[11]

In 1944, leaders at the National Association for the Advancement of Colored People (NAACP) obtained a confidential directive issued by Eisenhower on March 1 that made officers responsible for "scrupulous enforcement" of the principle, "Equal opportunities of service and of recreation are the right of every American soldier regardless of branch, race, color, or creed." Eisenhower particularly pushed for authority to allow Negro soldiers, normally restricted to logistical support, to volunteer for combat. In December 1944, at the time of the Battle of the Bulge in Europe, Ike needed all the troops he could get. General John C. H. Lee issued a directive, approved by Eisenhower, proclaiming: "The opportunity to volunteer will be extended to all soldiers without regard to color or race but preference will normally be given to individuals who have had some basic training in infantry." The War Department declared the order contrary to policy and forced Eisenhower to withdraw it, destroy the original message, and substitute a more innocuous statement.[12]

On January 7, 1945, Eisenhower resumed his campaign to

permit black soldiers to volunteer for combat. He complained to General Marshall that more than 100,000 Negroes were performing "back-breaking manual work" on docks, depots, and roads, but were denied the chance to serve on the front lines. To Eisenhower, this was unjust: "I feel that in existing circumstances I cannot deny the Negro volunteer a chance to serve in battle," Ike wrote to Marshall. Eisenhower finally persuaded Marshall to authorize a modest infantry unit. Nearly 2,500 Negroes initially volunteered, and some of them accepted a reduction in grade to qualify. Eventually, 4,562 Negro soldiers enlisted for combat duty.[13]

Eisenhower pressured his generals to filter these black units into the combat forces. General George S. Patton, commander of the Third Army in Europe, worried that his southern soldiers would rebel. "Our experience was just the opposite," Eisenhower recalled. "There was not a single objection brought to my attention. On the contrary from all sides there came heartwarming reports of the success of the experiment," including from Patton. Some of the black squads had Negro leaders, some white. "Some of these white units, by the way, were southern units," Eisenhower told a press conference in 1956. "This was the thing that convinced me that the thing could be done."[14] Amid the stresses of a great war, Eisenhower had quietly undermined the myth that Negroes were unwilling and inadequate warriors.

By the end of the war, Eisenhower's principles on race relations had crystallized. In 1946, Dr. Milton Eisenhower, then president of Kansas State University, asked his brother for suggestions for a course on citizenship he was instituting. Ike responded: "In presenting the objectives of the course I should bear down hard on *elimination of racial intolerance.*" The course, he wrote, should confront students with "the obligations of citizenship as well as its privileges, which could of course be done through the history of some of the sacrifices that have been made ever since 1215 to establish the equality of the citizen before the law."[15]

In 1947, Lawrence Dunbar Reddick, a curator at the New York Public Library, asked Eisenhower for a statement on the service of Negro soldiers in the war. Eisenhower advocated evaluating recruits purely on merit, and expressed his regret that the service of blacks in the army "has not always received the public recognition or realistic appreciation it merited." He declared: "Both as Chief of Staff and as an American citizen I oppose any discrimination in the rights and privileges awarded American soldiers based upon color or race."[16]

As postwar army chief of staff in 1946–47, Eisenhower sought partial integration, but army officials resisted. Eisenhower claimed that he "fought the staff on the issue." In the peacetime army, resistance to desegregation revolved around the social life of the army. The opponents argued, Ike recalled, "that through integration we would get into all kinds of difficulty in staging soldiers' dances and other social events." The pressure was "to get the soldiers home," so "little progress toward integration was made during that period." In early 1947, in response to inquiries from the NAACP, Eisenhower ordered units as small as companies to be integrated into previously all-white units, but integration of individuals was still forbidden by the government.[17]

During these postwar years, President Harry Truman laid important groundwork for presidential leadership in civil rights. On December 5, 1946, Truman issued an executive order establishing the President's Committee on Civil Rights. In October 1947, the committee issued its report—"To Secure These Rights." The report contained ten recommendations, including a civil rights commission, a civil rights division in the Justice Department, antilynching legislation; protection of the right to vote; a fair employment practices commission; and home rule for the District of Columbia.[18]

Eisenhower was succeeded by Omar N. Bradley as army chief of staff on February 7, 1948. Eisenhower was invited, prior to his assuming the presidency of Columbia University, to testify before the Senate Armed Services Committee concerning the postwar status of the army. Two days before Eisenhower was scheduled to testify on April 3, a civil rights leader endorsed the general's views on segregation in the military. Walter White, the executive secretary of the NAACP, published a column in which he recalled a three-hour conversation with Eisenhower in 1944, just prior to the invasion of Normandy. White concluded that, in regard to segregation in the military, "Eisenhower was implacable in his opposition to that system so we confined our discussion to practical means of abolishing it as swiftly as possible."[19]

Despite his personal views, segregation of the armed forces was still the policy of the United States government; Eisenhower, the obedient soldier, was unlikely to oppose government policy in front of a Senate committee. Concerning Negro troops, Eisenhower stated: "We found that they fought better when distributed in small units with the white troops." He continued, "I personally have always stood since that time for organizing the Negro down to include units no larger than platoons." Eisenhower sounded ambivalent about eliminating individual segregation. The Negro, he worried, was "less well educated than his brother citizen who is white, and if you make a complete amalgamation, what you are going to have is, in every company the Negro is going to be relegated to the minor jobs, and he is never going to get his promotion to such grades as technical sergeant, master sergeant, and so on, because the competition is too tough. If, on the other hand, he is in smaller units of his own, he can go up to that rate, and I believe he is entitled to the chance to show his wares." Eisenhower expressed doubts about the effectiveness of legislation to combat discrimination. "I do believe," he stated, "that if we attempt merely by passing a lot of laws to force someone to like someone else, we are just going to get into trouble."[20]

The general could not know that Harry Truman was planning a surprise. In July 1948, Truman's presidential campaign was in difficulty. Southern segregationists had bolted the Democratic Party and were running Governor Strom Thurmond of South Carolina for president, while former vice president Henry Wallace led a revolt on the left. Governor Dewey, whose campaign was again managed by Herbert Brownell, seemed poised to win the White House. Campaign strategist and White House counsel Clark Clifford implored Truman to take action to enlist the support of Negro voters in northern cities. On July 26—just days after the Democratic convention—Truman surprised the nation by signing Executive Order 9981, requiring equal treatment and opportunity for Negroes in the United States military.[21]

Eisenhower's April testimony, coming nearly four months before

Truman's executive order, would prove controversial for years to come. In the wake of Truman's order, Eisenhower's comments seemed remarkably conservative for a general who had advocated progressive policies during the war. Perhaps Eisenhower had not made his peace with the integration of individual soldiers in the military; his initiatives had focused on blending small black units into white divisions. He correctly recognized that, badly implemented, desegregation could make the lot of black soldiers even worse. Still, he had repeated a common stereotype in assuming that all black soldiers were uneducated and unable to compete with whites on merit. If Eisenhower had known about Truman's plans, he might have felt freer to reprise his 1947 statement opposing "any discrimination in the rights and privileges awarded American soldiers based upon color or race."[22]

What Manner of Man?

Eisenhower's experience with black soldiers provides a partial backdrop for his approach to civil rights. Who he was—as a man and a military commander—reveals even more. By 1952, Eisenhower was a unique presidential candidate who had developed well-honed ways of doing business. He possessed extraordinary executive and strategic planning skills. Ike had been the army's premier military staff officer, his service coveted by generals George Marshall and Douglas MacArthur. He developed a "staff system" that required competent specialists who were assigned clear-cut responsibilities. As supreme commander in Europe, Eisenhower did not make war himself—Eisenhower never commanded troops directly in the field—so he cultivated the habit of recruiting strong-minded and competent subordinates to whom responsibility could be delegated.[23]

Eisenhower's skills at delegation enabled him to oversee a remarkable span of issues. He would raise questions, make certain a subordinate understood a policy and its outer boundaries, and expect a timely report. Fred I. Greenstein finds that Eisenhower tailored his delegation to his subordinates, keeping some on a short leash and granting wide latitude to others, especially Brownell. General Andrew Goodpaster, Ike's staff secretary and national security aide in the White House, once said to him, "It must take guts to delegate." Eisenhower responded by quoting the adage from the German general von Moltke that "centralization is the refuge of fear."[24]

Eisenhower did not like "yes" people. The rule, according to Goodpaster, was "No concurrence through silence." Eisenhower was "a good listener" who asked questions, then often "reserved his judgment and said that he wanted to talk with others." He was notorious for listening intently at length in a meeting, then halting the proceedings and summarizing the subject in stark, sometimes profane terms.[25]

Eisenhower, the war leader, had to be prepared for anything an enemy might do. Contingency plans were routine in his world; he did not disdain subterfuge, whether military or political. For instance, prior to D-Day, Eisenhower approved activities and messages about a fictitious army that were designed to mislead the Germans into thinking the Allies would launch their invasion across the English Channel at Calais, when the real site was Normandy.[26] To Ike, misleading an opponent was acceptable and often essential—an approach he would apply as president to civil rights as well as foreign affairs.

Eisenhower's ready smile and courtly demeanor covered an intense, hard-driving personality. His temper was legendary; General Wilton ("Jerry") Persons, a longtime aide, likened Eisenhower's temper "to a skyrocket." "It would blow up," Persons recalled, "and then everything would be alright again." On his sixty-seventh birthday, Eisenhower wrote to a friend about how he had developed "patience and moderation." "For a man of my temperament," he said, "it wasn't easy." Ike's intense self-restraint regimen eventually produced a dispassionate, somewhat misleading public persona that some observers characterized as "aloof."[27]

The presidential candidate whom Herbert Brownell courted in 1952 was, in many respects, a loner, a man who had arduously reined in his temper and his response to criticism. Personally intense, Eisenhower projected the public image of a smiling, gentleman soldier who rarely criticized anyone, no matter how odious.

William Ewald, a former speechwriter who assisted the former president with his memoirs, captured Ike's prescription for handling personal attacks: "Don't see, don't feel, don't admit, and don't answer;
just ignore your attacker and keep smiling."[28] That formula would
serve him well in running for president. It also profoundly influenced perceptions of his leadership on civil rights.[29]

Eisenhower, the Candidate

Eisenhower's role in the defeat of the Nazis in Europe, his military
bearing, and his infectious smile made him the perfect candidate,
but the transition from general to politician was not easy. Ike did
not perceive himself as a party leader. Still, he was a master of bu-
reaucratic and international political skills. He had carefully plotted
his extraordinary rise to power in the army. As wartime Allied commander, he had employed his relational skills to hold the unruly
Western alliance together, dealing successfully with aggressive generals and egocentric politicians such as Churchill and Roosevelt.

In the process, Eisenhower, seeing his personal popularity as a
resource for leadership, learned to protect his own prestige. Herbert Brownell remembered Ike's "reluctance to associate himself
with difficult policy decisions," especially in civil rights, and admitted that sometimes Eisenhower's "techniques of delegation put us
out on the proverbial limb." Brownell recalled that White House
press secretary James Hagerty once complained to Eisenhower
about having to deliver some unwelcome news to a roomful of hostile reporters. Eisenhower responded: "Better you, Jim, than me."
Richard Nixon, Ike's vice president, later opined that Eisenhower
was "a far more complex and devious man than most people realized, and in the best sense of those words."[30]

Eisenhower called his political philosophy "the middle way," distinguishing his leadership from the New Deal on the left and Republican isolationism on the right. Abraham Lincoln provided him
a model for walking politically between the extremes. Brigadier
General Bradford G. Chynoweth once wrote Eisenhower and criticized Lincoln as a "radical Republican." "You call Lincoln a radical,"
Eisenhower responded, "but every bit of reading I have done on his

life convinces me that in many ways he was the greatest compromiser and the most astute master of expedience that we have known." Eisenhower concluded: "I believe that the true radical is the fellow who is standing in the middle and battling both extremes."[31] That point of view would eventually irritate civil rights activists, who would resent the implication that they were "extremists" equivalent to segregationists in the South.

The aspiring candidate disliked traditional political rhetoric, abhorring anything that smelled of demagoguery. A campaign staff member might urge Eisenhower to make a statement on an issue and his typical response would be, "I've already said it." He would stubbornly ignore advice to "repeat it and repeat it and repeat it and repeat it and repeat it."[32] That style, when he became president, sometimes was an obstacle to communicating his goals and achievements in civil rights.

Eisenhower's approach to political speech was not naïve; it was intentional. He described his distaste for demagoguery in a confidential letter in 1953: "I deplore and deprecate the table-pounding, name-calling methods that columnists so much love. This is not because of any failure to love a good fight; it merely represents my belief that such methods are normally futile." Eisenhower concluded: "I simply must be permitted to follow my own methods, because to adopt someone else's would be so unnatural as to create the conviction that I was acting falsely."[33]

Eisenhower preferred action to rhetoric. After World War II, a Negro newspaper reported that Eisenhower's high school teammates had once refused to play a football game against a team that included a Negro, and young Ike addressed his teammates in the dressing room on justice and fair play. Eisenhower later corrected the account, recalling that his teammates had individually resisted playing the center position opposite the black player. Ike normally played end, but "I played center that day for the only time in my life." He "shook hands with the chap both before and after the game." The rest of the team, Eisenhower recalled, was "a bit ashamed." "But," he declared, "I did *not* make a speech!"[34]

That was vintage Eisenhower, setting an example rather than preaching. Like the young football player, the mature general had little faith in the power of words; he had not won the war in Europe by making speeches.

Courting the South

On June 4, 1952, in Abilene, a powerful thunderstorm interrupted Eisenhower's speech launching his campaign. He touched on multiple issues but was vague on civil rights. He advocated the government's elimination of inequities wherever it had authority, but implied that the states should resolve most civil rights issues.[35]

Brownell brilliantly managed the Eisenhower candidacy at the Republican convention, putting the old guard on the defensive, beating them in delegate seating contests, and outperforming them in public relations. Civil rights was not a divisive issue within the party. The platform plank was ambiguous regarding civil rights, recognizing "the primary responsibility of each state to order and control its domestic institutions." The federal government could "take supplemental action within its constitutional jurisdiction to oppose discrimination against race, religion or national origin." The platform pledged the appointment of "qualified persons, without distinction of race, religion or national origin"; action toward eliminating lynching and the poll tax; "appropriate action to end segregation in the District of Columbia"; and legislation "to further just and equitable treatment in the area of discriminatory employment practices," and that would not duplicate state efforts.[36]

Confident that the general would win the election, Brownell left the campaign following the convention to return to his law practice. Eisenhower was faced with campaigning against the Democratic candidate, Governor Adlai Stevenson of Illinois, without the man whose advice he most trusted, a situation he eventually came to deplore. Ike himself decided to campaign extensively in the South, something a Republican presidential candidate had rarely done. On the stump, Eisenhower cited his years of army service in the South and his "southern friends"—a formulation certain to make civil rights activists, particularly African-American leaders, uneasy.[37]

The centerpiece of Eisenhower's courtship of the South was his opposition to a federal fair employment practices commission

(FEPC) that could require contractors with the federal government to practice nondiscrimination in hiring and promotion. The FEPC had been an issue for Negroes since 1941; President Roosevelt, by executive order, had established a fair employment practices committee prohibiting discrimination in defense industries during the war, and broadened it to include all government contracts in 1943. Even then the order was not enforced in the South. In peacetime, the wartime FEPC disappeared and efforts at passing a permanent measure were blocked by congressional conservatives.

Prior to his candidacy, Eisenhower had propounded a racial version of his "middle way": "While I would flatly oppose any use of national funds or power or influence that would attempt to discriminate among American citizens on the basis of color or creed, I would also oppose turning the federal government into a police state." When Eisenhower launched his candidacy in Abilene, he declared that action against discrimination in employment was something that belonged with the states, not the federal government.[38]

Ike's flirtation with the South produced embarrassing moments. Walter White, executive secretary of the NAACP, anxiously telegrammed the candidate about a full-page advertisement that appeared in a South Carolina paper announcing: "Eisenhower and the people are opposed to federal controlled and sponsored civil rights to eliminate segregation in our schools, and in our mills and offices." When White asked Eisenhower to repudiate the statement, Sherman Adams, the New Hampshire governor who eventually became Ike's White House chief of staff, responded that Eisenhower "had no knowledge of this particular advertisement to which you refer, and he most certainly does not subscribe to its content." The general, Adams wrote, "would not have consented to its publication." Fifty-four newspapers in the thirteen traditionally Democratic southern states endorsed Eisenhower, compared with twenty-four that endorsed Dewey in 1948. Three southern Democratic governors endorsed the general: James F. ("Jimmy") Byrnes of South Carolina, Robert Kennon of Louisiana, and Allan Shivers of Texas.[39]

President Truman, campaigning on behalf of Stevenson, attacked Eisenhower's "gradualist" approach to civil rights and called for a civil rights program backed by "the full force and power of the Federal

Government." Referring to Eisenhower's 1948 testimony, Truman fumed that "some of our greatest generals have said that our forces had to have segregated units," but experience "has proved that to be nonsense." Eisenhower responded with a defense of his efforts to integrate blacks into the front lines in World War II. "They fought with (Gen.) George Patton's army," he said, "and fought brilliantly." Eisenhower insisted that, following the war, he "fought for integration of them in the Army but, as you probably know, the general staff doesn't pay much attention to a former chief."[40]

Val Washington, the minority programs director for the Republican National Committee (RNC), valiantly defended Eisenhower's positions, insisting that Eisenhower was "upset" by black leaders depicting him as an advocate of military segregation, when he was not. Regarding an FEPC, Washington declared that Eisenhower opposed "all force legislation," but emphasized that the general's goal was the same: "freedom of opportunity in employment for all Americans." Washington produced a fourteen-point program, promising that the Republicans would end segregation in the nation's capital, abolish discrimination in federal employment, make important Negro appointments, and strengthen the civil rights section in the Justice Department. Washington invoked a favorite Eisenhower theme: "A Republican administration will not arouse false hopes of Negroes by promising what it never intends to deliver."[41]

Washington persuaded the National Council of Negro Democrats to endorse Eisenhower just prior to the election, but some black leaders continued to be suspicious. Roy Wilkins, the assistant executive secretary of the NAACP, visited Eisenhower at the general's invitation in his suite at the Commodore Hotel in New York. Wilkins found Eisenhower "tense" and "surrounded by aides," reading his demeanor as a sign he was not comfortable with black people.[42]

A month after Val Washington assumed his position at the RNC, he placed an African-American on the Eisenhower campaign train. E. Frederic Morrow was a World War II veteran and former NAACP staff member who was employed by the Columbia Broadcasting System's radio division. Morrow's life on the campaign trail was difficult; hotels and restaurants frequently denied him access. When

Eisenhower visited Morrow's home town of Hackensack, New Jersey, Morrow was campaigning elsewhere. The New Jersey Republican committee chairman labeled Morrow a troublemaker and castigated the candidate for appointing him to his staff. Eisenhower, Morrow later learned, had praised his service and had angrily told the committee members that "it was none of their damned business who he appointed to his personal staff."[43]

Morrow joined the train on Labor Day, September 5, 1952, when the Eisenhower campaign was, he opined, "running like a dry creek." Morrow made an awkward start by openly criticizing the first speech he heard the candidate deliver. He also informed Eisenhower that his 1948 congressional testimony had disillusioned the black community. Ike granted that he had probably relied too heavily in 1948 on feedback from generals with southern roots. "Fred, maybe you've got something there," he said. "Maybe these politicians are pulling my leg. Maybe we'll have to do something about getting the message across." Three days after Morrow's arrival, on September 8, Eisenhower delivered his most quoted declaration on civil rights: "I believe we should eliminate every vestige of segregation in the District of Columbia."[44]

A "Gap between Promise and Performance"

By the end of September, Eisenhower was upset with his campaign. A fund for the use of vice presidential candidate Richard Nixon had created a political uproar. Eisenhower called Herbert Brownell in the middle of the night to discuss Nixon's fate. Brownell recommended retaining the Californian on the ticket, advice that was vindicated when Nixon delivered a successful defense on television.

Eisenhower and Brownell also discussed the candidate's distress with the management of the campaign. The RNC had given Eisenhower a "take-it-or-leave-it" plan that forced him to frenetically campaign for congressmen and senators without regard to his health or his wife's needs. The GOP leadership had pushed him to campaign for Senator Joseph McCarthy, the anticommunist demagogue who had accused General Marshall, Ike's army mentor, of treason. Eisenhower had allowed himself to be pressured into deleting a statement defending Marshall from a speech, a decision Truman characterized as "one of the most shameful things I can ever remember." Eisenhower asked Brownell to return and serve as his personal liaison with the RNC. In early October, Brownell rejoined the campaign.[45] Once he resumed command, the candidate and his team regained their confidence.

Eisenhower's primary focus in the final days of the campaign was the ongoing war in Korea, but Brownell persuaded the candidate to shift his approach to civil rights. The New Yorker was unsympathetic to further wooing of the South. By October, southern politicians such as Jimmy Byrnes could not easily repudiate their endorsements. Brownell's shift in strategy was signaled when columnist Drew Pearson reported that "the Republican high command has decided on a very important right-about-face in regard to the Negro vote." Walter White told the NAACP board of directors: "Eisenhower brain-trusters have virtually decided to have their candidate reverse himself and come out 100% for civil rights."[46]

Eisenhower's October 17 speech in Newark, New Jersey, was designed as the centerpiece of a new plan for the candidate to speak out on civil rights. The day before, Ike's speechwriters, including Emmet John Hughes and Milton Eisenhower, had been in "a mad rush" to get the address written. Stephen Benedict, another writer, recalled that Eisenhower insisted he would not apologize for his refusal to endorse making laws on civil rights, especially creating an FEPC. He felt "very strongly the full power of the federal government ought to be used, as contrasted with laws."[47]

That was Eisenhower's civil rights strategy—the commitment to invoke federal authority he had first enunciated to Brownell on March 24. He and his aides perceived the Truman administration as "just talk and no action" in civil rights. In his Newark speech, Eisenhower accused the Democrats of courting black votes with "demagogic speech-making" and annual proposals for legislation that the party leaders knew would never pass the Congress. The Truman regime, the general declared, suffered from a "gap between promise and performance."[48]

Eisenhower charged that segregation in Washington, D.C., provided "an unfortunate demonstration of how this administration, after 20 years of talk about moving mountains, has not even brought forth a mouse." Truman shot back that the Republican candidate should be warned "that the President can't get things done in the District of Columbia simply by waving a wand."[49]

Victory

Eisenhower won the election, breaking the "solid South" by winning four states—Tennessee, Virginia, Florida, and Texas. Stevenson carried seven Deep South states plus Kentucky and West Virginia. Ike received 55 percent of the popular vote, and won in the electoral college by 442–89. Stevenson carried an estimated 79 percent of the black vote.[50]

On election day, Eisenhower sent for Brownell. Ike was staying at the Columbia University president's home (he had served as president of the school from 1948 to 1950 and had been on leave until 1952). The general, wearing his artist's smock, was painting a landscape. When Brownell informed Eisenhower that he was winning by a landslide, Ike responded that they had better get busy planning to run the White House. He intended to employ the staff system he had developed in the military, "with a Chief of Staff at my side." Eisenhower paused in his painting and looked Brownell in the eye: "And I want you to be Chief of Staff." Eisenhower could have paid the New Yorker no higher tribute. Brownell responded that he preferred to stay active as a lawyer, to which Eisenhower replied, "Well, how about being attorney general." For Eisenhower's future policies in civil rights, this was a momentous decision.[51]

For the time being, the war in Korea overshadowed other issues confronting the president-elect, but the sleeping giant was civil rights. Eisenhower, with his electoral victory and foreign policy credentials, could have ignored racial issues, but he had learned in the trenches that history does not stand still. He had defined a basic strategy—invoking federal authority—that would dictate his first presidential steps against discrimination. Most important, Herbert Brownell would be the general's field commander in the movement toward racial justice.

CHAPTER TWO

Invoking Federal Authority

I propose to use whatever authority exists in the office of the President to end segregation in the District of Columbia, including the Federal Government, and any segregation in the Armed Forces.
—DWIGHT D. EISENHOWER, FEBRUARY 2, 1953

Shortly after noon on January 20, 1953, Dwight Eisenhower took the oath to "preserve, protect and defend the Constitution of the United States." Then the new president stepped to the podium and gazed out at a sea of white faces and beyond, to a segregated city—one that Minnesota Democratic Senator Hubert Humphrey called "more southern than the southern cities." On that inauguration day, a Negro could not rent a room in a premier hotel, eat at a restaurant, attend a movie theater, or easily find a restroom in downtown Washington. Parks and bowling alleys were strictly segregated. The president-elect had requested that there be no segregation at inaugural events but many Washington establishments ignored his entreaty. Still, Ike's inauguration initiated his policy of opening numerous White House events to guests without regard to race.[1]

During the campaign, Eisenhower had pledged to eliminate "every vestige of segregation in the District of Columbia." At a news conference the previous December, a reporter had asked President Truman if he thought Eisenhower could issue an executive order to desegregate the capital. Truman replied: "You can be sure that if I thought I had the power it would have been done a long time ago." F. Joseph Donohue, the Democratic chairman of the District of Columbia's commissioners, was more hopeful. "I think Gen. Eisenhower will keep his promise," Donohue declared. "He not only will be able to do it, but he will do it." Donohue was right; Eisenhower intended to improve on the Truman record.[2]

Appointments for Civil Rights

Ike had told Herbert Brownell a year earlier that his "first order of business" would be to end racial discrimination wherever there was federal authority. Given his popularity, the new president could have ignored racial issues. Eisenhower owed no political debt to black voters, who had deserted the Republican Party in large numbers in the 1930s in response to New Deal programs. The Gallup Poll found that 21 percent of eligible Negro voters supported the general prior to the election but, due to barriers against black voting in the South, a much smaller percentage likely voted for him. Although white southerners had delivered four states to the Eisenhower electoral column, Ike was still committed to ending discrimination where he had authority.[3]

Eisenhower's leadership on civil rights began with his appointments. His staff system demanded strong subordinates to implement his policies. Herbert Brownell, his attorney general, staffed the Justice Department with other civil rights advocates, including another New Yorker, William P. Rogers, as deputy attorney general, and J. Lee Rankin of Nebraska as assistant attorney general. Brownell also selected Warren Olney III, a close associate of California Republican governor, Earl Warren, to head the department's criminal division, which included a civil rights section; Arthur Caldwell, a career officer, continued as chief of that subdivision. Philip Elman, who had crafted the Truman administration's brief in the *Brown* school desegregation cases before the Supreme Court, was retained in the solicitor general's office, reporting to Rankin until a solicitor general could be appointed. The nation now had a Justice Department fully committed to progress in civil rights.[4]

Eisenhower's White House team, for the most part, comple-
mented Brownell's at the Justice Department. Sherman Adams, an
assistant to the president who functioned as chief of staff, was rea-
sonably favorable to civil rights. Gerald Morgan, the president's
counsel, was supportive, as were James Hagerty, the press secretary,
and Tom Stephens, the appointments secretary, who were closely
allied with Brownell. Ann Brownell Sloane, Brownell's daughter, recalls that her father indicated that Stephens "could spirit HB in to
see the president at any time." Bryce Harlow, a congressional liaison, usually supported civil rights, although he worked closely with
the one alleged segregationist among senior White House staffers,
General Wilton ("Jerry") Persons of Alabama, who served as an assistant to Adams and managed congressional relations.[5]

Maxwell M. Rabb, a Massachusetts attorney and close associate
of Henry Cabot Lodge, Jr., the new ambassador to the United Nations, was the secretary to the cabinet, but Eisenhower also charged
him with coordinating Negro relations with the White House. Eisenhower disliked naming positions for interest groups, so Rabb bore
no title for this role. The president ordered Rabb to seek genuine
progress in civil rights, not empty gestures or legislation likely to fail
in Congress; Ike believed the executive branch should reform its
own policies before seeking congressional action.[6]

Black appointments were important, although the racial politics
of the time severely limited the options. Eisenhower had asked Val
Washington, a Brownell protégé at the Republican National Committee, to submit "a list of qualified Negroes for positions in the government." The president informed Sherman Adams that he wanted
qualified Negroes considered for sub-cabinet positions, and he
urged cabinet members to appoint at least one black to a position of
leadership. But bowing to the likelihood that the Senate would not
confirm a black appointee, Eisenhower did not nominate a Negro
to his cabinet.[7]

The administration initially appointed more than two dozen African-Americans to so-called top positions. Lois Lippman, a secretary, was the first Negro to serve in the White House in a capacity
other than janitor or messenger. In 1954, Eisenhower selected J.
Ernest Wilkins, a prestigious Chicago attorney, as assistant secretary

of labor for international affairs, the highest sub-cabinet post ever given to an African-American. Eisenhower appointed Wilkins as the black representative on presidential equal employment committees and, in 1957, on the Civil Rights Commission. On August 16, 1954, Wilkins attended a cabinet meeting in place of Secretary of Labor James P. Mitchell, and Rabb informed Eisenhower that Wilkins's presence marked "the first time in American History that a Negro has attended a Cabinet meeting."[8] In 1955, E. Frederic Morrow, who had been serving in the Commerce Department, became the first African-American appointed to serve on the White House executive staff. With Morrow's appointment, the *Pittsburgh Courier*, a pro-Eisenhower black newspaper, claimed that the administration had named sixty-five African-Americans to professional positions. A small group of black officeholders became Rabb's informal "equality committee," which regularly advised him and the president on racial issues.[9]

The administration was less aggressive with black ambassadorial appointments. Jesse Locker, a Cincinnati lawyer recommended by Ohio Republican Senators Robert A. Taft and John W. Bricker, was named ambassador to Liberia, the African nation founded by former American slaves. Locker ended up offending the Liberian government and bungling the most elementary diplomatic duties. Secretary of State John Foster Dulles was intending to replace Locker when the ambassador died in 1955. In 1958, Dulles nominated another Negro, Clifton R. Wharton, as ambassador to Romania, hoping to counter Soviet propaganda about racial discrimination in America.[10]

Home Rule and Desegregation

Dwight Eisenhower wanted to make the District of Columbia "the showpiece of our nation" in terms of racial integration. "Home rule"—the proposal to grant residents and their officers greater authority over the district's own governance—would be important in fulfilling this pledge. In 1953, congressional committees still ruled the district through financial appropriations, and it had no representation in Congress. The president appointed the district's three commissioners, two of whom required Senate confirmation, with the third assigned from the Army Corps of Engineers. Congress, however, was faced with a growing and increasingly restless Negro community in Washington that demanded more authority over the city's affairs.[11]

Given these conditions, two options for implementing desegregation in the district were available to Eisenhower. One was to attempt to persuade the Congress to approve home rule that would include authority applicable to desegregation, but congressional segregationists were likely to block such legislation. The other option was to work through the municipal government as it stood. In 1952, Congress had enhanced the power of the commissioners by transferring to the city the functions of more than fifty federal agencies. The legal basis for D.C. government action on desegregation rested on laws passed by Congress in the 1870s that had not been enforced for decades. These statutes forbade discrimination in public accommodations in the district, requiring such facilities to serve "any respectable, well-behaved person without regard to race, color or previous condition of servitude." When Eisenhower entered office, the validity of these "lost laws" was being tested in the courts.[12]

The Republicans won narrow control of Congress in the 1952 election. The new chairman of the Senate's district committee, Francis Case (R-South Dakota), announced a seven-point legislative program designed to authorize home rule for the District of Columbia and increase the number of commissioners from three to five, the aim being to add a woman and a Negro. Case and House district committee chair Sid Simpson (R-Illinois) met with Eisenhower on January 15, 1953. The president expressed support for Case's program and proclaimed that "not a single penny of Federal money should be spent in a way that would discriminate against anyone."[13]

Eisenhower initially declined to submit to Congress general civil rights legislation beyond Case's bill for home rule because he "did not believe that this is the best approach to the problem." Under Truman, the Democrats had made an annual ritual of proposing legislation that they knew could not be passed. However, Eisenhower's military experience had left him with a disdain for symbolic acts. He focused on what he could do, not belaboring what he could not do. His administration would set the example by invoking federal authority. The president repeatedly told Republican leaders that he believed that federal money should not support discrimination. On January 26, days before his first State of the Union address, Eisenhower reaffirmed to legislative leaders his intent to use "the full power of the president to do away with segregation in the District of Columbia and the Armed Forces."[14]

Herbert Brownell, working with Max Rabb, masterminded the Eisenhower plan to desegregate the district. If Congress was unlikely to pass home rule legislation that would facilitate desegregation, working through the municipal government still made sense. Brownell understood the limitations on the federal government's authority to act otherwise. Throughout the Eisenhower presidency, the attorney general would be pressured to intervene in the South on racial issues, but the Justice Department lacked authority to prosecute crimes in the states. The District of Columbia was different. The federal government's authority there, although circumscribed by congressional committees, was unquestioned.

The *Thompson* Case

The case concerning the district's "lost laws," *District of Columbia v. John R. Thompson Co., Inc.,* had been in the courts since 1950. On a January afternoon that year, four well-dressed blacks, led by eighty-six-year-old Mary Church Terrell, had entered the Thompson Cafeteria. They represented the Coordinating Committee for the Enforcement of the D.C. Anti-Discrimination Laws. When the four approached the checkout register with their trays of food, the manager told them, "We don't serve colored." The district took the Thompson Company to municipal court and lost, but won on appeal. Then the Thompson Company appealed to the U.S. Court of Appeals for the District of Columbia. On January 22, 1953—two days after Eisenhower's inauguration—the appeals court upheld Thompson's right to refuse service to Negroes. The Washington *Afro-American* quoted a White House source as saying that the court decision would "in no way affect the Chief Executive's pledges to rid D.C. of segregation."[15]

Still, the ruling threatened the administration's plan to collaborate with the district's municipal government to promote desegregation. Eisenhower ordered Brownell to seize control of the district's appeal to the Supreme Court. The *Afro-American* hailed the administration's decision to intervene in the *Thompson* case under the headline, "Ike Redeems Rights Pledge." Segregationist congressmen fiercely attacked the administration's intervention in the *Thompson* case. Representative James C. Davis (D-Georgia) charged that Brownell's brief could only have been presented "at the direction of the president." Davis accused the Eisenhower administration of trying to "outdeal the New Deal" by "appeasing radicals to get votes."[16]

Brownell's brief for the Supreme Court quoted Eisenhower's commitment to desegregate the district, and the NAACP's argument mirrored Eisenhower's vision: "The elimination of discrimination in places of public accommodation in the District of Columbia is especially significant to America's progress toward full equality for all persons." The attorney general argued to the Court that the January 22 appeals court ruling had generated "doubts and uncertainty" concerning whether Congress could legally delegate home rule powers to the district. Brownell asked the Supreme Court to decide the *Thompson* appeal before the end of the judicial term in June, so that the home rule legislation pending in Congress would not be jeopardized.[17]

The State of the Union

Eisenhower planned to formally announce his desegregation agenda in his first State of the Union message on February 2. Senator Case hoped it would include a presidential endorsement of home rule. Walter White, the executive secretary of the NAACP, thought the president had personally given him "assurances he would do all in his power to abolish segregation in the District and the rest of the nation," but he still worried that "the gang around the president" might oppose civil rights legislation.[18]

On February 2, Eisenhower declared: "I propose to use whatever authority exists in the office of the President to end segregation in the District of Columbia, including the Federal Government, and any segregation in the Armed Forces." The president endorsed D.C. home rule and the expansion of the number of district commissioners from three to five. "In this manner," he continued, "and by the leadership of the office of the President exercised through friendly conferences with those in authority in our States and cities, we expect to make true and rapid progress in civil rights and equality of employment opportunity."[19]

Eisenhower had chosen his words with care. He would use the authority he already possessed. For what he lacked, he would substitute presidential prestige and persuasion, even in the states. The *Washington Post*'s editorial page concluded that Eisenhower intended to provide "the kind of moral leadership which the Nation is entitled to expect from its President." Other responses were hostile. Senator Richard B. Russell, a powerful Georgia Democrat, announced his opposition to racial integration in the district's schools and the fire department. Senator Allen J. Ellender (D-Louisiana) insisted that "President Eisenhower's pledge to eliminate segregation in the District of Columbia is not, to my mind, capable of achievement within the presidential powers."[20]

Eisenhower and Spencer

Joseph Donohue, the Democratic chairman of the D.C. commissioners, honored the tradition that allowed a new president to appoint his own leader in the district. On January 22—the same day the appeals court ruled against desegregation of Washington restaurants—Donohue met with Eisenhower at 11:00 A.M. and delivered his letter of resignation, effective at a time of the president's choosing. Donohue was impressed with Eisenhower's understanding of district issues, including segregation. "He has something in his mind about the District," Donohue told reporters. "I can't discuss it, but he has something in mind."[21]

Donohue went on to speculate that "President Eisenhower might achieve non-segregation in the District through the use of his appointive power to the Board of Commissioners." The NAACP urged the president to ensure his goal of eliminating "every vestige of segregation" by appointing a Negro. Eisenhower, in his State of the Union address, had endorsed the proposal to increase the number of commissioners from three to five, which could lead to a black appointee. On February 9, the president and his Republican congressional leaders made that expansion a "must" among their legislative priorities. Bishop D. Ward Nichols of the African Methodist Episcopal Church met with Eisenhower a few days later and reported that the president had promised him "full consideration" of the appointment of an African-American.[22]

Southern congressmen ridiculed the proposal to augment the board of commissioners as reverse discrimination. The Washington *Evening Star* labeled the plan "unnecessary" and challenged the president to make the black appointment to the existing three-person panel. Eisenhower knew that appointing a Negro to the existing board would ensure a bruising and predictably futile battle in Congress. He had decided to avoid such a conflict so early in his term.[23]

Eisenhower and Brownell reviewed potential candidates for Donohue's position for several weeks. The *Evening Star* reported on "credible rumors of considerable tugging within the local Republican ranks as to whose candidate will receive presidential approval." Senator Case wanted Walter L. Fowler, the city's white budget officer, but the NAACP objected and identified nineteen acceptable candidates, including eleven Negroes. The organization's approved list included a white attorney named Samuel Spencer.[24]

Spencer was a Mississippi-born, Phi Beta Kappa graduate of Harvard University and its law school, and a decorated naval veteran of World War II. He had practiced law in New York before returning to Washington, D.C. Because of Spencer's work in the Eisenhower campaign, Brownell knew that the lawyer's position on segregation matched the president's. The former Eisenhower for President organization in the district, undoubtedly with Brownell's encouragement, instigated a vigorous campaign on Spencer's behalf.[25]

On March 25, Eisenhower called Spencer to the White House, asked him to serve, and sent his nomination to the Senate that afternoon. When Spencer emerged from a meeting with the president, reporters asked if he endorsed the president's commitment to eliminate "every vestige" of segregation from the capital. "I share his viewpoint," the nominee declared. Washington newspapers and civic leaders praised Spencer's nomination. Senate district committee chairman Case endorsed the appointment and scheduled hearings that began on March 31 and ended three days later with Senate confirmation. Joseph Donohue testified in support of Spencer before the committee and, in a gesture of unity, Renah F. Camalier, the remaining Democratic commissioner, announced that he would nominate Spencer for chairman of the board. Eisenhower was satisfied; he had avoided a struggle with Congress over district leadership and had secured his own man from the progressive wing of his party. The president and Spencer would develop a close relationship, with the commissioner frequently reporting directly to the president.[26]

Civil rights advocates implored the new commissioner to act decisively on the president's commitment to desegregation. Mary Church Terrell and her committee, who had taken the Thompson Cafeteria to court to enforce the "lost laws," publicly pressured Spencer, "as the president's first appointee to the board," that he should "endeavor to carry out his program to eliminate segregation." Congressman Jacob Javits (R-New York) pressed Spencer for his plans for fulfilling the Republican platform pledge on civil rights.[27]

The authority of the district commissioners was still ambiguous, especially with the *Thompson* case in the courts, but Eisenhower and Spencer acted where they had jurisdiction. In April, Eisenhower eliminated segregation in the military district of Washington, the army district created during World War II to protect the capital. Spencer, in consultation with Eisenhower, collaborated with the NAACP to draft an order to eliminate discrimination in employment in the district government. On May 19, the president addressed the tenth anniversary luncheon of the United Negro College Fund and vowed to end "second-class" citizenship in the United States, rejecting "any distinction based on race, creed or color."[28]

The *Thompson* Decision

On June 8, 1953, the Supreme Court ruled unanimously for the administration on *Thompson*. Writing for the Court's 8–0 majority, Associate Justice William O. Douglas validated the post–Civil War statute that prohibited discrimination in the district's eating places, and refuted the contention of the court of appeals that Congress could not grant home rule to the district. "The power of Congress to grant self-government to the District of Columbia," Douglas wrote, "would seem to be as great as its authority to do so in the case of territories."[29]

"D. C. Café Segregation Killed," the *Washington Post*'s headline proclaimed, and Attorney General Brownell hailed the *Thompson* opinion as a milestone in accomplishing the president's desegregation program. Elmer W. Henderson of the American Council on Human Rights (ACHR) called the decision "a mighty blow for democracy." Mary Church Terrell poignantly commented: "I will be 90 on the 23rd of September and will die happy that children of my group will not grow up thinking they are inferior because they are deprived of rights which children of other racial groups enjoy."[30]

Eisenhower joined in the celebration. On June 11, at a convention of Young Republicans, the president praised Brownell for winning a ruling that would facilitate desegregation in the District of Columbia. "We have taken substantial steps toward insuring equal civil rights to all of our citizens regardless of race or creed or color," Eisenhower said. "These actions have been designed to remove terrible injustices rather than to capture headlines. They are being taken, quietly and determinedly, wherever the authority of the Federal Government extends."[31]

Samuel Spencer's government exercised its new authority by declaring that restaurants must comply "immediately" with the Court's decision and that prosecution of violations would begin in "a day or so." A special board of commissioners meeting resulted in a police order requiring compliance by 8:00 A.M. on June 10. *The Afro-American* reported that "welcome" signs were out at Washington restaurants. The exuberant declaration in the newspaper's June 13 edition read: "Eat anywhere!"[32]

Spencer's initiatives convinced civil rights activists that he was serious about desegregation. The NAACP informed the White House
that its leaders had decided to work "through Commissioner Spencer." Ralph Rose, the head of the American Friends Service Committee, wrote the president: "Your appointee to the Board of
Commissioners of the District of Columbia, Samuel Spencer, has
become a close friend and a constant supporter of our efforts."[33]

The Eisenhowers personally reinforced Spencer's policies,
which were aimed at desegregating all Washington public accommodations and activities. Mrs. Eisenhower desegregated the annual
White House Easter egg roll. The president and Mrs. Eisenhower
had refused to attend motion pictures in the segregated movie
houses in the district. Eisenhower called the chief executives of the
major motion picture companies to the White House and enlisted
them to pressure the owners of downtown Washington movie theaters to admit black customers. He held a dinner for Mr. and Mrs.
Samuel Goldwyn of Metro-Goldwyn-Mayer on April 1, 1953, met
with Spyros Skouras of Twentieth Century–Fox on April 9, Jack
Warner of Warner Bros. on May 22, and Darryl Zanuck of Twentieth
Century–Fox on July 20, 1953. By October 1953, the *Afro-American*
broadened its slogan to "go anywhere" at the movies.[34]

Contracts and Discrimination in Employment

Eisenhower's frequent assertion that no federal money should be
spent in support of discrimination clashed with his campaign statements opposing a compulsory federal fair employment practices
commission (FEPC). Ike had addressed this issue in the 1952 campaign for mixed reasons—part principle, part politics. He was genu-
inely reluctant to overrule states' rights with a federal program and,
as a candidate, he had blatantly sought a political payoff in the
South for this position. Still, he believed that discrimination in employment and promotion violated constitutional principles.

Contracts with the federal government involved great sums of
money, and a campaign to eliminate discrimination in employment
by federal contractors might produce confrontations with powerful
congressmen. In April 1953, when reporters questioned the presi-

dent on the issue, Eisenhower sidestepped it, but he would eventually have to address the contradiction between his egalitarian principles and his rejection of compulsory regulations.[35]

Meanwhile, Brownell had been collaborating with NAACP leaders in developing the president's desegregation agenda. In May, he and Rabb hosted representatives from fifty organizations, comprising the NAACP-sponsored Leadership Conference on Civil Rights. Brownell promised this group that he would assist them in securing an audience with the president, and four NAACP leaders met with Eisenhower in July. Roy Wilkins, the editor of the NAACP's magazine, *The Crisis,* and normally a Democratic advocate, left his meeting with the president "unequivocally convinced of his sincerity" about minority rights.[36]

The president made a decision about his employment policy in early July—about the time he met with the NAACP leaders. They may have leaked Eisenhower's plan to the press. Adam Clayton Powell, Jr., the black Democratic congressman from Harlem, in New York City, said that Eisenhower had decided to create "a little FEPC." Powell's role in revealing this news was noteworthy; he was the handsome, charismatic minister of the Abyssinian Baptist Church, the largest Negro congregation in the world, and renowned as "Mr. Civil Rights." An internal White House document, almost certainly authored by Max Rabb, confirmed that the president's new committee was "in effect an FEPC."[37]

Eisenhower issued an executive order on August 13 creating the President's Committee on Government Contracts (PCGC). This was a dramatic step in fulfilling Eisenhower's commitment to invoke federal authority to end discrimination. The committee was given definite functions, whereas the Truman administration's Committee on Government Contract Compliance had been a study board with little authority. The new body could not force compliance; that would have required statutory authority. Eisenhower himself characterized its methods as "cooperation, persuasion, education, and negotiation." The president invested the committee with prestige by appointing Vice President Richard Nixon as its chairman. J. Ernest Wilkins, the black Chicago attorney who eventually became assistant secretary of labor, agreed to serve as vice chair. Eisenhower encountered difficulty in recruiting a southern member for the committee. Finally, Brownell identified a Republican lawyer from New Orleans, John Minor Wisdom, who had worked for Eisenhower's nomination in 1952 and, Max Rabb recalled, "was liberal and had a lot of courage." The remaining members of the PCGC included labor, business, and legal leaders.[38]

The news of the creation of the PCGC was electric in Washington's black community. The *Afro-American* proclaimed in a page one headline: "Eisenhower carries out 'little FEPC' promise." Elmer Henderson of the ACHR said he thought the new order was "in some respects stronger than that issued by President Truman." Walter White, the NAACP executive secretary, praised Eisenhower's action, saying: "He has reaffirmed the important principle that those who do business with the United States shall not refuse employment to qualified persons solely because of race, religion or national origin."[39]

In his letter to Nixon launching the new board, Eisenhower declared: "On no level of our national existence can inequality be justified. Within the Federal Government itself, however, tolerance of inequality would be odious." The president concluded: "What we cherish as an ideal for our nation as a whole must today be honestly exemplified by the Federal establishment." On August 19, Eisenhower met with the PCGC, after which Nixon informed the press that the president had challenged the committee to achieve "something concrete in connection with the problem of employment on Government contracts other than making a great show from a publicity standpoint."[40]

The PCGC threatened the South because contractors operating in states that practiced or permitted segregation might lose federal contracts. James F. Byrnes, the Democratic governor of South Carolina and an outspoken segregationist, had supported Eisenhower in the 1952 campaign, partly because of the general's opposition to a federal FEPC. In late July 1953, Eisenhower had paid his political debt by appointing Byrnes to the U.S. delegation to the United Nations. Byrnes, a former secretary of state under Truman, was qualified for the appointment, but Walter White called the nomination "shocking" and one of astonishing "ineptitude." White wired the chairman of the Senate Foreign Relations Committee that Byrnes's record as a segregationist was "so bad that he will become the immediate and exceedingly vulnerable target of Communist and other critics of American Democracy."[41]

The timing suggests that Ike also used this appointment to soften the impact on Byrnes of the impending creation of the PCGC. The day after issuing the executive order, Eisenhower wrote Byrnes in an attempt to ameliorate his reaction. The staff had warned Ike that his letter could become a notorious "Dear Jimmy" document. Eisenhower responded by labeling the letter "personal and confidential" because "our job is to convince, not publicize," and he affirmed his hope for enlisting Byrnes's support "in the enforcement of *federal* regulations."

In his letter, Eisenhower made no apology for moving "in the direction of complete justice." The president affirmed "the right to equal consideration in Federal employment, regardless of race or color." Eisenhower's soothing words did not sway Byrnes, who accused Eisenhower of "usurping the powers of Congress" and labeled the committee, in effect, "a Federal FEPC order." On September 3, Ike and Byrnes held a long phone conversation that Eisenhower reported to Nixon, as chair of the PCGC, along with a copy of his August 14 letter. Ike urged Nixon to make a public statement on the intent of the committee, since "it would be very helpful in quieting the fears that have been voiced by many, including Governor Byrnes."[42]

The NAACP's board of directors reflected the ambivalence of the organization's members toward Eisenhower's civil rights policies. On September 14, the board adopted a motion that crisply encompassed both positive and negative views, urging "that the President be commended for an appointment of the Government Contract Committee and condemned for appointment of James Byrnes as delegate to the United Nations."[43]

Progress in Employment

The first priority of the new contract committee was the District of Columbia. A special subcommittee, chaired alternately by the vice president and J. Ernest Wilkins, conducted closed-door meetings with Samuel Spencer and city aides. As a result, the district government announced on October 26 that, starting on November 16, 1953, new contracts with the city would require nondiscrimination in employment. Spencer achieved particular success with two major district employers, the Chesapeake & Potomac Telephone Company and the Capital Transit Company, both of which had denied blacks access to certain positions. Jacob Seidenberg, the staff director for the PCGC, achieved a breakthrough for Negro bus drivers with the transit firm by citing the president's "deep interest and concern." The contract committee's first report to the president in 1954 proclaimed: "For the first time in the 13-year history of Federal antidiscrimination efforts the policy of the District Government conforms with the national policy of equal economic opportunity."[44]

The PCGC's methods of quiet negotiation, backed by the president and the vice president, sometimes worked elsewhere in the nation. An Ohio segregationist complained to the president that, for the first time, there were Negro bus drivers in Youngstown. This was "the result of the letter written by Mr. Richard Nixon that all firms dealing with government contracts must hire personnel disregarding discrimination," the segregationist wrote. By early 1955, the PCGC had processed 104 complaints of employment discrimination, thirty-seven of which had been settled. On October 25 of that year, Eisenhower summoned top executives of seventy of the federal government's largest defense contractors to Washington for a meeting to persuade them, in the words of Labor Secretary James Mitchell, "to do more than they have done" in ending employment discrimination.[45]

Another employment issue concerned the practices of federal government agencies themselves. On November 25, 1953, Spencer reported to the president that the district commissioners had issued an order banning discrimination and segregation in employment, facilities, and services in twenty-three city agencies. Negro leaders criticized the board's order because it temporarily exempted several agencies, including the fire department.[46] Segregationists in Congress were adamant about preventing integration of the fire department; they wanted to avoid the prospect of black and white firefighters living and working closely together. Spencer hoped to put most of his nondiscrimination system in place before confronting this issue with powerful senators such as Richard Russell. The commissioner announced that integration would be ordered in the fire department "within months, rather than years." Spencer kept his word. On September 1, 1954, the board ordered the integration of the department and, on September 14, denied a plea for further delay, although it took years to effectively integrate the fire services.[47]

Ending discrimination in employment throughout the federal government, beyond district agencies, would take longer to achieve. Eisenhower inherited a Fair Employment Board, which was housed in the Civil Service Commission, and had been created by President's Truman's executive order in 1948. This board could overrule a department secretary, a prospect that frightened cabinet members. Upon receiving a complaint of discrimination in hiring or promotion, the Truman appointees, mostly in their seventies and eighties, could issue an order. If the department failed to comply, the board could send the problem directly to the president's desk, accompanied by publicity. If the president supported the cabinet member over the board, the dispute could escalate into a political controversy.[48]

Eisenhower established the President's Committee on Government Employment Policy (PCGE) by executive order on January 18, 1955. The new committee's role was primarily advisory: it could not issue mandatory orders. The final decision on any complaint remained with the particular cabinet secretary. Press Secretary James Hagerty argued that the new committee, established at the presidential level, would have greater influence than the Truman committee, which had been lodged in the Civil Service Commission. The five-member committee included two African-Americans: J. Ernest Wilkins and Archibald Carey, Jr., a Chicago associate of Wilkins. The committee's first tasks were to conduct a survey of the employment status of Negroes in the government and to seek ways to increase black employment in higher-level positions. By the time Eisenhower left office in 1961, the PCGE had addressed more than one thousand discrimination complaints, claiming corrective action in 96 percent of them.[49]

Progress in the District

Eisenhower's policies reaped praise, even during his first year in office. B'nai Brith honored the president's efforts at the organization's annual meeting on November 23, 1953, and Ike underscored his commitment "to diminish bigotry and intolerance and to end racial discrimination whether manifested by segregation or exclusion or denial of privileges." This would be done, he said, "without fanfare but with determination."[50]

Two days later, in a letter to the president, Samuel Spencer proudly summarized the administration's achievements in desegregating the District of Columbia. Blacks were legally free to eat in district restaurants and patronize movie theaters, the National Capital Housing Authority had begun to open public housing to Negroes, and the district commissioners had banned discrimination in employment by contractors and most of Washington's municipal agencies.[51]

When Republican legislative leaders met with Eisenhower December 17–19, 1953, they discussed their failure to pass home rule legislation for the District of Columbia. Senator Case proposed to submit a bill for the election of a mayor and a nine-person board of commissioners. Spencer demurred; he was concerned that the inevitable controversy in Congress might jeopardize the public works program he hoped to propose. Eisenhower was steadfast; the minutes read: "The president voiced his opposition to setting aside such civil rights legislation for a mere material program, and he suggested action for providing a District Delegate to Congress and election of an Advisory Council."[52] Eisenhower's resolve was demonstrated again the following week, when the *Afro-American* reported that the president had personally intervened in the Bureau of Printing and Engraving when that agency attempted to dismiss a number of Negro apprentices. As 1953 drew to a close, the NAACP lauded Eisenhower for "important civil rights advances," but noted residual challenges in the District of Columbia's hotels, housing, and fire department.[53]

Given the failure of home rule legislation, the administration remained cautious about appointing blacks to high office in the district. In 1955, Eisenhower appointed attorney George E. C. Hayes, a lawyer who had represented the district in the *Brown* cases before the Supreme Court, to the Public Utilities Commission.[54] The segregationists who controlled Senate committees after the Democratic congressional victory in 1954 probably would have refused to confirm a Negro to serve on the district's board of commissioners. In any event, Eisenhower chose not to confront that challenge and never nominated an African-American to that office. Still, black government appointees experienced dramatic change under Eisenhower's regime. A black White House staff member later recalled that, when he first came to Washington in 1953, he "could not eat a meal or have a glass of water in a restaurant outside the Negro area." Two years later, that repressive social order had vanished.[55]

Ending legal segregation was only the beginning. The district commission was criticized for delay in extending nondiscrimination beyond the city of Washington to the entire district. For years, incidents of discrimination plagued Washington Negroes at playgrounds, bowling alleys, railway terminals, restaurants, cemeteries, and institutions serving the aged and disabled. Max Rabb even reported an allegation that the district Red Cross was segregating blood plasma. In December 1954, complaints were so numerous that the commissioners announced their intent to haul violators into court. In June 1955, the NAACP asked the president to give his immediate attention "to serious pace retardation in your program of eliminating discrimination and segregation in the nation's capital."[56] Eisenhower's 1952 promise to eliminate "every vestige" of segregation in the District of Columbia had not been fully achieved. Still, the new president had devoted remarkable time and attention to the issue, with visible results.

"Washington has changed." In January 1955, that is what Negro residents of Washington, D.C., told journalist Samuel Hoskins, who had last visited the capital in 1948. Hoskins, writing in the *Afro-American,* was awed at the transformation: "One gets the feeling that if there is one man in all the District of Columbia singly dedicated to the awful responsibility that is his job, that man is President Eisenhower."[57]

Ralph Bunche, the influential undersecretary of the United Nations, was equally impressed. Max Rabb recalled that Bunche informed Eisenhower that he had once declined President Truman's invitation to serve as an assistant secretary of state. The reason: he refused to force his children to "live in a city that was so rotten with segregation." Now the black diplomat was certain his answer would be different because, under Eisenhower's leadership, Washington, D.C., "once again represents equality."[58]

Desegregating the Armed Forces

As much as Eisenhower did to desegregate the District of Columbia, he was even more determined to invoke his authority to end discrimination in the armed forces.

The assertion that President Truman desegregated the armed forces in 1948 has been a staple in American history textbooks for decades. Truman signed an executive order to that effect, but issuing the order and enforcing it were two different things. Truman was vague about the requirements and declined to set a deadline. General Omar N. Bradley, chairman of the Joint Chiefs of Staff, and Secretary of the Army Kenneth C. Royall resisted implementing the order. The navy and the marine corps declined to alter their racial policies, and the air force implemented only a limited program of compliance. During the war in Korea, military necessity facilitated some integration of combat units, but desegregation was uneven, at best, by 1953.[59]

Adam Clayton Powell, Jr., decried this lack of progress. The congressman set out to influence the Eisenhower administration, sending a telegram to the new president every week or two. In February 1953, he sent a telegram charging that twenty-one army, navy, and air force bases had segregated schools; civilian employees were still segregated on military bases; and forty-seven Veterans Administration hospitals still practiced segregation. The congressman released his message to the press before it reached the White House. Max Rabb, undoubtedly at Eisenhower's direction, went to Capitol Hill and admonished Powell for involving reporters before contacting the president. He assured the congressman that Eisenhower already had made plans to address his concerns. Powell apologized and agreed to work with the administration.[60]

Powell complained that the Truman administration had reneged on its promise to desegregate the military. He declared in
April 1953 that "two-thirds of the Army's all-Negro units were still
intact; 60% of Negroes in the Navy were servants in the segregated
messmen's branch." Ambitious Negroes were boycotting the navy,
Powell claimed, "because they are not interested in making the
world safe for democracy by shining shoes, nor are they interested
in fighting communism with frying pans." The New York congressman pressed the new president to enforce his "forthright stand on
segregation when federal funds are expended."[61]

Meanwhile, Eisenhower had already encountered opposition similar to what Truman had experienced, but the former general had the
prestige to command compliance from reluctant military subordinates. In a March 19 news conference, Eisenhower expressed his irritation with the delays in desegregating the military. He asserted that
"wherever Federal funds are expended for anything, I do not see how
any American can justify—legally, or logically, or morally—a discrimination in the expenditure of those funds as among our citizens. All
are taxed to provide those funds. If there is any benefit to be derived
from them, I think they must all share, regardless of such inconsequential factors as race and religion."[62]

Despite the military's legendary resistance to change, Eisenhower accomplished the racial transformation of the nation's
combat forces with breathtaking speed, although facilities involving
civilians, especially naval bases in the South, took longer. This was
done in the Eisenhower style, without press releases, focused on
quiet negotiations with leading military officers. Congressman
Powell discovered the last segregated army unit at West Point in the
spring of 1954; he called the unit to the attention of the White
House, and it was quickly desegregated. On October 30, 1954—
twenty-one months after Eisenhower's State of the Union pledge—
Secretary of Defense Charles Wilson formally announced that the
last racially segregated unit in the armed forces had been abolished.[63]

Desegregating Military Schools

Eisenhower did not limit desegregation to combat units, but extended the policy to all facets of military life. The schools that served military dependents presented a particularly complex problem. On January 15, 1953, five days before Eisenhower's inauguration, Senator Hubert Humphrey had demanded that the office of education, in the Department of Health, Education, and Welfare (HEW), explain why these schools, supported by federal funds, practiced racial separatism on four southern army bases.[64]

The task of desegregating these schools was formidable. Three categories of institutions were involved. Some schools were located on military bases and were funded exclusively by the federal government; these were most easily desegregated. Federal authority was more circumscribed at a second type of school—those that were located on military reservations or on federal land adjacent to a base and were supported by local and state funds with federal subsidies. The third, locally controlled schools located on nonfederal land, were the most numerous; while they received federal aid to compensate for serving military dependents, the federal government had no statutory authority over these schools. Whenever state or local money and supervision were involved, Eisenhower's declaration that federal funds should not support discrimination collided with the stone wall of southern segregation.[65]

Eisenhower encountered resistance in his own ranks. John A. Hannah, the new assistant secretary of defense for manpower and personnel, initially decided to follow the Truman administration's policy and deferred action on desegregating federally controlled schools on military bases. Eisenhower's March 19 declaration—that he could not justify, "legally, or logically, or morally," discrimination in the use of federal funds—forced Hannah to reconsider. On March 25, the White House released a memorandum from the president to the secretary of defense, revealing that Secretary of the Army Robert Stevens had pledged that federally operated schools on army bases would be opened in the fall "on a completely integrated basis," and that he would negotiate with local authorities concerning schools operated with state funds on federal property.

Secretary of Defense Wilson formally ordered on January 12, 1954, that "no new school shall be opened for operation on a segregated basis, and schools presently so conducted shall cease operating on a segregated basis, as soon as practicable, and under no circumstances later than September 1, 1955."[66]

The integration of schools operated solely by the federal government went smoothly. The second category—the schools operated by local school authorities on military bases or federal land—proved more difficult. As a consequence, the federal government assumed control of forty-two out of sixty-three such schools, mandating their desegregation. During this process, Secretary of the Army Stevens worried that replacing segregated schools with federally funded academies might be criticized as a waste of money and result in accreditation problems. Eisenhower dismissed that concern, responding that if state authorities would not provide integrated schools, "other arrangements will be considered."[67]

In less than three years, the Eisenhower administration integrated hundreds of classrooms, including numerous locally controlled schools in the South. In the context of the time, desegregating these schools for military dependents was a major achievement. Eisenhower's program was initiated prior to the historic school segregation ruling by the Supreme Court, *Brown v. Board of Education,* in 1954. The desegregation of military schools provides profound evidence regarding Eisenhower's personal stance on that issue.

Desegregating Hospitals and Naval Bases

Congressman Powell had also complained about segregation in Veterans Administration (VA) hospitals. J. T. Boone, the chief medical director for the navy, was resisting desegregation and sought a sympathetic hearing from General Persons, Sherman Adams's Alabama-born assistant in the White House. Boone informed Persons that the policy of the VA was "to permit the individual hospitals to be guided by the local customs of the areas in which they are located." The outgoing VA administrator, Carl R. Gray, Jr., supported Boone by arguing that it was "medically advantageous to give some recognition to local custom."

That justification for continued segregation infuriated Congressman Powell, and Eisenhower overruled Boone and Gray.[68]

The program to eliminate VA hospital segregation was launched in September 1953. One year later, Harvey V. Higley, Gray's successor as administrator, reported to the president that segregation had been eliminated in VA hospitals and related facilities. Eisenhower commended Higley and "all who cooperated with you in this program" and proclaimed that the government's leaders had demonstrated once again "their determination to have in America fair play and equal opportunity."[69]

Despite steady progress in the integration of combat units, the navy's reluctance to desegregate southern naval yards would test Eisenhower's resolve. Naval bases in the South employed thousands of civilians at installations ranging from Virginia to Texas. The admiralty had firmly resisted desegregation of personnel at southern bases. In January 1952—almost four years after Truman's executive order—the chief of the Navy's Office of Industrial Relations, Rear Admiral W. McL. Hague, announced that base segregation would continue if local laws or customs required it.

Robert Anderson, Eisenhower's new secretary of the navy, despite Eisenhower's March 19 statement of policy, endorsed Hague's policy in May 1953, informing General Persons: "The Navy must, therefore, in a very realistic way, recognize the customs and usages prevailing in certain geographical areas of our country which the Navy had no part in creating." Anderson told Clarence Mitchell of the NAACP that the navy would "measure the pace of non-segregation by the limits of what is practical and reasonable in each area."[70]

As a result, Anderson found himself in an awkward position with the president. Clarence Mitchell had written Anderson in March that the navy yards at Charleston, South Carolina, and Norfolk, Virginia, were rigidly segregating African-American employees, with separate drinking fountains, restrooms, and eating places. Two months later, on May 28, Mitchell informed Rabb that he still awaited an answer from Anderson, and that he expected the navy to respond to his letter "in a manner contrary to the President's public statements about the importance of eliminating racial discrimination." Rabb checked with Anderson, who replied that segregation had been viewed as "a practical answer to the problem which this department cannot correct by edict," a response that soon became public. Rabb brought this situation to Eisenhower's attention, who recalled later that he ordered Rabb to "track down any inconsistencies of this sort in the rest of the departments and agencies of the government." Rabb confirmed to the president that "some government agencies were neglecting their duty."[71]

When Adam Clayton Powell, Jr., charged that members of the administration were undermining the president's stand on segregation in the armed forces, Eisenhower assured the congressman that he would not permit the desegregation of federal facilities to be "obstructed" by his subordinates. "We have not taken and we shall not take a single backward step," the president declared. "There must be no second class citizens in this country." Powell called that pronouncement a second "Emancipation Proclamation."[72]

The NAACP board of directors chided the president on June 9, saying they were "shocked to learn that the Navy Secretary is continuing racial segregation in the yards at Charleston, S.C. and Norfolk, Va." Two days later, on June 11, Eisenhower dispatched Rabb to meet with Secretary Anderson and his chief officers. Rabb repeated Eisenhower's March 19 statement and emphasized: "President Eisenhower says he wants segregation at the bases to be terminated." In response, Anderson ordered Undersecretary of the Navy Charles S. Thomas to Norfolk to investigate, and Thomas sent his report to Eisenhower on June 23. Thomas recommended simply removing the signs that enforced Jim Crow segregation. The following weekend, in Norfolk—when most employees were absent—workmen quietly removed the signs from the water fountains. The second weekend, they painted over the "colored" and "whites" signs on the restrooms with the words "toilet facilities."[73]

The transformation of most of the naval bases was quietly implemented. By August 10, the newspapers had discovered that the president had reversed his secretary of the navy. Eisenhower, avoiding any hint of conflict, stated that Anderson was "pursuing the purpose of eliminating segregation." On August 20, a chastened Anderson issued an order for "complete elimination" of racial barriers at the forty-three naval bases in the South, with commanders required to submit a report by November 1 and every sixty days thereafter. Defense department sources informed reporters that this was the result of White House pressure. The practice of following local customs, these sources revealed, had become a "source of embarrassment" for the president.[74]

The Charleston, South Carolina, navy yard, in Jimmy Byrnes's domain, was the last holdout. Eisenhower had written Governor Byrnes on August 14, 1953, not only about the new committee on government contracts, but also about the need to change policies at the naval base. Byrnes reluctantly granted that the government possessed the authority to desegregate the naval facility, but he complained that this was an action that "not even President Truman deemed necessary at such installations."[75]

At the end of October, Anderson reported to the president that the desegregation of the Charleston shipyard was virtually complete, despite residual episodes of whites intimidating black employees. It was progress that he termed "most encouraging." Eisenhower summarized Anderson's report for the press, hiding his frustration that the South Carolina base alone, out of the sixty armed forces installations in the South, retained partial segregation. The president called this "a very encouraging report." By January 14, 1954, the Charleston navy yard had eliminated the remainder of its visible segregation requirements.[76]

Residual Problems in the Armed Forces

The effort to dismantle racial barriers in the armed forces was plagued by inconsistencies and incidents, especially when service personnel left their bases and ventured into segregated communities. In late 1953, forty-eight black soldiers were arrested in Columbia, South Carolina, when one of the men sat down by a white girl in a restaurant. The soldiers were fined $1,573 as a group for their involvement in the disturbance that followed, and the army concluded that the situation was beyond federal jurisdiction. The navy fired thirty white barbers in early 1954 at the Jacksonville, Florida, base for refusing to serve Negroes. In mid-1954, Airman Third Class Rodgers Priester wrote the president about visiting a Mississippi beach where a white man accosted him. "Boy, come here," the man shouted, and demanded, "What are you doing here?" The man ordered Priester to move to the "colored" beach by the Veterans Hospital. When Priester resisted, the police harassed and arrested the airman and his buddies. Incidents like these fueled growing African-American impatience with segregation in the civilian world. Black soldiers and their families increasingly pressured the government with demands for action at off-base housing, schools, and public accommodations.[77]

The National Guard presented a particularly difficult challenge. Governors controlled the guard in the states and jealously protected their authority. Eisenhower, compromising his position that federal money should never be spent to support discrimination, hesitated to confront the governors on this issue. There were problems even in the District of Columbia. Frederic Morrow reported to Max Rabb in September 1955 that the district National Guard, while ordered to desegregate, had engaged merely in "a display of integration." Some blacks believed that "Jim Crow" outfits were still ignoring the president's orders.[78]

Still, much had changed, both in the District of Columbia and the armed forces. In an August 1953 radio report to the nation, Eisenhower reaffirmed his civil rights policy: "We have used the power of the Federal Government, wherever it clearly extends, to combat and erase racial discrimination and segregation—so that no man of any color or creed will *ever* be able to cry, 'This is not a free land.'" That same month, the National Negro Council presented its 1953 Civil Rights Award of Honor to the president. The council cited Eisenhower's "distinguished leadership and unprecedented statesmanship in enforcement for the first time in eighty years of the District of Columbia Civil Rights Laws" and his "executive action in outlawing segregation in the armed services and discrimination in Government contracts."[79]

The following year, Adam Clayton Powell, Jr., summarized these developments in a draft of a *Reader's Digest* article. Powell rejoiced that there was not "a single all-Negro unit left in the Army." He acclaimed the desegregation of forty-seven VA hospitals and the integration of schools on military bases. Eisenhower's "silent revolution" had resulted in marine guards prowling naval bases at night with screwdrivers, removing "White Only" and "Colored" signs from drinking fountains, and painting over the signs on restrooms. At the end of three months, Powell reported, "In 21 naval plants employing 70,000 whites and Negroes, the only segregation remaining was a few washrooms in one station—and this was soon gone." Powell concluded: "Where there are laws relating to civil rights, the President is insistent on their enforcement."[80]

At a 1956 news conference, Eisenhower reflected on his efforts to desegregate army troops during World War II and why he came to believe "the thing could be done." "When we came in, in '53," he said, "it looked to us like it was time to take the bull by the horns and eliminate it all; and that is what we have done." When Dwight Eisenhower left office in 1961, five million servicemen, civilians, and their dependents had lived for years in a racially mixed military establishment. The armed forces had become the most integrated institution in American life and a beacon for progress in the larger society.[81]

Given his popularity, Eisenhower could have ignored the unfinished task of desegregating the armed forces, but he used his military prestige to effect compliance. Ike achieved in less than two years what President Truman had failed to accomplish in seven. He had done so in typical Eisenhower style, "without fanfare but with determination," working quietly with his subordinates. President Truman deserves credit for beginning the task of desegregating the armed forces, but he did not complete it; Dwight Eisenhower did, although Negroes continued to encounter discrimination in treatment and advancement well into the 1960s.[82]

In January 1954, Walter White sketched an outline for his report to the annual NAACP meeting. The executive secretary noted the transformation in the armed forces of the United States and wrote a note to himself: "Praise Eisenhower." The following month, Adam Clayton Powell, Jr., delivered the most ebullient endorsement of the new president's overall record: "The Honorable Dwight D. Eisenhower has done more to eliminate discrimination and to restore the Negro to the status of first class citizenship than any President since Abraham Lincoln."[83]

CHAPTER THREE

The President and *Brown*

The Supreme Court has spoken and I am sworn to uphold the
constitutional processes in this country; and I will obey.
—DWIGHT D. EISENHOWER, MAY 19, 1954

In January 1953, Eisenhower and Brownell knew a Supreme Court decision on school segregation was imminent. Plaintiffs from Kansas, Virginia, South Carolina, Delaware, and the District of Columbia had appealed lower court rulings denying approval of school desegregation to the Supreme Court in 1952, and the Court had consolidated these cases into *Brown v. Board of Education of Topeka*, named for the Kansas case. The justices had been expected to rule on *Brown* on June 8, when they struck down desegregation in Washington, D.C., restaurants in the *Thompson* case. Instead, they scheduled reargument of *Brown* for the fall and invited the new attorney general to present a brief. That guaranteed that the Eisenhower administration would become involved in *Brown*.[1]

The Supreme Court had already made rulings that addressed the failure of states to comply with the "separate but equal" doctrine of *Plessy v. Ferguson*. In 1938, the justices ruled in *Missouri ex. Rel. Gaines v. Canada* that the University of Missouri had violated the requirement by denying Negroes enrollment but paying their tuition to attend law schools in neighboring states. In 1950, in *Sweatt v. Painter*, the Court overturned a Texas law that had established a separate law school at a black institution to avoid admitting Negro students to the University of Texas law school. That same year, the

Court stuck down the University of Oklahoma's policy, which, while admitting a black student to the university's doctoral program in education, segregated the student on campus by requiring the man to sit in a separate row in classrooms, at a designated table in the lunchroom, and at a segregated desk in the library.[2]

The unanimous ruling in the *Thompson* restaurant case hinted at the direction the justices were moving, even under the leadership of a southern chief justice. Why, then, did the Court wait another year to rule on *Brown*? The *Washington Post* assumed at the time that the justices were "too divided to make a clear-cut decision." That report exaggerated the situation. The delay was rooted less in disagreement on the principle of desegregation than the justices' fear of the political upheaval that might result from such a decision. Justice William O. Douglas's meticulous notes on the justices' December 13, 1952, conference vividly captured the Court's fears. He quoted Hugo Black as worrying that "there may be violence" if the Court ruled against segregation. Felix Frankfurter and Robert Jackson viewed that possibility "with great alarm and thought that the Court should not decide the question if it was possible to avoid it." Chief Justice Fred M. Vinson concluded that the abolition of segregation in southern schools presented "serious practical problems." Thus, as a new term began in October 1953, the justices were more focused on the politics than on the merits of the issue.[3]

For reargument, the Court asked the parties five questions regarding the Fourteenth Amendment, which provided for equal protection of the laws but did not explicitly address school segregation. The first three addressed the intent of Congress and the ratifying legislatures. The final two questions concerned the politically contentious issues of implementation that had worried the justices the previous term. Assuming that the Court could legally abolish public school segregation, the fourth question addressed the "gradualism" issue: whether desegregation should be required immediately or should the Court "permit an effective gradual adjustment to be brought about from existing segregated systems to a system not based on color distinctions?" Finally, the justices inquired about enforcement methodologies: whether the Court must provide "detailed decrees" and "appoint a special master," or "remand to the courts of first instance"—the lower federal courts—the obligation to review suits, receive evidence, and make decrees. Once the principle in *Brown* was decided, the future of school desegregation would rest on the Court's answers to these enforcement questions.[4]

Eisenhower's Southern Friends

Two of the southern Democratic governors who had supported Eisenhower's candidacy in 1952 were anxious about the Supreme Court's invitation to Attorney General Brownell to present a brief. Fearing Brownell's liberalism on race, the governors mounted a campaign to influence the president. On July 16, Allan Shivers, the governor of Texas, wrote Eisenhower: "I see in this unusual Supreme Court invitation an attempt to embarrass you and your Attorney General." Shivers urged that the attorney general support community-based decisions on segregation. "There is nothing more local than the public school system," he wrote. Eisenhower's perfunctory response to Shivers gave no clue to his position.[5]

Governor Jimmy Byrnes of South Carolina was apprehensive about the president's, not just Brownell's, views on civil rights. Eisenhower's creation of the committee to eliminate discrimination in hiring by government contractors and his efforts to desegregate southern military bases and schools directly affected his state. On Monday, July 20, Byrnes had lunch with the president for the express purpose of discussing, as Eisenhower put it in his diary, "the possibility of a Supreme Court ruling that would abolish segregation in public schools of the country." Byrnes tried to convince the president that overturning *Plessy* would result in the abolition of public schools in the South, a possibility that would haunt Eisenhower throughout his presidency. Byrnes claimed that southerners could tolerate interaction with adult African-Americans but were violently opposed to mixing the races in school. Byrnes feared that the prospect of a larger Negro vote could seduce Eisenhower, so he presented a document analyzing the 1952 election and predicting that blacks would continue to vote as a block for the Democrats.

Eisenhower's response was evasive. "I told him," Ike confided to his diary, "that while I was not going to give in advance my attitude toward

a Supreme Court opinion I had not even seen and so could not know
in what terms it would be couched, that my convictions would not be
formed by political expediency." Eisenhower doubted the efficacy of
compulsion and agreed with Byrnes that improvement in race relations
needed local support. "Consequently," Ike concluded, "I believe that
Federal law imposed upon our states in such a way as to bring about a
conflict of the police powers of the states and of the nation, would set
back the cause of progress in race relations for a long, long time." Still,
Eisenhower reminded Byrnes of his constitutional duty: "I feel that my
oath of office, as well as my own convictions, requires me to eliminate
discrimination within the definite areas of Federal responsibility."
Byrnes had replied, "You can do no less."[6]

The southern governors' crusade troubled Eisenhower. When
Brownell visited Ike on vacation near Denver, Colorado, on August
17, the president quizzed him about the implications of his brief for
the separation of powers. Eisenhower feared that the attorney general's rendering an "opinion" on the intent of the Fourteenth
Amendment might "constitute an invasion of the duties, responsibilities and authority of the Supreme Court." On August 19, Eisenhower called Brownell to further discuss his concerns, but Brownell
convinced him that the administration could not evade the responsibility of responding to the Court's invitation. The justices would
inevitably ask, "Is school segregation constitutional?" Eisenhower
asked for the attorney general's view on that question and, Brownell
recalled, "I answered that in my professional opinion public school
segregation was unconstitutional and that the old *Plessy* case had
been wrongly decided." Eisenhower replied that if that was the attorney general's "professional opinion," he "should so state, if the
Court asked the question."[7]

This August 19 phone conversation is frequently cited as evidence that Eisenhower opposed school desegregation. Without
doubt, Eisenhower was more circumspect than his attorney general.
He was a constitutionalist who adhered to a traditional conception
of the separation of powers doctrine. Besides, he was troubled about
the political impact of a Court decision. Yet despite these concerns,
the president had already desegregated numerous schools for military dependents.

The conversation reflected Eisenhower's methodical style of decision-making. Ike appointed strong subordinates; when confronted with a policy question, he would raise every possible issue, listen carefully, and make a decision he would rarely reconsider. Eisenhower had not lightly reached his conclusion. The administration—including the president—was committed to the government arguing for overruling *Plessy v. Ferguson* before the Supreme Court of the United States.

A New Chief Justice

On Tuesday, September 8, Supreme Court Justice Hugo Black notified President Eisenhower that Chief Justice Fred Vinson was dead. On September 30, Eisenhower nominated Republican Governor Earl Warren of California to replace Vinson. That decision would eclipse the president's previous initiatives to desegregate Washington, D.C., and the armed forces, and to combat discrimination in employment. No subsequent president has made a judicial appointment of greater consequence for civil rights.[8]

The death of Chief Justice Vinson injected uncertainty into the pending deliberations on *Brown;* predicting the views and impact of a new chief justice would be difficult. Three weeks of speculation on his successor followed. Vinson was a Kentuckian by birth, yet Eisenhower never seriously considered appointing a southerner as chief justice. Ike believed that Franklin Roosevelt and Harry Truman had appointed justices of inferior quality, so he gave priority to high standards over regional representation. Eisenhower wrote the dean of Columbia University Law School that he wanted to "bring to the Court a man of broad experience, professional competence, and with an unimpeachable record and reputation for integrity." The president asserted to his brother, Milton, that his problem was "to get a man (a) of known and recognized integrity, (b) of wide experience in government, (c) of competence in the law, (d) of national stature in reputation so as to be useful in my effort to restore the Court to the high position of prestige it once enjoyed."[9]

The slate was not blank. A White House source revealed to the press that, right after the 1952 election, the president-elect had told

Governor Warren that he could have the first available vacancy on the Supreme Court. That pledge did not mean that Warren would be named chief justice. A sitting member could have been promoted, permitting the governor to assume the vacated associate's seat.[10]

Eisenhower wanted a healthy chief judicial officer no older than himself; Warren, about the president's age, qualified. The governor was an impressive figure, standing six feet, one inch tall, weighing over two hundred pounds, with thinning silver hair. Warren was known for greeting visitors with "a crushing handshake" and a "booming laugh." The Californian called himself a "progressive Republican" and, while he lacked experience as a judge or legal scholar, he had served as a district attorney and as attorney general of California. Warren had sought the Republican nomination for president three times. In 1946, he won both the Democratic and Republican endorsements for governor, and in 1948, he ran as the vice presidential candidate with New York Governor Thomas E. Dewey. Earl Warren was a major national figure in the Republican Party well before Dwight Eisenhower entered politics.[11]

Contrary to legend, Eisenhower and Brownell knew Warren's political views. Brownell had managed Dewey's 1948 campaign, and he and Warren were friends and frequently socialized. Eisenhower knew that Warren was in favor of civil rights and had publicly supported a fair employment practices commission (FEPC).[12]

Eisenhower charged Brownell with determining whether Warren should be appointed chief or associate justice. Together, they considered promoting two sitting justices, Harold H. Burton and Robert H. Jackson, but ruled both out due to age, health, and, in Burton's case, insufficient administrative skills. Eisenhower apparently contemplated appointing his secretary of state, John Foster Dulles as chief justice but, according to Brownell, did not formally offer him the position. New York's Governor Dewey was not considered. Eisenhower never directly indicated that he wanted a pro–civil rights chief justice, but the president knew that Brownell would not recommend a nominee who favored segregation.[13]

On Sunday, September 27, Eisenhower dispatched Brownell to meet with Warren at an air force base near Sacramento. The attorney general's assignment was to ascertain the governor's willingness, given his lack of judicial experience, to take the chief justice's job, and to confirm that Warren concurred with the president's commitment to the separation of powers. Eisenhower recalled that Brownell returned with unbounded enthusiasm for Warren's candidacy and told the president: "The man is absolutely not doctrinaire. He's flexible in his judgments, and he's a student, and I think we've got the top man." Brownell invited reporters to his house and leaked the news of Warren's possible appointment to test public reaction. The attorney general's zeal convinced the journalists that the decision had already been made. The public response was generally positive.[14]

On Wednesday, September 30, Eisenhower commenced his news conference by "confirming something that is certainly by no means news any more—that is, that I intend to designate Governor Earl Warren as Chief Justice of the United States." Then Eisenhower announced a second decision of transcendent importance: because Congress had already adjourned, he would make a recess appointment. Warren would assume the chief justice's mantle the following Monday, the first day of the new judicial term.[15]

The recess appointment was a bold and controversial action, recommended by Justice Felix Frankfurter. With Congress in recess, the earliest the new chief justice could be confirmed would be January, when the Senate reconvened. Delaying his appointment risked a four-to-four deadlocked decision on *Brown* or further postponement of the ruling. However, Warren's limited judicial experience made the recess appointment more controversial. Five professors at Harvard Law School opposed Eisenhower's decision as a violation of the Constitution, but the Justice Department upheld its legality.[16]

Columnist Arthur Krock endorsed the choice: "Governor Warren for years has demonstrated great tactical ability in handling difficult men and difficult situations." Walter White, the executive secretary of the NAACP, enthusiastically endorsed the nomination, noting Warren's public advocacy for civil rights, including asking the California legislature to establish an FEPC. The president knew he was appointing a chief justice who would not please southerners such as Jimmy Byrnes. A Warren appointment guaranteed a *Brown* ruling contrary to segregationist interests, and the *New York Times* repeated Byrnes's warning to Eisenhower that "if the high court declares segregation unconstitutional South Carolina would abolish its public school system."[17]

On the first Monday of October 1953, Justice Hugo Black escorted Governor Warren to the justices' chambers for introductions. Warren wore a long, surplus robe and tripped on it, recalling in later years that he "literally stumbled onto the bench." President and Mrs. Eisenhower were present, an unprecedented courtesy, as were Vice President Nixon and Attorney General Brownell. Justice Black administered the oath, and Warren, in a sonorous voice, declared that he would "administer justice without respect to persons, and do equal right to the poor and to the rich." That afternoon, the chief justice and his wife, Nina, visited the White House, where the High Court's new leader engaged in genial conversation with the president and the attorney general.[18]

Eisenhower was elated over his first appointment to the Supreme Court. Three days after Warren's installation, Ike confided to his diary that he expected Warren's confirmation by the Senate to be "immediate and overwhelming." His words reflected his enthusiasm: "If the Republicans as a body should try to repudiate him, I shall leave the Republican Party and try to organize an intelligent group of Independents, no matter how small."[19]

The Government Supports Desegregation

Earl Warren now began his preparation to receive briefs and hear arguments on *Brown* from attorneys representing the southern states and the District of Columbia, the Eisenhower administration's Department of Justice, and the legendary constellation of NAACP lawyers who had so brilliantly managed the plaintiffs' cases to this point. Thurgood Marshall, the director-counselor for the NAACP's Legal Defense Fund, was the preeminent strategist for the entire NAACP team, which included Assistant Counsel Robert L. Carter, Assistant Counsel Jack Greenberg, the District of Columbia NAACP's George E. C. Hayes and James M. Nabrit, Jr., and Southeast Regional Counsel Spottswood W. Robinson III. Marshall

was assisted by William T. Coleman, Jr., a prominent young Philadelphia attorney.[20]

In mid-November, the news Eisenhower and Brownell had
guarded since August became public—the Department of Justice
would oppose school segregation before the Supreme Court. This
news surfaced amid reports that both South Carolina and Georgia
were threatening to abolish their public schools if the Supreme
Court ruled against them.[21] Brownell called Eisenhower on Monday,
November 16, because Jimmy Byrnes was having dinner with the
president the following night and planned to see Brownell on
Wednesday. Fearing that education could become the responsibility
of the federal government, Ike asked, "What would happen if States
would abandon public education?" Brownell said that he would try
to convince Byrnes that a desegregation decision would take years
to implement, perhaps a decade or more. At Eisenhower's news
conference that Wednesday, a reporter asked about Brownell's brief:
"Do you plan to confer with him before he puts that brief in the
Court?" Eisenhower responded: "Indeed I do. We confer regularly,
and this subject comes up along with others, constantly."[22] That was
the reality; Eisenhower and Brownell discussed the *Brown* case "constantly."

Byrnes made one more desperate attempt to derail the momen-
tum toward a desegregation ruling. Two days after the president's
news conference, Byrnes and Governor Robert Kennon, the Louisiana Democrat who had supported Eisenhower in 1952, wrote separate letters to the president. Byrnes enclosed pages from John W.
Davis's brief for South Carolina, arguing that the courts had never
held that the Fourteenth Amendment prohibited school segregation. Byrnes noted that some South Carolina school districts enrolled ten African-American students to every white student and, in
the governor's view, such density made segregation essential. He asserted flatly that "the Court has no right to legislate."[23] But the
South Carolina governor had lost his argument with Eisenhower. In
his response, the president informed Byrnes and Kennon that he
had referred their materials to the attorney general—a clear signal
that Eisenhower was deferring to Brownell, not to segregationists.

On November 27, Brownell submitted his brief to the Court.

The document, prepared by Lee Rankin and Philip Elman under Brownell's supervision, supported overturning *Plessy v. Ferguson*. The intent of the Fourteenth Amendment, the brief contended, was to secure full equality before the law for Negroes. Therefore, the justices possessed the constitutional authority to end racial segregation in the schools. The Court had the duty "to enforce all rights arising under the Fourteenth Amendment without awaiting exercise of the independent enforcement power granted Congress." Brownell suggested a one-year transition period with allowance for reasonable extensions.[24]

Eisenhower knew that Byrnes would be upset. Once the brief was filed, Ike wrote the governor that he had turned over "full responsibility" for the case to the attorney general, effectively closing the door to further lobbying. Eisenhower's words bordered on patronizing: "I appreciate your intimate study and knowledge of the problem and count you among my warm personal friends." The president assured Byrnes that the Department of Justice would focus on "the legal aspects" of the case and that "no political consideration of any kind" would be involved. Ike shrewdly pledged that the attorney general would respect local control of schools "to the maximum degree consistent with his legal opinions." The president knew that what was "legal" was the core issue. Brownell's brief, with Eisenhower's acquiescence, had already made the case that school segregation was *illegal* under the Fourteenth Amendment.[25]

Eisenhower gave Byrnes the impression that he was simply following the lead of his attorney general, but that was disingenuous. Brownell, not Byrnes, was the president's trusted advisor on civil rights. Eisenhower validated that relationship by reading the draft of his letter to Byrnes to Brownell, who approved its content. The attorney general told Eisenhower that Chief Justice Warren had told him that the Justice Department's brief was "outstanding."[26]

Eisenhower took particular interest in the Washington, D.C., portion of the *Brown* case. Congress had established segregated schools in the district prior to ratification of the Fourteenth Amendment. Given congressional sovereignty, there was a question as to whether the amendment applied to Washington's schools. Therefore, the case for the desegregation of D.C. schools rested on the "due process" provision of the Fifth Amendment rather than on the Fourteenth. On November 5, Brownell had reported to the president that the district's board of education was badly split over desegregation and that the board's lawyer favored upholding the segregation laws passed by Congress. The Consolidated Parents Group, a black parents' organization represented by George Hayes and James Nabrit, was demanding immediate integration. The administration's brief in *Brown,* though more conservative in tone than the brief submitted by the NAACP, effectively supported the parents' position that segregation in district schools was unlawful.[27]

A Fearful Court

As they read the briefs, the justices realized that they were traversing a legal wilderness. Traditionally, the Supreme Court relied on two foundations for opinions: the Constitution and the precedents established in previous decisions. In the *Brown* case, the constitutional source was problematic. The Fourteenth Amendment was controversial in the South because, following the Civil War, it had been ratified while the rebellious states were under federal occupation. The intent of the amendment's framers was murky in regard to schools. Justice Douglas, a liberal jurist, ordered his clerk to review congressional intent on the Fourteenth Amendment, and determined "that the legislative history of the Amendment is, in a word, inconclusive." Precedent presented an even thornier problem because the monumental precursor was the 1896 decision in *Plessy v. Ferguson.*[28]

The parties to *Brown* had submitted their briefs in November. On December 7, 1953—two years and a day from when the justices had first heard arguments in the five school cases—the new chief justice formally called the Court into session for oral arguments. John Davis, the losing Democratic presidential candidate in 1924, had made dozens of arguments before the Supreme Court and presented the case against desegregation. Davis articulated the southern perspective on the constitutional issue: "The evidence demonstrates that the Congress which submitted and the State Legislatures which ratified the Fourteenth Amendment did not contemplate the abolition of segregation in the public schools."[29]

Thurgood Marshall, a former protégé of Charles Hamilton
Houston, dean of the Howard University law school, had founded
the NAACP's Legal Defense and Education Fund in 1940. In previ-
ous precedent-making Supreme Court cases—*Missouri, Sweatt,* and
McLaurin—Marshall and his colleagues had invoked the post–Civil
War constitutional amendments, especially the Fourteenth, with its
requirement for "equal protection of the laws." Marshall told the
Court that segregated education was a "sorry heritage from slavery."
Marshall argued that "in truth and in fact" separate schools could
not possibly be equal in their impact on African-American students.
Lee Rankin, representing the Eisenhower Justice Department, supported Marshall's position, and contended that the Supreme Court
had the authority and the duty to abolish segregation in the public
schools.

The justices, while nearing agreement on the principle of desegregation, were preoccupied with their fears of a hostile public reaction in the South to such a decision. Warren insisted that the
plaintiffs' lawyers avoid esoteric legal issues, because the Court was
primarily interested in the question of "its powers in the controversy." The justices understood that they risked validating the charge
that they were legislating from the bench. Numerous precedents
supported segregation, which would make a desegregation decision
even more contentious.[30]

According to Justice Douglas's notes on the conference five
days after the oral arguments, Warren contended that the "separate
but equal doctrine" leaned on the "basic premise that the Negro
race is inferior." Warren could not understand "how segregation
can be justified in this day and age." The other justices did not disagree, but they were still preoccupied with the fears of political upheaval that had haunted them the year before. Justice Stanley F.
Reed argued that "we should not move to change the law—if there
is to be a change Congress should do it." Justice Tom Clark feared
that "violence will follow in the south." Robert Jackson admitted
that it was "a political question" and contended that they could not
justify "elimination of segregation as a judicial act—if we have to
decide the question representative government has failed." Jackson
envisioned a situation where the radicals would want to put "all

Boards of education in jail." Justice Harold Burton countered that the problem was "a judicial one" and that equal protection meant the states could no longer do what they wanted. Noting the Court's decisions in 1950 regarding graduate institutions, Burton argued that the "principle applicable to graduate school is applicable to primary school." Justice Sherman Minton pointed out that the Negro's alleged inferiority was the justification for segregation. The Fourteenth Amendment, he insisted, "was intended to wipe out the badge of slavery." When that amendment proclaimed "equal" rights, it did not say "separate but equal." "Separate," Minton declared, was "a lawyer's addition to the language."[31]

Eisenhower and Brownell proceeded carefully, knowing a decision was near. Eisenhower avoided mentioning civil rights in his 1954 State of the Union address, excepting a one-sentence plea for home rule for the District of Columbia. Brownell informed the president on January 25 that a confidential source had informed him that the Court might decide the constitutionality issue in *Brown* in the spring but "put off remedies for fall." The president wryly suggested that the Court consider deferring enforcement until the issue would no longer be his administration's problem.[32]

Warren Molds Consensus

Eisenhower's expectation that Warren would be rapidly confirmed, once the Senate reconvened in January, clashed with congressional reality. Senator William Langer (R-North Dakota) chaired the Judiciary Committee and was unhappy because the White House had ignored his wishes on the appointment of postmasters in his state. Langer opened the hearings to attacks on Warren, including those from a law professor who argued that "the man has no judicial experience, and he is not a lawyer in any proper sense of the term." The senator dispatched investigators to California to investigate anonymous allegations that Warren was a drunk, was connected with organized crime, had protected corruption in his administration, had followed Marxist doctrine, had failed to prosecute illegal bookmakers, and had appointed dishonest judges. Southern senators were delighted with this turmoil, and Senator Olin Johnston (D-South

Carolina) demanded a full FBI investigation. Eisenhower stood by his nominee, calling him "one of the finest public servants this country has ever produced."[33]

Warren was finally confirmed by the Senate on March 1, 1954. Armed with the legitimacy of his confirmation, the chief justice asserted himself with his colleagues. By April, Warren had won the *Brown* argument on principle, encouraging unanimity by convincing the justices to distance themselves from the politics of the coming struggle. The chief justice recommended that the justices avoid requirements that would embroil the Court directly in the inevitably bitter conflicts over school desegregation. The Court, he insisted, should neither appoint a special master to oversee the enforcement of *Brown* in southern states, nor suggest to the lower courts that they appoint one. The justices should not set a date for completion of the program or recommend to the lower courts that they set a date. They should not require the lower courts to seek a plan from school districts and there should be no procedural requirements for the lower courts. Warren planned a "bare-bones" decree that would pass responsibility to the lower courts and avoid any definition of enforcement mechanisms. Justice Hugo Black, calling for "unanimous action," agreed that the "less we say the better." The justices would wait another year to spell out the ambiguous approach to enforcement they had largely agreed upon by May 1954.[34]

Under Warren's leadership, the Court had become an agent of social change. Years later, in January 1960, Justice Douglas recorded Felix Frankfurter's ruminations on the new chief justice's impact during 1953–54. Frankfurter recalled that he had urged the Court to consider school segregation cases as early as 1946, but would then have voted to uphold segregation because "public opinion had not been crystallized against it." Frankfurter said that the arrival of "the Eisenhower Court"—meaning Warren's appointment—convinced him that there had been "a change in public opinion, enabling him to vote against segregation."[35]

The Historic Decision

On May 17, 1954, the Supreme Court filed its opinion in *Brown v. Board of Education of Topeka.* Warren, the skilled politician, carefully staged the announcement. In his short opinion, the chief justice stated that the history of the Fourteenth Amendment furnished inconclusive evidence as to its intent with regard to segregation in schools. But the clock could not be turned back to 1868 or even 1896: "We must consider public education in the light of its full development and its present place in American life throughout the Nation."

The key, in Warren's opinion, was not precedent but the impact of segregation on black children. The chief justice proclaimed that "separate but equal" had no legitimate place in public education. "Separate educational facilities are inherently unequal," he declared. Therefore, the plaintiffs in *Brown* had been "deprived of the equal protection of the laws guaranteed by the Fourteenth Amendment."

Regarding the District of Columbia, Warren asserted that because the Court had decreed that segregated public schools were unconstitutional, "it would be unthinkable that the same Constitution would impose a lesser duty on the Federal Government." The chief justice concluded: "We hold that racial segregation in the public schools of the District of Columbia is a denial of the due process of law guaranteed by the Fifth Amendment to the Constitution."[36]

American race relations would never be quite the same after *Brown.* After the decision was read, Thurgood Marshall gave Lee Rankin a hug, grabbed his hat, and ran from the court to tell Jack Greenberg, Walter White, and Roy Wilkins. Marshall bounded into the NAACP offices, Roy Wilkins recalled, "with a grin as wide as Fifth Avenue." Marshall marched over to Wilkins and kissed him.[37]

The nation's newspapers hailed the significance of *Brown.* A leading black newspaper called *Brown* "the greatest victory for the Negro people since the Emancipation Proclamation." The *Pittsburgh Courier* emphasized that it would "stun and silence America's communist traducers behind the Iron Curtain." Washington's *Evening*

Star called the Court's decision a model of "wisdom and fairness." The *Washington Post* echoed Lincoln's Gettysburg address, proclaiming "a new birth of freedom." The response in the Deep South was predictably different; the *New Orleans Times-Picayune* warned that public school systems will face "considerable turmoil for some time to come."[38]

The Supreme Court, having proclaimed the principle of desegregation, skirted the tangled enforcement issue by deferring it to the Court's new term in October 1954. Warren had achieved unanimity by persuading the justices to put off and avoid such politically explosive requirements as timelines and detailed desegregation plans. The *Atlanta Constitution* commended the Court for providing this "cooling-off" period. The *New York Herald Tribune* concurred: "The court has wisely left the question of enforcement to decision at a later time." But the delay gave the segregationists time to organize their resistance. It gave new hope to die-hard southerners such as Jimmy Byrnes, who urged his followers to "exercise restraint" in the interim. Governor Herman Talmadge of Georgia proclaimed that "there will never be mixed schools while I am governor" and warned that integration would lead to bloodshed.[39]

Eisenhower Responds to *Brown*

Dwight Eisenhower had acted quietly but firmly the previous year to desegregate the schools of military dependents and to end discrimination in Washington, D.C., and the armed forces. Now, in the wake of the *Brown* decision, he responded in characteristic fashion—with action rather than public pronouncement.

The morning after the Court's decision, the District of Columbia commissioners came to the White House for a signing ceremony for a public works bill. Eisenhower seized the occasion to express his "very great interest" in desegregating the district's schools. He ordered the commissioners to make Washington, D.C., a "model for the nation," and provide him with regular progress reports. The commissioners met with the district board of education the next day, May 19. Superintendent of Schools Hobart M. Corning proposed an integration plan a week later, with a modest first phase planned for September, moving toward full integration in 1955. The *Afro-American*'s headline summed up the feelings of the district's black population: "Walls Crumbling."[40]

Eisenhower carefully planned what he would say publicly in response to the Court's decision. Given his view of the separation of powers, he deemed it inappropriate to comment on the merits of a Supreme Court decision. Politically, Eisenhower expected the same angry response in the South that the Supreme Court justices had feared. The president often reminded his peers that the South had lived under *Plessy* for nearly six decades, and that the adjustment to *Brown* would be difficult. He believed that the most effective way to enlist compliance by white southerners was to urge them to obey the law rather than to lecture them on the morality of the issue.

The day he met with the D.C. commissioners, May 18, Eisenhower informed his aides "that he would simply say the Supreme Court is the law of the land, that he had sworn to uphold the Constitution, and he would do so in this case." Ike worried aloud that Jimmy Byrnes's threat would materialize—that southern states would abolish public school systems and pass legislation to give financial aid to private schools. He feared that this "would not only handicap Negro children but would work to the detriment of the so-called 'poor whites' in the South."[41]

Eisenhower followed his plan precisely at his May 19 news conference. He declined to give advice to the South. Then Eisenhower made the pronouncement that, for decades to come, would generate controversy about his stance on *Brown:* "The Supreme Court has spoken and I am sworn to uphold the constitutional processes in this country; and I will obey." Eisenhower never budged from that position as president. A reporter then asked whether *Brown* would cause political difficulties for southern leaders who had supported the Republican ticket in 1952. Eisenhower responded, "The Supreme Court, as I understand it, is not under any administration." He said that he stood for "honest, decent government" and the southerners would have to decide whether "I have got any sense or haven't."[42] By any measure, this did not sound like a ringing endorsement of the Supreme Court's decision.

No Waiting in D.C.

Thanks to the president's leadership, the District of Columbia moved ahead. Seventeen organizations and numerous Negro leaders criticized the Corning plan for gradual desegregation and demanded immediate and complete integration of the schools. Despite that response, on May 25—one week after *Brown* was announced—the board of education approved Superintendent Corning's plan for the district's schools.[43]

On June 7, Samuel Spencer, the chairman of the district commissioners, wrote the president a "personal and confidential" letter, informing him that, due to "considerable criticism by colored organizations," the school board had reconsidered whether to require immediate integration. Superintendent Corning had stated that it would be physically impossible to redraw school district lines to facilitate full integration by September. The board voted five to three against immediate integration along color lines, with the three Negro members in favor. The board then formally adopted the Corning plan. Spencer met with Corning after the meeting and pressured him for accelerated action. The superintendent agreed to make integration effective in twenty-one of the 158 schools in September 1954, and guaranteed the completion of the full integration plan in 1955. Spencer promised the president: "I will continue to keep you informed of further developments."[44]

Prior to the beginning of school in September, the Federation of Citizens Associations, a coalition of anti-integration groups, filed suit in the district court to delay the board's plan on the grounds that the Supreme Court had not provided guidelines for enforcement. U.S. Assistant Attorney General Warren E. Burger told the court that he had intervened in the case "as a result of a direct order from President Eisenhower" and restated the president's commitment to making Washington a model for the nation. The case was dismissed.[45]

Meanwhile, Spencer notified Eisenhower that the first day of school in September 1954 took place without incident. On September 20, the commissioner reported that Corning had exceeded his original plan. Three-quarters of the schools—116 out of 158—had enrolled students of both races, and thirty-seven schools featured integrated teaching faculties. But Spencer's report ignored how much tokenism was involved in these initial desegregation efforts. Approximately 1,900 African-American students had been transferred to previously all-white schools, and the integration in former all-black schools was negligible.[46] Nevertheless, while most of the South was "stalling" on school integration, the Associated Press announced that desegregation was "advancing rapidly in District of Columbia schools." Eisenhower's commitment to ending segregation where there was federal authority had once again produced results. In early 1957, Senator Hubert Humphrey, a frequent critic of the president, would admit to a constituent that the "integration of the school system in the District has been effected rather smoothly."[47]

Brown II Arguments

On October 4, 1954, as its new term began, the Supreme Court issued a call for briefs on the implementation of *Brown*, in preparation for hearing oral arguments. Two plaintiffs declined to participate. The board of education of Topeka, Kansas, informed the Court that desegregation was already proceeding "as rapidly as is practicable." The District of Columbia reported its desegregation plan had been executed, although that plan was attacked for its "gradualist element" by the NAACP's Nabrit and Hayes. Once again the Court had invited the Justice Department to submit a brief. The briefs would be presented to the Court in November, with oral argument scheduled for December.[48]

Five days after the Court reconvened, Justice Robert Jackson died. Southerners hoped for the appointment of one of their own, but Eisenhower nominated a New York judge, a former law firm colleague of Attorney General Brownell. John Marshall Harlan II was the grandson and namesake of the John Marshall Harlan who had cast the lone dissenting vote in *Plessy v. Ferguson* in 1896. Southern Democrats delayed Harlan's appointment but Eisenhower refused to withdraw the nomination; he renominated Harlan in January 1955, when a new congress convened. The Senate confirmed Harlan 71–11 on March 16, in time for the new justice to participate in the decision that would come to be known as *Brown II*, spelling out requirements for implementing the original decision.[49]

Meanwhile, Eisenhower monitored the justices' struggles with the troublesome issues surrounding the enforcement of their May 17 decision. On October 23, he wrote his friend, Swede Hazlett, that "the segregation issue will, I think, become acute or tend to die out according to the character of the procedure orders that the Court will probably issue this winter." Eisenhower, relying on Brownell's sources, suspected what the justices would do: "My own guess is that they will be very moderate and accord a maximum of initiative to local courts."[50]

The NAACP brief, submitted in November, presented the justices with powerful arguments against gradualism. The NAACP lawyers implored the Court to "reiterate in the clearest possible language that segregation in public education is a denial of the equal protection of the laws." Desegregation should be immediate, require periodic reports to the lower courts, and establish "an outer time limit by which desegregation must be completed," no later than September 1956. Thurgood Marshall's brief called for the Court to "direct the issuance of decrees in each of these cases requiring desegregation by no later than September of 1955."[51]

The Eisenhower administration's brief, oriented more toward gradualism, was edited by the president of the United States—an extraordinary involvement. Brownell recalled that Eisenhower "actually wrote in his own handwriting some suggested language" for the document, which was prepared by the new solicitor general, Simon E. Sobeloff, a progressive advocate of civil rights causes in his home state of Maryland. Those who have seen that document, which is no longer available, report that Eisenhower toned down the Justice Department's rhetoric that might shame the South. Still, in the end, Ike signed off on a document that proposed an enforcement strategy more assertive than the cautious Court was ready to accept.[52]

At his November 23 news conference, Eisenhower gave the impression that he was uninvolved in preparing the administration's brief. Asked if he had any personal views related to the document, Eisenhower responded, "Not particularly." He noted that "the Attorney General is required to file his brief," but that, due to foreign travel, Brownell's submission might be delayed. Actually, Brownell was set to submit the brief the next day, a fact the president surely knew. Eisenhower's dissembling gave the impression that he did not know the document's content. He reprised his legalistic premise: "The Supreme Court has ruled what is the law in this case, what the Constitution means." "I am sure America wants to obey the Constitution," he continued, "but there is a very great practical problem involved, and there are certainly deep-seated emotions." Eisenhower predicted that the justices, in *Brown II,* would take into account these difficulties: "I don't believe they intend to be arbitrary, at least that is my understanding."[53]

If Eisenhower's editing muted the language of the government's brief, it was still compelling. "The constitutionality of racial segregation in the public schools is no longer in issue," the attorney general declared. His document described the deleterious effect on children of denying them what is "a fundamental human right, supported by considerations of morality as well as law." The brief challenged the Warren Court to spurn timidity, arguing that "where there are no solid obstacles to desegregation, delay is not justified and should not be permitted." Brownell warned against any order that "might have the practical effect of slowing down desegregation where it could be swiftly accomplished." The Court "should make it clear that any proposal for desegregation over an indefinite period of time will be unacceptable, and that there can be no justification anywhere for failure to make an immediate and substantial start toward desegregation, in a good-faith effort to end segregation as soon as feasible." The brief forcefully concluded: "Delay solely for the sake of delay is intolerable."

While leaving enforcement to the lower courts, the attorney general proposed that the lower courts order "the defendants to submit within 90 days a plan for ending, as soon as feasible, racial segregation of pupils in public schools subject to their authority or control." Failing the submission of such a plan, the lower courts should issue an order "directing admission of the plaintiffs and other children similarly situated to nonsegregated public schools at the beginning of the next school term." The attorney general urged close scrutiny of plans developed by school districts, requiring detailed progress reports on the implementation of those plans, with the lower courts reporting periodically to the Supreme Court.[54]

A Cautious Decision

The Justice Department's brief displeased the justices. The administration's proposal for specific guidelines and a timetable would force the Court into hands-on supervision amid political turmoil. Earl Warren was determined to avoid that. In a phone conversation, Brownell reported to Eisenhower that the justices—probably Warren in particular—felt that the president "was predicting what they were going to do." The use of "predicting" is misleading. The justices had not seen Ike's October letter to Hazlett, in which he predicted that the Court would delegate enforcement to the lower courts. The context of the phone conversation was the Justice Department's brief, to which Ike had contributed. Brownell probably meant that the justices believed the president, through the brief, was telling the justices what they *should* do. Eisenhower responded that he had tried to avoid that. The Court members were scheduled to attend their annual tea at the White House. Given their adverse reaction to the brief, Brownell suggested that the president "avoid discussion of segregation."[55]

For *Brown II,* Warren again planned a decision that laypersons could understand. On May 31, 1955, the justices issued their opinion, sending the enforcement issues to the lower courts with no requirements that would embroil the High Court in local cases. In the unanimous decision, Warren asserted only that the courts should require that segregated districts "make a prompt and reasonable start toward full compliance" with *Brown.* The chief justice provided the opponents of integration with a litany of excuses that school districts could invoke to slow the process. "Once such a start has been made," Warren wrote, "the courts may find that additional time is necessary to carry out the ruling in an effective manner." The parties could extend the time if there were issues related "to administration, arising from the physical condition of the school plant, the school transportation system, personnel, revision of school districts and attendance areas" and necessary "revision of local laws and regulations." Felix Frankfurter is credited with proposing the famous phrase associated with the May 31 decision—that desegregation should take place "with all deliberate speed." Thurgood Marshall is alleged to have translated this phrase as "S-L-O-W."[56]

When Brownell called the president to inform him of the Court's ruling, the attorney general said the justices had fulfilled Eisenhower's October prediction "almost exactly." The Court had sent the cases back to the district courts, which would "receive plans from local school boards and take into consideration all local factors." Brownell always believed that the Supreme Court's decision not to impose a timetable for compliance, like the ninety-day proposal made by the Justice Department, was a serious mistake. He concluded in his memoirs that "all deliberate speed" became, for the southerners, "some indefinite date in the future."[57]

Warren, in his memoirs, vigorously defended his approach. The former governor, perhaps still thinking like a politician, contended that proposals for immediate action ignored "the complexity of our federal system, the time it takes controversial litigation to proceed through the hierarchy of courts to the Supreme Court, the fact that the administration of the public school system is a state and local function so long as it does not contravene constitutional principles, that each state has its own system with different relationships between state and local government and that the relationship can be changed at will by the state government if there should be a determination to bypass or defeat the decision of the Supreme Court."[58]

The Supreme Court's year-long delay after *Brown I* in issuing the implementation decision had given the opponents of segregation time to mobilize; the new opinion sanctioned further delay. Without a timetable, the NAACP Legal Fund's lawyers would be forced to fight the desegregation battle school by school, district by district, without a timetable or other built-in mechanism to trigger federal court or Justice Department intervention. On June 4, 1955, they accepted that challenge. Thurgood Marshall's organization convened fifty-five leaders from sixteen southern states and the District of Columbia to plan for petitions in every segregated school district, to organize supporting groups, and, if necessary, to institute suits in federal court.[59]

Some of Eisenhower's subsequent discomfort with the Court's decision was rooted in *Brown II*. The Court-sanctioned excuses for delay presented his administration with a formidable problem while encouraging procrastination and conflict in the South. The executive branch had no statute authorizing action or any appropriation from Congress to finance measures aimed at ensuring compliance with *Brown*. Brownell contended that the Court's ruling in *Brown II* "was a major source of the enforcement problem for the executive branch."[60]

Dwight Eisenhower had acted resolutely in desegregating the District of Columbia and the armed forces, combating discrimination in employment, and in appointing two progressive justices to the Supreme Court. Deluged by demands for intervention in the years ahead, his administration would lack authority to intervene in the states except in the narrowest of circumstances. This prescription for turmoil would dominate the civil rights agenda for the remainder of the Eisenhower presidency.

In the aftermath of *Brown*, the president would be forced to move beyond his policy of eliminating discrimination where there was federal authority to act. *Brown* would eventually compel him to seek legislative authority to address enforcement in the states. Otherwise, when confronted with violent resistance to a federal court order, Eisenhower might be forced to send in the army. That prospect would trouble him from the moment *Brown* was announced.

CHAPTER FOUR

A Judiciary to Enforce *Brown*

*The lawyers of this country have not come to understand that I
do not consider federal judgeships as included in the list of
appointments subject to "patronage."*
—Dwight D. Eisenhower, March 23, 1956

Dwight Eisenhower's lasting contribution to the advancement of
civil rights was his judicial appointments. Ever the strategic
planner, Eisenhower preferred comprehensive, expansive approaches
to solving problems. That inclination was enshrined in the "broad
front" strategy he managed for the war in Europe and in his proposal for an interstate highway system. The president and Attorney
General Herbert Brownell embraced a similarly strategic approach
to civil rights—one aimed, as Brownell phrased it in his memoirs, at
the "reshaping of the federal judiciary" and "building the foundations of equality."[1]

The Eisenhower Process

Brownell recalled in his memoirs that Eisenhower, at the outset of
his presidency, "took an unusual personal interest in judicial appointments." Eisenhower told the attorney general that he wanted
his recommendations for judicial appointments to reflect "character and ability," not politics. They instituted the practice of having

the American Bar Association screen potential nominees for federal judgeships prior to any announcement, a process that was followed for the next fifty years. Until his heart attack in 1955, Eisenhower met personally with every federal court nominee who came to Washington for hearings.[2]

Eisenhower's predecessors had housed the process for identifying judicial candidates in the White House, relying primarily on the recommendations of senators and congressmen. Eisenhower depoliticized the process by delegating it to the attorney general. Warren Olney, head of the criminal division in the Justice Department, recalled that Brownell was very meticulous about judicial appointments. Olney quoted Brownell to the effect that "it's the judges that were going to give this administration its reputation, that they'll be here long after this administration goes."[3]

Eisenhower repeatedly turned down judgeship recommendations from politicians and friends. Early in his first term, the president rejected a nomination from Senator Robert A. Taft of Ohio, Ike's adversary for the 1952 Republican nomination, on the grounds that Taft's nominee was too old. Taft produced a younger candidate, Potter Stewart, whom Eisenhower eventually appointed to the Supreme Court. Ike expressed frustration to his brother Edgar "that even the lawyers of this country have not come to understand that I do not consider federal judgeships as included in the list of appointments subject to 'patronage.'"[4]

Eisenhower and Brownell agreed that, beyond Chief Justice Earl Warren, they would restrict nominations for the Supreme Court "to people who had served on either minor federal benches or on the supreme courts of the various states." After *Brown,* they may have concluded that this policy would mute controversy over appointments to the bench. Eisenhower publicly affirmed his policy in October 1954, telling a press conference that "for the Associate Justices, I should think it would be a good practice to bring in people who have had real experience on the courts."[5]

Eisenhower explored abandoning that principle when he considered Brownell as a possible nominee. In 1957, the president read a newspaper article chronicling Brownell's qualifications for the Supreme Court and pointedly asked the attorney general if they should stick with their agreement to confine nominations to sitting judges; Brownell responded that they should. Eisenhower pressed the point: if the attorney general had judicial ambitions, the president could appoint him to a vacancy on the appellate court in New York. Brownell responded that they "should just let things go as they were." Eisenhower observed in his diary: "It is entirely possible that he would like to be on the Supreme Court. But I think that on balance he prefers to go back to private practice some day and earn some money for himself and family."[6]

Ike considered Brownell again in 1958, after the attorney general had left the government, though he still lacked judicial experience. While he believed that the New Yorker would make a great justice, Eisenhower knew that the southern segregationists "would point out that he was Attorney General when the Supreme Court's integration orders conforming to the decision of 1954 were promulgated." Eisenhower never completely abandoned his vision of appointing Brownell to the Court. In December 1968, on his deathbed, Ike wrote a letter to President-elect Richard Nixon, recommending Brownell as a possible successor to Chief Justice Earl Warren.[7]

In any event, Eisenhower's policy of relying on the Justice Department to propose candidates for nomination to federal courts guaranteed moderately progressive nominees in regard to civil rights. The president knew that Brownell and his successor, William Rogers, would never knowingly recommend a segregationist for a federal bench.

Supreme Court Appointments

Eisenhower's Supreme Court appointments after Warren reveal more about his convictions on the *Brown* decision than any public statement.

Eisenhower appointed five justices to the Supreme Court. None were southerners or segregationists, despite enormous political pressures on Eisenhower to appoint such judges. Michael A. Kahn, an attorney and author who specializes in federal court cases, asserts that despite southern agitation after *Brown*, "Eisenhower defiantly nominated four justices who were pledged to uphold *Brown*." The president consciously made appointments that would entrench *Brown* in the judiciary and laid "a foundation for the Court's broad expansion of civil rights in the 1950's and 1960's." Kahn calls Eisenhower "the chief architect of the judicial edifice that withstood Southern and conservative efforts to undermine *Brown v. Board of Education*."[8]

When Justice Robert Jackson died of a heart attack on October 9, 1954, the country was in the midst of a congressional campaign. Partly because arguments were scheduled to commence on *Brown II*, Eisenhower waited until the election was over before announcing his nominee. The pressure from southerners, especially Jimmy Byrnes, was for the president to appoint someone who would work to overturn *Brown*, but speculation centered on former New York governor and presidential candidate Thomas E. Dewey, Secretary of State John Foster Dulles, and Herbert Brownell—liberal Republicans who would not have fulfilled segregationists' hopes. A White House source indicated to the press that Eisenhower, unlike with the nomination for chief justice a year earlier, was inclined to appoint a "career jurist" to the Court.[9]

Brownell recommended a former New York law firm colleague, John Marshall Harlan II, age fifty-five. Eisenhower had appointed Harlan to the Second Circuit Court of Appeals earlier in the year. The newspapers quoted White House Press Secretary James Hagerty to the effect that "the President had known Judge Harlan personally for some time." After Warren's appointment, Brownell and the president had begun to groom potential High Court nominees such as Harlan well in advance, appointing them to lower federal courts before moving them up the judicial ladder.[10]

Ike's selection of Harlan was striking in its symbolism. He was named for his grandfather, the justice who had cast the lone dissenting vote in *Plessy v. Ferguson* in 1896. The elder Harlan had argued that the Constitution was "color blind" and predicted that his minority opinion would someday prevail—a prophecy fulfilled on May 17, 1954. But his grandson's nomination quickly encountered difficulty. Senator James Eastland (D-Mississippi), who would become chairman of the Senate Judiciary Committee in 1956, informed

Brownell that Harlan had been accused of having "Communist sympathies," a charge that arose because the judiciary committee staff investigated the wrong man with the same name.[11]

When Harlan's appointment was not approved by the Senate in its postelection special session in 1954, Eisenhower resubmitted the nomination to the new Congress in January. The Judiciary Committee delayed its hearing on Harlan's nomination until February 23, a postponement Eisenhower called "unfortunate." The *New York Times* speculated that, if Harlan was not confirmed, the Supreme Court might delay the implementation of *Brown* until its following term, beginning in October 1955.[12] After Harlan was approved by the Judiciary Committee on March 9, Eastland spoke on the Senate floor for three hours, declaring that the appointment had been "dictated by Thomas E. Dewey." The senator claimed that the reason for his opposition was not segregation; he attacked Harlan's position on American sovereignty in foreign affairs, his limited judicial experience, and the judge's origins, stating that New York residents "possess views and philosophies which are different from the viewpoints of the rest of the country." Harlan was finally confirmed by the Senate on March 16, 1955, four months after Eisenhower's nomination, in time for Harlan to participate in *Brown II*.[13]

Eisenhower's third appointment to the High Court was just as remarkable. Eisenhower and Brownell had repeatedly discussed the possibility of appointing a Catholic, in a time when anti-Catholic prejudice still afflicted candidates for high office. In November 1954, the American bishops of the Catholic Church contemplated passing a resolution calling for the placing of a Catholic on the Supreme Court. Instead, Francis Cardinal Spellman of New York held a private conversation with Eisenhower. On December 2, Brownell recommended to Eisenhower that he appoint a Catholic to the next open seat unless it was Felix Frankfurter's, who occupied the so-called Jewish seat. In 1955, Eisenhower reminded Brownell: "I still want the name of some fine, prominent Catholic to nominate to the Bench."[14]

In 1956, in the midst of his reelection campaign, Eisenhower got his chance. Justice Sherman Minton, the lone Catholic on the Court, informed the president of his desire to retire. Unlike in 1952, civil rights was now a contentious electoral issue. The "Southern Manifesto," defying the *Brown* decision and signed by 101 congressmen, had been released in March. Racially explosive confrontations were under way in Mississippi and Alabama. Politically, Eisenhower could have avoided controversy by waiting to appoint a replacement until after the election.

Instead, Eisenhower and Brownell selected an associate justice from the New Jersey Supreme Court named William Joseph Brennan, a fifty-year-old Catholic. Brennan had been recommended by that state's respected chief justice, Arthur T. Vanderbilt, who told Eisenhower that Brennan had the best "judicial mind" he had ever known. A liberal Democrat, Brennan would, without doubt, uphold the *Brown* decision—hardly the kind of High Court member the segregationists wanted. The appointment also demonstrated how much Eisenhower had learned about presidential politics. The nomination appeared nonpartisan, yet Eisenhower selected a nominee from a northern state he intended to carry in the election. Once again, as with Earl Warren, Eisenhower made a recess appointment, announcing it on September 29 after Congress had adjourned for the election campaign. Brennan served for thirty-six years as one of the Court's respected, often controversial, liberals.[15]

Eisenhower's fourth appointment to the Court in 1957 was his least distinguished. Justice Stanley F. Reed informed the president of his intent to resign in January of that year. Eisenhower nominated Charles E. Whittaker, a fellow Kansan with a law degree from the University of Kansas City. Whittaker was not a close associate of the president and had ascended the judicial ladder based on his record as a judge. Whittaker had practiced law in Missouri and, in 1954, Eisenhower had appointed him United States district judge for the Western District of Missouri. In 1956, Eisenhower appointed him to the Eighth Circuit Court of Appeals. While he was relatively conservative, his appointment to the High Court did not begin to fulfill the demand of the southerners for someone more sympathetic to them on school desegregation. Whittaker's fragile health led to his retirement from the Supreme Court in 1962.[16]

After Brownell

Scholars have often assumed that Eisenhower's progressive court appointments were primarily Brownell's handiwork. Brownell certainly influenced Eisenhower, but the president's commitment to appointing quality judges transcended that relationship. Brownell left government service in 1957, and Eisenhower maintained a similar pattern of appointments with his new attorney general, William Rogers. The president again refused to appoint a southerner or a segregation sympathizer to the Supreme Court, and he avoided, in most cases, the appointment of opponents of *Brown* to the lower federal courts.[17]

Eisenhower was never quite as comfortable with Rogers as he had been with Brownell. When Rogers was promoted from his position as deputy attorney general, Eisenhower cautioned him: "I have always taken a deep personal interest in the appointment of Federal Judges. For this reason I should like that, before you submit a formal nomination for signature, you drop in to confer with me about the matter." Eisenhower emphasized to Rogers that "it has been my habit to look over such nominations very carefully before we have committed ourselves to making them."

A year later, Eisenhower was upset that Rogers was not consistently following those instructions. In January 1959, the president underscored to Rogers "how important I believe it is to anticipate vacancies in the Courts and make our selection and announcements of appointments before pressures begin to build up in favor of particular individuals. To delay is to make enemies all over the place— and very few friends." The following month, Eisenhower wrote a "personal and confidential" letter to Rogers, describing "disturbing flaws" in the way Rogers was selecting candidates for the federal judiciary. Eisenhower and his principal assistants, the president complained, were too often "uninformed as to vacancies, prospective vacancies, and possible candidates for some judicial position until it is far too late to have any flexibility in choice." The president went over the letter in person with Rogers, giving him step-by-step instructions on how to handle future appointments.[18]

Rogers attempted to adjust to Eisenhower's rigorous expecta-

tions, especially in the lone Supreme Court appointment he managed. When Harold H. Burton announced that he would retire in
October 1958, the southerners had yet another chance to persuade
Eisenhower to appoint one of their own. This was the year after the
president had sent troops into Little Rock, Arkansas, to uphold
court-ordered desegregation. Eisenhower could have taken this opportunity to appoint someone sympathetic to the South as a peace
offering.

Eisenhower never seriously considered appointing anyone to
the High Court in 1958 who would not support *Brown*. Initially, he
reviewed three potential nominees—Herbert Brownell, Warren
Burger, and Elbert Parr Tuttle, all supporters of desegregation.
Burger had served as assistant attorney general for three years
before Eisenhower appointed him to the U.S. Court of Appeals for
the District of Columbia in 1955. He was eventually elevated to chief
justice by Richard Nixon. Eisenhower put Tuttle, a Fifth Circuit
Court judge, on the list because "he is of Southern origin," although
Tuttle's appointment would not have pleased the segregationists; he
was a courageous supporter of *Brown* and desegregation.[19]

On October 7, Eisenhower received a telegram from a southern
GOP congressman, William C. Cramer of Florida. He urged Eisenhower to appoint "a southerner who is an outstanding constitutional lawyer, one who has ample judicial experience," to succeed
Justice Burton. Cramer's plea came too late. Eisenhower had already closed the southern door to the Court with his selection of
Potter Stewart. Born in Michigan, and Yale-educated, Stewart had
practiced law in New York and served in the navy during World War
II. He moved to Ohio in 1947 and, in 1954, Eisenhower had appointed him to the Sixth Circuit Court of Appeals. Burton's retirement was effective October 13, 1958, and Eisenhower, for the third
time with his five Supreme Court nominees, made a recess appointment.[20]

Eisenhower's nomination of Stewart to the Court touched off
another four-month-long controversy in the Senate, although the
judge's record was so distinguished that southerners could not
attack his competence. Senator Richard Russell (D-Georgia) led the
opposition, arguing that the appointment was "a part of a deliberate

policy by the Department of Justice to perpetuate some recent decisions of the Court in segregation rulings, which decisions were partly based on amicus curiae briefs submitted by the Justice Department." During his confirmation hearings, Stewart was asked about *Brown*. He told the committee members that they should not vote for him if they assumed he was "dedicated to the cause of overturning that decision." "Because," Stewart declared, "I am not."[21]

Reshaping the Judiciary: The Fifth Circuit

Eisenhower's determination to appoint progressive judges did not stop with the Supreme Court. In the Deep South, this meant confronting senators who normally controlled the appointment of federal judges. Brownell recalled that "candidates recommended by southern senators during this period almost always had a public record opposed to desegregation." So, Brownell's Justice Department made recommendations to Eisenhower without senatorial endorsements. Because the southern senators were invariably Democrats, Eisenhower could invoke party affiliation to justify ignoring their preferences. The Justice Department consistently recommended men of quality who, if not on record in favor of desegregation, were believed to be open-minded on that issue.[22]

The legal struggle to enforce *Brown* was centered on the federal courts that covered the Deep South—the fourth and fifth circuits. The United States Court of Appeals for the Fifth Judicial Circuit covered six states: Alabama, Florida, Georgia, Louisiana, Mississippi, and Texas, all part of the Confederacy during the Civil War. Herbert Brownell had recommended four judges, all supporters of desegregation, to serve in that circuit following the May 1954 *Brown* decision. Eisenhower appointed Elbert Parr Tuttle of Georgia in 1954, John Brown of Nebraska in 1955, and John Minor Wisdom of Louisiana in 1957 to the appeals court. He appointed the fourth judge, Frank M. Johnson, Jr., in October 1955 to the Alabama middle district court, a trial court subordinate to the Fifth Circuit. In 1956, Johnson issued the court order striking down segregated seating on Montgomery's public buses after Rosa Parks's refusal to give up her seat had launched a city-wide bus boycott. These Eisenhower appointees became a bulwark of support for desegregation efforts in the Fifth Circuit.[23]

John Minor Wisdom's appointment in 1957 was the result of a contest with segregationist Governor Robert Kennon of Louisiana, who sought the judicial position for himself. Wisdom had worked for the Eisenhower campaign in 1952 and had served with distinction on the President's Committee on Government Contracts. Kennon was one of the three southern Democratic governors who had endorsed Eisenhower for president in 1952. Judge Wayne Borah had announced his intent to retire from the Fifth Circuit in 1956. As early as 1954, Kennon had lobbied the president for the appointment, and Charles E. Wilson, Ike's secretary of defense, had supported his nomination. George C. Stafford, a Louisiana Negro leader, wrote to Eisenhower that his people were opposed to Kennon's nomination "because he is hostile and obnoxious to colored people in Louisiana." Despite Kennon's broad political support, the president never appointed the segregationist to the bench.

The selection of Wisdom over Kennon again signaled Eisenhower's alliance with the progressives on school desegregation. Tuttle, Brown, and Wisdom, along with a Truman appointee—Richard Taylor Rives—bore particular burdens at the appeals court level for court-ordered desegregation in the circuit. Burke Marshall, a former Yale University law professor and assistant attorney general for civil rights in the Kennedy administration, later wrote: "Those four judges, I think, have made as much of an imprint on American society and American law as any four judges below the Supreme Court have ever done on any court." Marshall concluded that "if it hadn't been for judges like that on the Fifth Circuit, I think *Brown* would have failed in the end."[24]

Eisenhower and Brownell came to regret one appointment because, in making it, they departed from their policy of ignoring southern senatorial recommendations. Ben F. Cameron of Mississippi, a former Democrat, appeared to have the right credentials for a position on the Fifth Circuit in 1955. Deputy Attorney General William Rogers, who was friendly with Mississippi's Senator Eastland, failed to perceive the danger signal in the senator's advocacy for Cameron, and did not unearth the nominee's segregationist leanings; John Minor Wisdom provided a reassuring endorsement. Unfortunately, Cameron turned out to be a strict states'-righter who opposed *Brown* and was committed to obstructing the rulings sought by Eisenhower's other appointees.[25]

Rogers's friendly relationship with Eastland resulted in another embarrassing incident. When Rogers succeeded Brownell in 1957, he asked Lawrence Walsh, an Eisenhower judicial appointee from the southern district of New York, to serve as his deputy. Brownell's relationship with the southern senators had been contentious, so Rogers asked Walsh to build a better relationship with Eastland, who now chaired the Senate Judiciary Committee. The fruit of that friendship was a proposal in 1959 for the administration to add twenty-five new federal judgeships to handle the crushing workload arising out of civil rights cases. Walsh promised to consult Eastland and other southern senators on nominations to the new positions, and Eastland convinced the majority leader, Senator Lyndon Johnson of Texas, to go along with the legislation creating the judgeships. Eastland apparently believed that southerners would get to nominate a number of judges without complying with the administration's usual prohibition against segregationists, a dramatic reversal of Brownell's previous policy.[26]

To Walsh's surprise, Attorney General Rogers abruptly wrote Eastland a letter that so offended him and Johnson that they killed the legislation. The letter revealed that Eisenhower had effectively vetoed the arrangement. The reasons for Eisenhower's discomfort were obvious. The Mississippi Democrat had consistently opposed Ike's judicial appointments in the South, and Walsh's bargain would give Eastland the chance to promote more judges like Ben Cameron. Eisenhower made one concession; he was willing, Rogers wrote, to "fill those vacancies so they will be divided evenly between the parties." But the president set a condition that was unacceptable to Eastland: he would require recommendations for "the best qualified men to fill these vacancies irrespective of party." Eastland knew what that meant. With Eisenhower, "best qualified" had consistently meant candidates who were opposed to segregation. Rogers emphasized that he was "not authorized" to make any other type of commitment.[27] As a result, the deal was never consummated.

Reshaping the Judiciary: The Fourth Circuit

Eisenhower's nomination of Simon E. Sobeloff to a seat on the Fourth Circuit in 1955 was particularly contentious. That circuit encompassed Virginia, Maryland, West Virginia, and North and South Carolina. Sobeloff, Jewish and born in Baltimore, had worked closely with Thurgood Marshall and openly opposed segregation in Maryland, including during his service as chief judge of the state court of appeals. He had become U.S. solicitor general in February 1954, had developed the *Brown II* brief (partially edited by Eisenhower) that the Justice Department submitted to the Supreme Court in November of that year, and had argued the administration's case for the enforcement of school desegregation before the High Court.

Eisenhower and Brownell apparently were grooming Sobeloff to fill the Jewish seat on the Supreme Court whenever Felix Frankfurter retired. Eisenhower was impressed with Sobeloff's work on *Brown II*. The president suggested to Brownell that they consider appointing him to the open position in the Fourth Circuit, wondering if "that would be better preparation for him than [the] present position of Solicitor General."[28]

Southern segregationists raised a furor over Sobeloff's nomination to the Fourth Circuit. The appointment placed Eisenhower directly at odds with South Carolina politicians—former governor Jimmy Byrnes, Senator J. Strom Thurmond, and Byrnes's successor as governor, George Bell Timmerman. The tradition had been to rotate circuit court appointments among the states, and the South Carolinians had insisted that it was time for another appointment from their state. Thurmond passionately lobbied Eisenhower for his candidate, Robert McCormick Figg, Jr., of Charleston. The senator had even recruited General Mark W. Clark, Eisenhower's World War II colleague, to endorse Figg. The general touted Figg's "capabilities, his unimpeachable character, integrity, and capacity to do this job should you see fit to give him the appointment. He is held in highest esteem here in South Carolina."[29]

After Eisenhower formally nominated Sobeloff to the appeals court on July 14, 1955, he was inundated with mail protesting the appointment. A North Carolina clergyman, who claimed to be "one of your strong supporters," wrote Ike the following week that the source of the appointment was "the attempt by the NAACP to integrate the negroes with the whites." He charged that Eisenhower was supporting that goal by resorting to "underhanded judicial means."[30]

By late July, the Sobeloff nomination was in trouble. Despite fierce southern opposition, Eisenhower and Brownell declined to withdraw the nomination. The president declared to the American Bar Association in August that he would not appoint any judge who would not "serve in the tradition of John Marshall," the revered chief justice who had served from 1801 to 1835. In November, after Congress had adjourned without confirming Sobeloff, Brownell spoke before a B'nai Brith dinner honoring the solicitor general and announced that he would be renominated in the new congressional term.[31]

Eisenhower resubmitted Sobeloff's nomination on January 12, 1956. When Harley M. Kilgore, a West Virginia Democrat and chair of the Senate Judiciary Committee, died at the end of February, James Eastland inherited the chairmanship, a post he would hold for the next two decades. Eastland's promotion appeared to doom the nomination. After two more months of foot-dragging by Eastland, Eisenhower deplored the committee's inaction on the Sobeloff nomination at his May 23 news conference. Ike asserted that he had nominated Sobeloff "on the same basis that I nominate every other individual to the Federal Courts. His records are brought to me, [and] I go through them from stem to stern."[32]

Finally, Lyndon Johnson of Texas, the Democratic majority leader, signaled the evolution of his views on civil rights. Attempting to position himself to run for president, Johnson urged Eastland to break the deadlock for the sake of the Democratic Party. The Judiciary Committee voted to approve the nomination on June 28. The struggle on the Senate floor continued until Johnson scheduled a marathon debate on July 16. The raucous session ended after 8:00 P.M. with Sobeloff confirmed by a 64–19 vote—one year after he had first been nominated.[33]

During the Sobeloff debate, another vacancy occurred on the

Fourth Circuit. Eisenhower refused to send the second nomination to the Senate until his first one was confirmed. Jimmy Byrnes lobbied Eisenhower for a South Carolina appointee to the second position, regardless of identity. Byrnes told Ike that he had heard that Assistant Attorney General Warren Burger had commented that "no lawyer would be appointed who participated in any way in the effort to continue segregated schools." Byrnes complained that this restriction ruled out judges who, prior to May 17, 1954, had ruled on what they thought was the Constitution. Eisenhower sent Byrnes a perfunctory letter saying, as usual, that he had referred Byrnes's letter "to the Attorney General." Brownell attempted to reassure Byrnes in a phone conversation, asserting that the alleged comment did not represent policy, nor was there any evidence that Burger had made it.[34]

After Sobeloff was approved, Strom Thurmond once again lobbied for Robert Figg for appointment to the new position. The senator visited White House Chief of Staff Sherman Adams in December 1956 to advocate fervently for his friend, saying in a follow-up telegram: "I shall be embarrassed if he is not appointed. However I would be embarrassed even more if our state should not receive the appointment."[35]

Eisenhower yielded to the demand that the next appointment go to South Carolina and, in February 1957, Brownell recommended Clement F. Haynsworth, Jr., a moderate Democrat, for the position. Despite the Justice Department's denial of the alleged Burger comment, it reflected the sentiment inside the administration: Haynsworth was another Eisenhower judicial nominee who had not been active "in the effort to continue segregated schools."[36]

A Judicial Foundation for Equality

Despite his aversion to appointing segregationist judges, Eisenhower did not break new ground in the appointment of Negroes to the federal courts. When asked in 1964 about this, Ike responded that he had instructed subordinates to seek "the very best people" regardless of religion, national origin, or color; however, he had not encouraged them to purposely recruit candidates representing such characteristics. In other words, affirmative action was not a policy he had considered or could conceivably implement at that time. Eisenhower had encountered enormous difficulties in getting white candidates such as Simon Sobeloff confirmed, so the odds were against the Senate confirming a black judicial nominee. Still, he and Brownell made one abortive effort. On July 13, 1956, Brownell wrote a memorandum recommending that Scovel Richardson be appointed United States district judge for the eastern district of Missouri. Eisenhower had previously appointed Richardson as chairman of the Federal Parole Board, the first Negro to hold that position. Prominent Missouri Republicans opposed Richardson's nomination to the federal district court, especially in an election year. Without their support, the appointment had no chance for success in the Senate, and Eisenhower did not submit the nomination. In 1957, Eisenhower named Richardson to a lifetime position on the U.S. Customs Court.[37]

Early in the Kennedy administration, Brownell, as president of the New York City Bar Association, testified at the confirmation hearing for one of President Kennedy's appointees. Following his testimony, Senator Eastland invited Brownell into his office for a drink. "Well, Jim," Brownell asked, "how are you getting along on the appointment of federal judges?" "Everything is fine now," Eastland replied. "It's much better than when you were here."[38]

Brownell believed that, by the end of the Eisenhower administration, the president "had established a beachhead in the southern states for the enforcement of the Supreme Court's civil rights decision; without it we would have faced a repeat of the Reconstruction period during which the courts played a major role in undoing the promise of the Fourteenth Amendment."[39]

The Eisenhower judges had momentous impact over the years. Simon Sobeloff led a three-judge panel in 1960 that declared Virginia's law closing desegregated schools unconstitutional, a blow to the "massive resistance" movement in the South. In 1962, Judge Elbert Tuttle led the struggle on the Fifth Circuit to secure the admission of James Meredith to the University of Mississippi, a decision that eventually caused President John F. Kennedy to send in troops. In 1965, Judge Frank M. Johnson, Jr., issued an order that directly affected the movement for passage of the Voting Rights Act that year. On March 7, protestors against voting discrimination, attempted to march from Selma, Alabama, to the state capitol at Montgomery. They were turned back by police using billy clubs, whips, and tear gas. The television coverage of the violence shocked the nation, prompting President Lyndon Johnson to address Congress on March 15 and propose a new voting rights act. Following one more abortive attempt, led by Martin Luther King, Jr., to march to Montgomery, Judge Johnson ordered Governor George Wallace to permit the marchers to complete their pilgrimage and, on March 25, they staged a nationally televised rally on the capitol steps. As a result of his appointment by President Eisenhower, Judge Johnson participated in numerous other landmark decisions during his illustrious forty-four-year career.[40]

Many more stories of these judges and their efforts to implement *Brown* and its desegregation principles have been chronicled by capable scholars. Their accounts of this titanic struggle fall short in one regard; they generally fail to recognize the central role that President Eisenhower played in appointing these "unlikely heroes."[41]

CHAPTER FIVE

The President
and the Chief Justice

*I wanted a man to serve as Chief Justice who felt the way we do
and who would be on the court for a long time. Therefore I
chose Warren.*

—DWIGHT D. EISENHOWER, JUNE 15, 1954

The importance of Earl Warren's appointment as chief justice
transcends the *Brown* decision. With his name attached to that
historic ruling, Warren assumed an iconic position that enabled him
to largely define how Dwight Eisenhower's leadership on civil rights
would be viewed by scholars and the media.

"I have always believed that President Eisenhower resented our
decision in *Brown v. Board of Education* and its progeny," Warren recorded in his memoirs.[1] The chief justice's opinion, posthumously
published in 1977, eight years after Eisenhower's death, has profoundly influenced the historiography of Eisenhower and civil
rights. The statement is more than a comment about a Court ruling;
it reflects Warren's bitterness toward the president who had appointed him.

Scholars and commentators frequently repeat the allegation
that Eisenhower was so shocked by the *Brown* ruling that he proclaimed the appointment of Earl Warren "the biggest damned fool
mistake I ever made." Herbert Brownell called this charge "apocry-
phal" and cast doubt on its authenticity, insisting he never heard

the president say anything comparable. Brownell traced the quotation to a 1969 oral history remark by Ralph H. Cake, a former Republican National Committeeman from Oregon and ardent opponent of Warren's selection as chief justice. Eisenhower's chief of staff, Sherman Adams, asserted that he never heard Ike say anything about Warren along the lines of, "Well if I'd known he was going to make these kinds of decisions, I never would have appointed him."[2]

Although Milton Eisenhower described his brother as "very fond of Governor Warren," he granted that Eisenhower did not approve of every Warren Court decision, and that with more years of experience, "he might not have appointed Governor Warren as Chief Justice." William Ewald, who assisted Eisenhower with his memoirs, confirmed that Ike could "blow off steam about Earl Warren and, in 1961, once named Warren as one of his worst appointments." In 1965, historian Stephen E. Ambrose interviewed Eisenhower for a biography and asked about his biggest mistake as president. Eisenhower replied: "The appointment of that S.O.B. Earl Warren."[3]

The core issue is whether Eisenhower's disillusionment with Warren was rooted in *Brown*. Brownell and Adams admitted that Eisenhower had qualms about the Warren Court, but they contended that those doubts were mainly focused on rulings regarding criminal law handed down after *Brown*, a conclusion Ambrose also embraced.[4]

The issue was born at the moment of Warren's nomination. Some news stories assumed that Eisenhower appointed Warren to the Supreme Court as a political reward for the governor's support at the 1952 Republican convention. Eisenhower insisted there was no bargain because Warren did not release the California delegation, pledged to him as a favorite son candidate. James Hagerty, Eisenhower's White House press secretary, said that the Warren appointment "was never a question of political debt. I think it was a question of getting the best man possible for any given job."[5]

According to Brownell, the president knew the California governor's record "in some detail," including that Warren was strong on civil rights and had publicly supported a fair employment practices commission (FEPC). Unlike Chief Justice Fred Vinson, who often voted against minority rights, Warren could be expected to support desegregation. Columnist James Reston reported that intimate friends of the California governor believed that, "if relieved from political pressures on the bench, his personal tendencies would be even more liberal than his political record."[6]

That probability would not have dismayed Eisenhower. Sherman Adams recalled that Eisenhower liked the governor and knew he was "liberal." According to Adams, the president understood that Warren would tend "on racial issues, for instance, to be more in accord with Eisenhower's views than would a justice picked from the South." Most important, Brownell, who Adams recalled "had great weight with the President," strongly supported Warren's appointment. Ever since their March 1952 encounter in Paris, Eisenhower had understood that the attorney's general's highest priority was progress toward racial justice. Adams would call the Supreme Court, starting with the Warren appointment, "a Brownell Court."[7]

A month after the first *Brown* decision, Eisenhower told Hagerty that he had seriously considered only two men for chief justice— Secretary of State John Foster Dulles and Warren. Although Eisenhower deemed Dulles too old for the bench, he discussed the position with his secretary of state who, according to Eisenhower's memoirs, eliminated himself; it is unlikely that Eisenhower would have chosen to disrupt his foreign policy team this early in his first term. As Eisenhower told Hagerty, "I wanted a man to serve as Chief Justice who felt the way we do and who would be on the court for a long time. Therefore I chose Warren."[8]

An Extraordinary Promise

Eisenhower maintained that he paid no political debt with Warren's appointment. Why, then, with qualified judicial candidates available, did Eisenhower make the California governor his first nominee, and risk the impression that he was playing politics with a Supreme Court appointment? Even brother Milton had opined to Ike that "the Chief Justice ought to be a man of judicial experience." Eisenhower justified the choice by citing Warren's qualities as a statesman and strong administrator, distinguishing the criteria for chief justice from that of other Court positions.[9]

The president was not violating sacred tradition in appointing a politician to the Court; the membership at the time of Vinson's death—the chief justice himself was a former congressman and Treasury secretary—included former senators Hugo Black and Harold Burton. Yet Eisenhower, given his own high standards, fretted about Warren's lack of judicial experience. Earlier, when Brownell encountered difficulty in filling the post of solicitor general, the president had suggested appointing Warren, on the grounds that the position would enhance the governor's credentials and provide him with experience arguing before the Court. On July 13, 1953, Brownell arranged for Warren to visit the White House for a luncheon with the president. Brownell remembered that Ike concluded that Warren was "a man of high ideals and common sense." Brownell then formally offered Warren the solicitor general's position. Later, while in Sweden on a family holiday, Warren sent Eisenhower and Brownell a coded message indicating his willingness to take the post. Chief Justice Vinson died before this plan could be implemented.[10]

The extraordinary fact is that Eisenhower promised to appoint—or at least strongly considered appointing—Warren to the Supreme Court *before* there was a vacancy. The parties—Eisenhower, Brownell, and Warren—confirm that a conversation took place right after the 1952 election. Eisenhower minimized the time gap in his memoirs, claiming that he made the pledge to Warren "a few months" prior to Chief Justice Vinson's death; it was, in reality, closer to ten. When speculation arose over a successor to Vinson, a White House source confirmed the arrangement with Warren to the press.[11]

Brownell provided the most detailed account. One evening following the 1952 election, Brownell was working late in his room in the Commodore Hotel in New York City, finalizing cabinet appointments. Eisenhower strode down the hall, marched into Brownell's room, and announced: "I want Governor Warren to know that we consider him a part of the Eisenhower team, so to speak." Brownell was taken aback and asked if Ike wanted Warren in the cabinet. No, said the president-elect, "I think he'd be a good man on the Supreme Court. What do you think?" Eisenhower pushed ahead: "Why don't we call him and tell him that we're closing up the cabinet, but that doesn't mean we haven't been considering him for a high post in the administration. I think I'll just say to him that I have him in mind for the first vacancy on the Supreme Court." Eisenhower placed the call. "Governor," Warren recalled Eisenhower saying, "I am back here selecting my Cabinet, and I wanted to tell you I won't have a place for you in it." Warren responded that he did not expect a cabinet appointment. Then, the president-elect divulged the purpose of his call: "I want you to know that I intend to offer you the first vacancy on the Supreme Court."[12]

In his memoirs, Eisenhower described the pledge more ambiguously, saying he informed Warren that he was "considering the possibility of appointing him to the Supreme Court and that I was definitely inclined to do so if, in the future, a vacancy should occur." Perhaps Eisenhower simply intended to keep Warren "in mind"— the phrase Brownell recalled him using prior to the call. Eisenhower asserted in his memoirs that he was not "definitely committed to any appointment." Warren, on the other hand, believed he heard a clear promise to appoint him to "the first vacancy" on the Court. Given Eisenhower's own account—that he "was definitely inclined" to appoint Warren—the governor could be excused for reaching that conclusion.[13]

Either way, the usually cautious general took an extraordinary step in November 1952. Eisenhower was not yet in office. There was no Supreme Court vacancy, nor was one anticipated. Eisenhower, months or potentially years in advance, had mortgaged his flexibility on one of the most significant decisions a president ever makes— an appointment to the Supreme Court.[14]

Eisenhower and Brownell used rigorous investigative processes in making subsequent judicial appointments. Insisting on candidates with judicial experience, Eisenhower never again appointed a full-time, practicing politician to the Supreme Court. His argument that Warren was a skilled administrator, while defensible, could have been a justification as well as a reason. Eisenhower was not impulsive; he was a planner by temperament and training. The phone call to Earl Warren was clearly intentional.

Swede Hazlett, Eisenhower's intimate Abilene friend, thought the appointment had political purposes. Months after Warren's confirmation, Hazlett wrote Ike and urged the president to depoliticize the next Supreme Court appointment. Eisenhower, irritated at the implication that politics was the reason for Warren's nomination, declared in a letter to Hazlett: "It most emphatically was not." He asserted that he chose Warren based on qualifications he had "studied and lived with for a number of weeks." He wanted a strong administrator and "a statesman." Eisenhower wrote that "I could not do my duty unless I appointed a man whose philosophy of government was somewhat along the lines of my own." Eisenhower continued to be adamant that he did not nominate Warren to pay a political debt. "So," he asserted in an interview, "I owed him nothing."[15]

Eisenhower's offer to the California governor—if not paying a debt—was undeniably *a political act*. Eisenhower's idealistic motives were not necessarily fraudulent; Ike frequently blended visionary motives with pragmatic political concerns. At a minimum, in telling Warren that he would consider him for the High Court, Eisenhower was enlisting Warren's goodwill as he began his administration.

Another possibility is that Eisenhower was already thinking about 1956 and a second term. Warren had been a candidate for president three times—in 1944, 1948, and 1952. Brownell believed, even after Warren became chief justice, that the Californian "had not given up the idea that he might be president." Warren, one of the Republican Party's most ambitious politicians, would be an unlikely candidate if he were safely planted in the nonpartisan position of chief justice of the United States.[16]

Eisenhower's 1952 commitment to Warren did not automatically mean the governor would be appointed chief justice. The president could have promoted a sitting justice, which would have opened up an associate position. The Court's membership was heavily Democratic, and Harold Burton was the lone Republican, but Eisenhower rejected promoting Burton because he was a poor administrator. Warren wanted the top job and lobbied for it. When Brownell interviewed Warren in California, the governor expressed his view that the chief justice's position was indeed "the next vacancy" Ike had promised.[17]

The feared attacks on Warren's qualifications quickly materialized. Eisenhower's mail, some of it inspired by columnist David Lawrence and broadcaster Fulton Lewis, Jr., bulged with complaints about Warren's judicial inexperience and the president's allegedly political reasons for the appointment. Lawrence contended that there were "at least a dozen men in America better qualified" than Warren to serve as chief justice. Lawyers constituted the largest group of critics. After two weeks, a tally of White House mail on the nomination counted eighty-five letters unfavorable to the appointment, with thirty-one favorable.[18]

Eisenhower sparred with his legally trained brother, Edgar, over Warren's qualifications. When Warren's appointment was first rumored, Edgar had complained that a Warren appointment would be a "tragedy" and result in "the loss of a lot of support." In response, Eisenhower expressed esteem that he rarely extended to any person. "To my mind," Eisenhower wrote, "he is a statesman. We have too few of these." He called Warren "a man of national stature" and expressed his belief that the governor was a man of "unimpeachable integrity." Ike similarly described Warren to his brother Milton as a man with "a national name for integrity, uprightness, and courage."[19]

Discomfort Over *Brown*

After Warren was confirmed, he and Eisenhower exchanged cordial, handwritten notes. Warren wrote: "The fact that you who have served our country so magnificently commissioned me in this service will be an added inspiration to always do my best." The president expressed confidence that Warren would fiercely fulfill "the single purpose of upholding justice in the land." The nation, the president wrote, was blessed "to have such a dedicated, able and devoted public servant in such an influential, responsible and honored position." While such notes are routine in public life, Ike's sentiments were undoubtedly genuine.[20]

What happened to destroy this warm relationship? Any explanation must take into account Eisenhower's response to *Brown*. Brownell had not discussed the school desegregation case with

Warren during his California visit. He and Eisenhower apparently thought it would be inappropriate to ask Warren to take a position on how he might decide any issue before the Court. In any event, they already knew Warren's views on civil rights.[21]

Earl Warren had reason to expect that Eisenhower would endorse a school desegregation decision. He had witnessed from afar the new president's commitment to racial justice—his desegregation of the District of Columbia, his program to reduce discrimination in government contracts and employment, and his initiatives in desegregating the armed forces, including the schools for military dependents. Warren knew that Eisenhower had either approved or, at a minimum, had acquiesced in the government's brief in *Brown* supporting desegregation of the schools. Above all, Eisenhower had enthusiastically defended Warren's appointment as chief justice.

Instead, when *Brown* was announced, Eisenhower delivered a statement that must have sounded cold-blooded and legalistic to Warren: "The Supreme Court has spoken and I am sworn to uphold the constitutional processes in this country; and I will obey." Warren had expended enormous personal effort in crafting a decision that transcended difficult precedents and powerful political pressures. The chief justice later bitterly complained that, while southern officials angrily resisted compliance with *Brown,* "no word of support emanated from the White House."[22]

Why did Eisenhower adopt this legalistic strategy? The primary reason was his constitutional philosophy. Eisenhower embraced a traditional interpretation of the separation of powers—the very subject he had instructed Brownell to question Warren about in the California interview. The president consistently honored this doctrine by avoiding criticism of Congress as well as the Court. As late as 1959, Eisenhower proclaimed: "The oath of the President is to support and defend the Constitution of the United States—not to interpret it." He wrote to a critic: "Do you have anything to suggest that a President should do, if he should personally disagree with a decision? I remind you that if ever he made such a disagreement public, then he would always be under the suspicion that in such cases he would probably not be interested in enforcing the law faithfully, even though his oath requires him to do so." Brownell later defended Eisenhower's approach, noting that although he and Ike disliked the Supreme Court's "all deliberate speed" order in *Brown II,* the president never aired his disapproval.[23]

Second, Eisenhower hoped to moderate the inevitable political backlash against *Brown* in the South. He frequently cited the difficulties that southern whites faced with *Brown,* after living nearly six decades under *Plessy v. Ferguson.* Eisenhower repeatedly preached: "You cannot change people's hearts merely by laws." This sentiment was sincere: Eisenhower empathized with the radical adjustment southerners were being forced to make. This was also the flag he waved to retain white southern support while quietly making judicial appointments and taking actions contrary to segregationist interests. Warren sarcastically characterized Ike's aphorism as one "dear to the hearts of those who are insensitive to the rights of minority groups."[24]

Eisenhower's aloof strategy collided with a growing public obsession with presidential rhetoric, especially on the question of race. The emerging television age, which Eisenhower embraced with his frequent news conferences, intensified preoccupation with presidential statements. Black activists, confronted with an unresponsive government, had come to place undue weight on the comments of the president. As Val Washington, the Republican National Committee's director of minority programs, put it, "Negroes, because of inequalities suffered, hang on every word of their president." The preaching tradition in many Negro churches encouraged blacks to equate passionate expression with personal commitment. Lacking legal redress, they anxiously measured white politicians by their words.[25]

That expectation did not match Eisenhower's strengths or mesh with his values. The Supreme Court's conservative *Brown II* decree had left the president with few tools to enforce the decision. What remained was "the bully pulpit," which Eisenhower resisted using. He was uncomfortable with the role of public educator, and had an implacable distaste for political demagoguery. Eisenhower's restrained rhetoric discouraged activists who hungered for a stronger presidential endorsement of *Brown.* To them, the president's aloof demeanor seemed to encourage the segregationists to resist the Court's ruling.

During all his professional life, Eisenhower had prized results over rhetoric. In the case of *Brown,* he hoped that imploring white southerners to obey the law, rather than insisting that they make a moral commitment, would provide a "middle way" for them to embrace the new order. For the segregationists, the president's message was not obscure; the law Eisenhower demanded that they obey was *Brown,* not *Plessy.*

Still, Warren deplored Eisenhower's refusal to use his popularity to evangelize the public for *Brown.* The chief justice believed that if the president had clearly stated "that it should be the duty of every good citizen to help rectify more than eighty years of wrongdoing by honoring that decision—if he had said something to this effect, we would have been relieved, in my opinion, of many of the racial problems which have continued to plague us. But he never even stated that he thought the decision was right until he had left the White House."[26]

The Rift

Earl Warren believed that, for Eisenhower, once *Brown* was decided, "with it went our cordial relations." Through the years, there were repeated rumors of a rift. The tensions were partially rooted in the two men's personal styles and backgrounds. "Eisenhower, with his military training," Brownell reflected, "kept his personal views and feelings separate and compartmentalized from his official views while he was in office." Warren, the gregarious politician, "spoke freely about his personal opinions." Washington social circles delighted in spreading Warren's not-so-private remarks. Eisenhower, on the other hand, frustrated reporters by reserving comment, a silence often interpreted as passive hostility to the chief justice and his Court's decisions.[27]

In 1955, a reporter asked Eisenhower about a speech in which Warren had expressed doubt that the Bill of Rights could now be approved. Eisenhower responded with bafflement, his manner betraying his belief that the chief justice should not be pontificating about such matters in public. "If it were up for passage today," the president said to reporters, "I would be one of those out campaigning for its adoption." Afterward, the president sent his staff scrambling for a copy of the chief justice's address. "This so bothered me," Eisenhower confessed to reporters the following week, that he had personally reviewed Warren's remarks. He reminded the press that he had previously assured them that he "had the greatest confidence in the Chief Justice's judgment, patriotism, and dedication." Ike pronounced himself relieved that Warren's actual speech had expressed "his faith in the good sense, the soundness of the American people" and that the chief justice was confident the Bill of Rights "would be adopted."[28]

In 1957, a reporter alleged that Eisenhower, at a private party, had angrily criticized the Supreme Court. Ike wrote to Warren, admitting that "in private conversation someone did hear me express amazement about one decision, but I have never even hinted at a feeling such as anger." The president's criticism had been in response to "Red Monday"—not *Brown* or school desegregation—wherein the Court had made controversial rulings regarding the prosecutions of Communist Party members. Eisenhower promised Warren that he would be more careful with his words and labeled the story "a distortion." Warren responded that the president need not have written and that "some columns are written in ignorance and others to deceive. Whatever the reason, if unfounded, they should be ignored."[29]

A particularly awkward moment arose at a news conference in 1959. Merriman Smith, a reporter for United Press International, informed the president that the chief justice had told friends "that your stand on school desegregation is too indecisive" and that Warren was "pained by what was described as your failure to take forceful action." Eisenhower barely contained his temper.

PRESIDENT: He is what?

MR. SMITH: Your failure to take—

PRESIDENT: What is his reaction?

SMITH: He is described this morning as being pained—

PRESIDENT: Oh, oh!

SMITH: —at what this story called your failure to take forceful action to implement the desegregation decision of

the Court. If the chief justice has made known his feelings in this matter, would you like to do the same
thing?

There followed an awkward silence. Then Eisenhower resorted
to the classic politician's reflex, blaming "irresponsible reporting."
He voiced his exasperation: "I have told you people a dozen times
or certainly frequently, exactly what I feel about a President commenting publicly upon decisions of the Supreme Court. Now, I have
regarded, and I am sure that everyone knows this also, I have regarded the Chief Justice as my personal friend for years. I know of
no personal rift of any kind, and therefore I would believe that
there is something that doesn't meet the eye here; and if the thing
which you speak is felt by the Chief Justice, I should think, and I am
quite sure, that he is capable of telling me himself and doesn't have
to take it to the public print." Eisenhower's irritation may have been
exacerbated by the fact that he was preparing, in a few days, to propose a seven-point civil rights program to Congress. When Warren
heard about the story and Eisenhower's outburst, he issued a terse
statement: "The story merits no comment. It is wholly without foundation."[30]

Eisenhower protested too much. There was a rift; Warren certainly believed there was. The strains on their relationship may have
involved presidential politics as much as *Brown*. Twice, prior to 1956,
the press had trumpeted the possibility of Warren running for president if Eisenhower did not seek reelection. Senator Robert Taft,
Eisenhower's previous adversary, had died at the end of July 1953.
Thomas E. Dewey, after losing two races for the presidency, was no
longer a viable candidate. Earl Warren enjoyed enhanced stature as
a result of *Brown*, especially in northern states, although he was despised in much of the South. Above all, Warren had wanted to be
president for a long time.

Eisenhower was besieged by party leaders and the press as to
whether he would run in 1956. A Gallup Poll in April 1955 had
identified Warren as a Republican who would have a chance of defeating Adlai Stevenson in the next election. Eisenhower apparently
believed that such speculation was unlikely without the acquies-

cence of the chief justice. When the rumors continued, Warren issued a statement calling the conjecture "a matter of embarrassment" because it undermined his responsibilities as chief justice. He insisted that his intent had always been to "leave politics permanently for service on the Court. That is still my purpose. It is irrevocable."[31]

That quieted the speculation until Eisenhower suffered a heart attack the following September. Political pundits presumed again that if Eisenhower did not run, Earl Warren would be the strongest Republican candidate. Eisenhower apparently continued to suspect that Warren was complicit in the rumors. He uncharacteristically criticized the chief justice in a news conference in early 1956, a month prior to announcing his own intentions. Asked about the possibility of a Warren candidacy, Ike cited his own resignation from the army when nominated by the Republicans, and stated, "We shouldn't get too great a confusion between politics and the Supreme Court." The president's implication was clear; Warren should resign from the Court if he wanted to run.[32]

A Shocking Incident

Warren's memoir contains the ultimate story denigrating Eisenhower's attitude toward civil rights. Warren claimed he became convinced of the president's opposition to school desegregation because of an incident at the White House on February 8, 1954—prior to the *Brown* decision in May. The chief justice was invited to one of Eisenhower's periodic "stag dinners"—informal gatherings of prominent officials, politicians, and personal friends of the president—at which the issues of the day could be discussed candidly off the record. These gatherings sometimes brought people together that, judged by modern standards, might seem inappropriate. Warren was the ranking guest and sat at the right hand of the president, "within speaking distance" of John W. Davis, the attorney for South Carolina in the *Brown* case. During the dinner, Warren related, "the President went to considerable lengths to tell me what a great man Mr. Davis was." When the meal was over and the guests filed into another room for coffee and drinks, the president, Warren recorded, took him by the arm and said, "These are not bad people. All they are concerned about is to see that their sweet little girls are not required to sit in school alongside some big overgrown Negroes."[33]

White males frequently repeated stereotypes like this in the 1950s, alleging black predatory sexual behavior. Still, modern readers are understandably disturbed for the words to have come, as Warren claimed, from the lips of the president of the United States. Most important, Warren interpreted the incident as an attempt to influence his decision on *Brown*. Political activists and historians alike have reported this episode as firm evidence of Eisenhower's opposition to civil rights. Warren's clear intent in recounting the episode was to portray Eisenhower as a racist.

Warren is the only source for this story. There are no corroborating witnesses. It is possible that Eisenhower said something like what Warren reported amid the small talk of the evening. Like many white contemporaries, Eisenhower was not immune to repeating racial stereotypes. An alternate interpretation is that he was explaining an attitude prevalent among white southerners; it was almost verbatim what Jimmy Byrnes had said at his luncheon meeting with the president the previous July 20. Ike had noted in his diary that Byrnes had told him that southerners could tolerate dealing with "adult Negroes," but they were "frightened at putting the children together."[34]

Even if Warren's account of Eisenhower's remark is accurate, it does not follow that Eisenhower tried to influence the chief justice on the *Brown* case. To do so would have been an uncharacteristic violation of the president's rigorous commitment to the separation of powers. Besides, Eisenhower knew too much about Warren's attitudes on racial matters to expect the chief justice to sympathize with that kind of remark. Eisenhower was usually careful with his speech. These considerations raise the question of whether the incident actually took place.

William Ewald, who helped Eisenhower write his memoirs, later insisted: "Eisenhower did not, repeat not, I am convinced, invite Warren to the White House to undermine the *Brown* decision." Ewald grants that, probably, "in a moment of thoughtless candor

Eisenhower did relay to the Chief Justice the southern horror of ad-
olescent miscegenation." Herbert Brownell generously interpreted
Eisenhower's statement as an expression of "his personal sympathy
for the mothers of young white children in the South who had been
reared in a segregated society and feared the unknown—the arrival
of a time when the public schools would be desegregated." Ewald
claimed that he heard Eisenhower say something similar a decade
later when he was assisting Ike at the former president's Gettysburg
home, but he found it incomprehensible to conclude that this
meant that Ike was "lobbying against desegregation—that leap is unthinkable."[35]

Eisenhower and *Brown*

Unearthing Eisenhower's real view of the *Brown* ruling is essential to
placing Earl Warren's critique in context. In a 1967 interview, Eisenhower admitted that, regarding most of the Warren Court decisions,
"I am on the opposite side." He admitted that he had not anticipated Warren's liberalism on issues related to criminal law, and he
made a statement that could support the "damned fool mistake"
legend: "Well, I made a mistake, that's all. I mean, I was fooled in
my own judgment."

Then, in the same interview, Eisenhower expressed a monumental caveat: "Strangely enough, the one where I agreed with him absolutely was the first one, in which he took a part, the '54 decision
about the integration of schools." Eisenhower made the same assertion in his memoirs. "Although," he wrote, "as President I never expressed either approbation or disapproval of a Court decision, in
this instance, there can be no question that the judgment of the
court was right."[36] Sherman Adams confirmed that Ike endorsed
Brown "in general principle" and "thought the Supreme Court decision was correct and personally he had no quarrel with it." In all
likelihood, Adams's statement illuminates Eisenhower's real view of
Brown: he agreed with the ruling in principle but was conflicted
about its methods, especially those in *Brown II.*[37]

Eisenhower's temperamental outbursts in private have furnished
ammunition to those who would deprecate his commitment to civil

rights. Despite his carefully cultivated, serene public image, the old soldier could explode in frustration and fill the air with profanity, saying things he would later regret. This trait furnishes context for the comments he allegedly made to two disillusioned speechwriters, Arthur Larson and Emmet John Hughes. Ike may have enjoyed baiting these idealistic young speechwriters, making provocative comments designed to provoke a response.

During much of 1956, Eisenhower was a contentious and cranky candidate—his ill temper exacerbated by the regimen and medication he endured after his 1955 heart attack and his colon surgery in June. He and Arthur Larson sparred about *Brown* on July 20, 1956, when they were preparing his acceptance speech for the Republican convention. In that conversation, Ike resorted to what Larson called "the oldest cliché in race relations dialogue," that political and economic opportunity did not mean "that a Negro should court my daughter."[38]

Emmet John Hughes, another speechwriter, recorded later in the 1956 election campaign that Eisenhower expressed his view that the "Supreme Court decision set back progress in the South at least 15 years." He bemoaned the damage done to his relationships with men like Jimmy Byrnes: "We used to be pretty good friends—now I've not heard from him not at all, no just once, in the past 18 months—all because of bitterness on this thing." Eisenhower, according to Hughes, fumed: "We can't demand *perfection* in these moral questions—it's not going to come—all we can do is keep working toward a goal—and keep it high. And the guy who tries to tell me that you can do these things by *force* is just plain *nuts*."[39]

Eisenhower made another angry comment to Larson about *Brown* on October 1, 1957, just after he had sent troops into Little Rock, Arkansas, to enforce a federal court order for school desegregation. He was preparing to meet with a group of southern governors protesting his action in Little Rock. Eisenhower was exhausted from the struggle with Congress during 1957 over civil rights legislation he had proposed. The Arkansas crisis had erupted right after the act's passage, and it had destroyed his much-needed September vacation in Rhode Island. Larson recorded that Eisenhower, irritated that he would once again have to defend his actions to hostile southern governors, said that he thought the Supreme Court's decision in *Brown* "was wrong." Ironically, after grumbling to Larson, Eisenhower walked into his meeting with the governors and firmly supported the enforcement of *Brown*.[40]

If Hughes's and Larson's reports are accurate, the argument over Eisenhower's support for *Brown* would appear to be settled. But it is not. There is no denying that Eisenhower was more comfortable with promoting political and economic equality for blacks, rather than integration. Beyond that, Ike was frequently frustrated by the bitter politics that followed in the wake of the *Brown* decision. The conflicts over school desegregation were relentless and maddening for a president who prided himself on orderly planning and efficient execution of those plans. His rants were responses to pressure and conflict—not his calm, more carefully considered thoughts.[41]

Eisenhower had qualms about the methods implied in the *Brown* ruling, partly because they placed children at the center of violent conflict. In 1956, he said to his personal secretary, Ann C. Whitman, that "the troubles brought about by the Supreme Court decision were the most important problem facing the government, domestically, today." Whitman asked the president what alternative the Court could have adopted. He replied that perhaps it could have demanded an end to segregation in the graduate schools, later in the colleges, then the high schools, "as a means of overcoming the passionate and inbred attitudes that they developed over generations."[42] Eisenhower's reasoning was "gradualist," but so was the Court's "all deliberate speed" formulation. Ike's comment to Whitman was not a formal, thought-out proposal so much as, in the midst of turmoil, he was wondering whether a more effective method could be found.

In July 1957, Ike, in a personal letter to Swede Hazlett, similarly concluded, "I think that no other single event has so disturbed the domestic scene in many years as did the Supreme Court's decision in 1954 in the school segregation case." He cited the impact on his administration: the decision had "put heavier responsibilities than before on the Federal government in the matter of assuring to each citizen his guaranteed Constitutional rights." Then Eisenhower, despite three years of frustrating experiences following the school desegregation decision, endorsed *Brown:* "The plan of the Supreme Court to accomplish integration gradually and sensibly seems to me to provide the only possible answer if we are to consider on the one hand the customs and fears of a great section of our population, and on the other the binding effect that Supreme Court decisions must have on all of us if our form of government is to survive and prosper." Eisenhower's conclusion was firm: "There must be respect for the Constitution—which means the Supreme Court's interpretation of the Constitution—or we shall have chaos."

To reinforce his point, Eisenhower shared an anecdote with Hazlett. A "violent exponent of the segregation doctrine" had visited the president's office and had insisted on the sanctity of the 1896 Supreme Court decision. Eisenhower asked him: "Then why is the 1954 decision not equally sacrosanct?" The man hesitated and said, "There were then wise men on the Court. Now we have politicians." Eisenhower replied: "Can you name one man on the 1896 Court who made the decision?" The visitor was embarrassed and dropped the subject.[43]

This letter to Hazlett echoed what Ike had said to his Abilene friend three years earlier, when he defended the Warren appointment and proclaimed: "I could not do my duty unless I appointed a man whose philosophy of government was somewhat along the lines of my own." Eisenhower enunciated that private defense of the Warren appointment—including the assertion that Warren's outlook paralleled his own—on October 23, 1954, five months *after* the *Brown* decision.[44]

Ultimately, the most compelling evidence for Eisenhower's support of *Brown* resides in his actions, not his rhetoric. This is the president who desegregated schools for military dependents before the *Brown* decision, and who, immediately after *Brown,* directed the commissioners of the District of Columbia to make Washington, D.C., a model for the nation in school desegregation. Moreover, he dispatched troops to Little Rock, Arkansas, to enforce a federal court order for school desegregation—a highly unlikely action by a president truly opposed to *Brown.*[45]

Warren and Eisenhower

The rift between Dwight Eisenhower and Earl Warren was detrimental to Eisenhower's reputation in civil rights. Warren resented the war hero who had destroyed his chance to be president. Eisenhower, with his legalistic rhetoric, deeply disappointed the chief justice he had appointed with such enthusiasm and who had skillfully engineered a unanimous decision in *Brown*. Scholars have routinely accepted Warren's judgment without questioning his motives or facts.

Eisenhower, more than Warren granted, made statements endorsing equality, but he consistently refused to focus his egalitarian platitudes on specific civil rights situations or Court decisions. Ike frustrated his political advisors because, once having made an idealistic statement, he was disinclined to repeat the sentiment for political effect.[46] Eisenhower was a gradualist and shared misconceptions about black people common to white politicians of his era. Still, Warren's attempt to depict him as a southern-style racist is unwarranted.

Warren alleged that resistance to *Brown* would have been overcome if only Eisenhower had "said something." Eisenhower's failure to speak out more forcefully on the great issue of his time merits criticism. A specific, passionate endorsement of *Brown* and a fervent indictment of the evils of segregation would have enhanced the president's reputation with the scholars of his administration. Still, Warren's insistence that an Eisenhower pronouncement would have negated massive resistance in the South was naïve. The segregationists were not going to surrender their cause because the president "said something."

Warren was legitimately disappointed in Eisenhower's cautious, legalistic statements about *Brown*, but his assertions lack balance. His memoirs do not acknowledge Eisenhower's desegregation of the nation's capital and the armed forces. The former chief justice says that Lyndon Johnson "sponsored and had passed the first Civil Rights Bill in many decades," when in fact Eisenhower proposed the legislation that became the Civil Rights Act of 1957.[47] Warren ignored Eisenhower's decision to send troops to Little Rock in 1957, an event he never commented about in public, possibly for the same separation-of-powers reasons that inhibited Eisenhower. Warren's most glaring omission was his disregard for the quality and importance of Eisenhower's judicial appointments, including those to his own bench. Eisenhower's contribution to the judicial enforcement of *Brown* was not as important to Warren as an offhand remark he alleges the president made at a White House dinner in 1954.[48]

Eisenhower wrote respectfully in his memoirs about the chief justice. He defended Warren's role in *Brown*, contending that the Californian's tenure on the Court was so brief at that point that he could not have swayed the other justices unless there was a constitutional reason. The former president concluded: "I have questioned many eminent lawyers on the soundness of this decision, and without exception they have expressed the opinion that it conformed to the Constitution of the United States."[49]

William Ewald insists that Eisenhower was honest in his memoirs. As president, Ike may have confused observers with his legalistic statements, but "the one thing I find him absolutely incapable of is making up an answer in which he did not believe and setting it down in a book to burnish his image. In the end, though not without qualms, I believe he would have voted with Earl Warren."[50] The evidence, so profoundly present in Eisenhower's actions, supports that conclusion.

CHAPTER SIX

Confronting Southern Resistance

In no event should the President, I believe, answer any
questions indicating that the Federal Government has even
considered the use of Federal troops in the South.
—HERBERT BROWNELL'S ADVICE TO EISENHOWER
  FOR HIS MARCH 7, 1956, NEWS CONFERENCE

D wight Eisenhower had reason to be pleased at the beginning of
1955. He had ended the Korean War, avoided being drawn
into war in Indochina, skillfully managed the Cold War with the
Soviet Union, and played a role in discrediting Joseph McCarthy,
the demagogic Wisconsin Republican senator. On January 18, he
issued an executive order creating the President's Committee on
Government Employment Policy, a body committed to reducing
racial discrimination in federal positions. Eisenhower's self-
confidence was further reflected in his decision to conduct the first
filmed press conference in the history of the presidency on January
19. Afterward, Eisenhower told Press Secretary James Hagerty that
he had purposely recognized an African-American reporter, Alice A.
Dunnigan of the Associated Negro Press, for a question.[1]

On January 28, Attorney General Brownell reported to the cabinet regarding what the administration had done, in Eisenhower's
1952 campaign phrase, to close the "gap between promise and performance" in civil rights. He cited the Supreme Court's school de-

segregation decision and the administration's efforts to reduce discrimination in employment, and he proudly announced to the cabinet that there were "no longer any all-Negro units in the Services." Washington, D.C., was desegregating its schools and public accommodations, and had implemented a nondiscrimination policy in contracts and in its own employment. In response to Brownell's report, Max Rabb, the secretary to the cabinet, invited the members to celebrate the disparity "between the quiet success of this Administration and the noisy lack of accomplishment of the previous one."[2]

For the moment, the administration enjoyed modest recognition of its accomplishments. Roy Wilkins, slated to be Walter White's successor as NAACP executive secretary, called 1954 "the year of the great decision" in *Brown*. "For its unanimous and unequivocal decision on this basic moral issue, unqualified praise should go to the United States Supreme Court," Wilkins stated. "So, too, do we owe a debt of gratitude to President Eisenhower for his firm stand against racial segregation." Wilkins predicted that more blacks would vote for Republicans in 1956 because "there is in the White House a man who is steadily winning their admiration by his forthright pronouncements on civil rights and by the leadership he has given in his branch of the government."[3]

Rabb found more signs that the administration's reputation in civil rights was on the rise. In April 1955, he sent to the president a 1953 *Washington Post* editorial in which the paper had criticized Eisenhower for doing "relatively little" in civil rights. The paper's editors had just retracted that critique and now extolled Eisenhower's role in desegregating Washington, D.C., and his support for the district's government in combating discrimination in employment. The *Post* proclaimed that civil rights had become "one of the strongest features of the Eisenhower Administration—and the community and the country are healthier for it."[4]

The Anti-Segregation Amendments

The euphoria would not last. Brownell's report to the cabinet had ignored the increasingly hostile response to *Brown* in the South. The coming year would be shaped by rising expectations in the black community and growing violence in the South. Brownell and Eisenhower did not anticipate how little gratitude and how much criticism they would reap in the months ahead.

Eisenhower disdained symbolic actions that might have elicited more goodwill in the black community. He declined to attend or send a personal message to a celebration planned by civil rights organizations for the first anniversary of *Brown* on May 17, 1955. In June, NAACP leaders praised Eisenhower but criticized his party for doing "nothing in the 83rd Congress after the sweeping victory of 1952."[5] The GOP, when in control of Congress, had proposed no general civil rights legislation. That was because Eisenhower did not want it; he still scorned what he viewed as the annual Democratic charade of offering bills that had no chance for passage. Ike preferred his policy of ending discrimination wherever there was federal authority, thereby avoiding a confrontation with congressmen who could derail his legislative program.

That legislative program included a proposal for funding school construction that would embroil him in civil rights controversy. The program was linked with the issue of school desegregation. Due to the *Brown* cases, the capital had been flooded with horrific stories of shabby Negro schools; white southerners would rebel against sending their students to those schools under desegregation plans. But Southern governors confronted a financial crisis if they tried to rapidly build schools that were both integrated and adequate.

On February 3, 1954, three months before *Brown*, Val Peterson, the federal civil defense administrator and former governor of Nebraska, had written Max Rabb advocating support for states inclined toward integration by developing a program to "assist them in rebuilding their public school systems." "Warmth, sympathy, solid helpfulness should be offered," Peterson suggested. Once the Supreme Court's decision was announced, he continued, "the administration should be ready to announce a constructive program the President can vigorously advance." Eisenhower eventually embraced a version of the Peterson plan; it fit his preference for programs that were not overtly racial, yet promised progress.[6]

In his January 6, 1955, State of the Union address, Eisenhower cited "an unprecedented classroom shortage" caused by population growth, increased school attendance, a longer school year, and—pointedly—the "additional responsibilities of schools," an oblique reference to *Brown*'s requirements for desegregation. On February 8, Eisenhower proposed a three-year, $7 billion school construction program, asserting that "millions of children still attend schools which are unsafe or which permit learning only part-time or under conditions of serious over-crowding." He wanted the funds to go to school districts with "proved need and proved lack of local income." Eisenhower knew that this category included segregated Negro schools, but he avoided singling them out in proposing his "emergency plan."[7]

Congressman Adam Clayton Powell, Jr. (D-New York), acting on behalf of the NAACP, began an effort to attach an anti-segregation amendment to the school construction legislation. Eisenhower was certain that his legislation could not be passed bearing such an amendment, so his administration embraced the argument that the Powell amendment was not needed because the federal courts would eventually settle any disputes over construction funds for segregated school districts. Bryce Harlow, the White House congressional liaison, valiantly tried to clarify the administration's case for congressmen. He underscored that the "matter is in the hands of the courts." Therefore, "when and if it becomes unconstitutional to provide Federal funds, the Executive Branch would have to terminate grants with or without a Powell Amendment."[8]

In his June 8, 1955, news conference, the president expressed his growing exasperation with Powell's amendments: "If you get an idea of real importance, a substantive subject, and you want to get it enacted into law, then I believe the Congress and I believe our people should have a right to decide upon that issue by itself, and not be clouding it with amendments that are extraneous." "Extraneous" was not a term that would please the black community. The following month, Eisenhower called the Powell amendment "extraneous" again, "for the simple reason that we need the schools." He reminded the reporters that the Supreme Court had ruled and that segregation issues could be taken to the district courts. "Now," he complained, "why do we go muddying the water?"[9]

Congressman Powell sent Eisenhower telegrams on June 19 and 20, requesting a meeting on the amendment issue. Eisenhower responded with a blunt letter. "It is a fact of history," he wrote, "that no legislation, however meritorious, containing such a provision has ever passed the Senate." The president pledged "to work toward the eventual elimination of segregation from our national life." "But," he concluded, "school construction legislation containing a non-segregation provision cannot now become law. . . . The building of schools critically needed cannot be put off without damage to children of all races."[10]

The school construction bill failed to pass in 1955 with or without the Powell amendment, but Eisenhower stubbornly resubmitted it in 1956 and 1957. In May 1957, he lectured the Republican legislative leaders "at length" about meeting "the great need that existed for catching up with the backlog in school construction created by the depression and two wars—things for which the Federal Government must take some responsibility." Ike described conditions in the schools as "deplorable" and said that "he didn't believe in pledging one thing and later backing off it." His lecture did not convince his party's congressional leaders. Joseph W. Martin, Jr., of Massachusetts, the Republican minority leader in the House, informed the president that the Democrats would never allow the measure to pass.[11]

Eisenhower failed to obtain passage of school construction legislation, even without the Powell amendment, in the three years following his 1955 proposal. This outcome may have reflected southern congressmen's suspicions about the administration's motives. The segregationists understood that Eisenhower and Brownell would probably do what Val Peterson had suggested—use federal construction funds to pressure compliance with *Brown*. Meanwhile, Eisenhower, abhorring symbolic actions for political effect, had squandered some of his support among black leaders in a lost cause. Brownell later concluded that Congressman Powell's amendment tactic "served a useful purpose, and over the long run it dramatized an issue that should be dramatized," but Eisenhower never embraced that point of view.[12]

Conflict in the South

By mid-1955, Val Washington, the Republican National Committee's minority troubleshooter, had become concerned about the president's declining stock with black voters. At his urging, the White

House belatedly redeemed a promise to E. Frederic Morrow, made after the 1952 election, to place him on the White House staff. With Morrow's promotion, the administration trumpeted the claim that he was "the first Negro ever to be named to a presidential staff in an executive capacity."[13] On July 28, 1955, Washington sent a report to the president asserting that the party had made good on its vows to Negroes during the 1952 campaign. "With the appointment of E. Frederic Morrow on the White House staff," Washington wrote, "the fourteen promises have been fulfilled."[14]

Val Washington had reason to be concerned. A Gallup Poll, published on August 7, identified five criticisms of the president by respondents, including: "Encourages segregation." Max Rabb called that finding "outrageous." He concluded that "we are probably to blame. We have been more than tender in soft-pedalling our accomplishments." Rabb grumbled that the only time the president discussed civil rights was when he addressed the anti-segregation amendments to legislation, and then Negroes felt as if the president were scolding them instead of the segregationists. Looking toward the next election, Rabb warned: "Perhaps it is time to give some serious thought to this whole problem."[15]

Val Washington countered the Gallup Poll by releasing a progress report on the party's fulfillment of the fourteen points on August 9. The president's accompanying letter, dated August 1, affirmed: "We believe in the equal dignity of all our people, whatever their racial origin or background may be; in the equal right to freedom and opportunity and the benefits of our common citizenship." Eisenhower admitted that "much must still be done," but "all of us have reason for just pride in the tremendous advances of the past thirty months." The *Washington Post* titled a news story, "Ike Cites Far Advances in Field of Civil Rights."[16]

Two events in late 1955 intensified black pressures on the administration. On August 28, fourteen-year-old Emmett Till was murdered in Money, Mississippi, for allegedly inappropriate behavior with a white woman in a store. The killing became an emotional cause in the black community. Emmett Till's mother, Mamie E. Bradley, left her son's mutilated body on open display for days, and she toured the country to appear at rallies. J. Edgar Hoover, the FBI director, cited "confidential sources," saying that Mrs. Bradley was being exploited by the Communist Party; even Max Rabb complained that Till's mother had "permitted herself to be the instrument of the Communist party." Till's mother wired the White House seeking help in punishing her son's killers, but the Justice Department advised the president not to respond.[17]

Frederic Morrow was distraught as the furor over Emmett Till raged around him. Morrow concluded that "there was no visible evidence that the Administration was remotely concerned." Stacks of mail poured into his office "berating the President for his failure to denounce the breakdown of law and order" and charging Morrow with "Uncle Tomism." Val Washington wrote Sherman Adams that the Till affair was "one of the most delicate problems I have had in my entire political career." He pled for "someone in the Federal government to say something—if no more than words of encouragement."[18]

On September 23, an all-white jury acquitted the defendants in the Till murder. The next day, while Ike and Mamie were visiting Mrs. Eisenhower's mother in Denver, the president suffered a heart attack. Eisenhower did not return to the White House until November 11. The publicity concerning the Till murder did not abate. Mrs. Bradley spoke at rallies attended by thousands in major cities, raising funds for the NAACP. By year's end, the White House had received three thousand communications as well as petitions with eleven thousand names protesting the murder. The Washington *Evening Star* cynically characterized the administration's response to the question of who killed Emmett Till: "Silence. Silence. Silence."[19]

Herbert Brownell bemoaned the government's "lack of authority" in the Till case, and told an interviewer years later that he "could never find any evidence that would allow us to act under any federal statute." Warren Olney, head of the Justice Department's criminal division, complained that the critics could not comprehend "the fact that there wasn't anything that we had any legal authority to do." Morrow wrote Rabb a long memorandum on November 29 about the Till matter, predicting "a dangerous racial conflagration" and expressing "disappointment that no word has come from the

White House deploring this situation." Rabb called Morrow into his office for what Morrow interpreted as "a tongue-lashing." Rabb complained that African-Americans were not showing proper gratitude for what the president had done.[20]

Two days after Morrow wrote his memorandum, on December 1, 1955, a forty-two-year-old Negro seamstress employed by a Montgomery, Alabama, department store stepped aboard a Montgomery bus. When asked to give up her temporary seat to a white person and move to the back of the bus, Rosa Parks refused. She was arrested and taken to jail. "In that moment," Roy Wilkins recalled, "the Montgomery bus boycott was born." The next day an estimated 90 percent of the city's blacks refused to use the buses.[21]

The Eisenhower administration concluded that the bus boycott was like the Till case—"strictly a State matter in which Federal authorities apparently have no jurisdiction." Although there were concerns that the boycott might escalate into the "racial conflagration" that Morrow had feared, the nonviolent strategy that the Negro leaders adopted reduced the danger. Their tactics propelled a twenty-six-year-old preacher and eloquent advocate of nonviolence, Dr. Martin Luther King, Jr., into national prominence as leader of the bus boycott.[22]

Meanwhile, southern resistance to school desegregation was growing. According to the NAACP, no public schools had been desegregated in eight southern states during 1955, and economic intimidation—threatening the advocates of desegregation with losing their jobs, credit, or essential farming and business supplies—was increasing. The NAACP estimated that the number of registered Negro voters in Mississippi had declined from 22,000 to 8,000 during the year. Most important, racial violence was increasing. In Mississippi, no lynchings had been recorded in the previous five years; in 1955, there were three.[23]

The growing racial tensions in the South during Eisenhower's third year in office, combined with Eisenhower's response to the Powell amendment controversy, had taken a toll on the administration's reputation in civil rights. The administration's lack of authority to intervene in the Emmett Till murder and the Montgomery bus boycott—as well as a reluctance to comment—gave the impres-

sion of an administration increasingly indifferent about the movement for equality.

Eisenhower's original strategy—to abolish segregation and discrimination wherever there was clear federal authority—had been
eclipsed by events. Herbert Brownell had become convinced that he
would need to persuade Eisenhower to embrace what he had previously resisted: legislation granting the federal government authority
to enforce civil rights in the states.

Eisenhower, the Candidate?

Meanwhile, the press speculated about whether Eisenhower would
run for a second term in 1956. The president's heart attack on September 24, 1955, had revived discussion of Earl Warren as a possible
presidential candidate. Moderate and liberal GOP leaders thought a
healthy Warren might be a stronger Republican candidate than a
president recovering from a life-threatening illness.[24]

Invoking Warren as a potential candidate was certain to stoke
Eisenhower's competitive fires. On December 14, 1955, at his Get-
tysburg farm, Eisenhower reviewed possible Republican candidates
with James Hagerty, his press secretary. That inventory included
Thomas Dewey, Treasury Secretary George Humphrey, Herbert
Brownell, Sherman Adams, former navy secretary Robert Anderson,
and the president's brother Milton, who, despite his prominence as
an educator, was an unlikely candidate in anyone's mind but Ike's.
Hagerty inquired, "Mr. President, what about Warren?" Ike snapped:
"Not a chance." He predicted that the chief justice would make the
Court his life's work, and concluded: "I do not think I would approve of a Chief Justice stepping down from the bench to run for
office." Eisenhower had eliminated the most viable candidate mentioned in their conversation. When Hagerty said that his favorite
ticket was still "Eisenhower-Nixon," the president laughed and replied, "Listen Jim, I haven't said I'm not going to be a candidate.
I'm just trying to get some thoughts."

Hagerty concluded that Eisenhower had already decided; running would be "his duty regardless of his health to try to keep this
nation free of war and on the right path." Throughout his career,

Eisenhower had frequently cloaked his ambition in a soldierly call to serve his country. Sherman Adams, years later, put it more bluntly: "The real reason a President wants to run again is because he doesn't think anybody else can do as good a job as he's doing." That analysis fit Dwight Eisenhower.[25]

Earlier in December, a Gallup Poll had provided discouraging news for Republicans hoping to attract black votes in 1956. Despite Eisenhower's civil rights efforts, the percentage of African-American voters loyal to the Democratic Party had increased since 1951. Sherman Adams asked Max Rabb, Eisenhower's White House troubleshooter on Negro issues, and his black equality committee to review the poll. Rabb, Frederic Morrow recalled, was "a thoroughly unhappy man" about the survey "and he let us know it in no uncertain terms." Morrow, Val Washington, the RNC's minority programs director, and Joseph Douglas, an HEW staff member, added to Rabb's discomfort, criticizing "the failure of any prominent member of the Administration to speak out against, and deplore, the present condition of terrorism and economic sanction against the Negroes in Mississippi."[26]

The Brownell Civil Rights Plan

Eisenhower and Brownell were worried about more than black votes. *Brown* had thrust racial conflict into the schools; because they were under state and local control, the federal government lacked authority to intervene. Violent protests might force the president to send in troops to put down disorder. Eisenhower and Brownell believed that the president had the authority to do so, but the army was a blunt instrument. Ike believed that military force should be a last resort, yet he intended to be prepared. The army's strategic capabilities plan for 1956 included the requirement for a "domestic disturbance plan," held strictly "confidential." The plan avoided the use of inflammatory phrases like "race riots" or "domestic violence," but it ordered riot training for the troops. That stipulation almost certainly originated with the president or had his approval.[27]

Brownell's increased concern with civil rights legislation was driven by his president's need to find alternatives to using the army.

Clarence Mitchell, the NAACP's Washington, D.C., chief, tried to persuade the attorney general that, in an election year, the Republican Party could offer something to black voters that the Democrats could not—a civil rights bill. But a presidential election year was hardly a propitious time to push such controversial legislation. The Democrats were split, and the *New York Times* assumed that the GOP would make no proposals because Eisenhower was "on record as opposed to compulsory civil rights programs."[28] That assessment did not reckon with Herbert Brownell.

Brownell recalled in his memoirs that he approached Eisenhower with a legislative proposal in December 1955. It was probably earlier, because his legislative proposals were debated in the December 2 cabinet meeting that, in Eisenhower's absence, discussed the content of his upcoming State of the Union address. Brownell's proposed legislation had four parts: 1) the appointment of a civil rights commission to investigate charges of voting discrimination, with authority to hold hearings with subpoena power and to propose legislation; 2) the creation of a civil rights division in the Justice Department, headed by an assistant attorney general, replacing the three-man section housed in the criminal division; 3) authority for the attorney general to initiate civil suits to protect constitutional rights beyond voting, including suits aimed at school desegregation; and 4) enforcement machinery to protect the right to vote in federal elections. Part three would, in Brownell's words, "give the attorney general unprecedented power to enforce civil rights."[29]

Brownell made a crucial distinction between civil and criminal prosecutions in his proposed legislation.* He perceived civil rights enforcement as unworkable as long as it required treating all viola-

---

* In American common law, a "crime" is radically different from a "civil" violation or a breach of contract. Criminal conviction entails moral condemnation and may result in imprisonment or some other kind of punitive action. A civil penalty does not reflect such moral censure, although it can result in a court order regulating conduct, requiring compensation, or otherwise dictating a remedy for a situation. Criminal cases often require a jury trial in which unanimous jury verdicts are required for conviction, based on evidence that establishes a defendant's guilt "beyond a reasonable doubt." Civil cases are often tried by a judge, without a jury, and verdicts are based on a "preponderance" of the evidence.

tors as criminals and prosecution by the Justice Department's criminal division. Civil remedies would minimize humiliation for southern citizens but still grant the courts the power to issue and enforce injunctions. Besides, all-white juries in criminal trials in the South in the 1950s frequently refused to convict white defendants. Brownell believed that the path to progress lay in trying more cases in front of a judge, thereby avoiding jury trials.

Eisenhower recognized that Brownell's legislation might provide alternatives to his abhorred option of military intervention to quell disorder. The problem was that Ike wanted to be reelected, and a fervent endorsement of civil rights legislation would embroil him in controversy. Therefore, Eisenhower supported Brownell's plan on the condition that he, as a candidate, could keep his distance from the measure when it was submitted to the Congress in 1956; but he agreed to prepare the ground in his State of the Union address.[30]

On January 5, 1956, in the State of the Union address, Eisenhower extolled the success of his exercise of federal authority on behalf of civil rights, announcing to the Congress that "in Executive Branch operations throughout the nation, elimination of discrimination and segregation is all but completed." But Eisenhower noted "that Negro citizens are being deprived of their right to vote and are likewise being subjected to unwarranted economic pressures," and he called for the creation of a bipartisan commission to investigate such irregularities. Eisenhower proclaimed his determination "to assure our citizens equality in justice, in opportunity and in civil rights." "We must expand this effort on every front," the president asserted. "We must strive to have every person judged and measured by what he is, rather than his color, race, or religion." Then Eisenhower announced that "there will soon be recommended to the Congress a program further to advance the efforts of the Government, within the area of Federal responsibility, to accomplish these objectives." For the first time, Dwight Eisenhower had endorsed civil rights legislation.[31]

Senator Richard Russell, the Georgia Democrat, was quick to denounce Eisenhower's statement as "cheap politics" aimed at attracting Negro votes and "part of the campaign to vilify the South."

Jimmy Byrnes predicted that the president's attempt to curry black votes would fail. The Mississippi senators, John Stennis and James Eastland, denied that Congress had any jurisdiction over voting in the states. The NAACP leadership decried the absence of an anti-lynching proposal and a commitment to denying federal education funds to states resisting desegregation.[32]

A Warren Candidacy?

Eisenhower still had not announced whether he would run for reelection. Ike's longtime practice, as he confided to Milton the previous year, was "to wait until the last possible moment before announcing any positive decision." On January 8, Eisenhower hinted to the press about his personal plans, saying he felt much stronger. He toyed with the reporters' questions. "I have not made up my mind to make any announcement as of this moment," he said, but "I am certainly not trying to be coy."[33]

Renewed rumors of a Warren candidacy pushed Eisenhower toward disclosure. In a January 25 news conference, a reporter cited Warren as a potential Republican candidate and wondered if the chief justice's return to politics would set a negative precedent. Eisenhower's irritation was palpable. "The second I was nominated by the Republican Party, I resigned from the Army," he asserted. "Now, I just don't believe we ought to cross over, we oughtn't to get the military and the civil powers tangled up. We shouldn't get too great a confusion between politics and the Supreme Court." Eisenhower said that "every official," obviously including Warren, had "a responsibility to do his part in keeping these separations."[34]

Eisenhower apparently believed that Warren was complicit in the rumors. The chief justice pulled Jim Hagerty aside at a party to express his annoyance at the president's January 25 comments. Hearing about Warren's complaint, Eisenhower rehearsed a shrewd argument in his diary—that he would say he agreed with Warren's April 1955 statement that "the Supreme Court and politics should not be mixed." Warren had a right to run, he wrote, and "it would be a great relief to me." But if Warren "indicated himself as receptive to the nomination, he should resign from the Supreme Court."[35]

The Warren controversy escalated at the president's February 8 news conference. A reporter commented that "some people got the idea that you were opposed to Warren as the Republican candidate, if you don't run yourself." Eisenhower bristled: "Opposed? For goodness sake, I appointed him as Chief Justice of the United States; and there is no office in all the world that I respect more." Eisenhower rehashed his respect and "very deep affection" for the chief justice. Then he delivered the case he had rehearsed, quoting Warren as having "argued for the complete separation of the judiciary and politics." The president concluded: "Now, there are many ways in which he could be a candidate. And if he were, he would have no opposition from me; of that I assure you." Eisenhower's response was disingenuous. He had already decided to enter the race. For all their other issues, Eisenhower and Warren were still political rivals for the presidency of the United States.[36]

As Eisenhower moved toward announcing his candidacy, the state of Alabama presented him with situations that might require military action. In response to a federal court order, the previously all-white University of Alabama admitted Autherine Lucy, a twenty-six-year-old black student, whose admission on February 1 resulted in mob violence. On March 1, the university expelled Lucy for disciplinary reasons and the judge who had ordered her reinstatement lifted his order. Exhausted, Lucy did not appeal; in this case, violent resistance to desegregation had succeeded.[37]

In Montgomery, Alabama, the bus boycott continued, and bombs exploded at the homes of boycott leaders, including the residence of Martin Luther King, Jr. On February 21, a grand jury indicted 115 Negroes under a 1921 law that made conspiracy to interfere with a business a misdemeanor. Frederic Morrow, besieged with demands that the administration do something, believed that the two Alabama situations had "developed a new keg of racial dynamite to be exploded at any moment."[38]

It was in this charged environment that Eisenhower prepared to announce his candidacy for a second term. He had already been endorsed by the nation's best-known Negro spokesman. Adam Clayton Powell, Jr., had announced on February 13 that he would support the president against the probable Democratic candidate, Adlai Ste-

venson. Eisenhower, Powell declared, had made "the greatest contribution to civil rights in the history of the United States."[39]

Eisenhower scheduled the announcement of his candidacy for
a February 29 press conference. Ike's overriding concern in his pre-
conference briefing was not his candidacy, but whether he would
be forced to take military action in Alabama. Attorney General
Brownell urged that they not "force the situation—best to wait."
Eisenhower framed the military question: whether "the Federal Government could step in if there was mob action." What would he do
"if the judge issues a certain writ and the U.S. marshal is not permitted to execute?" Gerald Morgan, the president's counsel, responded
that "the Executive has the obligation to protect the U.S. Marshal in
the performance of his duties." Andrew Goodpaster, staff secretary
to the president and national security aide, cited legal precedent for
the military to give aid to the civil power. The president grumbled
that "the Army can protect the U.S. Marshal but the State can close
the school." If southern states abolished public schools, he lamented, "then only wealthy boys and girls in the state could be educated."[40]

Eisenhower announced his candidacy at the news conference
later that day. Asked with whom he had discussed his decision, Ike
quipped: "Everybody that I thought was my friend, and some that I
wasn't so sure of." Earl Warren's name inevitably came up, and a reporter noted that Vice President Nixon had called Warren "a Republican Chief Justice." Eisenhower kept Warren firmly locked in
his judicial restraints: "Once a man has passed into the Supreme
Court, he is an American citizen and nothing else in my book until
he comes out of that Court." Eisenhower denied that the chief justice any longer had "a political designation." Eisenhower wanted
Warren out of politics—permanently.[41]

Now that Eisenhower was officially a candidate, Brownell warned
the president to be cautious in addressing civil rights questions. He
urged the president to avoid specifics at his next news conference
on several civil rights issues by deferring, as appropriate, to the
courts, the states, the attorney general, or the Congress. Regarding
the University of Alabama situation, Brownell added an urgent note:
"In no event should the President, I believe, answer any questions

indicating that the Federal Government has even considered the use of Federal troops in the South."[42]

Hoover versus Brownell

Once he announced his candidacy, Eisenhower moved to fulfill his State of the Union pledge to address civil rights legislation. The president scheduled reports from FBI Director J. Edgar Hoover and Brownell for the March 9, 1956, cabinet meeting. That set the stage for a confrontation between Hoover and Brownell.[43]

Hoover went first. He made the case, using the example of communist efforts to exploit the Emmett Till murder, that communists had captured the civil rights movement. "The area of danger," he declared, "lies in friction between extremists on both sides ready with violence." The communists, Hoover contended, were intent on "forcing the Administration to take a stand on civil rights legislation with the present Congress," promoting a civil rights division in the Department of Justice and a commission on civil rights. Hoover had framed the issue so that Brownell's legislative proposals would implement the agenda of the Communist Party.[44]

Undaunted, Brownell stated that his proposal was "in keeping with the President's message." He explained the four-part legislation he had earlier presented to Eisenhower: a civil rights commission, a civil rights division in the Justice Department, authority for the attorney general to "protect all of the rights guaranteed by the Constitution" (destined to become the most controversial provision), and mechanisms for prosecution of voting rights violations. Brownell concluded: "I believe that the enactment of all this legislation not only will give us the means to meet, fully and intelligently, our responsibility for the safeguarding of Constitutional rights in this country, but will demonstrate to the world at large our determination to secure equal justice under law for all people."[45]

Eisenhower had known for months what Brownell would propose. He wanted alternatives to military action to put down racial disorder, and that concern dictated his response in the cabinet meeting. Brownell had argued for his menu of civil remedies because, as the attorney general put it, the "worst thing would be to use force—send troops in." In response, Eisenhower said: "In the long run, the Constitution, as interpreted by the Supreme Court, is going to be enforced. That's my duty." The president criticized the southern states for saying, "We defy." When several cabinet members criticized the proposed legislation, Eisenhower repeated: "I took my oath of office to uphold it and that is what I am going to do." He added: "We are asking for non-violent things—civil law." The South, he continued, had made "big mistakes" in the Lucy case and in "opposing the moderate demand" of blacks for riding Montgomery buses. The focus on civil remedies, the president said, was "so moderate."[46] That was indeed the case, given Ike's private scenarios for having to use troops.

Harold Stassen, the former Minnesota governor and the president's special assistant, asserted that the "great danger is in moving too fast." Eisenhower challenged Stassen: "Where do you think that the Attorney General's suggestions are moving too rapidly? They look to me like amelioration." Stassen said that Brownell knew that the legislation could not be passed that year and that any bill sent to Congress "will only inspire deadlock." Brownell countered that, given the president's statements, the Congress expected the administration to drop "the other shoe." Eisenhower expressed his hope that the legislative proposals would "pour oil on the troubled waters of the situation." Brownell made his argument for civil remedies again, contending that presently the Justice Department had no recourse but to "throw people in jail. These would allow us to take a moderate action."

Eisenhower summarized the discussion: "I think that this is such a moderate approach—especially the emphasis on civil recourse rather than criminal—that it will ameliorate the situation in the South. Certainly no one could object to the proposal for the new Assistant Attorney General." He continued: "I believe that Herb Brownell should put forward what he has got here, but with a statement that many Americans understandably are separated by deep emotions on the subject." Eisenhower reminded the cabinet members that southerners had not been breaking the law for six decades before *Brown*. "People have a right to disagree with the Supreme Court decision," he stated, "since the Supreme Court has disagreed with its own decision of 60 years standing—but, of course, the new decision should now be carried out."

Brownell revealed that he and the president had agreed that the Justice Department would present the legislative proposal without a formal presidential message. That would, to some degree, insulate Eisenhower from controversy; Brownell would be the president's civil rights lightning rod. Ike instructed Brownell to bring the proposals back for a final reading. Thanks to the president's support, Brownell escaped the difficult cabinet meeting with his legislative program intact. He added softer language to a new draft, adopting the more empathetic tone Eisenhower wanted without altering the substance of his program.[47]

A few days after the March 9 cabinet meeting, Senator Strom Thurmond (D-South Carolina) released the "Southern Manifesto," a document eventually signed by more than one hundred members of Congress. The manifesto pledged unyielding resistance to *Brown,* seeking "a reversal of this decision which is contrary to the Constitution."[48] Eisenhower delivered a warning to the manifesto signatories in his March 14 news conference. The southern congressmen, the president noted, had asserted they would "use every legal means," not "nullification." The latter, the president stated, would be "a very bad spot for the simple reason that I am sworn to defend and uphold the Constitution of the United States and, of course, I can never abandon or refuse to carry out my own duty." Eisenhower combined that admonition with a call for moderation and patience. "Extremists on neither side are going to help this situation," he said, "and we can only believe that the good sense, the common sense, of Americans will bring this thing along."[49]

On March 20, Eisenhower and Brownell presented the attorney general's civil rights proposals to the Republican legislative leaders. They confirmed what Eisenhower and Brownell already knew—that civil rights legislation had little hope of passage in an election year.[50]

Enlisting Billy Graham

In his quest for alternatives to force, Ike attempted to enlist southern religious leaders in the cause of ameliorating racial hostility. The day of the March legislative leaders meeting, Eisenhower met with evangelist Billy Graham for forty-five minutes. Graham, who had already banned segregation in his crusades, recalled that "the president was deeply concerned about the rising racial tension and he felt strongly that the church could make a tremendous contribution toward the bettering of race relations."[51]

Eisenhower's subsequent letter to the evangelist proposed "certain practical measures that would be considered by Federal Judges in the South as evidence of progress toward desegregation." He asked if Graham would encourage the election of a few qualified Negroes to official positions, encourage university admission on merit, and support flexible plans for transportation, "so that we do not have the spectacle of Negroes in considerable numbers waiting for a ride on a public conveyance, while numerous seats are held vacant for possible white customers." These things, Eisenhower suggested, "could properly be mentioned in a pulpit."

Graham shared the president's "personal" letter widely. Eisenhower, a bit upset, wrote the evangelist that he had been "completely confident that you would hold confidential any suggestions I made; otherwise I could not have written as I did." Graham pledged to make an effort with the leaders of the major southern denominations, but he worried about "rumors that Republican strategy will be to go all out in winning the Negro vote in the North regardless of the South's feelings."[52]

A Cabinet in Conflict

On March 23, the cabinet reconvened for another session on civil rights legislation. The critics of Brownell's proposals had been lobbying the president. Ike informed the attorney general that cabinet members were having a "terrible time" getting through his legislative proposals, especially part three, which empowered the attorney general to prosecute general civil rights violations. Eisenhower still hoped that provision could be "an ameliorating move." Brownell insisted that the existing law requiring criminal penalties was unworkable because it provided for only one option—putting violators "in jail."

Secretary of State John Foster Dulles urged Brownell to "go a bit slow to accomplish by law what is essentially a social matter." The government, he opined, could not impose the conscience of half the country on the other half. Dulles feared that part three, "if literally applied, would send a large portion of white southerners to jail. Just can't do that." Eisenhower responded that southern Democrats were so rigid "that anything ameliorating we propose and regard as an advance gets attacked." He wanted to reinforce the "conscience" of America "and try to get southern conscience closer to it."

Eisenhower hesitated, then admitted that he was "at sea." Activists wanted him to force the University of Alabama to accept Autherine Lucy, but the government had no authority to intervene. Ike worried, as he always had, that southerners would shut down their educational system, and that "could be chaos." He fretted about "how deep this emotion" was in the south. Yet "I constantly try to get people to look forward to make some advance."

Eisenhower repeated his contention that providing southerners with civil rather than criminal penalties was "moderating." Marion Folsom, the HEW secretary, countered, "They won't see it that way." Eisenhower responded that the government "must enforce law—or would you ignore it?" Secretary of Defense Charles Wilson suggested putting the controversial parts of the proposed legislation on the agenda for the proposed civil rights commission to study. That proposition tempted the president, but Brownell declared, "That would be moderation but no progress." Folsom contended that the legislation would never get passed anyway because "any broadening of authority is going to be resented." Frustrated, Eisenhower decided the cabinet could reach no conclusion and asked Brownell to see him outside the meeting.[53]

Later that day, Brownell, Sherman Adams, Gerald Morgan, and Max Rabb met with a troubled president in the Oval Office. Eisenhower reviewed additional revisions Brownell had made to the proposals. According to Morgan's notes, the president stated that "the proposed program was perhaps the best that could be devised under the circumstances, and told the Attorney General to go ahead with it if he wished." Morgan and Adams demurred, suggesting that "the statement should not go up unless and until the president was more convinced in his own mind that it was the right thing to do." Then Eisenhower dismissed everyone but Brownell. The attorney general needed just five minutes. Morgan recorded: "When the Attorney General came out, he reported that the President had given the proposed statement a complete okay."[54]

That was a bit misleading. Eisenhower had asked Brownell to make changes to his proposals in both tone and substance before he testified before the House Judiciary Committee. The attorney general removed potentially inflammatory language and agreed to formally submit to Congress only the two less controversial parts of his proposed legislation—the commission and the civil rights division—but be prepared to discuss the other two informally. Brownell delivered the final version of his written testimony to the president on Saturday, April 8, before testifying on the following Monday.[55]

Brownell Testifies

What happened next is extraordinary; Brownell played shrewd congressional politics with the House Judiciary Committee. Eisenhower may have known what he planned, since he had received the attorney general's written testimony in advance, never repudiated Brownell's actions, and praised the proposals to legislative leaders the following week.

Brownell was set to formally submit only his first two proposals—for a civil rights commission and a civil rights division in the Justice Department. But his written statement elaborated expansively on the two provisions he was not, at this time, formally proposing (parts three and four of his original proposals), giving the attorney general broad authority to file civil suits to prosecute violations of general constitutional rights as well as the right to vote. The attorney general's statement described voting violations where criminal penalties were unworkable, for example, in making potential Negro voters explain the Constitution or count how many bubbles are found in a bar of soap. In such cases, under existing law, the Justice Department would be forced to take criminal action rather than initiate a civil action that might be more likely to secure results.[56]

Brownell then began his oral testimony by quoting the president's State of the Union address. He had conspired in advance with New York Republican Congressman Kenneth Keating, an old political ally, to put the two remaining provisions he was not formally proposing on the agenda. Keating asked if the department had considered problems other than those that would be addressed by the commission and civil rights division, and "would the Department be able to draft any legislation to meet them?" Brownell was ready with parts three and four: "Yes, we certainly could, and indeed we have. We have drafts right here."

Brownell stated that administration policy on school desegregation would emphasize litigation rather than legislation, making prosecutions a primary responsibility of the new civil rights division. When asked about antilynching legislation, Brownell testified, "We are not in favor of extending the Federal jurisdiction to murder." However, mob action was something else, and Brownell hinted at the possibility of military intervention: "I want to make this clear, that so far as mob violence is concerned, or the so-called hooded-action crimes, that we think the Federal Government should have complete authority there to prevent mob violence based on racial discrimination."[57]

Brownell had never been so far out on what he called Eisenhower's "proverbial limb." He made these proposals from the Justice Department, rather than in a formal presidential message.[58] Despite the president's election-year aloofness, Eisenhower and Brownell had crossed a critical juncture in their quest for legal alternatives to landing troops in the South.

Some critics complained that Brownell's proposals were "too little and too late"; Thurgood Marshall did not concur. He deemed it unfair to criticize Brownell "without condemning the Democratic leadership in Congress for holding up action in the pending civil rights laws." Marshall understood what he called "the terrific difficulties of successful criminal prosecutions for violation of existing civil rights statutes in many areas of the South." He concluded that

Brownell's "request for authority to bring injunctive proceedings on behalf of the United States" would be "a step forward."[59]

The Eisenhower Coalition

The week after Brownell's testimony, Eisenhower told worried Republican congressmen that he had "personally gone over the whole proposal very carefully and he couldn't imagine anything more moderate." He complained that hostile southerners had not even read the proposals. Once again, Ike worried aloud about being forced to use troops to enforce federal court orders. He lamented that "civil rights extremists never stop to consider that although you can send in troops, troops can't make anyone operate schools. Private schools could be set up, and Negroes would get no education at all."[60]

By May 1956, the Eisenhower administration's civil rights proposals had begun to undermine old alliances in Congress. For decades, a conservative coalition of southern Democrats and conservative Republicans had blocked civil rights legislation. Senator Hubert Humphrey, the Minnesota Democrat, began to envision an alliance that would replace the old "coalition of resistance." Humphrey wrote Roy Wilkins that "if the Eisenhower administration will just jar loose four votes in the Senate Judiciary Committee and about fifteen to twenty votes from the Republican side of the [a]isle, we will pass these bills. That will be the happiest day of my life."[61]

Eisenhower underwent colon surgery on June 9. On July 10, he was back, urging Republican leaders to push ahead on the civil rights legislation because the bill, the meeting's minutes recorded, "was, to his mind, the most moderate thing we could have asked for and he thought the real criticism was going to come because of its lack of vigor."[62] But Eisenhower's failure to publicly endorse the bill outside legislative meetings embarrassed the bill's advocates. He finally authorized congressional liaison Bryce Harlow to inform Democratic Representative James Roosevelt of California of his endorsement of the bill, and Roosevelt read Harlow's letter on the floor of the House. Kenneth Keating, Brownell's Republican colleague from

New York, was shocked on hearing a Democrat announce this news. Keating insisted on a letter of his own and declared that "any other signature than the President's will *not* do." Eisenhower responded with a note: "I would like to have it made clear to your colleagues that I subscribe fully to the bill now before the House and am earnestly hopeful that it will be approved."[63]

The new coalition pushed the legislation rapidly through the House, and it passed 276–126 on July 23, with 168 Republicans supporting the bill, and twenty-four opposed. The Senate leadership, anxious to adjourn in an election year, quickly agreed that there was insufficient time for the Senate to act on the bill. Eisenhower and Brownell had anticipated that outcome, but they had tested the legislative waters. The new coalition, a committed president, and shrewd strategies for the manipulation of Senate rules held hope for a different outcome in 1957.[64]

The Republican Platform

By August, the Republican convention was on the horizon, with delegates facing an inevitable tussle over the civil rights plank in the platform. These pressures were beginning to irritate Eisenhower. On August 6, Ann Whitman recorded that an agitated Eisenhower "hit some golf balls," walked around the exterior of the White House, and was "still in bad temper." He wondered aloud "why anyone would want such a job as that of the President."[65]

In the August 8 pre–press conference briefing, the White House staff urged the president "to stay out of all platform plan discussion" with the press, especially while the Democrats were struggling with their own platform on civil rights. Asked by reporters if he thought the Republican platform should specifically endorse *Brown*, Eisenhower dissembled, saying he had not "given any thought of my own as to whether it should just state it in that way." Ike was not being candid. He was fully prepared to dictate the content of the civil rights plank. A week earlier, he had pressured Senator Prescott Bush of Connecticut, the GOP platform committee chairman, to make sure the document stated that "civil rights will not be achieved by law alone."[66]

Southern GOP delegates pressured the platform committee, contending that a strong civil rights plank might hurt Republican chances to pick up a Senate seat in Kentucky and several House seats. The newspapers noted that "for the first time at a Republican convention, the sort of political horse-trading over civil rights that has characterized recent Democratic conventions was beginning to develop." Ike frantically sought to head off a Democratic-style split. Warren Olney, head of the Justice Department's criminal division, which housed civil rights, worked on draft after draft of the platform but "had great difficulty getting those things approved in the White House." On August 19, Eisenhower, in a particularly bad mood, called Brownell and reminded him of their public strategy in the brief for *Brown I*—that they had pretended that "the Attorney General was appearing as a lawyer, not as a member of the Eisenhower Administration." Eisenhower noted that "he had always denied that the Administration took a stand on the matter." At such moments, Ike, as he put it to Brownell, was torn "between the compulsion of duty on one side, and his firm conviction, on the other that because of the Supreme Court's ruling, the whole issue had been set back badly." Eisenhower insisted that the party not "concur" with the Court's ruling but employ the milder term, "accepts." He petulantly told Brownell to tell Senators Prescott Bush and Everett Dirksen (R-Illinois) that if they did not comply with his wishes, he might refuse to go to San Francisco for the convention. That ill-tempered rant aside, Eisenhower got what he wanted. The platform stated that the GOP "accepts" the Supreme Court's decision in *Brown* and that Republicans "concur" that "school desegregation should be accomplished with 'all deliberate speed.'"[67]

Roy Wilkins, usually allied with the Democrats, confessed that "on balance, the Republican platform was a shade better than that of the Democrats—but only a thin shade." That "thin shade" was what Eisenhower wanted. Despite the GOP's compromises, southern Democrats attacked the platform, charging that it allied the Eisenhower administration with "iniquitous" civil rights proposals that threatened the South's "way of life."[68]

Adam Clayton Powell, Jr., did not agree with his Democratic colleagues. On August 12, he delivered a speech titled "Why This Dem-

ocrat Is for President Eisenhower." Powell derided the bargain that
Adlai Stevenson had allegedly made with the South, asserting, "I
don't like anybody that is pledged to Eastland." Powell emotionally
recalled: "Four years ago in Washington, I couldn't eat in any place
except a Jim Crow restaurant. I couldn't get a room in a hotel. I
couldn't get into any theater except a Negro one. But Dwight D.
Eisenhower overnight made Washington, D.C., better for all people
than New York City."[69]

Once the platform fight was over, Eisenhower moved in a more
progressive direction. He took Frederic Morrow's advice and selected a professor of history at North Carolina College—Dr. Helen
Edmonds, whose skin was dark enough to show on the black-and-
white television sets of the day—to second his nomination. Eisenhower trumpeted his civil rights record in his August 23 acceptance
speech, reminding the delegates that "the Republican Party was created in a devout belief in equal justice and equal opportunity for all
in a nation of free men and women." The Republican record, Eisenhower declared, rested "not on words and promises, but on accomplishment."[70]

A Scenario for Military Intervention

Just as the election campaign got under way in September 1956,
school desegregation crises erupted in Texas. Governor Allan Shivers, an Eisenhower supporter in 1952, ordered Texas Rangers to bar
Negro students from entering Mansfield High School in compliance with a federal court order, and to prevent the integration of
Texarkana Junior College. But Eisenhower had no intention of
sending troops to Texas—a state he intended to carry in the election. Instead, sounding much like J. Edgar Hoover, he stated how
important he thought it was "that extremists on both sides do not
defeat what we know is a reasonable, logical conclusion to this whole
affair, which is recognition of equality of men." Thurgood Marshall
complained to the president: "Surely you do not mean to equate
lawless mobs with federal courts as 'extremists.'"[71]

Partly in response to the Texas situation, Eisenhower sketched
out a scenario at his September 11 news conference that foreshad-

owed his actions a year later in Little Rock, Arkansas. First, a federal court would issue an order for students to enter a school, but violence could prevent their attendance. Then the federal court would decide if the violent persons were in contempt of court. If they were, the Justice Department would be asked to assist with the case. Then, Eisenhower concluded, "I assume that it is the job of the U.S. Marshal to serve warrants and take the men, the offenders, to jail or to pay their fines or whatever happens." He did not state that if such a situation turned overwhelmingly violent, he might have to send in troops.

Then Eisenhower, so crassly political about civil rights during much of the campaign, confounded his critics with a move to the left. Supreme Court Justice Sherman Minton had announced that he would retire, effective October 15. On September 11, reporters had asked if Eisenhower would appoint a southerner to Minton's seat. The president responded that there were already two southerners on the Court, an obvious reference to Hugo Black of Alabama and Stanley Reed of Kentucky, who had supported the *Brown* decision. On September 19, Eisenhower nominated William J. Brennan, Jr.—a Catholic Democrat and justice of the New Jersey Supreme Court. This shrewd bipartisan appointment sent a signal to the segregationists. This was the second High Court appointment Eisenhower had made since the *Brown* decision—the first being New Yorker John Marshall Harlan II, the grandson of the dissenting justice in *Plessy v. Ferguson* in 1896. Despite intense agitation for a southerner, Eisenhower had nominated another liberal northerner.[72]

Campaigning on Civil Rights

On September 19, the same day that Eisenhower nominated Brennan to the Supreme Court, he opened his campaign for reelection with a television address. Focusing on world peace, he also called for "understanding and tolerance among all races and creeds," and reiterated his policy of securing "wherever the authority of the Federal Government extends, equality of rights and opportunity for all men regardless of race or color."[73]

As in 1952, Eisenhower in 1956 shifted the discussion of his campaign in the final month toward civil rights and appealed more directly for black votes. Eisenhower invited E. Frederic Morrow to sit with him in the presidential box at the opening game of the World Series. Morrow arranged for a parade of leading black Republicans to visit with the president. On October 23, Cora M. Brown, a Michigan Democrat, came to the White House and announced her support for Eisenhower. Portia Washington Pittman, president of the Booker T. Washington Foundation, pledged her support, and the president instructed Morrow to send her a campaign logo brooch and earrings.[74]

The Eisenhower campaign's publicity regarding the president's role in desegregating the armed forces annoyed the Democrats. In a Harlem speech, Adlai Stevenson, the Democratic nominee, accused Eisenhower of misleading the public because it was a Democratic administration that had begun desegregating the armed forces. Ike responded in a news conference that, during World War II, he "was the first combat commander that ever used Negroes incorporated actually into white units on the battlefield," and he described his conflict with General Patton over that initiative. Eisenhower said that he had concluded, by the time he took office, that "it was time to take the bull by the horns, and eliminate it all."[75]

Eisenhower had a political weapon in reserve. On October 11, he summoned Adam Clayton Powell, Jr., to a meeting that included Hagerty, Val Washington, and Bernard Shanley, the president's appointments secretary. Powell said that he was "prepared to lead an independent movement for the President on a nationwide basis and take an active part in the balance of the campaign." The congressman launched an "Independent Democrats for Eisenhower" organization at a news conference on October 19, claiming that 25 percent of Negroes had shifted their allegiance to Eisenhower and predicting that another 10 percent would switch by election day.[76]

The day after he met with Powell, Eisenhower, in a televised question-and-answer program, responded to Stevenson's charge that he had been "virtually silent" on civil rights. The president stated that "the United States is never going to be completely easy with its conscience until we are according to everyone that equality before the law and that equality and opportunity that is visualized by our Constitution." All the Supreme Court had done, he said, was "to devise a method by which this would eventually be brought about in our schools." Eisenhower cited his desegregation of Washington, D.C., and contrasted his style of leadership with the Democrats: "We have been pursuing this quietly, not tub-thumping, and we have not tried to claim political credit. This is a matter of justice, not of anything else."[77]

That was Ike's constant theme in the closing days of the campaign. At a rally in Seattle, Eisenhower asserted that the GOP's approach to civil rights was based on "the principle of talking less and doing more." The president proclaimed to a Madison Square Garden crowd in New York that Republicans had discovered "the true way to advance the cause of civil rights: less oratory, and more action."[78]

Four days after his meeting with Eisenhower, Powell spoke passionately in Harlem about his conversation with the president. The congressman recalled that he had asked the president what the government would do if a school district refused to obey a federal court order to desegregate its schools. Powell quoted Eisenhower as saying: "Mr. Powell, I advocate that the Federal Court shall get Federal marshals, swear in deputies if they need them, go out and arrest anyone who refused to obey their orders, bring them before the court, try them for contempt, and if they're guilty put them in prison." A black congressman suggesting that the president wanted to send southerners to jail produced a political uproar. The White House asked Powell to retract the statement and he did so, claiming that the president had not made the remarks in their meeting. He had, he said, "inadvertently confused this interview with my recollection of what the President said at his public press conference on September 11th when he did mention the subject of enforcement of school integration."[79]

That was a clever response. Eisenhower, on September 11, had indeed made a statement about U.S. marshals serving warrants and taking "the men, the offenders to jail." Bernard Shanley's notes on the October 11 meeting indicate that "the President explained again his position on the integration problem as he has done so often in press conferences." Congressman Powell probably quoted the president accurately in his speech.

Now, in the heat of the presidential campaign, Democrats spread rumors that Powell had made a deal with the Eisenhower administration to avoid prosecution for alleged income tax evasion. Powell called the charge "a complete lie," pointing to the fact that three of his secretaries had been indicted and jailed. As the campaign neared its climax, the man reputed to be the "most compelling Negro orator in the world" campaigned for Eisenhower across the nation while Jimmy Byrnes, the president's old southern friend, stumped for an independent ticket headed by Virginia Senator Harry F. Byrd.[80]

Civil rights was the least of Eisenhower's problems as the campaign ended. On October 23, the Hungarians revolted against Soviet rule and were brutally suppressed by the Red Army. In the midst of this crisis, on October 29, Israel, Britain, and France launched a war against Egypt to regain control of the Suez Canal.

On Sunday, October 28, Eisenhower underwent a physical checkup. A good report left the president in high spirits. He called in his speechwriters and made changes in three speeches scheduled for Monday. Ann Whitman noted that Ike had dictated two paragraphs on civil rights that were "much stronger than anything anyone around here had dared suggest."[81] Two days before the election, the Gallup Poll published findings on the shifts in voting groups since the 1952 election, showing that black support for the Eisenhower-Nixon ticket had moved from 21 percent in 1952 to 42 percent.[82]

Eisenhower won in a landslide on November 6; Stevenson carried only seven states, all in the Deep South except for Missouri. The president carried the Electoral College 457 to 73, including Texas, Louisiana, Florida, Tennessee, and Kentucky. The *New York Times* reported that, especially in the South, black voters had returned to the Republican Party and had possibly carried the four southern states for Eisenhower. The trend was less pronounced in the North. The night of the election, Sherman Adams gave Frederic Morrow, who had campaigned in black communities, a big smile and a handshake, and said: "A job well done, son."[83] There was one problem; despite Eisenhower's personal victory, the Republicans failed to win either house of Congress.[84]

Powell paid a price for supporting Eisenhower. After the election, the Democrats moved to deprive him of his seniority and committee assignments in the House. Roy Wilkins protested to the Speaker of the House that the members of the States Rights Party in 1948 and the southern Democrats who had supported Eisenhower in 1952 had not lost their party privileges. These actions, he charged, were contemplated "because of Mr. Powell's race and because of his efforts to secure civil rights legislation."[85]

Toward 1957

On November 13, the Supreme Court ruled on the Montgomery, Alabama, bus boycott and upheld a lower court decision that declared state and local laws segregating buses unconstitutional. The next day, a weary Eisenhower prepared for his first news conference following the election. He did not welcome another Supreme Court decision that would complicate his life. Ike blustered to his staff that, on some issues, he was more of a "States Righter" than the Court, and he worried that hostile reaction in the South to the new decision might reverse rather than advance the welfare of blacks. Fearing "a general strike" in the South, the president sarcastically noted that the Court did not submit its decisions to him for approval. Eisenhower's laments were fueled by the prospect that had haunted him throughout 1956—that he might be forced to use the army to put down disorder in the South. "Eventually a District Court is going to cite someone for contempt," he fretted, "and then we are going to be up against it." Civil rights never came up at the press conference; the reporters were preoccupied with the crises in the Middle East and Hungary.[86]

Despite his grumbling, Eisenhower had won an overwhelming personal electoral victory. He had simultaneously collaborated with Brownell to place civil rights legislation on the congressional agenda, molding a Republican-led coalition of legislators that might make the difference in a nonelection year. The *New York Times* predicted that Eisenhower would use his electoral landslide to push his program with Congress, including "a basic repetition of the Administration program on civil rights." But the paper went on to note that 1956 was the first election since 1848 in which a reelected president had failed to carry either house of Congress. Southern Democrats would resist Eisenhower's civil rights program, "especially in the light of election returns that showed Southern Negroes jumping into the Republican column."[87]

The newspaper's assessment of the administration's intent was accurate. Eisenhower and Brownell had agreed to resubmit the civil rights legislation to the new Congress. Enhanced civil authority still constituted Eisenhower's best hope for avoiding military intervention in the South. The prospect of being forced to send troops into the former Confederacy would become more urgent in 1957.[88]

CHAPTER SEVEN

The Civil Rights Act of 1957

I believe that the United States must make certain that every citizen who is entitled to vote under the Constitution is given actually that right. I believe also that in sustaining that right, we must sustain the power of the Federal judges in whose hands such cases would fall.

—Dwight D. Eisenhower, July 31, 1957, news conference

The election was over. After a year of mixed signals from the White House, Eisenhower was ready to do his duty on civil rights legislation. He met with Republican legislative leaders on December 31, 1956, and concurred when Attorney General Herbert Brownell told them of "the Administration's intent to request four items that were not acted upon by the Senate last year." On New Year's Day, 1957, the *New York Times* page one story left no doubt: "President Pushes Civil Rights Plan at G.O.P. Parley."[1]

The New Civil Rights Coalition

"Steadily we are moving closer to the goal of fair and equal treatment of citizens without regard to race or color," Eisenhower told Congress in his State of the Union address on January 10, 1957, "but unhappily much remains to be done." The president used his message to describe all four parts of the previous years' legislation: appointment of a bipartisan civil rights commission, creation of a civil rights division in the Justice Department, authority for the attorney general "to seek from the civil courts preventive relief in civil rights cases," and protection of voting rights. Eisenhower could not know at this point what a bone of contention part three, the enhancement of the attorney general's powers, would become during the congressional session. He firmly concluded: "I urge that the Congress enact this legislation."[2]

Roy Wilkins wired Eisenhower that the NAACP deplored his failure to mention the "rising tide of hate-inspired violence" and noted that, the night before the president's address, four black churches in Montgomery, Alabama, had been bombed. Senator Hubert Humphrey complained to columnist Drew Pearson that Eisenhower's proposals "were facsimiles of the very bills which we had introduced here in the Senate in every session of the Congress since 1949." He grumbled: "I don't mind them adopting our legislative children, but it bothers me when they start to claim paternity." But Humphrey recognized that Eisenhower and Brownell had transformed the legislative landscape. The Minnesota Democrat lobbied Senate Majority Leader Lyndon Johnson "to give us some support on these civil rights bills, or at least to let us fight it out." Humphrey told columnist Stewart Alsop that he had warned Johnson that "the informal but highly effective coalition between the Southern Democrats and the Republicans was soon to come to an end." Senator William Knowland, the conservative Republican minority leader from California, was the key player. "As long as Dick Russell and Bill Knowland worked together," Humphrey recalled, "there was not a chance for civil rights to succeed. The day that the Republicans decided that civil rights legislation should be passed, that coalition came to an end and the success of a civil rights program was assured."[3]

Eisenhower was apparently responsible for Knowland's conversion. He had complained to Brownell in 1954 that "Knowland is the biggest disappointment I have found since I have been in politics." Just what happened between the two men is not documented but, at an April 1957 news conference, reporters asked the president whether Knowland should resign as minority leader "because he is opposed to so much of your program." Eisenhower rejected that proposition. He had firmly committed himself to civil rights legislation, and Knowland understood that his duty, as minority leader, was to support that cause. In a letter to a friend, Senator Humphrey stated that, beyond Knowland's conservatism, a problem in passing civil rights legislation was "the aloofness of President Eisenhower."[4] In fact, the president was much less detached than Humphrey thought.

Humphrey was willing to work with the administration. "If we go too far, we will get nothing," he asserted to Paul Ziffren, a prominent California attorney. "Concentrate attention upon the bill to protect the right to vote. If federal action can be used to protect the right of that franchise, then we have started to win the civil rights battle." Humphrey urged Democrats to embrace the administration's proposals. "Simply because Brownell and Ike support them, doesn't make them meaningless or bad bills," he wrote. Humphrey pressed the point with Walter Reuther, president of the United Auto Workers. "A bill to protect the right to vote is not meaningless," he said, "and anyone who says it is, is just playing to the galleries or being a demagogue."[5]

The new Eisenhower coalition was already at work. Two days after Ike's State of the Union speech, the *New York Times* reported that civil rights advocates had reached an agreement with Lyndon Johnson to conduct around-the-clock sessions in the Senate to exhaust filibustering southerners and, if necessary, to invoke cloture—the Senate rule requiring the approval of a two-thirds majority of the Senate's membership or, in 1957, sixty-four votes—to end debate.[6] Johnson, who wanted a mild civil rights bill to advance his presidential ambitions, pledged he would not bar the legislation from getting to the Senate floor, nor would he participate in a filibuster or oppose efforts to break off debate. Roy Wilkins remembered the dilemma when working with the opportunistic Texan: "With Johnson, you never knew if he was out to lift your heart or your wallet."[7]

The Legislative Struggle Begins

Eisenhower entered his office at 8:40 A.M. on January 20, 1957, and announced to Ann Whitman that he "had not made one substantial change in his Inaugural address and that no pages needed to be retyped." Whitman called this "the most outstanding event of the past four years, from a secretary's worm's eye viewpoint." But Eisenhower was not serene. He dictated a letter to his brother Edgar, describing the president's job as "nothing but frustration." Whitman listened as Ike "fussed for about a half hour about the responsibilities he was again undertaking." She suggested he would have been more upset if he were turning the office over to Adlai Stevenson. At the ceremony, Chief Justice Earl Warren, Eisenhower's contentious appointee, administered the oath. The president's speech focused almost exclusively on foreign affairs, with no mention of civil rights.[8]

Once Eisenhower was inaugurated, Brownell and Eisenhower pushed their civil rights agenda. Brownell told a Republican gathering that the president's proposed program would "stop practices and subterfuges by which our Negro citizens are deprived of their right to vote." He promised that the Eisenhower civil rights program would be "pressed vigorously" in the Congress. The president himself asserted "emphatically" to White House reporters that "I want a civil rights bill of the character that we recommended to the Congress. It is nothing that is inimical to the interests of anyone. It is intended to preserve rights without arousing passions and without disturbing the rights of anybody else. I think it is a very decent and very needful piece of legislation." The segregationists struck back early and hard. Witnesses before the House Judiciary Committee claimed that the president's program would produce a "Soviet type Gestapo" that would constantly investigate, interfere with the states, and intimidate citizens. Congressman Henderson Lanham, a Georgia Democrat, said that Josef Stalin, the late Soviet dictator, could not have invented a more tyrannical program.[9]

The southerners quickly settled on two strategies. One tactic was to charge that the legislation would empower the president to use troops in the South. Attorney General Brownell lost his temper when, in a hearing, Senator Sam J. Ervin (D-North Carolina) harassed him with that argument. Brownell rejected the "implication that the President would act recklessly, if not unconstitutionally." He declared, "I personally cannot stay here and allow any such implication to stand."[10]

The other tactic, designed by Lyndon Johnson, was to argue that the legislation would deny the constitutional right to a trial by jury. The Eisenhower bill sought to replace unworkable criminal provisions with civil suits, which could be tried before a judge without a jury, resulting in a court order rather than a criminal conviction. Such injunctive orders could be obtained and implemented to remedy a situation in a more timely fashion, when criminal prosecutions often took weeks or months with uncertain outcomes. The segregationists stood this proposition on its head, insisting that these civil suits would be criminal prosecutions in disguise, once a defendant was cited for contempt for refusing to comply with a court order. Therefore, the southerners insisted that a jury trial was a constitutional imperative. In the Deep South, where juries were all white, a jury trial provision would guarantee a "not guilty" verdict in most civil rights cases, as well as significant delay. The tactic communicated a stark reality; the congressional segregationists had developed a fraudulent rationale to justify encouraging their constituents to defy federal court orders.[11]

The civil rights bill made rapid progress in the House of Representatives. With House passage assured, the southern members of the Senate Judiciary Committee engaged in what Clarence Mitchell, the director of the Washington, D.C., NAACP chapter, called "deception and filibuster" to delay a vote. On April 9, Knowland complained about "Democratic footdragging" and the opposition's "apparent determination to keep this subject off the floor until mid-May." If time ran out, as it had the previous year, no bill could be passed.[12]

Pressure from African-American Leaders

Martin Luther King, Jr., did not intend to remain silent about the prospect of another legislative failure. The twenty-eight-year-old King represented a new generation of African-American leaders. Buoyed by the *Brown* decision and the Montgomery bus boycott, these black activists were more assertive, skilled in dealing with white power brokers, and firmly insistent on a civil rights bill. Building on his Montgomery experience, the clergyman launched the Southern Christian Leadership Conference (SCLC), an umbrella organization for local civil rights organizations, most of them led by Negro ministers. The organization's January 11, 1957, communication to the president, under King's name, depicted a "state of terror" in the South. "In Tennessee, Negro children have been attacked," King wrote. "In Florida, stoning and cross burning are used to obstruct justice." In Alabama, churches and homes had been bombed and Negroes, including women, had been beaten. King implored Eisenhower to make a speech in the South and use "the weight of your great office to point out to the people of the South the moral nature of the problem." Max Rabb assured King that the president did "not condone these acts of violence and, when a federal statute is involved, the federal government stands ready to act speedily."[13]

Eisenhower's public comment on King's telegram was dismissive. The president, sounding as if he would rather play golf than discuss civil rights, told the press he had "a pretty good and sizable agenda" on his desk, and "I insist on going for a bit of recreation every once in a while, and I do that because I think it is necessary to keep up to the state of fitness essential to this job." Eisenhower maintained that he had expressed himself on civil rights in both the North and the South and "I don't know what another speech would do about the thing right now." On February 14, King, in another telegram to the president, pronounced Eisenhower's comments "a profound disappointment to the millions of Americans of goodwill, north and south, who earnestly are looking to you for leadership and guidance in this period of inevitable social change." He announced that his new organization would organize "a pilgrimage of prayer" to Washington. "If you cannot come south to relieve our harassed people," he wrote Eisenhower, "we shall have to lead our people to you in the capitol."[14]

Eisenhower's response had been more calculating than callous. Having just delivered his civil rights proposal to the Congress, he studiously avoided any appearance of embracing King's agenda.

King scheduled his pilgrimage event in Washington for May 17—the third anniversary of the Supreme Court's school desegregation decision. Despite warnings from J. Edgar Hoover that communists had infiltrated the event, Max Rabb, working with Adam Clayton Powell, Jr., Clarence Mitchell, and Roy Wilkins, reported to Sherman Adams that they had successfully changed the meeting from a protest march "into an occasion where there will be an observance of the anniversary of the school decision through prayer. The President, I am assured, will not be adversely affected."[15]

King sought a meeting with the president while in Washington for the prayer event. Rabb called the civil rights leader at the Statler Hotel in New York and bluntly told him "that it would be disastrous for the Civil Rights Bill" for him to visit the White House at this point. Rabb said they would set the time "in a month or so," after the fate of the legislation was resolved. King agreed and said he would not publicly demand the appointment.[16]

However, King was able to arrange a meeting with Vice President Richard Nixon, whom he had met in Ghana in March, when they had attended a celebration of that African nation's independence from British colonial rule. King and Nixon met for two hours on June 13. King urged the vice president to speak in the South and to press Republican congressmen to pass the civil rights bill. Instead of a speech, Nixon offered to hold a meeting of the committee on government contracts, which he chaired, in a southern city. King pledged to the vice president that his own group, the SCLC, would "urge Negroes to hold unswervingly to non-violence in word, thought and deed." Rabb informed Sherman Adams that "the Vice President was very much impressed with Reverend King and thinks the President would enjoy talking to him. He is not, he says, a man who believes in violent and retaliatory pro-Negro actions, but sponsors an evolutionary but progressive march forward."[17]

The president's commitment to meet with black leaders was now on record, to be scheduled after the fate of the civil rights bill was determined. On June 25, the staff was still saying: "Cannot hold meeting at this time. Civil rights bill is first priority and no excuse should be provided for pro-segregationists to postpone action on this legislation."[18]

The Jury Trial Issue

Eisenhower's leadership style grated on his Democratic allies in the Senate. Hubert Humphrey could not comprehend Eisenhower's reluctance to bluntly assert, "I am against segregation. I firmly believe that the Supreme Court decision of 1954 was correct, legally and morally." Frederic Morrow's black constituents demanded that the president speak out against violence in the South. Morrow tried to explain Eisenhower's reasoning: "Having spoken on this question many times, and having made his position very clear, he feels that he does not have to pick a specific time and a specific place to make a specific speech on this issue." In the heat of the legislative fight, Morrow said, such a speech "would divide this country in a manner similar to that during the period of the Civil War!" Morrow captured the staff's frustrations in dealing with Eisenhower's stubbornness: "No kind of pressure, from any source, can make the President speak out more forcibly than he already has on this question."[19]

The Eisenhower coalition's leaders in the Senate were not so timid. Paul Douglas, the liberal Democratic senator from Illinois, provided his colleagues with voting statistics showing shameless discrimination against blacks in the South, but the southerners focused their opposition on the absence of a jury trial provision in the legislation. Douglas and Hubert Humphrey sparred with Senator Ervin, who called the civil injunctions in the bill "a new, unique, and radical departure from the precedents of our law" and "abhorrent to those who love our constitutional and legal systems." Democratic Senator Harry Byrd of Virginia insisted that the Eisenhower program was a "travesty of justice to attempt the protection of civil rights for any one group through a process which denies a liberty equally precious—that of trial by jury."[20]

The sticking point that southern Democrats exploited was what would happen if a citizen or group, as the result of a civil suit, refused to comply with a judge's order. That would constitute "contempt of court." That, the segregationists contended, would move the case from civil into criminal legal territory. Douglas maintained that there was "no constitutional guaranty of jury trial in contempt proceedings—it is doubtful whether Congress could constitutionally provide for jury trials as broadly as the opponents of the civil-rights bill propose." He pled for understanding: "The aim of these provisions in the civil-rights bill is prevention of violations or deprivations of constitutional rights, not punishment. To equate these provisions with criminal prosecutions is to confuse and misread their meaning and effect."[21]

President Eisenhower and Attorney General Herbert Brownell, Jr., consulted frequently on government policies, especially civil rights. They had discussed civil rights in depth in Paris in 1952 when Brownell persuaded Ike to formally announce his candidacy for president. As attorney general, Brownell masterminded Eisenhower's civil rights initiatives and developed rigorous standards for the appointment of federal judges.

In 1955, Eisenhower appointed E. Frederic Morrow as the first black to serve in an executive position in the White House. Morrow had campaigned with Eisenhower in 1952 and had served in the Commerce Department. He was assigned more direct responsibility for White House relations with Negroes in 1958. Morrow's role as the sole black executive in the White House often proved uncomfortable for him.

President Eisenhower and his wife, Mamie, greeted Earl Warren and his wife, Nina, at the White House after Warren was sworn in as chief justice of the Supreme Court on October 5, 1953. This was a time of warm feelings between the president and the new chief justice, but, within two years, their relationship would cool because of presidential politics and Eisenhower's legalistic response to the Court's *Brown v. Board of Education* decision.

The Supreme Court justices met for their annual tea with Eisenhower and administration officials at the White House in November 1953, six months before they would rule on the *Brown* school desegregation case. Front row: William O. Douglas, Stanley F. Reed, Chief Justice Earl Warren, President Eisenhower, Hugo Black, Felix Frankfurter. Back row: third from left, Robert H. Jackson, Tom C. Clark, Sherman Minton, Harold H. Burton, unknown, Attorney General Brownell.

Eisenhower addressed a meeting of the NAACP in Washington, D.C., on March 10, 1954, celebrating the dedication of the nation's founders "to the proposition that all men are created equal." He renewed his pledge that wherever there was clear federal authority, he would act "to bring into living reality this expression of equality among all men." Preferring quiet action to grandstanding, Eisenhower chose not to recite the details of his desegregation of the District of Columbia and the armed forces.

NAACP lawyers George E. C. Hayes, Thurgood Marshall, and James M. Nabrit, Jr., who had argued *Brown* before the Supreme Court, celebrated the May 17, 1954, school desegregation decision. Nabrit and Hayes represented Negro plaintiffs from the District of Columbia while Marshall argued the case for Clarendon County, South Carolina, in addition to serving as the primary strategist for the NAACP team.

Adam Clayton Powell, Jr., the Democratic congressman from Harlem in New York City, met with the press on October 11, 1956, after discussing the president's re-election campaign with Eisenhower at the White House. Powell, who had already endorsed Ike, would campaign across the nation for Eisenhower in the remaining weeks before the election.

Senator Lyndon B. Johnson, speaking with reporters after consulting with Eisenhower at the White House. Johnson played a pivotal role as Senate majority leader in securing passage of the Civil Rights Act of 1957, but joined southern segregationists in eliminating the provisions in Eisenhower's proposals that would have protected constitutional rights beyond voting. As a result, Roy Wilkins, executive secretary of the NAACP, disparaged the 1957 act as "a small crumb from Congress."

On September 4, 1957, an Arkansas National Guard officer, on orders of Governor Orval Faubus, blocked black students from entering Central High School in Little Rock. On August 30, federal district judge Ronald N. Davies had ordered the Little Rock school board to admit nine Negro students. In response, Faubus had called out the National Guard, but Judge Davies ordered the school authorities to proceed with desegregation. A jeering, violent mob of 400 persons harassed the students while the guardsmen, blocking their admittance, did little to protect them.

Eisenhower signed the Civil Rights Act of 1957 on September 9, 1957, in Newport, Rhode Island, where he was vacationing. The act, the first civil rights legislation in 82 years, became law as the Little Rock school desegregation crisis was unfolding. The president chose to sign the legislation quietly, without a formal ceremony.

LEFT: Eisenhower, Governor Orval Faubus, and Arkansas Congressman Brooks Hays met at the Newport, Rhode Island, naval base on September 14, 1957. Hays had brokered the meeting in an attempt to defuse the Little Rock crisis. After the meeting, Eisenhower believed he had secured Faubus's agreement to change the orders of his National Guard soldiers, but when Faubus returned to Arkansas, he reneged on the agreement. On September 20, the federal district court ordered Faubus to cease obstruction of its desegregation order, and the governor withdrew the National Guard. On September 23, the black students were threatened by a violent mob and had to be withdrawn from the school for their own protection.

RIGHT: Declaring that "mob rule cannot be allowed to override the decisions of our courts," Eisenhower addressed the nation on September 24, 1957, from the White House after sending federal troops to Little Rock. Eisenhower had mobilized the 101st Airborne Division, an army unit that had been trained to handle riots in anticipation of anti-desegregation violence in the South. This was the first time that federal troops had been deployed in a former Confederate state since Reconstruction following the Civil War.

Soldiers of the 101st Airborne Division escorted Negro students into Little Rock's Central High School in late September 1957. Eisenhower ordered withdrawal of half of the army troops in mid-October and the remainder by Thanksgiving. They were replaced by federalized Arkansas National Guard troops, who would remain on duty until the end of the school year.

14

FBI Director J. Edgar Hoover and Herbert Brownell congratulated Attorney General William P. Rogers (center) after he was sworn in as Brownell's successor in November 1958. Eisenhower was not as comfortable with Rogers as he had been with Brownell, but Rogers was a strong supporter of civil rights and the primary author of the legislation that became the Civil Rights Act of 1960.

Eisenhower urged black leaders to have "patience and forbearance" when he addressed the National Negro Publishers Association on May 12, 1958. E. Frederic Morrow, who had arranged the president's appearance, was distressed at Eisenhower's words. Against a backdrop of violence and "massive resistance" by segregationists in the South, black leaders were not receptive to a call for "patience." Eisenhower's words elicited a firestorm of criticism and led to increased demands that the president meet with Negro leaders.

Eisenhower met with Negro leaders on June 23, 1958, at the White House. Left to right: Lester Granger (Urban League), Martin Luther King, Jr. (Southern Christian Leadership Conference), E. Frederic Morrow (White House assistant), President Eisenhower, A. Philip Randolph (Leadership Conference on Civil Rights), Attorney General William Rogers, Rocco Siciliano (White House assistant), and Roy Wilkins (NAACP). The leaders asked Eisenhower for aggressive enforcement of existing laws, new civil rights legislation, and Justice Department investigation of bombings in the South.

17

Eisenhower signed the Civil Rights Act of 1960 on May 6, 1960, in the presence of Attorney General William Rogers and Deputy Attorney General Lawrence E. Walsh, noting that the legislation protected the "key constitutional right of every American, the right to vote without discrimination on account of race or color." The act authorized the appointment of voting referees by federal courts where there was a pattern of discrimination against Negroes in state or federal elections, and enabled the FBI to investigate "hate" bombings of schools and places of worship. These provisions established a foundation for the legislative breakthroughs that Eisenhower's successors achieved in the 1960s.

On May 15, a reporter asked Eisenhower if his advocacy of the civil rights bill "would hurt the Republican chances of winning more seats in the South." Eisenhower repeated his view that "the civil rights bill is a very moderate thing, done in all decency and in a simple attempt to study the matter, see where the Federal responsibilities lie, and to move in strict accordance with the Supreme Court's decision, and no faster and no further." When pressed about the jury trial issue, Eisenhower said he was "not enough of a lawyer to discuss that thing one way or the other," but the authority of the federal courts "must be upheld."[22]

The jury trial argument was so politically powerful that Republicans had difficulty keeping their own members in line. Representative Keating of New York reported to Eisenhower and Republican legislative leaders in early June that, in the House, "many Republicans would oppose the entire bill, and some others would vote for the jury trial amendment by failure to understand exactly what was involved." According to the minutes of the meeting, Eisenhower complained that "it was a mystery to him how any Republicans could oppose such mild proposals as these."[23]

The legislative process moved forward amid threats of violence. John Kasper, a notorious agitator who had instigated violence in 1956 over school desegregation in Clinton, Tennessee, burned crosses on the lawns of several Supreme Court justices. One Sunday, Herbert Brownell awoke to noise outside his home. Outside the front door, he smelled kerosene that had been dumped around the house, but the perpetrators were frightened away before they could start a fire. Thereafter, the FBI provided protection for the Brownell family.[24]

The Bypass Strategy

On June 1, the House of Representatives passed the civil rights bill, 286–126, a slightly wider margin than in 1956. The Senate now became the battleground. As long as the bill languished in James Eastland's Judiciary Committee, it would never pass. Vice President Nixon and the administration's allies in the Senate had already devised a strategy with Lyndon Johnson to bypass the committee once the bill cleared the House. Johnson, wanting to advance his presidential ambitions, pursued a cosmetic bill, without enforcement teeth, that would diminish opposition to his candidacy in the North but not alienate his southern base.[25]

On June 15, Eisenhower called Johnson and learned that "tempers were flaring already and could be worse." The majority leader intended to get fifteen appropriation bills through the Senate before the struggle for the civil rights bill began in earnest. Once that was done, Johnson continued, "you can let us fight July and August and if necessary into September." Eisenhower insisted that his was the "mildest civil rights bill possible." He was "a little struck back on his heels" by the fury surrounding the bill.[26]

In his June 19 news conference, Eisenhower expressed satisfaction that the bill had passed the House, and he studiously avoided discussion of the plan to bypass the Judiciary Committee. A reporter asked if Eisenhower would urge the Senate to remain in session until the southern filibuster could be broken and the bill passed. Eisenhower claimed, with doubtful veracity, that "this point hasn't come up and I have not discussed that with the leaders." He declined to comment on the procedures of the Congress "because it is their business, and it is not for me to interfere to say how they shall do things." "That civil rights action bill," Eisenhower asserted, "was designed and conceived in the thought of conciliation and moderation, not of persecution of anybody."

Then Eisenhower publicly addressed the issue that had motivated him to propose civil rights legislation, his desire to avoid the use of troops. "It seems to me," he explained, "that after the unanimous decision by the Supreme Court about segregation many things could have happened." He recalled that reporters had asked at that time, "Did I contemplate sending the Army into the South to enforce this decision?" Rather than such radical action, Eisenhower stressed that his legislation met the need "for moderation and the development of a plan that everybody of good will could support. Now, I have been very badly disappointed that some people see in this program an opportunity to disturb their own rights, or to interfere in their own social order, in an unjust and improper way. To my mind, this is a very moderate, decent thing to do, and I hope that some thinking on the part of all of us will lead others to believe the same way."[27]

That same day, the civil rights coalition prepared to implement the bypass strategy. The plan called for Vice President Nixon, presiding over the Senate, to ask the clerk to use a low voice in reading the House bill's title. That would constitute a first reading of the legislation. A southern senator would inevitably raise a point of order, objecting to this surreptitious strategy for slipping the bill into consideration, but the vice president, as presiding officer, would overrule the objection. Then his ruling would be appealed to the entire body for a vote that the civil rights bloc believed it could win. After the second reading the next day, the bill would be placed on the Senate calendar, and the southerners could be expected to launch a filibuster. In turn, the coalition would seek cloture, confident they had the votes to limit debate.[28]

All proceeded according to plan. Senator Richard Russell raised the point of order. The Senate voted forty-five to thirty-nine to support the vice president's ruling and initiate the steps to place the House legislation directly on the Senate calendar. This ended a five-month stalemate in the Judiciary Committee. The new Eisenhower coalition was reflected in the vote total; thirty-four of the forty-five votes against Russell's point of order were Republican, and five Republicans voted with Russell and the Democrats. The outcome convinced the *New York Times* that Eisenhower was taking "a stronger role" in disciplining his party on congressional issues ranging "from spending to civil rights."[29]

A States' Rights President?

Once the civil rights bill was safely on the Senate calendar, Eisenhower set out to reassure the southerners. His vehicle was an address on June 24 to the Governors' Conference in Williamsburg, Virginia. There, in the heart of the restored colonial village, Eisenhower celebrated the American colonists' struggle against tyranny to vindicate a timeless principle: "Those who would be and would stay free must stand eternal watch against excessive concentration of power in government." He held up the Soviet Union as the ultimate example of government concentration and warned against "the march of political power toward Washington."

Eisenhower's states' rights discourse included a warning. He noted that "like nature, people and their governments are intolerant of vacuums. Every State failure to meet a pressing public need has created the opportunity, developed the excuse and fed the temptation for the national government to poach on the States' preserves." "I believe deeply in States' rights," he avowed. "I believe that the preservation of our States as vigorous, powerful governmental units is essential to permanent individual freedom and the growth of our national strength." But, he continued, "It is idle to champion States' rights without upholding States' responsibilities as well." Eisenhower warned that the alternative to state responsibility was "new vacuums into which the Federal Government will plunge ever more deeply, impelled by popular pressures and transient political expediencies."[30]

Eisenhower's civil rights bill was designed to fill one such vacuum, although he did not speak about it in these terms. He had finally made a speech in a southern city—but it was not the kind of address Martin Luther King, Jr., had wanted. The president had passed up an opportunity to lobby the governors on his civil rights legislation, and instead assumed a states' rights posture in the presence of governors who had defied *Brown*.

Eisenhower's comments generated immediate controversy. Civil rights advocates accused him of pandering to segregationist governors, while southerners found Eisenhower's legislative program inconsistent with his preachments at Williamsburg. The White House staff anxiously issued a white paper, clarifying that "the Administration civil rights program is not in any way inconsistent with the position taken by the President in his Williamsburg speech." The paper argued that "if a state discharges its obligations under the 14th and 15th Amendments, there will be no room for federal intervention." The administration wanted "legal weapons" to support liberty for "all races and classes." Finally, "we cannot ever afford in the name of states rights to permit local oppression of any race or group; the guarantee of equal protection of the laws is a national standard from which no state can be left free to depart."[31]

In Eisenhower's June 26 news conference, reporters pressed the president on the "contradiction" between his states' rights rhetoric at Williamsburg and his civil rights bill granting expanded authority to the attorney general. The president countered that "the civil rights program is eminently reasonable and moderate." He emphasized the legislation's intent to "proceed on civil rather than criminal channels." But he recognized that the opposition, promoting a jury trial amendment, had made much out of the fact that a federal judge "could commit a man for contempt of court if his orders were not obeyed." Eisenhower insisted that the bill was "a very moderate decent thing, and is designed to bring about better understanding and not persecute anybody."[32]

The Senate Fight

Once the bill was on the Senate docket, Senator Richard Russell of Georgia marshaled his prestige to attempt to defeat it. Now fifty-nine years old, Russell had served in the Senate for twenty-four years. He was described by a *New York Times* columnist as "a tall, patrician, hawk-faced, quiet and lonely politician with neither wife nor child and not an ounce of the cheery gregariousness that so often marks the men of his profession"—"a southern gentleman of a vanishing school." Russell repeatedly told his friends that the South was the target of "conscious hate." The *Times* called the senator the "Leader of a Lost Cause," whose mission could no longer "be to win any fight but to lose fights as slowly as possible, one by one, and so to hold back a little longer the oncoming certainty of a compulsory Federal civil rights program in his native South."[33]

Russell rose on the Senate floor on July 2 and asked no interruption of his remarks. In the silent chamber, Russell attacked the president's assertion that the civil rights bill was a "moderate, decent" measure. Focusing on part three, which would empower the attorney general to enforce school desegregation, he charged that Brownell had devised a "deceptive piece of legislation" that was "cunningly designed" to authorize the attorney general "to destroy the system of separation of the races in the Southern States at the point of a bayonet." Russell dredged up images of "the bayonet rule of reconstruction days" after the Civil War. The senator expressed doubt that "the full implications of the bill have ever been explained to President Eisenhower."[34]

Russell's remarks disturbed Eisenhower. The day after the sena-tor's speech, Eisenhower remarked to his staff in his pre–news con-ference meeting that he had thought that the bill's language "provided for the A.G. to use troops only in the event of restriction on voting," but it appeared that the opposition could interpret it to mean "any civil right." Eisenhower recalled that "that was not the way the Attorney General explained it to him."[35] Eisenhower's ad-mission was extraordinary: he and Brownell had discussed the use of troops to enforce voting rights, not just to put down disorder, but school desegregation was the burning issue. In his conversations with the president, Brownell had undoubtedly emphasized Ike's highest priority, the right to vote. But they both knew that school desegregation could force them to send in troops. Eisenhower's concern was mostly political; a threat of military action to enforce school desegregation might cause Congress to reject the entire leg-islative program.

At the news conference, Eisenhower was under siege. A reporter asked if in fact the civil rights bill was "a cunning device, as Senator Russell called it, to enforce integration of the races in the South." Eisenhower responded that he viewed the legislation as "a very mod-erate move." Asked if he would support refocusing the legislation on the right to vote rather than school desegregation, Eisenhower made a remark that would haunt him the rest of his presidency. He said, "I was reading part of that bill this morning, and there were certain phrases I didn't completely understand. So, before I made any more remarks on that, I would want to talk to the Attorney Gen-eral and see exactly what they do mean." Eisenhower was comment-ing on the language of the bill, not its substance, but the southerners seized on Eisenhower's comment. He had walked into Richard Rus-sell's trap, set when the senator claimed that the implications of the legislation had never been explained to the president.[36]

Eisenhower was troubled after the news conference. He was not ig-norant of the bill—he had reviewed it many times, even citing its provi-sions in his State of the Union message. In his news conference, he had ungraciously passed the onus for its implications on to the attorney general. He called Brownell, worried that the language of part three, intended to expand the attorney general's authority to protect constitutional rights, might be "so general that it scares people to death." Frustrated, Ike decided to escape to Gettysburg that evening. He had a cough he could not shake. Ann Whitman recorded that the president was worried about many things that night—his cough, his son John's future, and he was "certainly very worried about civil rights."[37]

In retrospect, the irony of the controversy over part three of the civil rights bill would prove extraordinary. Russell had been prophetic. Three months later, Eisenhower would send troops into Little Rock, Arkansas, to enforce a federal court order for school desegregation, not voting rights violations. The Georgia senator understood, to Eisenhower's discomfort, the president's willingness to act to uphold the federal courts.

The Russell speech reverberated in the July 9 meeting of the Republican legislative leaders. Their commitment to fight for part three of the bill was weakening. When Illinois Senator Everett Dirksen quoted Russell's description of part three as a "Force Act," Brownell replied that the president already possessed the authority to enforce federal law with troops. Representative Charles Halleck of Indiana asked how important part three was. Brownell said "it would serve to extend civil rights to things other than the right to vote." School desegregation was the issue; Eisenhower noted that "the only new thing in the picture was the Supreme Court decision and the Administration wanted to make certain that Federal court orders are not flouted." Eisenhower again called the bill "very moderate." He emphasized that "the Executive has a constitutional responsibility to support the Courts." The legislators thought compromise was inevitable. Eisenhower ruled out a deal for the moment, saying that he would consider clarifying language, "but there were four essential points that must be kept in it."[38]

Eisenhower did not tell the Republican leaders that he had decided to meet with Senator Russell. The day after the legislative meeting, Eisenhower spent nearly an hour with the senator. According to Ann Whitman's notes, the president indicated "that he would be willing to listen to clarifying amendments to the Bill as it stands." Whitman, watching her boss with Russell, recalled other times when Eisenhower seemed "not at all unsympathetic to the position people like Senator Russell take." Whenever she challenged him, he had always countered, "I have lived in the South, remember." She added that he was "adamant" that "the right to vote must be protected."[39]

Compromise

By July 16, Republican legislative leaders were openly discussing amendments to the civil rights bill. The president told the leaders, regarding part three, that "the intent is simply that the orders of the federal courts will be supported," thereby assisting school boards in implementing their response to the Supreme Court's mandate for desegregation "with all deliberate speed." Eisenhower conceded that "if we got simply the voting rights, that would not be a hollow victory," and he added that clarification of part three "would not be harmful."[40]

That day, senators voted seventy-one to eighteen to make the civil rights bill the pending business of the United States Senate. The Eisenhower coalition's victorious vote included forty-two Republicans and twenty-nine Democrats. Lyndon Johnson voted with the majority, as did Democratic Senators Estes Kefauver and Albert Gore of Tennessee and Ralph Yarborough of Texas. Eisenhower issued a statement at his news conference later that day touting all four parts of the bill, including part three, which he described as "a reasonable program of assistance in efforts to protect other constitutional rights of our citizens." He hinted at compromise, saying that "the details of the language changes are a legislative matter. I would hope, however, that the Senate, in whatever clarification it may determine to make, will keep the measure an effective piece of legislation to carry out these four objectives—each one of which is consistent with simple justice and equality afforded to every citizen under the Constitution of the United States."[41]

Merriman Smith, United Press International's respected reporter, asked if the president believed he had the authority to use the military to enforce school integration in the South. Eisenhower affirmed that he had the authority, but responded: "I can't imagine any set of circumstances that would ever induce me to send Federal troops into a Federal court and into any area to enforce the orders of a Federal court, because I believe that common sense of America will never require it." The comment was misleading; he and Brownell had rehearsed a variety of scenarios that might require military intervention. Asked about possible amendments to the bill, Eisenhower hinted at his openness to change, saying that "the voting right is something that should be emphasized."[42]

With compromise in the air, Max Rabb confronted near rebellion among the African-Americans with whom he regularly worked. On July 12, Frederic Morrow had written Sherman Adams: "Negro citizens are alarmed over reports that the Administration will 'soften' the requirements of the Administration bill on civil rights before Congress." He was hearing "talk of Administration capitulation to the South," and feared the Republicans could lose both the legislation and thousands of votes. Val Washington, the Republican National Committee's minority programs director, wrote to both Rabb and Adams that he was "troubled by the compromise talk on the Civil Rights Bill." Washington hurled the president's words back at him in a personal communication: "Let me say that your Civil Rights Bill is a very moderate one, so what is there to compromise?"[43]

Lyndon Johnson answered that question by appealing in person to the president. Johnson painted a stark picture; he told Eisenhower that he had the votes to kill the bill if part three remained in the legislation. Eisenhower was convinced and agreed to drop the provision. The Senate, responding to the president's decision, engaged in the formality of voting fifty-two to thirty-eight to strike part three from the bill. Ike had made this decision without consulting Brownell—a rarity in their relationship. Brownell called it "a political decision," designed not only to get some kind of civil rights bill but also to protect other administration legislation from retaliation.[44]

The southerners had won one battle. Now they redoubled their efforts to attach a jury trial requirement to part four, which had been designed to protect voting rights by empowering the attorney general to initiate civil suits in federal courts. This was too much for Eisenhower. The southerners, including Lyndon Johnson, cynically attempted to portray the civil suits as criminal prosecutions in disguise, thereby requiring a jury trial. Johnson had already practiced legislative blackmail, coercing Ike to abandon part three and repudiate his attorney general. On July 23, the Republican legislative leaders agreed with the president that they should reject "any attempt to incorporate a jury trial amendment in the right to vote section of the bill and thus nullify the purpose of the legislation."[45]

A week later, Eisenhower was still angry; he complained to Republican legislative leaders that the opposition was misrepresenting part four (providing for civil suits to protect voting rights) just as they had part three, outrageously accusing him of trying to impose a "Gestapo." The issue, as with part three, was what would happen if someone refused to obey a court order and was cited for contempt. William Rogers, the deputy attorney general, confirmed to the Republican leaders that contempt proceedings had never required juries and that a provision requiring jury trials would enable the South to continue to deny the right to vote to blacks. Eisenhower was in no mood to back down, assuring Republican legislative leaders that his questions were not "any sign of weakening."[46]

The press questioned the president on the jury trial issue the following day. Eisenhower responded, "I believe that the United States must make certain that every citizen who is entitled to vote under the Constitution is given actually that right. I believe also that in sustaining that right, we must sustain the power of the Federal judges in whose hands such cases would fall. So, I do not believe in any amendment to the section 4 of the bill."[47]

But Lyndon Johnson, as majority leader, firmly supported Richard Russell on the jury trial issue and, as a result, William Knowland of California, the minority leader, was losing the president's battle in the Senate. The *New York Times* reported "a rupture between Senators Knowland and Johnson, who had been working in harmony on procedural matters as the two party leaders." At the climax of the debate, Knowland dramatically shouted to the Senate: "Support President Dwight D. Eisenhower!" Johnson shot back that "the people will never accept that a man can be publicly branded as a criminal without a jury trial."[48]

The Jury Trial Vote

On August 1, the Senate voted fifty-one to forty-two to amend the civil rights bill to require a jury trial for the prosecution of criminal contempt for voting rights violations. Twelve Republicans joined thirty-nine Democrats to provide the winning margin, with nine Democrats and thirty-three Republicans in opposition. Even liberal Democrats such as Minnesota's Hubert Humphrey and Illinois's Paul Douglas had voted in favor of the amendment. Administration forces had suffered a major defeat.[49]

Richard Nixon called this "one of the saddest days in the history of the Senate because it was a vote against the right to vote." Ann Whitman called it "the blackest of days" because key Republicans had voted "against the President." In the August 2 cabinet meeting, Eisenhower was furious. There was "not much forgiveness in my soul," he fumed. "We've taken political defeats in [the] past four years, but this one is the worst." The president had particularly bitter words for Republican senators who voted with the majority.[50]

Eisenhower issued a statement that same day: "Rarely in our entire legislative history have so many extraneous issues been introduced into the debate in order to confuse both legislators and the public." Eisenhower pronounced the result "bitterly disappointing" and decried the fact that "many fellow Americans will continue, in effect, to be disenfranchised." Eisenhower's support of the federal courts was never more evident. He believed that requiring a jury trial to prosecute voting rights violations would weaken the entire judicial system and "make largely ineffective the basic purpose of the bill—that of protecting promptly and effectively every American in his right to vote."[51]

The *New York Times* headlined its article "Eisenhower Irate" and reported that the president "left no doubt today that he would rather have no civil rights bill at all than accept weakening Senate amendments." White House aides described Eisenhower as "angrier than at any time before in his four and one-half years in the White House" and hinted that he might veto the bill. Senator Charles E. Potter (R-Michigan) described Ike's mood succinctly: "Damn unhappy!" Eisenhower wrote to Robert Woodruff, one of his southern friends, about this "depressing" week. "I think the country took an awful beating," he lamented, "in the second defeat that the civil rights bill took in the Senate."[52]

Lyndon Johnson and Hubert Humphrey, aware of Eisenhower's wrath, began to fear that the president might veto whatever bill came out of the congressional conference that would be held to reconcile the House and Senate bills. In that case, Negroes would blame the Democrats. Humphrey tried to rekindle hope with a press release stating: "Contrary to what some Republican spokesmen are saying, the civil rights bill is not dead." "It can only be killed," he contended, "if Republicans show they are more interested in stirring up a partisan issue than getting some constructive action, however little it may be." Humphrey repeated: "The civil rights bill is wounded, but it is not dead."[53]

Val Washington blamed Lyndon Johnson for the situation. On August 6, he sent an open letter to the majority leader, declaring that the civil rights bill "was emasculated by the adroit handling of you with the aid of other Democrat leaders." Johnson had voted to send the bill to the Judiciary Committee, had voted to strike part three, and had supported the trial by jury, "which would automatically eliminate any chance for Negroes to be protected in most Southern states." Washington articulated the Negro perspective on jury trials in the South: "If a Southern jury would not convict confessed kidnappers of Emmett Till after he was found murdered, why would they convict an election official for refusing to give a Negro his right of suffrage?" He ridiculed Johnson's alleged "change of heart" and contended that "neither you, nor any of your Southern colleagues would vote for this bill unless you know it is meaningless and ineffective."[54]

Weak as the amended bill was, NAACP lobbyists and Democratic liberals reluctantly decided to try to "get something" by passing the entire bill as amended. In the August 6 legislative meeting, Eisenhower responded that "we ought to stand firm" on passing a bill intact, minus part three. That segment of the original bill had "beclouded the issue," he said, but if blacks could get the right to vote, then they could protect themselves, and the Republican Party "can stand on that." "I stand on this," the president declared: "After Section III went out, we should have the rest." The legislative leaders pledged to attempt to get the voting rights provision restored to its original form, without the requirement for a jury trial, if the bill was sent to a congressional conference committee.[55]

Val Washington and Frederic Morrow implored Eisenhower to veto any "fake" bill. Morrow contended that "an emasculated civil rights bill is worse than none at all." He found it "shocking" that some NAACP executives were "requesting civil rights supporters on the Hill to vote for this watered-down measure on the grounds that half a loaf is better than no bread at all." "It is strange," Morrow confided to his diary, "to see the NAACP agreeing with men of the South like Senator James Eastland of Mississippi, Lyndon Johnson, and Senator Richard Russell of Georgia!"[56]

To Veto or Not

On August 7, Ike pondered the problems with a veto. Ann Whitman's notes reflect a president who realized that he would be criticized for a veto because the bill "has been sold as a step forward to the American people. On the other hand, people who should know say that if he signs, there will be no forward civil rights legislation for the next decade or so." Eisenhower relieved his stress in the usual manner; Whitman recorded that the "President hit golf balls."[57]

Liberal Democrats were embarrassed at their capitulation and tried to shift the blame to Eisenhower. Hubert Humphrey contended that there would have been a different outcome "if the President had thrown his full weight and prestige behind this bill." Eisenhower "vacillated and oscillated, procrastinated and dawdled. He was hesitant and confused. With this type of leadership, it is no wonder that Administration supporters were unable to maintain the initiative in this fight." The Minnesota senator found it safer to criticize the president than his mentor, Lyndon Johnson, who was directly responsible for the jury trial amendment. Humphrey had voted against the deletion of part three and initially against the jury trial amendment. But then, he confessed, "I voted for the bill in its final form not because I liked it, but because I am a realist, and I knew that this was the best bill we could get. This bill, even in its present form, is better than no bill at all."[58]

Discouraged Republican legislative leaders met with Eisenhower on August 13. Joseph Martin, Jr., of Massachusetts, the House minority leader, suggested dropping the civil rights bill and resubmitting it in 1958. Eisenhower remained silent for a long time. Then he exploded, probably coloring the air with the profanity for which he was notorious when losing his temper. Ike noted that "three very respectable Negroes" had written him, including Dr. Ralph Bunche, the United Nations undersecretary, "that I should never sign a sham bill." He stormed: "Hell of a thing. Here are 18 southern senators who can bamboozle [the] entire Senate." Deputy Attorney General William Rogers foresaw "no middle ground; Lyndon won't buy any language at this point." Knowland insisted "the 85th Congress will never do a no-jury trial" and urged that they pursue "the art of the possible."

Eisenhower heaped scorn on the liberals who had voted for the jury trial amendment and now insisted on passage of the amended bill, no matter how weak it was. He demanded: "Why have liberals put so much heat on to get a bill—after abandoning all of their principles? Why?" Then, "if this goes to conference, don't these liberal Democrats who have joined southern Democrats have to reverse their positions? They've found a phony issue on which to coalesce for 1958 elections. If we fight them, we can not only do something to help civil rights but break up their coalition. They will have to take the blame for defeating this."

Eisenhower was angriest with Johnson, and he ridiculed "all this talk" about LBJ being a "great leader." Ike raged: "When someone tries to hit me over the head with a brickbat, I start looking around for something to hit him with." The minutes read: "The President spoke at length in favor of fighting it out to the end to prevent the pseudo liberals from getting away with their sudden alliance with the Southerners on a sham bill."[59]

The Final Strategy

Eisenhower's tirade motivated the Republican leadership to settle on what columnist James Reston called "a bold, and perhaps even dangerous gamble": they would prolong the exhausting debate over civil rights in order to get a stronger bill. The plan was to sow discord in Democratic ranks by resubmitting part three of the original bill—the section that Richard Russell had so fiercely attacked and that Johnson had persuaded Eisenhower to drop—enhancing the authority of the attorney general to prosecute the violation of any constitutional right, including school desegregation. They would put out the word that the president would veto any bill that did not restore part three. Then, if the bill went down to defeat, the Republicans could openly blame the Democrats.[60]

This was a hollow political ploy because Eisenhower had already given up on part three, but the threatened revival of that controversy made the Democrats uncomfortable. As so often happens with legislation, the outcome was determined more by fatigue and crass political calculation than the substance of the issue. The southerners' campaign for a jury trial amendment had been designed to assure their constituents that they supported continued resistance to federal court orders for desegregation, especially in the schools. Their political objective had been achieved with the August 1 vote, but Lyndon Johnson still wanted some kind of bill. As a result of Eisenhower's threatened veto, LBJ was faced with the possibility of being unable to pass any civil rights legislation to support his presidential candidacy and civil rights advocates could blame him personally for the failure.

The Justice Department broke the deadlock with a plan that, only two weeks before, the southerners would have rejected. On August 16, White House counsel Gerald Morgan transmitted to the president a proposal that, in contempt cases related to voting rights, a federal judge could try a defendant without a jury as long as the projected punishment did not exceed a fine of three hundred dollars or imprisonment of ninety days. This surprising overture, adopting a formula already in place in the District of Columbia, revived hope for retrieving something workable from the bill passed by the Senate. If the new proposal was accepted, the Republicans would drop the ruse of reviving part three because they would have achieved the ability to prosecute some voting rights violations by means of civil, not criminal, suits before a judge, without a jury. Just how this would work was left vague, effectively granting authority to the particular federal judge to make the decision. By August 17 a

New York Times editorial was predicting that "some sort of Federal civil rights bill will be passed within the week." Lyndon Johnson managed to leave the impression he had crafted the compromise proposal, and the newspaper praised Johnson's parliamentary skills when the Eisenhower administration had actually broken the stalemate. The *Times* editorial writer wearily concluded: "This would be the first law of its kind in nearly three generations. It is worth trying. Half a loaf really is better than no bread."[61]

Having riled the Democrats, Eisenhower hinted at compromise. At his August 21 news conference, he rejected the "all or nothing" stance of both sides. The pending Senate bill bearing the jury trial amendment, he stated, was "not strong enough, and I would like to see it stronger." Eisenhower said that Republican leaders were prepared to make a proposal (the Justice Department plan) "that would represent a position between the one that I took originally, and the one that is now in the Senate version." Eisenhower concluded: "I can't conceive of anything worse than making the basic right of so many millions of our citizens just a part of political snarling as to who is to blame for this and who is to get the credit for that."[62]

On August 23, Lyndon Johnson was ready to end the struggle. The majority leader called Eisenhower and said that he thought he could get key people to agree "to a compromise on the civil rights bill of $300 and 45 days" as the trigger for requiring a jury trial in contempt citations. He asked Eisenhower to see if his leaders would agree and Ike asked for ten minutes. He called Knowland and Martin off the floor, secured their agreement, and called Johnson back to confirm the deal.[63] After contentious debate for two years over civil versus criminal law, both sides agreed to a bill that left that elusive distinction to the discretion of federal prosecutors and judges, based on a financial and incarceration formula that would, in practice, prove difficult to implement.

On August 26, Eisenhower and Johnson met for breakfast. Johnson recommended that Ike have a private meeting with Richard Russell, "off the record," to seek his support on matters beyond civil rights. Russell, Johnson implied, was privately more in tune with the administration on civil rights than it might appear. He hoped that "the 12 Republican senators who voted against the Administration on [the] previous civil rights bill will now vote for the compromise."[64]

Final Passage

At 10:53 P.M. on August 29, the Senate passed the final version of the civil rights bill by a vote of sixty to fifteen. Thirty-seven Republicans and twenty-three Democrats—the Eisenhower civil rights coalition—supported the bill. Fifteen southern Democrats opposed it. Strom Thurmond had conducted a twenty-four-hour filibuster but, his voice hoarse and weak, gave up at 9:12 P.M.[65]

Congressman Adam Clayton Powell, Jr., issued a press release from Germany, declaring that Eisenhower had "kept his word to me 100 percent." He recalled that on October 11, 1956, Eisenhower had promised the congressman that he would call for civil rights legislation in his next State of the Union message, spell it out specifically, press for early consideration, and push his legislative leaders to fight for it. "This completely vindicates my support of President Eisenhower," Powell asserted. "Personally, I am proud to have campaigned for one who has kept every word to me. After 80 years of political slavery, this is the second emancipation."[66]

Martin Luther King, Jr., acknowledged in a letter to Vice President Nixon that "many sincere leaders, both Negro and white, feel that no bill is better than the present bill." King thought otherwise: "After considering all angles I have come to the conclusion that the present bill is far better than no bill at all." King foresaw that "the full effect of the Civil Rights bill will depend in large degree upon a program of sustained mass movement on the part of Negroes. History has demonstrated that inadequate legislation supported by mass action can accomplish more than adequate legislation which remains unenforced for the lack of a determined mass movement."[67]

The *New York Times* credited the compromise on jury trials to Lyndon Johnson and William Knowland, not to Eisenhower. This reflected Johnson's active courtship of the press, while Eisenhower and Brownell consistently avoided boasting to reporters. It is undeniable that LBJ played an important role in the passage of the bill. But Val Washington was right: Johnson had wanted an act that

would be "meaningless and ineffective" but provide a fig leaf of re-
spectability for his presidential candidacy.[68]

The night after passage, Johnson called the president to report
that the Senate was ready to adjourn. He and Mrs. Johnson had sent
flowers to Mrs. Eisenhower, who was recuperating from surgery.
Johnson said "he imagined the president was just as glad to see
them go as they were to go." Johnson, for all his grandstanding,
knew where credit belonged. Ann Whitman noted: "He thanked the
President especially for the call that unlocked the civil rights bill."[69]

The Civil Rights Act of 1957 contained enduring provisions.
Fifty years later, the Civil Rights Commission and the Civil Rights Division in the Justice Department still exist. While part three, designed to give the attorney general authority to file suits to protect all
constitutional rights, including school desegregation, had been jet-
tisoned, the debate laid the groundwork for stronger legislation in
the 1960s. Weak as part four protecting voting rights was, it authorized the Justice Department to seek civil, not just criminal, federal
court injunctions against discrimination in voting, and persons cited
for contempt could still be prosecuted under the criminal provisions.
Most important, the congressional barrier to civil rights legislation
had been breached; never again could southern segregationists
guarantee blockage of legislation to protect the rights of African-
Americans.

Dwight Eisenhower received even less credit for his legislative
achievement as the years passed. Historians increasingly made
Lyndon Johnson—the man who had killed part three and champi-
oned the jury trial provision—the hero of the tale, enhancing his
reputation as a parliamentary genius. Eisenhower and Brownell had
laid a foundation for the stronger civil rights legislation in 1964–65,
in which Johnson certainly played a major role as president. If their
full proposal had been enacted in 1957, especially the broad enforcement powers envisioned in part three, the nation would have
been years ahead in the struggle for equality. Roy Wilkins called the
1957 civil rights act "a small crumb from Congress," but it was still
the first crumb in eighty-two years.[70] Without Eisenhower's and
Brownell's leadership, that would not have happened.

CHAPTER EIGHT

The Little Rock Crisis

The Federal Constitution will be upheld by me by every legal means at my command.
—DWIGHT D. EISENHOWER, SEPTEMBER 5, 1957

On Monday, September 2, 1957, in a 10:30 P.M. radio speech, Democratic Governor Orval Faubus of Arkansas announced that he had ordered units of his state's National Guard to surround Central High School in Little Rock, preparatory to classes beginning the morning of September 3. Faubus claimed that he was sending the troops to prevent violence, but his real purpose was to prevent nine African-American children from entering the school in fulfillment of a federal court desegregation order.[1]

This news was not welcome at the White House. Eisenhower was weary from the struggle to pass the civil rights act. The president needed a vacation, as did Mrs. Eisenhower, who was recovering from surgery, and they were scheduled to depart on Wednesday, September 4, "for a rest" at the Newport, Rhode Island, naval base. "Rest" to Eisenhower meant golf. He liked the course at the Newport Country Club and looked forward, according to Sherman Adams, "to entertaining a few friends whom he could beat when his game was right."[2] Thanks to Governor Faubus, Ike's stay in Newport would not be much of a vacation.

A Defiant Governor

A crisis in Little Rock had been simmering for some time. The city's school board had adopted a plan on May 24, 1955, for gradual integration of the schools. The plan had called for implementation in fall 1957 and then only in the city's high schools. Negro students were not eligible to enroll in the city's high schools until 1957 but, in January 1956, twenty-seven African-American students attempted to register ahead of schedule and were turned away. On February 8 of that year, the NAACP filed suit on behalf of those students but Arkansas' western district federal judge, John E. Miller, dismissed the suit. The Arkansas legislature passed bills on February 19, 1957, that abolished mandatory attendance at integrated schools and authorized funds for the state to use to fight integration. Governor Faubus, armed with these laws, tried to convince the Little Rock school board to rescind its integration plan, but the board refused. On April 27, 1957, the Eighth Circuit Court of Appeals upheld Judge Miller's ruling against the NAACP's suit and approved the school board's original plan to implement limited integration in September 1957.[3]

Unless Faubus acted, integration of Central High School would take place on Tuesday, September 3. On August 27, Faubus supporters filed suit with Judge Murray O. Reed, a Faubus appointee, in the Pulaski County Court for an injunction to delay integration at Central High on the grounds that there was danger of violence. Then Faubus called the U.S. Department of Justice to ascertain what it would do if he blocked integration when classes began. On August 28, Deputy Attorney General William Rogers dispatched Arthur Caldwell, the head of the civil rights section in the criminal division and a native Arkansan, to talk with Faubus. Faubus admitted to Caldwell that he had no solid evidence that there was a conspiracy to commit violence to prevent integration of the school. Caldwell told Faubus that the department would not sanction any effort by the governor to prevent integration.[4]

Judge Reed issued an injunction on August 29 blocking integration of Central High School, but on Friday, August 30, Judge Ronald N. Davies, the recently assigned federal district court judge for Ar-

kansas's eastern district, nullified Reed's injunction and ordered the
school board to admit nine Negro students on the opening day of
school. Faubus responded by calling out the National Guard on
September 2 and, in response, the school board capitulated and
asked that no Negro students "attempt to attend Central or any
white high school until this dilemma is legally resolved." Judge
Davies, despite the governor's action, immediately ordered the
school board to proceed with its integration plan.[5]

On September 3, as he prepared for a news conference prior to
departing the capital, Eisenhower worried about the situation in Arkansas. He wondered aloud to his staff whether the federal government had the legal authority to intervene in Little Rock, given that
the suit to enroll the students at Central High School was a private
action, filed by the NAACP on behalf of the Negro parents. The
press reported that the Justice Department had concluded that the
government could not act unless Judge Davies requested intervention.[6]

At the news conference, Eisenhower professed ignorance of the
Arkansas situation and said he had referred the matter to the attorney general. That was a classic Eisenhower dodge—pretending ignorance to sidestep controversy about an issue that he and Brownell
had thoroughly discussed. Ike repeated the little homily that he frequently gave to skirt civil rights issues: "You cannot change people's
hearts merely by laws." Eisenhower noted that the Supreme Court
had established the precedent in *Brown II* for a gradual process of
integration to be determined by the courts. Then, according to the
New York Times, the president offered "the most direct comment" he
had ever made about the Supreme Court's 1954 decision. The
Court, he said, had explained "the emotional difficulties that would
be encountered by Negroes" who attended "equal but separate
schools, and I think probably their reasoning was correct, at least I
have no quarrel with it." He reiterated that "we are going to whip
this thing in the long run by Americans being true to themselves
and not merely by law." Eisenhower then cited the "strong emotions
on the other side." The Arkansas segregationists should have noted
that the president placed them "on the other side" from himself
and the Supreme Court on the desegregation of schools.[7]

Despite Eisenhower's dissembling with the press, Brownell had already secured the president's approval to issue a public warning to the governor of Arkansas. His department had planned for a contingency such as the one in Little Rock ever since the Supreme Court's 1954 *Brown* decision. On Wednesday, September 4, the attorney general announced an investigation of Faubus's claims of impending violence as a rationale for deploying the National Guard. The investigation would be conducted jointly by the FBI and the United States attorney's and marshal's offices, under the supervision of Judge Davies. Brownell underlined the potential dangers for the governor of Arkansas if he continued his defiance: Faubus could be cited for contempt of court, he could be prosecuted for a federal crime, or federal funds could be withheld from the Arkansas National Guard. Lastly, Brownell said, "the President could use Federal troops or the National Guard units of any state to enforce the court order." The attorney general then provided a detailed legal rationale for military action and said he was in constant communication with the president, who would make such a decision.

James Hagerty, Ike's press secretary, issued a statement from the White House reinforcing the attorney general's announcement and noting that the president had directed the attorney general to keep "in close touch" with the situation and "and advise him by telephoning of future developments." Meanwhile, General Maxwell D. Taylor, the army chief of staff, ordered the 101st Airborne Division, based in Kentucky, to begin contingency planning, including riot management, in preparation for deployment if ordered by the president.[8]

That same day, September 4, the nine black students attempted to enter Central High School. The guardsmen blocked their way while a crowd of four hundred men and women jeered, booed, and yelled "go home, niggers" and chanted "Two, four, six, eight, we ain't gonna integrate!" Elizabeth Eckford, barely five feet tall, arms full of books, anxiously searched for a place to enter the school building, but tall, armed soldiers blocked her way. When a crowd of fifty protestors closed in on Elizabeth, the guardsmen did nothing to restrain them. "Get her, get the nigger out of here. Hang her black ass," someone in the crowd shouted. Terrence Roberts, another would-be student, later found Elizabeth sitting on a bus bench "in a state of shock," waiting for a ride home. A man chased Melba Pattillo and her mother, seized the girl's sleeve, and shouted, "We got us a nigger right here!" Another yelled, "They're getting away! Those niggers are getting away!" A man carrying a rope joined in the chase. Another tore Melba's mother's blouse and a man close to the girl swung at her with a large tree branch, but missed. Melba and her mother jumped in their car and drove away as a man pounded on the hood and another threw a brick at the windshield. Terrence Roberts had begun to walk home when suddenly he heard footsteps and saw a white male coming toward him. The boy prepared to defend himself, but the man assured him he was not hostile and apologized for the hateful white people gathered at the school. He told Terrence that not all white people were against desegregating the high school.[9]

In a more tranquil environment—Newport, Rhode Island—a city prepared to welcome the first family. Flags and patriotic bunting were generously displayed. The president and first lady landed at Quonset Point naval station about 11:30 A.M. and were greeted by Governor Dennis J. Roberts before boarding the presidential yacht for the ten-mile trip across Narragansett Bay.[10]

The Eisenhowers had barely settled into the commandant's residence in Newport when, on Thursday, September 5, Governor Faubus sent the president a long, angry telegram. Faubus accused federal authorities of plotting to arrest him, charged that his telephone was being tapped, and blamed federal agents for any violence that might occur at Central High School. Eisenhower's response was brusque: "When I became President, I took an oath to support and defend the Constitution of the United States. The only assurance I can give you is that the Federal Constitution will be upheld by me by every legal means at my command." "Legal means," given Brownell's pronouncement of the previous day, clearly included troops. Faubus responded that he would cooperate "in upholding the Constitution of Arkansas and the Nation." The order of the governor's words betrayed his priorities; his state came before the nation.[11]

The situation deteriorated rapidly. Black leaders pressured the president. Wiley Branton, the NAACP attorney who had filed the original complaint in February 1956, warned the president: "If the Supreme Court is to be defied this way, we are getting back to Civil War conditions." Branton's boss, Roy Wilkins, reinforced this prophecy, wiring Eisenhower on September 5 that the doctrine that states could nullify the Constitution and federal rulings "threatens the entire concept of a federal union and endangers a wide variety of rights and privileges of the citizens of the United States wherever they may live." A few days later, Martin Luther King, Jr., urged Eisenhower to take a strong stand because indecisiveness "will set the process of integration back fifty years."[12]

Brownell Enters the Case

On Saturday, September 7, Judge Davies denied the request of the Little Rock school board to vacate his order to proceed with integration at Central High School. That day, Eisenhower flew back to Washington to consult with Brownell. The attorney general was adamant that Faubus obey the court order. Sherman Adams later described Brownell as "a man of great tenacity" and one "who could not be shaken when his mind was firmly made up, as it was on the Little Rock issue." After conferring with Brownell, the president returned to Newport.[13]

On Monday, September 9, at 8:10 A.M., the president signed the 1957 Civil Rights Act in his small Newport office, located on the second floor of the base headquarters building. The office overlooked Narragansett Bay—the same bay where, early in the nation's history, ships had been loaded with rum for sale or barter as part of the West African slave trade. With a stern expression, Eisenhower signed the act.[14]

Later the same day, Judge Davies asked the attorney general to enter the Little Rock case, and Brownell informed the president that his department would comply. The following day, Brownell, acting as a friend of the court, applied for a temporary injunction against the deployment of the National Guard at Central High School. Davies set September 20 for Faubus to appear in court to defend his actions obstructing desegregation. Jim Hagerty issued a statement saying that the president "deplored" the violence in the

South and that the White House was considering a number of steps if the court order were disobeyed.[15]

Brownell's legal rationale for federal action had been carefully prepared. The Supreme Court's instructions in *Brown II* dictated four principles. First, "the Executive Branch of the Federal Government does not participate in the formulation of plans affecting desegregation," but the lower courts could invite the government to participate in litigation. The second principle stated that "the period of time within which any such plan should be put into effect likewise must be proposed by the local authorities and approved by the Courts." This bow to local initiative was a result of the Supreme Court's "all deliberate speed" dictum in *Brown II*. The final two principles addressed situations like the one in Little Rock. Principle three proclaimed that "a final order of a Federal Court giving effect to a desegregation public school plan must be obeyed by State authorities and all citizens as the law of the land." The last principle addressed state nullification: "Powers of a State Governor may not be used to defeat a valid order of a Federal Court." This doctrine would deny a governor, "under a pretext of maintaining order," the authority to "interpose military force or permit mob violence to occur so as to prevent the final order of a Federal Court from being carried out." That would constitute "obstruction of justice" and the president would be "obliged to use whatever means may be required" to enforce the court order.[16]

Eisenhower knew these legal guidelines by heart. A year earlier, in a September 11, 1956, press conference, the president had described a sequence of events that, based on these principles, could lead to federal intervention. That scenario had been precisely played out in Little Rock.[17]

Meanwhile, Eisenhower was bombarded with proposals for action. Democratic Senator Hubert Humphrey of Minnesota urged the president to travel to Little Rock and "personally take those colored children by the hand and lead them into school where they belong." James P. Felstiner, a Harvard University researcher, disagreed: "You cannot go into court, nor can you lead a Negro child into a school room. But you can clearly state in words of a man that you believe that the battle is for freedom and that you are still dedicated and devoted to the effort to obtain victory for your own people." Democratic Governor Foster Furcolo of Massachusetts proposed that the president appoint a bipartisan committee of governors to assist in the situation. Eisenhower curtly rejected such schemes. When Furcolo called Sherman Adams, Hagerty recalled, "Governor Adams listened. Period. Then he thanked the Governor and hung up."[18]

An Attempt at Mediation

On Wednesday, September 11, Brooks Hays, a Democratic congressman from Arkansas, called his friend Sherman Adams at the White House and offered to arrange a meeting between Eisenhower and Faubus. Adams informed Hays that Eisenhower would not want to meet "with a state governor who was standing in open defiance of the Constitution." Besides, Adams knew that Brownell would oppose such a meeting. To address the attorney general's objections, Adams and Hays decided that Faubus would need to send a telegram to Eisenhower stating his willingness to comply with the court order.

Adams called Eisenhower in Newport and communicated Hays's proposal. Brownell had argued to Adams that they should not "encourage" such a telegram and that Faubus had "soiled" himself and did not deserve a meeting with the president. Adams told the president that he thought "the Governor realizes he has made a mistake and is looking for a way out." Accepting that assumption, Eisenhower overruled Brownell. Ike confided to Adams that the attorney general and his staff didn't understand "the seething in the south."[19]

Eisenhower agreed to see Faubus on the condition that the governor publicly abandon his defiant attitude. To ensure this, the president proceeded to stage-manage the meeting. He phoned Brownell to dictate specific wording for Faubus's telegram requesting the meeting. Eisenhower also promised the attorney general that he could be present to make his case to Faubus, but Ike struggled with his states' rights convictions. He warned Brownell that, in any public statements, they must respect a governor's right to call out the National Guard to prevent violence. That stance should be "crystal clear," Eisenhower declared, "or we will find ourselves in trouble with public opinion." Brownell noted that Hays's attempt to set up a meeting was the fifth attempt, but Eisenhower thought that now was the time.[20]

Brownell worked with Adams on the president's prescribed wording of Faubus's telegram asking for the meeting while Hays communicated with Faubus on the other end of the telephone line. "It required a little negotiation, a few extra calls," Hays recalled, "to get the exact language the President wanted." This awkward exercise allowed the president and the governor to maintain the appearance that they had not talked to each other. "Sherman was telling me the president would insist upon this particular phrase," the congressman recalled, "whatever it was, and I had gone back, and the Governor had responded, 'Yes, I'll sign that.'" At long last, Hays phoned Adams with a draft statement that Adams accepted.[21]

Later that Wednesday, just as Eisenhower began a round of golf at the Newport Country Club, Hagerty arrived, carrying a telegram from Faubus. But the message was not quite the same as the one that Hays had read to Adams. Eisenhower had insisted that the governor pledge to "obey all proper orders of our Courts." Faubus left himself an escape hatch. The governor said he would comply with the order by Judge Davies "consistent with my responsibilities under the Constitution of the United States, and that of Arkansas." Adams and Brownell were not on the golf course to point out this discrepancy. The president and Hagerty sat down in a golf cart and Eisenhower composed an answer. He suggested September 13 or 14 for a meeting. Hagerty told reporters that the governor's telegram had reached the White House "without advance notice," and he denied reports that Adams had communicated with Governor Faubus in advance, which was only technically accurate because the negotiations had been channeled through Brooks Hays.[22]

At this point, Faubus's manipulation of the message did not matter. Eisenhower had decided to hold the meeting and attempt to avoid a military confrontation in Arkansas. Eisenhower and Brownell had no illusions, although Eisenhower was more hopeful. They knew how devious Faubus had been. The attorney general had received a 746-page report from the FBI and a 400-page report from his department, the result of the investigation he had announced on September 4, detailing Faubus's spurious claims of potential violence.[23]

On Thursday, September 12, Hagerty announced the plans for the summit meeting. Faubus would arrive at the vacation White House at 9:00 A.M. on Saturday, the 14th. When asked if Brooks Hays had played a role in setting up the meeting, Hagerty said, "None that I know of." One reporter asked Hagerty if Faubus would be invited to stay overnight to play some golf. That drew laughter. There would be no golf on Saturday.[24]

Later that day, Eisenhower's attempt to micromanage the event almost unraveled. Charles Von Fremd, a commentator for the Columbia Broadcasting System, citing a White House source, claimed that Faubus, by agreeing to meet with the president, was "throwing in the sponge." Hagerty, speaking for Eisenhower, angrily denounced the report and insisted that none of the aides involved with setting up the meeting had "made any such statement." Nevertheless, Von Fremd insisted that the White House leadership expected that Faubus, after meeting with the president, would obey the court order and "that segregation in the Little Rock high school will be ended."[25]

Eisenhower's plans for a rest in Newport had been shattered as he shouldered the multiple burdens of the presidency. Those pressures included the negative impact of Little Rock on the international situation. On Thursday, Eisenhower initialed a document detailing Soviet propaganda broadcasts that had accused the U.S. ambassador to the United Nations, Henry Cabot Lodge, Jr., of "lies" and "slander" for criticizing the Soviet occupation of Hungary in late 1956 while "the cries of Negro children, ill-treated by the whites, rise from the Southern states and drown out his voice." Eisenhower felt harassed and later grumbled to the cabinet about a "feeling of nakedness" in the Little Rock crisis.[26]

On Friday, September 13, the day before the meeting with Faubus, Eisenhower dictated his frustrations in a letter to Henry Luce, the publishing magnate. Ike admitted that he had made "a grave mistake" in calculating what his second term would demand "in the way of a continuous toll upon my strength, patience, and sense of humor." He had assumed that the two-term limit would free him from some of the stresses of his first term. "The opposite is the case," the president wearily concluded: "The demands that I 'do something' seem to grow." Then this man, so steeped in military discipline, thought about how that sounded. As a matter of honor, he rarely complained, exhibited frustration, or expressed anger to someone outside his inner circle. Eisenhower turned to Ann Whitman and said, "No, don't put it in. I will say it to him sometime."[27]

Critics assumed that Eisenhower was naïve in thinking that he could persuade Faubus to change course in a personal meeting. But the evidence is more complex. Eisenhower understood that he was dealing with a man who had not kept his word in the wording of the telegram requesting the meeting. The attorney general had undoubtedly informed the president about the reports from FBI agents who had found no evidence to support Faubus's contention that violent agitators were advancing toward Little Rock. Eisenhower understood that Faubus had contrived the confrontation to test the government's ability to enforce the Supreme Court's decision, as well as to promote his own political ambitions.[28]

More important, Eisenhower was making a final attempt to manage a situation wherein he might have to use force. He had already communicated to Faubus his intent to uphold the Constitution "by every legal means" at his command. Eisenhower and Brownell had decided that, while they could not legally violate a governor's right to prevent violence, they could intervene to protect children. They had often discussed the possibility of using troops in such situations. If the meeting with the governor worked, fine. If not, the critics could not say that Eisenhower had been unwilling to talk with a southern governor before coercing compliance.[29]

The Meeting

Faubus and Congressman Hays left Arkansas the evening of the 13th. Reporters asked about the rumor that Faubus would "throw in the sponge" when he met with Eisenhower. Faubus feigned searching through his belongings and laughed: "I'm not taking a sponge with me, am I?" According to Hays, Faubus was "pensive" and unusually quiet throughout the flight. Back in Newport, meanwhile, Eisenhower was managing stress in his usual way—by playing golf. That morning, the press reported that the president had swung his clubs in fog so heavy that some greens were not visible from the tee.[30]

As the morning of Saturday, September 14, dawned, Ann Whitman witnessed "a great frenzy" at the Newport White House. Adams, Brownell, and Gerald Morgan, the president's special counsel, arrived about 7:45 A.M. and met with Eisenhower and Hagerty. Adams then stayed with the president to discuss other White House business.[31]

The Faubus party arrived by helicopter at 8:50 A.M. Hagerty and Adams witnessed the landing with a group of reporters. Congressman Hays introduced Faubus; they posed for pictures with the White House officials and then strolled with them up a gravel path to the base headquarters. Eisenhower, Morgan, and Brownell were waiting for Faubus in the outer office. They chatted informally for a few minutes about the governor's trip and the history of the naval base. Then, Eisenhower took Faubus into what Whitman called "the President's tiny office"—the same one in which he had signed the civil rights act—and closed the door. For the next twenty minutes, the two men sat alone—the governor of Arkansas and the president of the United States. The air was thick with the tensions of more than a century of racial conflict between North and South.[32]

According to Faubus, Eisenhower did most of the talking. The governor later complained that the president "lectured me in the beginning." "Well, at first he was going to tell me off," Faubus recalled, "like a general tells a lieutenant." He remembered Eisenhower saying, in effect: "This is the way it is and this has got to be done and that's got to be done, and I could see that he didn't understand it at all from a legal standpoint." The governor explained Eisenhower's blunt words by snidely concluding that the president "was anxious to get back to the golf course."[33]

Eisenhower's own notes, dictated almost a month later, indicate that he offered the governor a face-saving solution. Faubus would not have to withdraw the National Guard troops. He could simply change their orders from preventing integration to preserving the peace and allowing the children to attend school. Faubus worried aloud about "ugly plans that were afoot in Arkansas" and requested a delay "to give the tempers a chance to cool off, to give emotions a chance to subside." Eisenhower later told Adams that Faubus seemed perplexed about what to do, perceiving that federal law conflicted with his duties as the governor of Arkansas.[34]

Eisenhower recalled that he delivered an ultimatum, warning Faubus about the consequences of opposing him. No one, Eisenhower said, would benefit from "a trial of strength between the President and a Governor." The government was committed to upholding the Supreme Court's decision. If Arkansas opposed federal authority, the outcome would be that "the State would lose." Eisenhower recalled that he said he "did not want to see any Governor humiliated."

Their private talk finished, Eisenhower and Faubus stood up and strode into the outer office, where Adams, Hays, Brownell, and Morgan were waiting. Hays recalled that Faubus "looked unhappy"; the governor's grim expression communicated that his time with the president had been "slow going." Hagerty arrived a few moments later. Ann Whitman waited outside the door. The chairs were arranged in a circle with Faubus sitting on the president's right—a positioning that spawned laughter when Hagerty later described it to the press. Faubus felt surrounded and patronized, like "a country boy, governor of a small state."[35]

The meeting was long and difficult. According to Faubus, the president summarized his private conversation with Faubus and turned to Brownell. "Herb," Faubus recalled that Eisenhower began, "can't you go down there and ask the court to postpone the implementation of this order for a few days, ten days or three weeks, in conference with them, whatever time it might be decided is best to try to solve the problem?" Brownell responded: "No, that's impossible. It isn't legally possible." The governor did not have to approve of the desegregation decision, but he would have to obey it. Faubus, Adams recalled, listened "in inscrutable silence."[36]

Eisenhower had known what Brownell would say before he asked the question. Ike had thrown the attorney general a fat pitch that he could hit over the fence while preserving, in Faubus's eyes, his own neutrality. The governor later claimed that the president looked "nonplussed" but "accepted the attorney general's statement as final." Faubus alleged that Brownell "lied to the President of the United States" and that Eisenhower "found out later on that Brownell had erroneously advised him on that question and that is why he fired him." Eisenhower did not fire Brownell. The attorney general had already told Eisenhower he wanted to leave the government for private life—a plan that was postponed by the Little Rock crisis.[37]

The specter of civil war haunted the room when Eisenhower produced a letter from a businessman who had advised him to remove every southern officer from command in the army "because they were going to stage a revolution over this very thing." Eisenhower wanted to know how far Faubus would go in using force to oppose the government. After much wrangling, Eisenhower believed that the governor capitulated: "I got definitely the understanding that he was going back to Arkansas to act within a matter of hours to revoke his orders to the Guard to prevent re-entry of the Negro children into the school."[38]

Hagerty met with the press at 11:22 A.M. and described the meeting with Faubus as "friendly and constructive." Ann Whitman thought otherwise: "I got the impression that the meeting had not gone as well as had been hoped, that the Federal government would have to be as tough as possible in the situation." Whitman had not heard Eisenhower's suggestion that Faubus change the orders of the guard, so she concluded: "The test comes tomorrow morning when we will know whether Governor Faubus will, or will not, withdraw the troops."[39]

One task remained. As a condition for holding the meeting, Eisenhower had required that the parties issue statements to the press. These, including the governor's, were to be cleared with the president. Brooks Hays encountered difficulty with Faubus. Two hours passed with no statement from the governor. Finally, Hays negotiated a statement over the phone, talking back and forth with Adams and then with Faubus. The result, Adams concluded, was "far short of what we wanted."[40]

Faubus's statement called the meeting "friendly and constructive"—the same phrase that Hagerty had used. He termed the 1954 Supreme Court decision "the law of the land" and said that it "must be obeyed." The governor was vague about whether he would comply with the court order to admit the nine students to Central High School. He reasserted his responsibility for preventing violence and contended that "the national Administration has no thought of challenging this fact." In effect, Faubus had not budged from his original position. Potential violence was his excuse. Delay was his strategy. His statement said nothing about changing the orders of the National Guard, which Eisenhower had proposed.[41]

Eisenhower's statement said that he was "gratified" by Faubus's "constructive and cooperative attitude." "The Governor stated his intention to respect the decisions of the United States District Court," the president said, "and to give his full cooperation in carrying out his responsibilities in respect to these decisions." Eisenhower, mindful of his cautionary comment to Brownell on September 11, recognized "the inescapable responsibility resting upon the Governor to preserve law and order in his state." But the president pressured Faubus with his expectations: "I am sure it is the desire of the Governor not only to observe the supreme law of the land but to use the influence of his office in orderly progress of the plans which are already the subject of the order of the Court."[42]

Perhaps Eisenhower was naïve in thinking he had an agreement. Adams interpreted the president's statement as "hopeful and somewhat optimistic." Whitman's pessimistic reading may have reflected Eisenhower's private concerns. Brownell was not fooled. He had been convinced from the outset that Faubus would use every means at his command to sabotage the federal court order.[43]

When Faubus issued his statement, a reporter asked him whether the National Guard soldiers would still be in place at Central High when school opened the following Monday morning. Faubus replied: "That is a problem I will have to take care of when I return to Little Rock."[44]

The Crisis Deepens

Faubus did nothing. The National Guard remained at the school, preventing the Negro students from attending. Faubus did not accept Eisenhower's suggestion that he change the guard's orders. Indeed, the governor had decided to defer action until his scheduled appearance in federal court on Friday, September 20.

Eisenhower was furious. Brownell recalled how the president's famous temper erupted after Faubus "reneged on his promise to let black children enter the schools there." At such moments, "Eisenhower would start getting red from the neck up and he certainly knew all of the right curse words." According to Brownell, Eisenhower phoned him and said: "You were right. Faubus broke his word."[45]

Brooks Hays felt betrayed. Arthur Caldwell, a good friend, chided Hays for his gullibility about the governor's intentions. The congressman was now labeled an "integrationist" in Arkansas, a tag that would defeat him in the next election. Hays's effort reminded Caldwell of a sign he kept on his desk: "Blessed are the peacemakers for they catch hell from both sides."[46]

Eisenhower's political opponents attacked him for staging a fruitless meeting with the Arkansas governor. The day after the meeting with Faubus, the Democratic Party Advisory Council—including former president Truman and Adlai Stevenson—called the results of the meeting "disappointing to all Americans who believe that respect for the Law of the land must be paramount." The group charged that Eisenhower had "failed in his duty" and proclaimed that "the first responsibility of a Governor" was to uphold the Constitution. On September 17, Senator Humphrey joined the chorus of critics, charging to a constituent that "when the entire country is looking to the President for leadership, he hesitates and does nothing."[47]

Republican Senator Prescott Bush of Connecticut released a statement defending the president. The National Republican Club protested: "It was the Democrat Party that fought the President's Civil Rights Bill in the last congress, and it has been a divided Democrat party, through the years, that has blocked civil rights legislation." The club asked the haunting question, burdened with the nation's history: "What would they have President Eisenhower do, rush in federal troops to do battle with Governor Faubus' state Guard and set the stage for civil war?"[48]

The responses from black leaders were mixed. On September 17, Roy Wilkins told Max Rabb: "The President has done magnificently in the Little Rock crisis." The NAACP executive secretary characterized the angry southerners as "separatists, fighting desperately to justify the slave system and the master-slave psychology and thus—in a fashion—to gloss over the fact of Appomattox and the fact of the Civil War amendments to the constitution." Congressman Adam Clayton Powell, Jr., exploited the situation. On Wednesday, September 18, he demanded "an immediate appointment" with the president, noting that Eisenhower had already conferred with Senator Richard Russell (on the civil rights act) and Governor Faubus. Eisenhower himself labored over the wording of a response to Powell, initially preferring to reject the request. Richard Nixon persuaded the president to wire Powell that he would ask the staff to make plans to meet with him.[49]

Eisenhower was clear on the issues. On September 19, the day before Faubus was to appear in court, the president reminded a critic that the Supreme Court had ruled that "the segregation of Negro children in public schools solely because of their race was a deprivation of the equal protection of the laws in violation of the Constitution of the United States." To Eisenhower, the legalities were irrefutable: "The authority of the Supreme Court as the final arbiter of the Constitution in cases that come before it has been established since the early days of the Republic. It is therefore incumbent upon all officials to enforce the Constitution as interpreted by the highest court."[50]

This angry president was getting restless about the stalemate in Little Rock. He had called Sherman Adams the morning of the 19th and wondered whether he should issue a statement. Adams and Brownell recommended against it. They agreed that Faubus was not going to enforce the court order. Adams told Hagerty that he should simply tell the press that the matter was with the federal district court and "that it would be improper to comment while the particular proceedings are going forward." The press secretary was authorized to say that "the President is deeply disappointed that voluntary means have not been found to comply with the Court's orders."[51]

Eisenhower waited for Faubus to defy Judge Davies in court. General Andrew Goodpaster, Eisenhower's staff secretary, reflected his commander's thinking and transmitted those perceptions to Hagerty; if the court issued an order and Governor Faubus defied it, "then an obligation falls upon the Federal government to require Faubus to do so by whatever means may be necessary. At that time the President should speak to the country." "Whatever means" obviously implied the use of troops.[52]

On Friday, September 20, Faubus appeared in person in Judge Davies's courtroom and argued that he had acted to prevent violence and that the federal court could not prevent his doing so. Davies rejected that argument and ordered Faubus to cease barring the students from entering the school with National Guard troops or by any other means. The governor's attorneys walked out of the courtroom in protest.[53]

Eisenhower called Brownell at 3:30 P.M. and listened to a detailed account of the courtroom confrontation. Brownell had concluded beforehand that Faubus would either withdraw the guard or defy the court order; "In either case it calls for decisions on the President's part." Eisenhower, worried about the possibility that Faubus would close the school, asked, "Can he do that legally?" Brownell responded that he would investigate that question. This was the fear that Eisenhower had so frequently voiced—that segregationist leaders might abolish the public schools in the South rather than submit to court-ordered desegregation. Then both African-American and poor white children would suffer.

Ann Whitman, monitoring the phone conversation, noted that Brownell was planning to talk with Secretary of the Army Wilber Brucker about using troops. Whitman recorded: "The President is loath to use troops—thinks movement might spread—violence would come. There is no doubt whatever about the authority of the President to call out the troops, although he 'cannot use them to preserve law and order' but can use them to see that the children are protected."[54]

At 4:35 P.M. that Friday, Hagerty sparred with an agitated press corps. Asked if he still viewed the Faubus meeting as constructive, the press secretary replied, "Yes I do." Hagerty refused to discuss the government's alternatives or characterize the president's reaction to Faubus's lawyers walking out of the courtroom. When Hagerty tried to end the press briefing, a reporter asked when there would be more news: "What about tomorrow?" That would be Saturday, the press secretary said, "a day of rest." The reporters broke into laughter. Hagerty sighed: "A day of rest, I doubt it."[55]

Governor Faubus announced his response to the judge's order on television the evening of September 20. He would comply with the court order and withdraw the National Guard. Then Faubus departed for the Southern Governors Conference in Georgia. Eisenhower apparently harbored some faint hope that the crisis was over. At 8:30 A.M. on Saturday, the 21st, he released a short statement:

> The action by the Governor of Arkansas in withdrawing the detachment of Arkansas National Guard troops from the Little Rock high school is a necessary step in the right direction. I am confident that the citizens of the City of Little Rock and the State of Arkansas will welcome this opportunity to demonstrate that in their city and in their state proper orders of a United States Court will be executed promptly and without disorder.

But events were no longer moving "in the right direction." Congressman Hays called Sherman Adams from Little Rock and relayed the fears of Mayor Woodrow Wilson Mann and Superintendent of Schools Virgil Blossom that the Little Rock police could not handle the mob they believed would appear at the school on Monday. Later that day, Hagerty released another statement by an increasingly worried president, his anxiety undoubtedly fueled by these reports from the usually reliable Hays. Faubus's defiance of integration had finally mobilized the anti-integration mob he had predicted. Eisenhower pled with the citizens of Arkansas to "vigorously oppose any violence by extremists." He challenged them to think about "the ordeal to which the nine Negro children who have been prevented from attending Central High School have been subjected." The president expressed confidence that the citizens of Arkansas would allow the court order to "be executed promptly and without disorder."[56]

But Eisenhower was not confident. By withdrawing the guard, Faubus had once again ignored Eisenhower's proposal that the governor change the guard's orders. Faubus had intended to use the troops solely to prevent integration. He had dismissed the soldiers, left the state, and, in effect, invited extremists to prove how right he was about needing troops to prevent violence.

That weekend, Eisenhower tried to salvage the ragged remnants of his alleged vacation. On Sunday evening, September 22—the ninety-fifth anniversary of Abraham Lincoln's 1862 preliminary emancipation proclamation—the president of the United States cooked steaks out on the patio and played bridge.[57]

CHAPTER NINE

Military Intervention in Little Rock

Mob rule cannot be allowed to override the decisions of our courts.
—DwIGHT D. EISENHOWER, SEPTEMBER 24, 1957

Monday, September 23, 1957, was a busy day for the president of the United States. At 7:17 A.M., he boarded a helicopter to return to Washington, where he spoke to conferences at two Washington hotels without mentioning Little Rock.[1]

That morning chaos reigned at Central High School. A mob gathered, determined to keep the African-American students from entering the school. A newsman reported: "This was a mob with a job to do and the leadership to do it." The men were dressed in gray and khaki work clothes, straw hats and work shoes; "obvious ringleaders" were organizing the crowd. One was Jimmy Karam, the state athletic commissioner and close associate of Governor Faubus. Karam's wife was with Faubus and the Arkansas delegation at the southern governors' conference.

At the south side of the school, the crowd intercepted four Negro newsmen. A white man stopped them: "You're not going into our school." The reporters replied that they did not wish to enter. A mob leader called out: "Kill them, kill them!" Several men beat two of the reporters. During the melee, eight of the Negro students slipped through a side door of the school. A woman saw them: "Oh, my god, they're going in. The niggers are in." She fell to her knees and covered her face. The Negro reporters had, in effect, distracted the rioters while the students entered. A mob ringleader bellowed: "Come on, let's go in the school and drag them out." A white girl ran down the street and shouted hysterically: "The niggers got in. They tricked us. The niggers got in." When the police arrested the girl, protest leaders cried: "Look at that. They arrest a white girl and let the niggers in our school."

A Negro reporter tried to photograph the mob, but Karam led a group that chased the photographer. A white man kicked the photographer twice and Karam jumped into the street and bellowed: "The nigger started it. He struck him first." One police officer, in frustration, slammed his billy club to the ground, threw his badge on the street, and walked away.[2]

Another black man accompanied the ninth student, who never was able to enter the school. When rioters chased them, the youth was able to escape, but a reporter from the *Arkansas Democrat* witnessed an "extremely brutal" beating of the man. The riot continued for more than three hours. At noon, Virgil Blossom, the superintendent of schools, called Arthur Caldwell, the chief of the civil rights section in the Justice Department, and pled for federal assistance. Blossom estimated the size of the mob at 1,500 persons. Eventually, the crowd broke through the police barricades surrounding the school and the police removed the students from the school for their own protection.[3]

Following his ceremonial appearances in Washington, Eisenhower returned to Newport. He had instructed Brownell to call him if the situation worsened. Eisenhower boarded his yacht to cross the bay to the country club, intent on playing golf. When he landed, he received an urgent message from the attorney general, ordered the boat turned around, and returned to his quarters.[4]

Despite his efforts to manage the crisis, the president now looked indecisive and ineffective. Eisenhower's meeting with Faubus had failed. Faubus had done what the public erroneously assumed that the president had requested—pull out the National Guard troops. The press knew nothing about Ike's ultimatum to the governor at Newport and his demand that Faubus change the orders of the guard. The situation had turned violent, just as Faubus had predicted.

The Decision

According to journalist Roland P. Burnham, Woodrow Wilson Mann, the mayor of Little Rock, was "in deep despair." Mann asked Burnham what he should do. Burnham responded that the mayor had no choice but to appeal to the president. Mann was hesitant. Finally, he told Burnham: "You do it. Tell him you're me." Burnham reached Maxwell Rabb at the White House and Rabb instructed him to send a telegram to the president.[5]

At 3:44 P.M., Eisenhower received a frantic wire from Mayor Mann, who declared that the mob at Central High School "was no spontaneous assembly" and alleged that followers of Governor Faubus had "agitated, aroused, and assembled" the mob. The mayor identified Jimmy Karam, "a political and social intimate of Governor Faubus," as a principal agitator.[6]

Eisenhower was incensed. His rage was still evident, just beneath the surface, in his memoirs. "The issue had now become clear both in fact and in law," Eisenhower wrote. "Cruel mob force had frustrated the execution of an order of a United States court, and the Governor of the state was sitting by, refusing to lift a finger to support the local authorities." Eisenhower concluded: "There was only one justification for the use of troops: to uphold the law. Though Faubus denied it, I, as President of the United States, now had that justification and the clear obligation to act."[7]

Eisenhower and Brownell had already begun preparations for intervention before they received Mann's telegram. Ike had contemplated the use of the army in Little Rock ever since September 4, when he had approved Brownell's statement indicating that possibility. A presidential decision to send troops into a southern state for the first time since Reconstruction would be controversial. Eisenhower and Brownell, in their contingency planning, had identified steps that would be codified in three documents; Ike now ordered the attorney general to draft all three—a statement, a proclamation, and an address to the nation. The statement would provide a legal rationale for intervention, the proclamation would order citizens to cease resistance and would invoke the authority to mobilize troops, and the speech would explain the president's actions to the public once the army had been dispatched. The speech would be of particular importance for a president who was usually reluctant to use the "bully pulpit." On September 19, national security aide Andrew Goodpaster had alerted Hagerty that the Little Rock situation might require military action; if it did, "at that time the President should speak to the country."[8]

Given these assignments, Brownell canceled his scheduled 4:30 P.M. flight from Washington to New York City to attend a boxing match. At 4:48 P.M., Jim Hagerty called in the press to read aloud the first of the three documents, the president's statement, because he lacked time to mimeograph copies. Although Brownell had drafted the statement, it was vintage Eisenhower, rippling with the crisp, vivid language Eisenhower employed when in command and intending "to make several things clear." The first two points were particularly emphatic: "The Federal law and orders of a United States District Court implementing that law cannot be flouted with impunity by an individual or any mob of extremists"; the second read, "I will use the full power of the United States including whatever force may be necessary to prevent any obstruction of the law and to carry out the orders of the Federal Court." The pledge to use "the full power of the United States" and "whatever force may be necessary" left no doubt: Eisenhower had decided to coerce compliance with the federal court order. The presidential anger flashed in point three: "It will be a sad day for this country—both at home and abroad—if school children can safely attend their classes only under the protection of armed guards."[9]

At 6:45 P.M., Hagerty distributed a formal proclamation signed by the president, titled, "OBSTRUCTION OF JUSTICE IN THE STATE OF ARKANSAS." The document declared that persons in Arkansas had "willfully obstructed" the orders of the federal court. The key sentence read: "Now, THEREFORE, I Dwight D. Eisenhower, President of the United States, under and by virtue of the authority vested in me by the Constitution . . . do command all persons engaged in such obstruction of justice to cease and desist therefrom, and to disperse forthwith."[10]

The remainder of the proclamation set forth the precedents for presidential action. Eisenhower and the Justice Department had agreed to cite a 1792 law that George Washington had invoked to put down the Whiskey Rebellion in 1794, along with Grover Cleveland's use of an updated 1807 law to enforce a federal injunction against the Pullman strike in 1894—the latter action contrary to the wishes of a state governor. An extraordinary precedent was left unstated—Lincoln's use of force against the southern states that had illegally seceded from the Union in 1861.[11]

Eisenhower still intended to proceed one step at a time. A reporter asked Hagerty whether, if the proclamation was defied, it would mean "sending in troops?" Hagerty hedged and said the proclamation applied "to calling out the troops" and did "not necessarily mean sending in." The reporters ridiculed this parsing of words, but Hagerty insisted that there was "a very vast distinction" and concluded: "This has to be issued before a President can use military force. It does not mean inevitably that he is going to." Hagerty declined to comment when a reporter asked: "If these mobs continue their violence tomorrow then you will call out the troops?"[12] Perhaps Eisenhower clung to a faint hope that the proclamation itself would result in a cessation of violence in Little Rock. That was not to be. The president would be forced to move from words to action.

As Tuesday, September 24, dawned, Eisenhower prepared to act. At 8:35 A.M., he held a long phone conversation with his attorney general. Ike told Brownell that he should continue working on the address to the nation, but no announcement should be made until they learned what was happening in Little Rock that morning. Ann Whitman noted that Eisenhower had "softened" some language in a draft he had already received.

The president and the attorney general also discussed military options. Army Chief of Staff General Maxwell Taylor preferred using National Guard rather than army troops. Eisenhower thought otherwise. He feared that the use of Arkansas guard units in Little Rock might pit "brother against brother."

Eisenhower, obviously thinking about golf, wondered aloud whether he should stay in his office during the morning. Finally, he and Brownell agreed that would look as though the president "was frozen waiting for something to happen," and that the president should go about his "normal routine." But Eisenhower ignored Brownell's advice. He was, in fact, "frozen"—waiting for word on Little Rock. He called his spiritual advisor, the Reverend Billy Graham, who told the president that sending troops was "the only thing you can do." Fifteen minutes after the president hung up the phone with Brownell, Hagerty told the press that the administration was waiting to see if the president's proclamation would be obeyed: "If it is not obeyed by those to which it was directed, additional action will be taken by the President on behalf of the United States."[13]

Eisenhower and his advisors debated where he should deliver his address to the nation. General Alfred M. Gruenther, Ike's former chief of staff in the army and successor as Supreme Allied Commander in Europe, urged the president to return to Washington. Eisenhower demurred, saying that he did not want "to exaggerate the significance of the admittedly serious situation in Arkansas." Then the president wavered: "On the other hand, for a number of reasons I wish I were back there. My work would be a lot easier to do."[14]

That issue surfaced when Hagerty met with reporters. One asked, "Jim, is the President going to terminate his Newport vacation because of this situation?" Hagerty responded, "No," and repeated the argument that Eisenhower had used with Gruenther, reminding the reporters that "wherever the President of the United States is, there is the office of the White House."[15]

A short while later, at 9:16 A.M., Eisenhower received a second frantic telegram from Mayor Mann in Little Rock: "The immediate need for federal troops is urgent. The mob is much larger in numbers at 8AM than at any time yesterday. People are converging on the scene from all directions. Mob is armed and engaging in fisticuffs and other acts of violence. Situation is out of control and police cannot disperse the mob. I am pleading to you as President of the United States in the interest of humanity, law and order and because of democracy world wide to provide the necessary federal troops within several hours. Action by you will restore peace and order and compliance with your proclamation."[16]

The president was ready to act. In Newport, Brownell met with Hagerty and Adams at 10:15 A.M. At 11:20, Eisenhower joined the group. At 11:45, Eisenhower read the telegram from the Little Rock mayor to California Senator William Knowland on the phone and told the Republican minority leader what he had decided. At 12:08 P.M., Ann Whitman recorded that "the President said definitely he would sign the order for the Federal troops to go into Little Rock."[17]

At 12:15, the president called General Taylor. Eisenhower had made a final decision on the composition of the military force he would send to Arkansas. The National Guard could not be ready soon enough to defuse the crisis, and Ike was uncertain of the Arkansas guard's loyalty. The army could respond within six hours, so Eisenhower chose a force that he knew would be loyal to him—the 101st Airborne Division. There was nostalgia as well as military calculation in his choice. That division had won fame in World War II under General Taylor's leadership. Eisenhower had paid a legendary personal visit to the troops in 1944, just prior to the D-Day attack on Normandy and had joked and talked with the soldiers, most of whom he expected to die that day. The successors to those troops, trained to handle riots, would remain on duty in Little Rock until the situation was stabilized. Then the 101st would be replaced by federalized Arkansas National Guard soldiers if they demonstrated they were ready. Major General Edwin A. Walker, a decorated combat veteran with a reputation for toughness, would be in overall command of both the regular army and the federalized National Guard troops.[18]

Eisenhower reversed his decision to stay in Rhode Island. Radio and television communications in Providence were inadequate. More important, Eisenhower had come to agree with Knowland that the address needed "the dignity of the White House behind it—that it did not sound well to have it said that the speech came from the Vacation White House." A weary Eisenhower, still wanting to preserve his phantom vacation, had argued that proposition with the senator. Ann Whitman recorded that the "President said he was not going to do so; weakened and said he might." One hour after Eisenhower had written General Gruenther that he would not return to Washington, Whitman recorded that "he agreed to go."[19]

At 12:22 P.M., Eisenhower signed the executive order dispatching troops to Arkansas. At 12:30, Hagerty informed the press. The order recapped the proclamation of the previous day and invoked "the authority vested in me by the Constitution and Statutes of the United States." The document nationalized the Arkansas National Guard and authorized the secretary of defense to enforce the federal court orders and to use armed forces if necessary. One reporter asked Hagerty: "Will this end the President's little vacation here then?" Hagerty exclaimed: "Little vacation!" Another asked: "Did the President say anything as he signed this order?" "No," responded the press secretary.[20]

The first of fifty-two aircraft carrying approximately one thousand troops departed from Fort Campbell in Kentucky at 3:30 P.M. Two hours later, the army announced that five hundred men of the 101st Airborne Division would land in Little Rock "within the hour."[21] For the first time since Reconstruction, federal troops would patrol the streets in a former Confederate state.

Eisenhower had told Ann Whitman that they should leave for the capital about the same hour as the troops took flight. Eisenhower boarded the helicopter at 3:12 P.M. and was back in the White House at 5:05 P.M., working on his address to the nation. At 6:40 P.M., twenty-six vehicles carrying troops of the 101st arrived at Central High School. The soldiers, carrying carbines and billy clubs, were in place by 6:55 P.M. Although Negro soldiers served in the 101st Division, none were deployed at Central High School that evening or the following day; they remained at a nearby armory, prepared to protect the homes of the nine students.[22]

The Speech

Meanwhile, Faubus regaled his colleagues at the southern governors' conference with protestations of his willingness to protect law and order in Little Rock. His allies made one last attempt to prevent military action. They sent the president the text of a resolution supporting Faubus, scheduled for action by the entire conference on the 25th. The resolution was released to the press at 6:30 P.M. on the 24th, timed to undercut Eisenhower's speech.[23]

Eisenhower ignored the ploy. His course was set. He worked on drafts of the address with Brownell, editing out sentences that he thought might shame the South. At 5:31 P.M., Secretary of State Dulles called to encourage the president to "put in a few more sentences in this draft speech emphasizing the harm done abroad." Dulles dictated several sentences to Ann Whitman that became part of the speech. Ike phoned Mamie in Newport at 8:34 P.M., minutes before he was to deliver the address.[24]

Eisenhower entered the Oval Office wearing a gray single-breasted suit with a blue shirt and tie. Toward 9:00 P.M., the president sat down, flanked by portraits of the men whom Eisenhower regarded as America's greatest heroes—Benjamin Franklin, George Washington, Abraham Lincoln, and Robert E. Lee. He had decided not to use a teleprompter and stared down at the manuscript, which had been typed in large print on thick paper. The opening paragraph had been added at the last minute. The signal was given, and the president looked into the cameras and began to speak deliberately, removing his glasses occasionally to look up and emphasize a point.[25]

> To make this talk I have come to the President's office in the White House. I could have spoken from Rhode Island where I have been staying recently, but I felt that, in speaking from the house of Lincoln, of Jackson and of Wilson, my words would better convey both the sadness I feel in the action I was compelled today to take and the firmness with which I intend to pursue this course until the orders of the Federal Court at Little Rock can be executed without unlawful interference.

Eisenhower had carefully chosen these words. His consistent stance on civil rights, to the dismay of his liberal critics, had been to avoid saying anything that would further inflame feelings in the South. Yet, at this moment, with soldiers on the ground in Arkansas, Eisenhower chose to invoke the name of the president who had made bloody war on the South.

Eisenhower said he had taken his action because "demagogic extremists and disorderly mobs" had "deliberately prevented the

carrying out of proper orders from a Federal Court" and had ignored his proclamation. His responsibility was "inescapable." The
president declared: "Mob rule cannot be allowed to override the decisions of our courts."

Eisenhower sought common ground with white southerners by
using language, especially the word "our," that critics would later portray as pandering to the South or reflecting the president's disagreement with the Supreme Court decision: "Our personal opinions about
the decision have no bearing on the matter of enforcement; the responsibility and authority of the Supreme Court to interpret the Constitution are very clear." This was ever Eisenhower's stance in regard to
the 1954 *Brown* decision. He insisted that the law, interpreted by the
Court, had to be obeyed. "The very basis of our individual rights and
freedoms rests," he asserted, "upon the certainty that the President
and the Executive Branch of Government will support and insure the
carrying out of the decisions of the Federal Courts, even, when necessary with all the means at the President's command."

Eisenhower expressed empathy for the South, a region where "I
have many warm friends, some of them in the City of Little Rock."
He expressed his belief that "the overwhelming majority of the
people in the South—including those of Arkansas and of Little
Rock—are of good will, united in their efforts to preserve and respect the law even when they disagree with it."

The president used Dulles's phrases to describe the impact of
the Little Rock crisis "in the eyes of the world." He asserted that "it
would be difficult to exaggerate the harm that is being done to the
prestige and influence, and indeed to the safety, of our nation and
the world."[26]

> Our enemies are gloating over this incident and using it ev-
> erywhere to misrepresent our whole nation. We are por-
> trayed as a violator of those standards of conduct which the
> people of the world united to proclaim in the Charter of the
> United Nations. There they affirmed "faith in fundamental
> human rights" and "in the dignity and worth of the human
> person" and they did so "without distinction as to race, sex,
> language or religion."

Eisenhower challenged the citizens of Arkansas to end resistance immediately. If that happened, the troops would no longer be necessary. He concluded the address with the closing words from the Pledge of Allegiance, which Eisenhower had personally penciled into the final draft: "One nation, indivisible, with liberty and justice for all." After finishing his address, Ike called Mamie.[27]

The Response

In Little Rock, the world of the nine African-American students had changed. Melba Pattillo wrote that night in her diary: "I don't know how to go to school with soldiers." She prayed: "Please show me. P.S. Please help the soldiers to keep the mobs away from me." Melba turned out the light and went to sleep. Suddenly, she was jolted awake by the doorbell and loud voices. Melba's mother, Lois, put her hand over her daughter's mouth and motioned her to get up. The doorbell kept ringing. Her grandmother picked up a shotgun and called out, "Who is it?" She whispered to her family: "White men. It's white men wearing black hats. What are they doing on our front porch at this time of night?" Then she called through the door: "State your business, gentlemen, or I'll be forced to do mine." "We're from the Office of the President of the United States; please open your door," one of the men said. "We have a message from your President." The men displayed identification and told Melba's mother: "Let your daughter go back to school, and she will be protected."[28]

A reporter described the scene at Central High School on the morning of September 25 as "chilling." "The force of law shows nakedly on the point of a bayonet," the newsman observed. The crowd that gathered numbered about 1,500. The troops dispersed groups of civilians as soon as they formed. A soldier accidentally pricked a man with a bayonet. Another man tried to wrestle a rifle from a soldier, who struck him on the head with the rifle butt.

At 9:25 A.M.—forty minutes after the bell signaling the start of school—jeeps arrived at Central High's main entrance and thirty soldiers accompanied the nine students up the wide steps and into the school. Shortly after 10:00 A.M., police received a call claiming that a bomb had been planted in the school. A second phone message led to a temporary evacuation of the building. There was no particular trouble among students in the school, although thirty to fifty left after the black students entered and approximately 750 had failed to appear for school that morning. The Negro students reported no serious incidents. Gloria Ray said "my classmates were very nice to me," and she had made some friends. Terrence Roberts reported that "everyone acted nice" and added, "I didn't have any trouble."

Outside, agitators taunted the soldiers. A woman lowered her car window and cried "Heil Hitler" to the soldiers of the division that had captured Hitler's refuge in Germany in 1945. A bus driver opened his door and yelled, "All you need now is a Russian flag." A Negro delivery boy was forced to flee into a house when the crowd threatened him and smashed his bicycle. A man stood on the steps of the school and announced: "Gentlemen, you've just observed how the Communist dictatorship works." By midday, the crowd around the school had dwindled to about twenty-five. That night, sooner than originally planned, National Guard troops relieved the army soldiers who had been on duty at the school for more than twenty-four hours. By the next day of school, September 26, the angry crowd had disappeared.[29]

The day after Eisenhower's speech, Ann Whitman recorded that "the reaction to the action and speech was about even, with a sharp delineation as to geographical location of the sender of the messages." The polls were encouraging. The Trendex poll published on September 26 indicated that 68.4 percent of the country (77.5 percent outside the South) approved of the president's action in sending troops to Little Rock. In the South, the results were reversed, with 62.6 percent disapproving. The following week, the Gallup Poll reported that 64 percent of the public believed that the president had done the "right thing." The South responded to the same question with 36 percent approval. One flurry of adverse publicity surrounded the fact that the president had left "under God" out of the concluding phrase of the Pledge of Allegiance.[30]

Eisenhower's ambivalent public image on civil rights was reflected in a report in the *New York World-Telegram*. The headline proclaimed that the speech showed "The Real Eisenhower." Andrew Tully called Eisenhower "the duty-bound soldier and man of huge patience" who had resisted pressures to act more quickly, and who finally "descended on the Little Rock mob with the wrath of the loyal soldier." Tully noted: "This was a man who quite possibly disagreed with the Supreme Court decision." The impression that Ike "quite possibly disagreed" with *Brown* resurfaced even when his action in sending troops was a resounding affirmation of the Court's decision.[31]

Columnist Walter Lippmann accused Eisenhower of failing to state "the real case of the United States Government"—that the situation had begun not with mob violence, but with Governor Faubus's orders to the National Guard. This misframing of the issue, Lippmann wrote, resulted in making Eisenhower vulnerable to the charge "that he is doing something he promised not to do—namely to impose integration with Federal troops." Lippmann believed that the president's advisors had "served him badly." The columnist ridiculed the president for attempting to manage the crisis "by remote control" from Rhode Island.[32]

The morning after his address to the nation, Eisenhower and his team left the White House at 6:55 A.M. The president was determined to play golf. On the day after the speech, Ann Whitman recorded that Ike "played 18 holes of golf and practiced putting, chipping and driving for almost two additional hours." Eisenhower could not get in an uninterrupted golf game, thanks to Little Rock. At 1:10 P.M., he received a formal request by phone for a meeting from a delegation of Southern governors who wanted to see Eisenhower on the 26th. He set the meeting for Tuesday, October 1, at 2:30 P.M. "to discuss the problems of school integration"—a broader agenda than the governors wanted. Hagerty announced the meeting to the press at 5:22 P.M. and told reporters that it was "not in our plans" to include Governor Faubus. Eisenhower's delay of the meeting reflected his disdain for such encounters and his desire to recover a few days of his vacation. There would be one appointment the next day, with Henry Ford II—and even the auto magnate would be expected to play golf with the president.[33]

Orval Faubus returned to Arkansas that day, September 25,

boarding a Georgia National Guard plane and transferring at Birmingham, Alabama, to an Arkansas National Guard plane. In the
midst of changing planes, the governor was informed that the president had federalized the Arkansas National Guard. "Well," Faubus
quipped, "I guess I'll be flying home in one of the president's planes
now." On Thursday evening, September 26, Faubus addressed the
state on radio and television, proclaiming: "We are now an occupied
territory."[34]

The peaceful day that Eisenhower had planned for September
26 was not to be. First, the administration's contingency plans for a
larger conflict in the South produced an embarrassing gaffe. The
army announced that units "throughout the southern states have
been placed on special alert to deal with any possible outbreaks in
connection with school segregation." The alert covered task forces
in North Carolina, Georgia, Louisiana, and Kansas. A spokesman
explained that the alert was ordered after "disorders and threats of
difficulties arose in widely scattered localities in connection with efforts to integrate the schools." He went on to note that the troops in
the southern states had received training in "military aid to civilian
powers."[35]

The order, if known to Eisenhower in advance, was not meant to
be public. Eisenhower's preparation notes for a later news conference indicate that he did not know. "As soon as the President heard"
about the military alert, the notes record, "the order was revoked."
This incident presented Eisenhower's enemies with more ammunition. Governor Faubus exploited the special alert in the climax of
his September 26 speech, and ignored the fact that it had been revoked four hours earlier. The governor left the impression that the
troop deployment to Little Rock was the first step in a larger military occupation of the South.[36]

Was the alert a mistake, made by anxious army leaders? Eisenhower certainly did not want a public impression that he was prepared to make numerous other military interventions in the South.
Still, the news about "disorders and threats of difficulties" was too
specific for this to be merely an error. The president, not just the
military, worried about the possibility of a larger military confrontation. Hagerty, who often manipulated the truth to protect his boss,

insisted to the press that the White House had not authorized the order and had no knowledge of it until it appeared on the news wires. Secretary of the Army Brucker likewise insisted that he learned about the order after its issuance.[37]

Who then issued the order? When, on September 27, the Senate Armed Services Committee, chaired by Senator Richard Russell, demanded a copy of it, Secretary Brucker declined, characterizing the order as "a precautionary training directive," and claimed that the troops had not been "alerted" in "the military sense of the word." Brucker admitted that the Little Rock situation had precipitated the order. As to who, specifically, had issued the alert, Brucker responded that he and General Maxwell Taylor, the army's chief officer, were "responsible" and he would not want to hold subordinate officers who were "engaged in executing the lawful orders of their superiors" accountable.[38]

The controversy over the alert reveals the practical limits on presidential authority and resources. What if another situation like Little Rock erupted? Former South Carolina governor Jimmy Byrnes declared: "The President has given the world the impression that civil war exists and the United States Government has declared war on Arkansas." Byrnes predicted that "when integration is attempted in rural areas in many Southern states, conditions will be worse than in Little Rock." Representative Carl Elliott (D-Alabama) called Eisenhower's action "illegal, unwarranted and unwise" and invoked southern memories of the Civil War. "Troops used as occupying forces," he said, "are a hated symbol throughout the old Confederacy." Elliott described the reality that confronted the president: "There are not enough troops to occupy every high school campus in the south."[39]

The other event that derailed the peaceful day Eisenhower had planned for September 26 was a telegram from Senator Russell. Released to the press by Russell, the telegram protested "the high-handed and illegal methods being employed by the armed forces of the United States under your command who are carrying out your orders to mix the races in the public schools of Little Rock, Arkansas." The senator alleged that the troops in Little Rock were "applying tactics which must have been copied from the manual issued the officers of Hitler's storm troopers." The senator described alleged episodes of brutality and declared: "There are millions of patriotic people in this country who will strongly resent the strong armed totalitarian police-state methods being employed at Little Rock."

That red flush must have crept up the president's neck again when he read the telegram. Eisenhower composed what Sherman Adams called an "indignant" reply. Actually, Eisenhower's response was restrained. He wrote the senator: "Few times in my life have I felt as saddened as when the obligations of my office required me to order the use of force with a state to carry out the decisions of a Federal Court." The action was necessary, he said, because the state had misused the National Guard, had encouraged "mobs of extremists" to violate the law, and had failed "to protect against mobs persons who are peaceably exercising their right under the Constitution." Eisenhower declared, in language that echoed Lincoln's a century earlier, "Failure to act in such a case would be tantamount to acquiescence in anarchy and the dissolution of the union." Eisenhower could not let Russell's invocation of the Nazis pass: "I must say that I completely fail to comprehend your comparison of our troops to Hitler's storm troopers. In one case military power was used to further the ambitions and purposes of a ruthless dictator; in the other to preserve the institutions of free government."[40]

A flood of other responses to Eisenhower's intervention rolled into the White House. Pratt Remmel, the former mayor of Little Rock, wired the president that he had made "a wonderful speech" and that his "action had to be taken." One supporter telegraphed: "Hell hath no fury like the anger of a righteous man scorned. Go to it. The nation is in your corner." That message elicited a response from Eisenhower: "I assure you I feel considerably less satisfaction than does a fighter in the ring." Ike felt "duty bound to make the decision I made."[41]

The Soviet Union exploited what it called "racist outrages" in the United States for propaganda purposes. Moscow's radio commentators pointed to "Negro persecution" and recounted "new acts of anti-Negro terror and oppression" in Little Rock. Eisenhower's use of troops was "merely an attempt to distract attention from the real root of the tragedy by staging a farce" to influence world opinion.[42]

Some supporters of Eisenhower made him uncomfortable—among them the Communist Party of Illinois and Robert Nathan, national chairman of the liberal Americans for Democratic Action (ADA). Others were not so kind, even in Eisenhower's own party. Mississippi State Republican Chairman Wirt A. Yerger charged Eisenhower "with joining hands with the NAACP and the Democratic High Command in a scheme to destroy the Constitution of the United States." Another alleged that Eisenhower's "illegal, ill-advised use of troops at Little Rock makes the United States a military dictatorship." One correspondent accused the president of stirring up "all the old resentments of the Civil War." A World War II veteran returned his medals to his former supreme commander, writing: "I am ashamed that I ever wore them."[43]

Senator Olin D. Johnston (D-South Carolina) advocated what amounted to civil war, calling for "warrants to be issued for the arrest of Federal soldiers responsible for unnecessary bludgeoning of Arkansas citizens and unlawful invasion of their homes." Johnston urged Governor Faubus to "proclaim a state of insurrection" and force a showdown with the president by calling out the Arkansas National Guard himself. George Aiken, a Republican senator from Vermont, stated that the president was "undoubtedly within his rights in authorizing the use of Federal troops there." Senator Wayne Morse, an Oregon Democrat, praised Eisenhower's decision as "a constitutional and needed exercise of his Presidential duty." Senator Patrick V. McNamara (D-Michigan) lamented: "It's damned near time he took some positive action." Lyndon Johnson straddled the issue without endorsing Eisenhower's action, saying "I think there should be no troops from either side patrolling our school campuses."[44]

The parents of the nine students in Little Rock wrote Eisenhower that his actions had "strengthened our faith in democracy." American freedom could survive, they wrote, only if all persons were granted "freedom and equality of opportunity." The parents believed that the president had "demonstrated admirably to us[,] the nation and the world how profoundly you believe in this concept."[45]

A few days after he had labeled the president "wishy-washy" on

Little Rock, Martin Luther King, Jr., wrote Eisenhower that "the overwhelming majority of southerners, Negro and white, stand firmly behind your resolute action." King went on to say, "in the long run, justice finally must spring from a new moral climate, yet spiritual forces cannot emerge in a situation of mob violence." Eisenhower responded in typically legalistic terms that did not address the "moral climate." "I share your confidence," the president wrote, "that Americans everywhere remain devoted to our tradition of adherence to orderly processes of law."[46]

King worried that white violence against blacks would eventually elicit a violent reaction from African-Americans. He challenged the Negro community in Little Rock to adhere to nonviolence. "You must meet physical force with soul force," he urged the Little Rock leaders. "History is on your side. World opinion is with you. The moral conscience of millions of white Americans is with you. Keep struggling with this faith and the tragic midnight of anarchy and mob rule which encompasses your city at this time will be transformed into the glowing daybreak of freedom and justice."[47]

Louis Armstrong sent the most colorful telegram to Eisenhower: "Daddy, if and when you decide to take those little Negro children personally into Central High School along with your marvelous troops, please take me along."[48]

Return to Washington

The situation in Little Rock required constant vigilance. Ann Whitman recorded in her diary that "the President decided to terminate his Newport visit, and on Monday, September 30th we engaged in the gigantic maneuver of moving the equipment and staff back to Washington. It always surprises me that so few things go wrong."[49]

Eisenhower was scheduled to meet in the Oval Office the following day with governors Frank Clement of Tennessee, LeRoy Collins of Florida, Luther Hodges of North Carolina, and Theodore McKeldin of Maryland. Governor Marvin Griffin of Georgia, an "out and out segregationist," was a member of the committee but, according to Whitman's notes, "refused to attend the conference because he said the President had broadened the scope to include the entire integration question, whereas all he wanted to discuss was the Little Rock issue." Hagerty, Adams, and John Howard Pyle, the White House liaison with the governors, were to attend. Brownell, so despised by the southern governors, would be available in Adams's office if needed.[50]

The president was cranky and frustrated as he prepared for the meeting with the southern governors on Tuesday, October 1. Arthur Larson, a special assistant and speechwriter, recorded that Eisenhower, in that agitated mood, fumed about the effects of the Supreme Court's desegregation decision on his presidency and growled that "he thought it was wrong." He said that he wanted to avoid pushing for integration in the meeting and, Larson's notes record, stick with "his constitutional duty of seeing that lawful court orders are obeyed."[51]

Having vented his frustrations to Larson, Eisenhower strode resolutely into his office, greeted the governors, and enunciated a position that echoed precisely the legal principles he and Brownell had agreed upon: "The 1954 decision of the Supreme Court relating to public school integration is now the law of the land." As president, he was "duty bound to see that it is carried out whenever and wherever a District Court of the United States acts to implement that decision." Eisenhower asserted that governors are sworn to uphold the Constitution and that, "under a pretext of maintaining law and order, no State Governor can interpose military force or permit mob violence to occur so as to prevent an order of a Federal court from being carried out." Governor Faubus had done just that in Little Rock. Eisenhower concluded: "In such a case the obligation of the President under the Constitution is inescapable." Eisenhower said he would withdraw troops if the governor and state authorities met their responsibilities. He had crossed out language in his prepared notes that would require Faubus to "permit the Negro children to attend Central High School," and he adhered to his legalistic line that demanded virtually the same thing, insisting that Governor Faubus not cause any "obstruction to carrying out the orders of the United States District Court."[52]

After talking with Eisenhower, the governors conferred separately and again engaged in the endlessly unrewarding exercise of drafting a statement for Faubus to sign. Faubus later remembered that "they called me, I don't know how many times that day, and then they read a statement they wanted me to issue." The statement read: "I now declare that I will assume full responsibility for the maintenance of law and order and that the orders of the Federal Court will not be obstructed." Brownell thought that such a statement would communicate honorable intent on the part of the Arkansas governor, and Eisenhower approved it. If Faubus issued the statement as drafted, the president said he would direct the secretary of defense to withdraw the troops and return control of the Arkansas National Guard to the governor. Implementation awaited the formal release of the statement in Little Rock.[53]

After Faubus's previous deceptions, why would either Eisenhower or Brownell think that they could trust him now? Or did they endorse the statement in full confidence that Faubus would never really agree? Everyone waited for Faubus to respond. According to Adams, "It was a long wait." That evening the president and Mrs. Eisenhower attended a dinner at the home of Secretary of State Dulles honoring Charles Wilson, the retiring secretary of defense. Finally, the statement came from Little Rock, and Adams interrupted the dinner to inform Eisenhower.

At 8:30 P.M., Eisenhower, Adams, Hagerty, Brownell, and Pyle reviewed the telegram. Faubus wrote: "I now declare that upon withdrawal of federal troops I will again assume full responsibility, in cooperation with local authorities, for the maintenance of law and order and the orders of the Federal Court will not be obstructed by me." The four men quickly concluded that the governor had resorted to another devious ploy. Faubus had appended to Eisenhower's approved statement—"I now declare that I will assume full responsibility for the maintenance of law and order"—a phrase stipulating "upon withdrawal of federal troops." Eisenhower found two more additions that infuriated him. As he stated in his memoirs, "This wire was worthless: the word 'again' gave Faubus an escape route to his earlier means of 'keeping the peace,' namely, stationing the National Guard around the school to keep the Negroes out; the words 'by me' suggested that he might willingly let others do the obstructing."

Adams recalled that the governors were "nonplussed" at Faubus's response. Governor McKeldin accused Faubus of "double-crossing" the committee. Eisenhower, Adams, and Hagerty prepared a response that was released that night:

> The statement issued this evening by the Governor of Arkansas does not constitute in my opinion the assurance that he intends to use his full powers as Governor to prevent the obstruction of the orders of the United States District Court. Under the circumstances, the President of the United States has no recourse at the present time except to maintain Federal surveillance of the situation.

Brownell was not surprised. He had fully expected Faubus to be as deceitful as he had been in Newport. Perhaps Brownell and Eisenhower never intended to withdraw the troops. They may have used the governors to set up Faubus for another public demonstration of his duplicity. The press jumped on the perception that Faubus "broke faith" with the governors' committee. On Wednesday, October 2, Faubus held a news conference at which he refused to alter his position.[54]

The President and the Press

On October 3, a weary Eisenhower faced the press, hoping "to play down the Little Rock situation, to be as quiet as possible about it." But reporters bombarded the president with questions about the "impasse" in Arkansas. Eisenhower described two conditions that could lead to the withdrawal of the troops. One would be "satisfactory and unequivocal assurances that the orders of the Federal Court would not be obstructed, and that peace and order would be maintained in connection therewith." The second would be "peaceful conditions" that would allow the local police to say: "There will be no difficulty that we can't control in the carrying out of this court's orders."

Then Eisenhower returned to his legalistic theme—that this matter was about obeying the law, not desegregation. "The problem grew out of the segregation problem," he remarked, "but the troops are not there as a part of the segregation problem. They are there to uphold the courts of the land under a law that was passed in 1792." Eisenhower insisted: "That is why they are there, and for no other purpose, and it is merely incidental that the problem grew out of the segregation problem."

Eisenhower, when pressed, refused to say that he would not use troops again in any comparable situation in the South, deriding the question as "hypothetical." Then a reporter asked a tough question about the president's leadership: "Sir, you probably are aware that some of your critics feel you were too slow in asserting a vigorous leadership in this integration crisis. Do you feel, sir, that the results would be any different if you had acted sooner instead of, as your critics say, letting things drift?" Eisenhower shot back: "I am astonished how many people know exactly what the President of the United States should do." That retort drew laughter. Eisenhower denied that he had acted indecisively. He contended that his administration had studied the problem from the time the Supreme Court made its decision in 1954—implying that the administration's strategies had been planned years in advance. In response to another question, Eisenhower replied: "No one can deplore more than I do the sending of Federal troops anywhere."

Journalist Sarah McClendon pressed the president: "Sir, you said yourself that you can't legislate emotions; and, as you just said, it isn't good to use troops; and you said that we need education, and you said a while back we needed patience. We saw patience did not work. Now, what will you do? Many people are asking, what will you do?" Eisenhower's response was tentative: "I don't know really much more that can be done." He explained that he had written church leaders and had met with educators and the southern governors' group. "Now," he said, "the leadership of the White House can be exercised only, as I see it, through giving the convictions of the President and exhorting citizens to remember America as well as their own private prejudices." Eisenhower missed another chance to elaborate on his personal convictions and address, in ringing moral terms, those "private prejudices" about race.

The president was eloquent about the courts, however. "These courts are not here merely to enforce integration," he said. "These

courts are our bulwarks, our shield against autocratic government."
Then Eisenhower pronounced his vision for the future.

> There is a very great division on the destiny of the races in
> the United States, how they should act, particularly when we
> come into the social aspects of our lives as opposed merely to
> the economic and the legal. But those quarrels will—as some
> others in the past in our country—eventually be settled. But
> we will, the population itself on the whole, will remember its
> respect for law, and it will be settled on that basis.[55]

Eisenhower's responses to the reporters' questions were unin-
spiring. He seemed to have no blueprint for his next steps. This was
a tired man who had traveled to Newport for a vacation a month
earlier and had returned to Washington more exhausted than ever.

Adding to the president's burdens, Little Rock was shoved off the
front pages on October 4 by news that the Soviet Union had successfully launched a satellite into space. "Sputnik" immediately altered
the international landscape and the preoccupations of the public.
Eisenhower was still thinking about Little Rock as he prepared for his
next news conference on October 9 (he reviewed the FBI reports and
expected to answer charges that Faubus had made about soldiers entering girls' dressing rooms). Eisenhower also anticipated questions
about the army alert that he had countermanded on September 26.
But Sputnik I, not Little Rock, commanded the reporters' attention
that day, and Little Rock was hardly mentioned.[56]

Withdrawing the Troops

By early October, the president's political opponents had successfully spread the perception that, despite his extraordinary intervention in Little Rock, Eisenhower had acted indecisively. On October
3, a reporter had quoted those critics as saying that Ike was guilty of
"letting things drift" until he had run out of options. Adlai Stevenson called the Little Rock crisis a "disaster" and concluded, somewhat condescendingly, that "at this point the president had no
choice" but to use troops.[57]

Senator Hubert Humphrey, unlike some of his Democratic colleagues, supported Eisenhower's action in Little Rock and wrote a
friend on October 14 that the president had acted "under statutes
approved by the Congress, and which are compatible with the Constitution." But Humphrey reinforced the allegation of Eisenhower's
indecisiveness, a myth that would become the conventional wisdom
for historians of the Little Rock crisis. "I only regret," Humphrey
wrote, "that the President was so slow in grasping the true nature of
the situation that troops had to be called out." The Democratic Party's Advisory Council, which included Stevenson and Truman, declared on October 21: "The failure of President Eisenhower to take
an early and firm position for observance of the provision of the
Constitution and laws of the United States has been substantially responsible for the trouble at Little Rock." The council made no mention of Governor Faubus, the Democrat who had precipitated the
crisis.[58]

To Eisenhower, the charge that he had mismanaged the crisis
was incomprehensible. Years later, he still resented the criticism
from "some of the great liberals—the Democratic Advisory Committee or whatever they called it." In a 1967 interview, Ike noted that
President John F. Kennedy had "the same problem" at the University of Mississippi in 1962. Kennedy, he grumbled, "had a couple of
people killed, but the Democratic Advisory Committee didn't say a
damn word about it."[59]

But there were limits to what Eisenhower could do. Just after
Eisenhower sent the troops into Little Rock, Senator James Eastland
of Mississippi told a white citizens council meeting that Eisenhower
had "lit the fires of hate between the races." Eastland's strategy for
confronting this new federal aggressiveness in law enforcement was
to simply wait until the government withdrew its troops. "The use of
an army will not win," Eastland said, "because the soldiers cannot
stay in Little Rock all the time."[60] That was true. The president could
not maintain an endless occupation of even one school—Central
High School in Little Rock—let alone send troops to every other
school in the South.

On October 14, his sixty-seventh birthday, Eisenhower phoned
Brownell and discussed the possibility of withdrawing the 101st divi-

sion if General Edwin Walker believed that the local authorities could maintain order. That afternoon, Eisenhower met with Brownell, Brucker, and the military leaders. Ike wanted to move rapidly and considered withdrawing the troops to "see what happens." The group finally agreed to withdraw half of the 101st, keep 1,800 National Guard troops under federal control, and release the rest to Arkansas. On October 23, the African-American students were able to leave Central High without military escort. Three weeks later, the National Guard assumed control of the Central High School area. Eisenhower agreed on November 18 to withdraw the remaining 101st division units by Thanksgiving.[61]

Tuesday, November 19, was "Equal Opportunity Day," the anniversary of Lincoln's 1863 Gettysburg Address. Eisenhower issued a statement, repeating Lincoln's words, that "it is altogether fitting and proper" to use this anniversary "to rededicate ourselves to the firm establishment of equal opportunity for all."[62] On November 25—just as the last of the 101st Airborne Division soldiers prepared to depart from Little Rock—Ann Whitman walked into the Oval Office and found Ike slumped over his desk, muttering incoherently. The president had suffered a stroke.[63]

CHAPTER TEN

Rising Expectations

There is no chance that there will be great divergences between
what the Attorney General expresses and what I believe.
—PRESIDENT DWIGHT D. EISENHOWER COMMENTING
ON THE JUSTICE DEPARTMENT'S BRIEF FOR *COOPER V. AARON*,
AUGUST 27, 1958

The president of the United States missed a state dinner for the King of Morocco on November 25, 1957, reportedly due to "a chill." Later, the White House revealed that Eisenhower had suffered a "cerebral arterial occlusion," a "slight stroke." In the weeks after his intervention in Little Rock, Eisenhower's stresses had multiplied. On October 23, his trusted civil rights advisor, Herbert Brownell, resigned, citing "family obligations and professional commitments." The president's "very deep regret" in his response was heartfelt: the New Yorker had been both his political strategist and his conscience on civil rights. For Ike, Brownell was nearly irreplaceable.

Eisenhower nominated Brownell's deputy, William Rogers, to succeed him. Rogers's liberalism would hardly mollify the South. Another New Yorker, he had been with Brownell since 1953, and the *New York Times* found "no hint of disagreement between them," although their personalities and management styles were distinctive. Rogers would never be as close to Eisenhower as Brownell had been.[1]

The administration planned no new civil rights proposals for

1958; the Justice Department was intent on implementing the Civil Rights Act of 1957. Without Brownell's assistance, Eisenhower struggled with filling the membership of the Civil Rights Commission that the act had created. Ike invited Adlai Stevenson to serve, but he declined. Eventually, the commission's six members included three southerners and one Negro, the assistant secretary of labor, J. Ernest Wilkins.[2] Eisenhower selected retired Supreme Court Justice Stanley F. Reed, a Kentuckian and a Democrat, to chair the commission—a symbolic appointment because Reed had participated in the *Brown* ruling in 1954. A month after his nomination, the former justice panicked and withdrew, fearing his appointment would diminish "respect for the impartiality of the Federal judiciary" and be "incompatible with my obligations as a judge." Reed's successor was John Hannah, the president of the University of Michigan, who, as assistant secretary of defense, had helped Eisenhower desegregate the armed forces.[3]

Eisenhower nominated another northerner to lead the new Civil Rights Division in the Justice Department. W. Wilson White, a Philadelphia native, had headed the Office of Legal Counsel in the Justice Department and was a controversial nominee. His office had prepared the legal brief President Eisenhower used to justify sending troops into Little Rock. The Senate Judiciary Committee held up White's appointment for nine months.[4]

Ike confided to his brother Arthur in early November that the preceding months had been a period of "steadily mounting crises and pressures, culminating in the Little Rock situation" and the Soviet space satellite. "When I wake up in the morning," he wrote, "I sometimes wonder just what new problem can possibly be laid on my desk during the day to come; there always seems to be an even more complex one than I could have imagined." His September vacation in Newport had been "hardly worthy of the name."[5]

Eisenhower complained to Swede Hazlett on November 18 that he had failed to convince southerners that he was just trying to enforce the law in Little Rock. "The biggest worry of all," Eisenhower wrote, "is the constant question of 'doing the right thing.'" Ike told Hazlett that "physically I seem to stand up under the burden remarkably well. Yesterday I think the doctor said my blood pressure was 130 over 80 and my pulse something on the order of 66." A week later, Eisenhower suffered the third major illness of his presidency.[6]

Eisenhower delivered his sixth State of the Union address on January 9, 1958, without uttering a word about civil rights—a remarkable omission in view of his action in Little Rock. On January 15, Eisenhower held his first news conference since the stroke. A reporter asked about his health and Eisenhower insisted that he felt "very well indeed." He said that the past five years had not been "very much rougher than I anticipated." When asked about Little Rock, Eisenhower expressed hope that local officials would maintain order so the National Guard, still under federal control, could be withdrawn.[7]

Rising Black Expectations

Eisenhower, already adjusting to Brownell's departure, lost another key player on his civil rights team on April 24. Max Rabb, the president's liaison with black appointees, NAACP leaders, and Adam Clayton Powell, Jr., resigned. The next morning, Sherman Adams called Frederic Morrow into his office and told him that "the President has agreed that from this point you will handle all correspondence and problems coming into the White House dealing with Civil Rights and Negro Affairs." Morrow was uncomfortable with this new role, feeling that he had become the "house captive," an embarrassing position vis-à-vis his black constituency.[8]

In May, Eisenhower decided it was time to get the Little Rock episode behind him. The remainder of the federal troops had been withdrawn on November 27, 1957, two days after the president's stroke. On Thursday, May 8, 1958, he announced that the National Guard would leave Central High School at the end of the school term on May 28. Eisenhower expressed his hope "that state and local officials and citizens will assume their full responsibility and duty for seeing that the orders of the Federal Court are not obstructed."[9] On May 27, the day before the National Guard was scheduled to depart, Ernest Green would become the first black student to graduate from Central High School, joining six hundred senior classmates in commencement ceremonies.[10]

The week after his announcement, Eisenhower sparred with reporters regarding school desegregation. May Craig, a Washington
correspondent for Gannett newspapers, asked whether the president intended to follow the Little Rock pattern in other states resis-
tant to desegregation. Eisenhower asked what she meant: "Sending
in Federal troops," she replied. "For what?" the president snapped.
"As you said, to obey a court order," she responded. Eisenhower
seized on that phrase: "That is right, to obey a court order; and that
is the point. I did not send troops anywhere because of an argument
or a statement by a governor about segregation. There was a court
order, and there was not only mob interference with the execution
of that order, but there was a statement by the Governor that he
would not intervene to see that that court order would be exercised." Eisenhower refused to rule out the use of troops if comparable circumstances arose. "Now, what is a President going to do? That
is a question you people answer for yourselves. I answered it for
myself." As the *New York Times* reported, "It was made plainer than
ever today by President Eisenhower that he would use his full powers
whenever necessary to enforce school integration orders of the Federal courts."[11]

Morrow's first major responsibility, after assuming Rabb's duties,
was to complete arrangements for the president's address to the National Negro Publishers Association in Washington on May 12.
Morrow tried to prepare the president for this difficult audience,
warning him about phrases that might be offensive, like "you
people."[12] The event started auspiciously, with thunderous applause.
The association cited Eisenhower for "the prestige and power he
has used in behalf of civil rights." Eisenhower told the group that
every American "must have respect for the law. He must know that
he is equal before the law. He must have respect for the courts. He
must have respect for others." He repeated his homily that the problems of discrimination could not be solved by law alone, "because
they are buried in the human heart."

Then, laying aside his notes, Eisenhower took off his reading
glasses and talked informally about the need for Negroes to practice
"patience and forbearance." At the word, "patience," Fred Morrow
felt sick and wished he could slip out of the auditorium. That eve-

ning, Roy Wilkins, the NAACP's executive director, fiercely attacked the president for his counsel of "patience." Thurgood Marshall, responding to Eisenhower's remarks about the limits of law, asserted that such statements ignored the fact that "the whole racial structure in the South was created by law." Law "kept whites and Negroes apart. And these barriers should be removed by law."[13]

Jackie Robinson, who had courageously integrated major league baseball, reacted angrily. On hearing the word "patience," Robinson said he felt like standing up and shouting, "Oh no! Not again!" Negroes, he wrote Ike, had been "the most patient of all people." They could not "wait for the hearts of men to change." Robinson concluded: "You unwittingly crush the spirit of freedom in Negroes by constantly urging forbearance and give hope to those pro-segregation leaders like Governor Faubus who would take from us even those freedoms we now enjoy."

Eisenhower was nonplussed at this reaction; he did not intend "patience and forbearance" to substitute for action. Ike had tried to speak from the heart, to communicate that he was doing all he could, but he was not tuned in to black sensitivities amid rising expectations. "I am firmly on record," the president wrote Robinson, "as believing that every citizen—of every race and creed—deserves to enjoy equal civil rights and liberties, for there can be no such citizen in a democracy as a half-free citizen." Robinson shot back that many black leaders and the masses believed "that you favor patience alone rather than patience backed up when necessary with law enforcement."[14]

Eisenhower's use of a single word—"patience"—had caused listeners to forget that, a few months earlier, he had sent troops into the South to enforce a court order for school desegregation.

A Meeting with Black Leaders

Eisenhower stumbled rhetorically in part because he rarely talked with blacks. In the 1950s, excepting some ceremonial occasions, it was unprecedented for Negro leaders to sit down with a president for serious policy discussions. The demand that Ike hold such a meeting with African-American leaders already had a tortured history. In July 1957, Max Rabb had promised a meeting with the president to Martin Luther King, Jr., once the Civil Rights Act was passed. When Eisenhower had met with Governor Orval Faubus on September 14, 1957, Adam Clayton Powell, Jr., had complained to the press that the president met "only with white persons on the South's school integration problem." Roy Wilkins was just as sarcastic: "When you were troubled over the expressed views of Senator Richard B. Russell on the civil rights bill you granted him a hearing. When you were troubled over the actions of Governor Orval E. Faubus of Arkansas, you granted him a hearing." Richard Nixon had interceded with the president after calls from Wilkins and Jackie Robinson, and Eisenhower agreed to schedule a meeting with black leaders.[15]

Eisenhower's aides quickly discovered how contentious the guest list for such a gathering could be. On the same day that the president sent troops into Little Rock, Robert C. Durham, a New York Republican, urged the White House to avoid including Martin Luther King, Jr., "as well as anyone from the NAACP." The staff repeatedly changed the date for the meeting. First, it was scheduled for October 15, but Jackie Robinson, apparently thinking of Little Rock, recommended waiting "until everything is normal." On October 17, Powell, thoroughly frustrated, wired the president that more than a month had passed since he was promised a meeting, and "the situation is deteriorating hourly." Powell was assured by Sherman Adams "that the meeting you mentioned is going to be held, and further that it will be held at the earliest date deemed advisable by the President." Rabb, after talking with Wilkins and Powell, determined that the meeting should be delayed until November. On November 5, Martin Luther King, Jr., and SCLC leaders commended President Eisenhower for his stand in Little Rock but argued that the crisis "points a dramatic finger to the urgent necessity for the President to confer with Negro leaders from across the nation." By then, the staff was planning for the meeting "sometime late in November." But Eisenhower took ill on November 25. As a result, the gathering was indefinitely postponed.[16]

The following year, Martin Luther King, Jr., attempted to end the impasse. On May 29, 1958, the twenty-nine-year-old King wired the president that due to "continued violence in the south and the dreadful prospect that some areas may close schools rather than obey federal court orders to desegregate in September, we urgently renew our request that you grant an immediate conference to Negro leaders in an effort to resolve these problems." King reminded Eisenhower of his promise "quite sometime ago."[17]

Eisenhower responded this time. Sherman Adams asked Rocco C. Siciliano, the president's special assistant for personnel management, to review the question of a meeting, assisted by Frederic Morrow. He, Morrow, and Lawrence Walsh, the deputy attorney general, met with King on June 9. They eventually agreed that the meeting should include King; A. Philip Randolph, founder of the Leadership Conference on Civil Rights (LCCR); Roy Wilkins, executive director of the NAACP; and Lester Granger, head of the Urban League, but not Adam Clayton Powell, Jr., who had been indicted the previous month for income tax evasion. In addition to Eisenhower, Attorney General Rogers, Morrow, and Siciliano would attend. The meeting was set for Monday, June 23 at 11:15 A.M.[18]

As the meeting began, Randolph handed the president a written statement and commended the president for his action in Little Rock. He stated, according to Siciliano's notes, that the group had "the firm conviction that the President was a man of courage and integrity who had shown leadership and had brought about accomplishment in this field."

The leaders asked Eisenhower for aggressive actions, including a White House conference on the enforcement of school desegregation, stronger civil rights legislation, and Justice Department intervention to investigate bombings in the South. The group implored the president to make it clear "in statement and act that he believes in the principle that federal money should not be used to underwrite segregation in violation of the federal constitutional rights of millions of Negro citizens." These proposals groaned with the constitutional issues that had plagued Eisenhower's efforts. Martin Luther King, Jr., expressed his belief that such actions would "mobilize the emotions of the spirit which, in turn, would aid in the fight for abolishment of segregation." Roy Wilkins praised Eisenhower's efforts with the armed forces and the civil rights bill. To him, the right to vote was the "most effective and bloodless way" to address the issues. Granger confronted Eisenhower with the rising expectations in the black community; blacks increasingly felt that, despite some earlier progress, "suddenly, it appears stopped." This, he asserted, was the reason for the angry response to the president's call for "patience" in his May 12 address.

After listening at length, Eisenhower spoke; his words reflected the perceptual gulf between the president and the Negro leaders. According to Siciliano's notes, Ike said he "was extremely dismayed to hear that after five and a half years of effort and action in this field these gentlemen were saying that bitterness on the part of the Negro people was at its height." Ike wondered if more action would produce only more bitterness. Granger assured the president that the anger was not directed at him but at the communities where there was resistance. Eisenhower reinforced "the need for diligent and careful perusal by the Federal Government of any actions in this field." Rogers affirmed that the president had asked him to take "aggressive actions in all matters affecting the Federal Authority."[19]

The next day, the *New York Times* ran a page one picture of the president with the Negro leaders. Siciliano provided the president with an upbeat assessment. The men had been "more than enthusiastic about their reception, the length of time granted for the meeting, the willingness to be heard and the willingness to speak, and the intense and sympathetic attention given them." He characterized their interaction with the press after the meeting as "faithful and honest." Siciliano concluded: "I am convinced that this meeting was an unqualified success—even if success in this area is built on sand."[20]

The president's agenda in mid-1958 included much more than civil rights. The Middle East was in turmoil. On July 14, a bloody military coup took place in Iraq. On July 15, Eisenhower dispatched five thousand American troops to Lebanon to counter what the administration called "indirect aggression" promoted by the Soviet Union.[21] Besides managing the crisis in Lebanon, he was contemplating a summit meeting in the United States with Nikita Khrushchev, the premier of the Soviet Union.

But the plight of black Americans constantly intruded on the president's global concerns. On August 5, J. Ernest Wilkins came to the White House to counsel with Eisenhower about the Labor Department position to which Ike had appointed him. Wilkins had been Eisenhower's favorite black appointee; Ike had appointed him to serve as assistant secretary of labor, as vice chair of the President's Committee on Government Contracts, as a member of the President's Committee on Government Employment, and as the sole Negro on the Civil Rights Commission created by the 1957 Civil Rights Act. The Negro press was alleging that Secretary of Labor James P. Mitchell was trying to force Wilkins to resign so the son of Henry Cabot Lodge, Jr., the United States ambassador to the United Nations, could have his position. Ann Whitman's notes described Wilkins that day as "very emotional (he had been ill)." Later that month, Eisenhower admitted to the press that he and Wilkins had held a conversation about his possible resignation, but "I have never urged him to nor asked him to, or anything else." It is unclear whether Wilkins's situation reflected racial bias in the Department of Labor, his rapidly declining health, or some mixture of the two. Wilkins resigned three months after consulting with Eisenhower and he died on January 19, 1959.[22]

The day after Eisenhower's consultation with J. Ernest Wilkins, a reporter asked him about school desegregation and whether the president had plans to address racial tensions as the new school year approached. Eisenhower asserted that "mere law will never solve this problem." He lamented that "if I could think of anything I thought would be effective in August or in the 2 or 3 weeks before the schools start, why, I certainly shouldn't hesitate to do it."[23]

Another Little Rock Intervention?

Eisenhower could not put Little Rock behind him; Governor Faubus was still blocking desegregation. Faubus finally found a federal judge who would do his bidding. At his urging, on February 20, 1958, the Little Rock school board had appealed to Judge Harry J. Lemley, serving the eastern district of Arkansas, for a moratorium on desegregation to avoid violence. Lemley ruled on June 21, 1958, that Little Rock could suspend school integration for two and a half years, meaning that the few black students attending Central High School would be forced to return to a colored school. NAACP lawyers immediately filed suit with the Eighth Circuit Court of Appeals in St. Louis, and Wilson White, as acting head of the Justice Department's Civil Rights Division, joined in that appeal. The case was labeled *Cooper v. Aaron,* named for the chairman of the Little Rock school board and John Aaron, a Negro student in the suit.[24]

The possibility of military intervention again in Little Rock beclouded the confirmation hearings for W. Wilson White, who was awaiting Senate approval as assistant attorney general for civil rights. In July, Senator John McClellan (D-Arkansas) pressed White on whether the government might again use troops in Little Rock or elsewhere. White said that the Justice Department did not want to enforce school integration "at the point of a bayonet." McClellan insisted: "Can you say it will not happen?" White responded that, while it probably would not happen, he could not rule out the use of troops. The situation grew tense when Governor Faubus won an overwhelming victory in the Democratic primary election, a guarantee of general election victory, on July 29 by campaigning on his determination to continue to fight federal court–ordered desegregation.[25]

Eisenhower and Rogers desperately wanted to avoid military intervention again in Little Rock, but they planned for every contingency. On August 18, assuming the court of appeals would reverse Lemley, Rogers told the president that "the principal objective of the plans of the Department is to avoid the necessity for use of military forces at the school." Governor Faubus's reelection campaign that fall and the Lemley ruling had emboldened the opposition. If Faubus called out the National Guard again to block school desegregation, Rogers told Eisenhower, the Justice Department would file a petition with the district court seeking contempt charges. These charges could be tried by the court without a jury as a civil contempt case under the 1957 Civil Rights Act. Heavy fines could be imposed for each day of continued contempt of court. If the Guard was not mobilized but mob violence ensued, the department would file a petition against "known agitators" in Little Rock and the school board, seeking to arrest and convict ring leaders. Again, civil contempt could be tried without a jury. In addition, the local police would be augmented with federal marshals but, Rogers warned the president, "it is not considered feasible for the deputy marshals alone to preserve order against a large and determined mob such as the mob which gathered on September 23 and 24, 1957." The implication was clear—Eisenhower might be forced to use troops again.[26]

Later on August 18, the United States Eighth Circuit Court of Appeals reversed Lemley and ordered that desegregation continue in Little Rock. The court granted a thirty-day stay of its order during which an appeal could be filed with the Supreme Court. The NAACP immediately asked the High Court to vacate that stay, and the High Court scheduled a special session for August 28.[27]

Dwight Eisenhower decided to do something unusual for him— speak out on a court case still in progress. On Wednesday, August 20, the president, dressed in a tan suit with a brown and white polka-dot tie, strode resolutely into his news conference. His countenance was solemn and he carried a written statement. Citing the Eighth Circuit's decision, Eisenhower underlined "the solemn duty that all Americans have to comply with the final orders of the court." The suppression of lawless violence was "the responsibility of each state" and no state could "by action or deliberate failure to act permit violence to frustrate the preservation of individual rights as determined by a court decree." Eisenhower underscored his willingness to use force if necessary: "Defiance of this duty would present the most serious problem, but there can be no equivocation as to the responsibility of the Federal government in such an event." He invoked 1957: "My feelings are exactly as they were a year ago." To emphasize the point, Eisenhower quoted from the speech he gave on September 24, 1957, after sending troops into Little Rock: "The very basis of our individual rights and freedoms rests upon the certainty that the President and the Executive Branch of Government will support and insure the carrying out of the decisions of the Federal Courts."[28]

Anthony Lewis, a *New York Times* reporter, pressed the president on whether "you personally favor the beginning of an end to segregated schools." Eisenhower repeated his dictum—that he was "sworn to one thing, to defend the Constitution of the United

States, and execute its laws." Then, in irritation, Eisenhower stumbled: "I have an oath; I expect to carry it out. And the mere fact that I could disagree very violently with a decision, and would so express myself, then my own duty would be much more difficult to carry out I think. So I think it is just not good business for me to do so." Ike had unwittingly handed his adversaries a phrase—that he might "disagree very violently with a decision"—they could use to argue that he did not support school desegregation.[29]

Despite that verbal miscue, Eisenhower's tone was so uncompromising that the *New York Times* did not misunderstand his message: "This was no casual statement by President Eisenhower today. It was carefully worked out in the Department of Justice with the specific purpose of making clear in advance the determination of the Federal Government to take whatever action is necessary to maintain order and permit compliance with the integration order." The editors concluded that the president intended "no equivocation" about whether he would be willing to use force again.[30]

Orval Faubus was not counting on the Supreme Court to support the Little Rock school board's appeal. He responded to Eisenhower's August 20 statement by introducing bills in the Arkansas legislature on August 26, giving him sweeping powers to close any school desegregated by the federal courts. The legislature authorized the governor to transfer state aid from a closed school to a private institution, approve the transfer of white students in an integrated school to another school, and postpone the opening of the Little Rock schools from September 2 to September 15. If the Supreme Court ruled against him, Faubus now possessed the emergency powers to close the schools.[31]

On Wednesday, August 27, Eisenhower met with the press. A reporter asked if the Justice Department, in response to the Supreme Court's invitation, would present a brief that reflected the president's personal convictions. Eisenhower cited his statement of August 20 and declared: "And I am sure of this: that in the general case there is no chance that there will be great divergences between what the Attorney General expresses and what I believe."

Robert G. Spivak, a reporter for the *New York Post*, pressed the president on "his personal views on school integration," quoting a fellow journalist as saying that Eisenhower "wishes the Supreme Court had never handed down its decision. He also thinks integration should proceed much more slowly. That is what he has told friends in private." Spivak asked if that story was correct. Eisenhower replied, "No, that story is not correct." If he had said anything like "slower," he had meant that it would take "reason and sense and education, and a lot of other developments that go hand in hand if this process is going to have any real acceptance in the United States." Eisenhower reiterated that there were no significant differences between his personal views and those of the Justice Department. "So I would assume that any brief would try to reflect the views that all of us, so far as I know, have held from the beginning." The Associated Press (AP) headed its release: "President Eisenhower gave public indication today that he feels school integration efforts may be moving too fast." Despite that distortion, the AP noted that Eisenhower "denied he ever said he wished the Supreme Court had not made its 1954 decision."[32]

Cooper v. Aaron

The Supreme Court met on August 28, just as Eisenhower was preparing to leave for Newport, Rhode Island. Ike wrote a former assistant that "the specter of a month haunted by school difficulties is always with me."[33]

A *New York Times* article on the High Court's hearing cited the Justice Department's brief—which Eisenhower had insisted reflected his views—noting, "U.S. Opposes Delay in Integration." Thurgood Marshall and J. Lee Rankin, the latter now serving as U.S. solicitor general, argued against the Lemley ruling that would delay desegregation in Little Rock until 1961. Rankin denied that any legitimate argument was possible over the definition of the law. "Is it what the Governor says today or a Senator says tomorrow or a Governor in a neighboring state says the following day? The law is established." Rankin pointed out that "Negroes did nothing to cause this situation," which had been caused by "a relatively small group of people who were opposed to the implementation of this decree of the court."[34]

The attorney for the Little Rock school board quoted the press report alleging that President Eisenhower had said desegregation should move more slowly. "That's exactly what we're asking," Richard Butler argued before the Court, so that in two and a half years, "a national policy could be established." That remark roused Felix Frankfurter, who snarled, "Why aren't two decisions of this court a national policy?" Earl Warren reminded the attorney that *Brown II* had ruled that constitutional rights could not be abrogated by local action. Rankin declared: "This country cannot exist without recognizing that, when the Supreme Court speaks, that is the law." If violent groups could dictate the law, that would send the wrong message to schoolchildren. They should be taught to honor constitutional rights—"not just the rights that I like and want for me, or that you like or want for you, but all of them, for every man and woman." The Court, asking for additional briefs and arguments, deferred its decision until September 11.[35]

Attorney General Rogers anticipated that the justices would uphold the Eighth Circuit's ruling, so he and Eisenhower took steps to prevent violence in the wake of a Supreme Court ruling. On September 7, he released letters to the chairman of the Little Rock school board and to the Little Rock mayor, announcing that the Department of Justice would assist in maintaining order by a "temporary expansion of the present staff of the United States Marshal's office." On September 11—the day the Supreme Court reconvened—the attorney general announced that Judge Lemley, whose ruling had been the flashpoint for the current controversy, had suddenly decided to retire, and that Judge John E. Miller, the federal judge for Arkansas' western district, would replace him. It appeared as if the Justice Department had pressured Lemley, seventy-four and in frail health, to resign prior to High Court action. Rogers also announced that "members of the legal staff of the Department of Justice have arrived in Little Rock, Arkansas, in order to make their services available in connection with the pending school integration litigation." An expanded team of deputy federal marshals would land in Little Rock by Friday morning, September 12, the day the Supreme Court's decision was expected. Eisenhower and the Justice Department had put the opponents of desegregation on notice that forces were in place to thwart their defiance, with federal troops a last resort.[36]

The hearing before the Court on September 11 focused on the purpose of the proposed delay of school desegregation in Little Rock. Solicitor General Rankin extolled the "precious" rights of the Negro children to attend desegregated schools and contended that the students' constitutional rights must be granted "forthwith." Butler argued that the school board was caught between "two sovereignties." Rankin responded that only one sovereignty—the United States government and its Supreme Court—could prevail. "There is nothing to that stuff," he declared, "and that is all it is."[37]

On Friday, September 12, the Supreme Court unanimously denied the Little Rock school board's appeal for delay in the desegregation of Central High School. Recognizing its need to act before the school year began, the Court ruled without issuing a written opinion, which it said it would deliver on September 29. Governor Faubus immediately issued a proclamation ordering the four Little Rock high schools closed the following Monday, when they were scheduled to begin the school year.[38]

In Newport, President Eisenhower issued a statement two hours after the Court's opinion was announced. The president appealed "to the sense of civic responsibility that animates the vast majority of our citizenry to avoid defiance of the Court's orders in this matter." If the courts are defied, he said, "then anarchy results." His statement called on state and local officials to do their "duty" and maintain peace so that "lawless elements will not be able by force and violence" to deny schoolchildren their Constitutional rights. America, he said "is a government of laws. Let us keep it that way." Eisenhower's usual appeal to the hearts of citizens was missing; this time he adhered strictly to the law.[39]

Roy Wilkins applauded the *Cooper* decision because it "makes clear that the basic human rights of individual citizens cannot be abridged or denied, because of threats or violent acts of those who uphold racial discrimination and segregation." Senator Richard Russell insisted that the South would not "surrender to the dictates of the N.A.A.C.P." The segregationists were obsessed by the possibility that Eisenhower might use troops again to uphold the Court's ruling. Ernest Vandiver, the Democratic nominee for governor of Georgia, declared that his state would continue school segregation "regardless of the threat by the Federal Government to send a legion of Federal marshals swarming over us or regardless of the threat to use armed troops against us." Senator McClellan of Arkansas asked: "Is the Supreme Court saying that it, implemented by Federal bayonets, is the 'supreme power' in the land?"[40]

Confronting School Closings

On Friday, September 12—the day of the Supreme Court's decision—Eisenhower returned to Washington from Newport for a round of conferences and to make a statement on the defense of the Nationalist Chinese islands of Quemoy and Matsu. The next day, Eisenhower penned a letter to Nikita Khrushchev concerning the Chinese shelling of Taiwan.[41]

The administration had two options regarding Faubus's order to close the schools. One was to ask the federal district court to hold the governor in contempt of the previous year's ruling by Judge Ronald N. Davies, which had prohibited Faubus from blocking the desegregation of Central High School. The alternative was to encourage a suit by Little Rock residents, which had the political advantage of originating from the community. Eisenhower and Rogers chose the latter. Rogers traveled to Newport on Tuesday, September 16, talked with the president for forty minutes, and issued a statement citing the efforts by citizens in Arkansas and Virginia, whose governor had also closed schools, to file suits designed to persuade state officials to open their schools. Out of respect for those efforts, "the Department is withholding making a decision as to any appropriate legal moves at this time." President Eisenhower, Rogers noted, "authorized the statement in its entirety."[42]

Rogers revealed that seventy-five federal marshals had been recruited for special enforcement work in Little Rock. The *New York Times* reported that the administration hoped for "enough clamor from the parents of children barred from school to bring about a solution of the integration thing." Rogers hinted at military action: he did not "want to leave the impression that we would not at the

same time take whatever appropriate legal steps we could take."
Governor Faubus had signaled that he was willing to hold another
meeting with the president, and when a reporter asked James
Hagerty, the White House press secretary, if he knew the president's
response, he said that the president "hasn't any reaction."

On Monday, September 22, Sherman Adams flew to Newport to
tender his resignation as chief of staff. Eisenhower appointed retired Major General Wilton "Jerry" Persons, Adams's deputy, to succeed him. While Eisenhower and Persons had worked together for
many years, the Alabaman was reputed to be the most reluctant supporter of civil rights in the White House. Frederic Morrow recalled
that, soon after Adams resigned, Persons asked him not to bring
him civil rights issues because "this damn civil rights black business
has broken up my family!"[43]

On Wednesday, September 24, the first anniversary of his ordering troops into Little Rock, Eisenhower publicly supported the parents who had fought school closings. He released his response to a
telegram from J. Albert Rolston, chairman of a committee seeking
to reopen the schools in Charlottesville, Virginia. "I deeply regret
the action of Virginia and Arkansas in closing schools that are subject to integration orders of the Federal Courts," the president
wrote. The impact of such closings on the children and the nation
"could be disastrous." "Most of us in the United States, as part of
our religious faith," he continued, "believe that all men are equal in
the sight of God. Indeed our forefathers enshrined this belief in the
Declaration of Independence as self-evident truth." The nation, he
said, must "constantly strive to achieve this ideal of the equality of
man." The school closings tactic, Eisenhower declared, "represents
a material setback not only in that progress, but in what we have
come to regard as a fundamental human right—the right to a public
education."[44]

Rogers reported to the president on September 25 that the
Little Rock school board had petitioned the district court for authority to lease Central High School to a private corporation, and
that the Justice Department would immediately file a brief opposing
that petition. The attorney general argued that either the Court
should deny the right of the board to lease the high school or, if the

Court decided otherwise, instruct the board that a lease would "explicitly require the operator to permit the Negro students eligible under the School Board's plan to attend Central High School." Rogers called the leasing plan "sham and artifice" to avoid compliance with the Supreme Court's order. In his brief, he argued that the Little Rock Private School Corporation had "no educational experience and no academic accreditation. They own no school, they employ no teachers and they have no financial resources of their own which would permit them to buy or rent a school or employ teachers."[45]

Later on September 25, federal Judge John E. Miller, Lemley's successor, shocked the Justice Department by declining to interfere with the Little Rock school board's plan to lease Central High School, holding that state laws were supreme in this matter.[46] The NAACP, with the Justice Department's support, appealed Miller's ruling to the Court of Appeals for the Eighth Circuit. The circuit court ruled in favor of the NAACP on Monday, September 29, the same day that the Supreme Court issued its written decision in *Cooper v. Aaron*, documenting its verbal mandate of September 12.[47] But neither judicial decision could legally bar Governor Faubus from closing the Little Rock high schools for the 1958–59 school year.

Attorney General Rogers marked a portion of the High Court's opinion for Eisenhower to read: "The constitutional rights of respondents are not to be sacrificed or yielded to the violence and disorder which have followed upon the actions of the Governor and Legislature." The ruling reinforced the Fourteenth Amendment's mandate that no state could "deny to any person within its jurisdiction the equal protection of the laws." The decision was firm in its language: "No state legislator or executive or judicial officer can war against the Constitution without violating his undertaking to support it." The opinion, written by Chief Justice Earl Warren, noted that since *Brown*, three new justices had come to sit on the Court: "They are at one with the Justices still on the Court who participated in that basic decision as to its correctness, and that decision is now unanimously reaffirmed." Each justice personally signed the opinion, underscoring their unanimity in unprecedented fashion.[48]

That day, Eisenhower submitted his final Supreme Court nomination. Again, it was one that would reinforce the unanimous support of *Brown* on the Supreme Court. He appointed another northerner, Potter Stewart of Ohio, a judge on the Sixth Circuit Court of Appeals. Because Congress had adjourned for the upcoming congressional elections, Eisenhower made his third recess appointment to the Court. Stewart openly told the Senate Judiciary Committee the following year that he would not support the overturning of *Brown*.[49]

At his October 1 news conference, Eisenhower read a statement in which he noted that the Supreme Court "once again has spoken with unanimity on the matter of equality of opportunity for education in the nation's public schools." All Americans must "recognize their duty of complying with the rulings of the highest court in the land." Anything else "would be fraught with grave consequences to our nation." Eisenhower celebrated "the concept of equal justice under law" in one of his most idealistic declarations: "We must never forget that the rights of all of us depend upon respect for the lawfully determined rights of each of us. As one nation, we must assure to all our people, whatever their color or creed, the enjoyment of their Constitutional rights and the full measure of the law's protection. We must be faithful to our Constitutional ideals and go forward in good faith with the unremitting task of translating them into reality."[50]

Two days later, Eisenhower wrote Ralph McGill, editor of the *Atlanta Constitution:* "I have had more than the usual number of things on my plate and, of course, one of the principal points of concern has been the series of maneuvers in the integration issue." He agreed with McGill, who in a letter had suggested that it was possible "that the schools must be closed for a period before there is hope of acceptance of the decision." Ike hoped that students themselves, desiring to have their music groups and athletic teams back, would press for a change. Still, he was "heartened by the shrinking perimeter of the area where prejudices of this kind run so deep. This is a difficult period for all of us, but there must, somewhere, be the common sense and the good will on the part of all to bring about a solution."[51]

The 1958 Congressional Campaign

Civil rights was a contentious issue in the 1958 congressional election campaigns. Blacks registered discontent with both parties. A
Cleveland gas station mechanic, changing a flat tire, was asked by a
reporter how he planned to vote. He thought for a moment, then
said: "You really want to know how I'd like to vote? I'd like to vote
for the whole United States Supreme Court, that's how I'd like to
vote. When it comes to this integration and civil rights stuff, neither
party is worth a damn." A survey conducted by the *New York Times*
confirmed an increase in this attitude in six key states—New York,
Maryland, New Jersey, Pennsylvania, Ohio, Michigan, and California—although blacks remained overwhelmingly loyal to the Democratic Party. While Negro voters criticized the Democrats for not
dealing with the segregationists in the South, they were equally critical of President Eisenhower's perceived lack of support for the Supreme Court's 1954 decision. The survey indicated that more blacks
were taking a "put up or shut up" approach to the major parties.[52]

Eisenhower campaigned on his record on civil rights. The Republican Party, he said on October 22, stood for "the universality of civil
rights; that everyone has the same Constitutional rights—economic
and political—in this country that anyone else does, regardless of race
or religion." He cited *Brown* and the 1957 Civil Rights Act's protection
for voting. These laws and rulings could be effective, the president declared, "only as the whole population, in its heart and its intelligence,
understands that this principle of equality is important to the United
States and must be sustained." Harry Truman challenged Eisenhower
on his claims of progress in civil rights. The former president asserted
that "firm and foresighted leadership might accomplish this without
calling on the Army for help," an obvious reference to Eisenhower's intervention in Little Rock. Truman not only accused Eisenhower of
failed leadership, he held the president responsible for the violence
and bombings in the South. Republican spokesmen Senator Clifford
Case of New Jersey and Val Washington of the RNC accused Truman of
"recklessness and irresponsibility" on the civil rights issue. They high-
lighted the schism in the Democratic Party, noting Truman's opposition to the expulsion of Orval Faubus and other segregationists from

the Democratic Party. Val Washington ridiculed Truman's praise for Speaker of the House Sam Rayburn, Lyndon Johnson, and Richard Russell. He complained that Rayburn had never voted for a civil rights bill, Johnson did so only in 1957, and Richard Russell was "perhaps the most dangerous man in the United States Senate as far as Negro rights are involved."[53]

Eisenhower was not a strong party leader, and the 1958 election on November 5 validated that assessment. A Gallup Poll just prior to the election found voters favoring the Democrats 57 percent to 43 percent. The Democrats gained thirteen seats in the Senate for a sixty-four to thirty-four majority, and forty-seven seats in the House, resulting in a margin of 283 to 153.[54]

The White House staff had been determined, following Eisenhower's stroke, to reduce presidential stresses in 1958; that hope had been trumped by events. Turmoil in the Middle East and Eisenhower's landing of troops in Lebanon, controversy over the Soviet Union's apparent lead in space satellites, the Chinese shelling of the offshore islands of Quemoy and Matsu, and other Cold War tensions had demanded his attention and energies. In civil rights, he had received little credit for his military intervention in Little Rock and, despite a landmark Supreme Court decision in *Cooper v. Aaron*, Governor Faubus had closed the city's high schools for the 1958–59 school year. The leaders of Ike's original civil rights team—Herbert Brownell and Max Rabb—were gone, replaced by less experienced personnel. The departure of the immensely competent Sherman Adams, his chief of staff, touched every issue that came to the office of the president.

Eisenhower had been surprised by the rising expectations among Negroes, symbolized by the angry reception to his "patience" speech in May and his June 23 meeting with Negro leaders. Despite continuing tensions in Little Rock, Ike had been able to avoid sending the army into the South again, but he reluctantly concluded, as he had in 1956, that more aggressive legislative action would be essential to racial peace. Eisenhower's strategy for 1959 would be predicated on his previously expressed conviction that if blacks could get the right to vote, then they could protect themselves, and the Republican Party "can stand on that."[55]

CHAPTER ELEVEN

The Final Act

I am deeply sympathetic with the efforts of any group to enjoy the rights of equality that are guaranteed by the Constitution.
—DWIGHT D. EISENHOWER ON LUNCH-COUNTER SIT-INS IN THE SOUTH, MARCH 16, 1960

Despite the Republicans' electoral defeat in 1958, the shift toward the left in the new Congress enhanced the prospects for civil rights legislation in 1959. The closing of schools in Arkansas and Virginia, along with a looming presidential election in 1960, created a more receptive climate. "Neither party," the *New York Times*'s Anthony Lewis suggested, "will want to be caught with a Congressional record of weakness on civil rights just before 1960." The Justice Department was considering legislation, Lewis reported, but "President Eisenhower would have to be convinced before anything went up to the Capitol as an Administration proposal."[1]

Eisenhower was already convinced. He and Attorney General Rogers had decided to transform congressional defeat into an opportunity in civil rights. Eisenhower had promised action to the African-American leaders who met with him in June 1958. Instead of coasting through his final two years in office, Eisenhower reenlisted in the congressional civil rights wars. He had maintained his distance from Herbert Brownell's proposals in 1956; this time the president would lead the charge.

At his first postelection news conference on December 10, 1958, Eisenhower announced that he would ask the new Congress to extend the life of the Civil Rights Commission. In Alabama, officials had refused to cooperate with the commission's investigation of voting irregularities in that state, declining to make voting records available or appear at hearings. Ike called Alabama's defiance of commission requests "reprehensible" and declared: "The right to vote does belong to any citizen that can qualify for the voting privilege, and all of us should stand for that." Five days later, Rogers informed Republican legislative leaders that the president would herald the new program in the State of the Union message. Ike laboriously edited the content of that message, insisting on agreement among his subordinates, despite "a wide divergence of views as to what our civil rights program should be."[2]

On January 9, 1959, Eisenhower discussed equality before the Congress with rare eloquence. He placed American civil rights in the context of global human rights and said that "in voting, in public education, in access to jobs" and other areas of discrimination, the world was "watching our conduct." "The image of America abroad," the president asserted, "is not improved when school children, through closing of some of our schools and through no fault of their own, are deprived of their opportunity of an education." He affirmed that "whenever the supremacy of the Constitution of the United States is challenged I shall continue to take every action necessary to uphold it." For Eisenhower, "every action necessary" continued to include, however onerous, the option of military force.

In his address, the president invoked the Fourteenth Amendment and its guarantee "to every individual, regardless of race, religion, or national origin, the equal protection of the laws." "This inspiring objective" could only be fulfilled "by our leadership in teaching, persuading, demonstrating, and in enforcing the law." Equal justice was essential so "the world will come to know that it is free men who carry forward the true promise of human progress and dignity." "We march in the noblest of causes," Eisenhower declared, "human freedom."[3]

The week after his address to Congress, Eisenhower appeared at the National Press Club, taking questions rather than making a speech. Asked about civil rights legislation affecting school segregation, Eisenhower responded that his first priority was to protect the right to vote. In areas where state authority dominates, "we run into difficulties," he said. "One of them is the closing of schools. To my mind this is tragic." Eisenhower asserted that if black voting rights were protected, that would empower Negroes to address other problems.[4]

The following week, Senate Majority Leader Lyndon Johnson filed his own "conciliation" civil rights bill. Johnson's proposals would establish a community conciliation service, extend the life of the Civil Rights Commission to 1961, empower the attorney general to subpoena witnesses and voting records to investigate charges of voting discrimination, "and make it a federal crime to transport explosives across a state line for the purpose of damaging a business, educational, religious, charitable, or civic building."[5]

Eisenhower and Rogers were prepared to go well beyond Johnson's weak bill. On January 28, Rogers delivered draft legislation to the president that, in the context of the 1950s, was expansive. Similar to Johnson's bill, it called for an extension of the Civil Rights Commission, retention of voting records for three years, and criminal penalties for crossing state lines to engage in bombings. But Rogers's draft asked for strong criminal penalties for "preventing, obstructing, impeding or interfering" with federal court orders protecting the right to vote and the admission of students involved in desegregating schools. The draft also called for statutory recognition of the President's Committee on Government Contracts (dedicated to eliminating employment discrimination), a guarantee of free public education to children of armed forces personnel (addressing off-base segregated schools), and denial of federal aid to school districts that tried to convert public school buildings into private academies.

Other strong provisions of the administration's draft were missing from LBJ's proposals. One would empower the attorney general to sue in court on behalf of any person denied the equal protection of the laws; this resembled part three of the 1957 bill, which part Eisenhower had dropped to placate Richard Russell. Most surprising, another provision would authorize the Department of Health, Education, and Welfare to provide grants to defray the costs of desegregation in states where, on May 17, 1954 (the date of *Brown*), schools had been segregated by law. This proposal, if passed, would constitute an explicit congressional endorsement of *Brown*.[6]

DDE and LBJ

Eisenhower set February 5 as the target date for submitting his legislative proposals in a special message to Congress. Given the thirty-seat Democratic majority in the Senate, Ike needed Lyndon Johnson's cooperation more than ever. In 1957, the majority leader had helped break the logjam on civil rights legislation, but he had coerced the president into dropping part three and had betrayed Eisenhower's trust on the jury trial issue. Ike understood that Johnson, planning to run for president, would want to put his stamp on any new legislation yet make it so weak that it would not alienate his southern colleagues.

On February 2, Johnson—who had suffered a heart attack in 1955, the same year as Eisenhower—was honored in the president's office as "Heart Man of the Year." Eisenhower pulled him aside afterward to discuss civil rights legislation. Johnson complained about the difficulty of dealing with Senator Paul Douglas (D-Illinois), a strong civil rights advocate, on one hand, and James Eastland, the Mississippi Democrat who chaired the Judiciary Committee, on the other. Still, Johnson thought seventy-five senators might support a moderate bill. Afterward, Ann Whitman noted that members of Eisenhower's staff expressed to one another their distrust of LBJ, who they thought was "extraordinarily ambitious" and "trying to get the President to take him off the hook on the issue."[7]

The following day, Eisenhower pushed his own legislative team to support his civil rights program. Republican congressional leaders were reluctant. Charles Halleck, the House minority leader from Indiana, worried about "the dissension created by new legislation." Senator Styles Bridges of New Hampshire feared the civil rights bill could sabotage any attempt to get southern support on the budget. Eisenhower listened quietly, then asserted that "the Administration must advance some moderate and constructive proposal in view of the provisions of our Constitution, the Supreme Court decision, and the large number of citizens not enjoying their proper rights."

While he disliked "arguments and dissension," Ike said that his proposals were "essentially moderate and something the Administration must do." Eisenhower admitted that some provisions might not
pass, but he wanted to spread "a little oil on troubled waters." A
chastened Bridges granted that "submission of the civil rights pack-
age might well be the thing to do." The *New York Times* reported that
the GOP leadership's response to the president's program was
"mixed" but that meeting participants had agreed that "the Executive Branch seemed solidly agreed on the civil rights program."[8]

Eisenhower met again with Johnson on February 4. The majority leader reported that Senator J. William Fulbright (D-Arkansas)
was distressed because he had heard that the president might insist
on enhancing the attorney general's powers. White House staff
members again worried among themselves that Johnson was un-
trustworthy and would "go out of the White House saying that he
was responsible for the Civil Rights message as it went up." But Ann
Whitman observed that Ike had decided that he had "to live with
Johnson."[9]

Eisenhower had learned in 1957 to include provisions he could
trade off for support. So, the president agreed with Johnson to drop
the section enhancing the attorney general's powers, so similar to
part three in the 1957 bill. This would give the majority leader an
early victory he could boast about to his southern allies. Ike himself
laboriously edited the draft special message to eliminate inflammatory language. Eisenhower focused his discussion on a provision for
prosecuting "the use of force or threats of force to obstruct Court
orders in school desegregation cases." While the protection of
voting rights was a priority, the president's message, including the
grants to states to facilitate desegregation, emphasized school desegregation to a striking degree.[10]

Eisenhower's Message

On February 5, three days after his first meeting with Johnson, the
president submitted his message on civil rights to Congress. Eisenhower invoked the Fourteenth Amendment: "Two principles basic
to our system of government are that the rule of law is supreme, and

that every individual regardless of his race, religion, or national origin is entitled to the equal protection of the laws." While progress depended "not on laws alone but on building a better understanding," the president endorsed "the goal of full equality under law for all people." The *New York Times* called the Eisenhower proposals "a broad civil rights program" that "included a declaration of support for the Supreme Court's 1954 decision holding public school segregation unconstitutional." Anthony Lewis noted the administration's commitment "to deal explicitly with the controversial school program" by means of grants that "would pay half of the local bills for pupil-placement, social or other services 'occasioned by desegregation.'" While the language of the bill did not explicitly endorse *Brown,* it still provided "strong psychological support for the implementation of the Supreme Court decision."[11]

A *Times* editorial found the president's proposals too progressive to satisfy Lyndon Johnson and insufficiently radical to satisfy Paul Douglas. Johnson, the editorial writer opined, "had done all he could to avoid the school integration issue. President Eisenhower does not propose to avoid that issue." The majority leader was "sympathetic with those Senators who would rather not obey all the laws of the land and conform to the decisions of the Supreme Court—at least, not right away." The *Times* concluded: "If the President and his supporters in Congress stick to the letter of the principles of yesterday's message, some progress will be made."[12]

Eisenhower knew he faced a difficult fight. He could not trust Johnson and he embraced no illusions about his other Senate adversaries. In a "personal and confidential" letter to Ralph McGill, editor of the *Atlanta Constitution,* Eisenhower called Olin Johnston and Strom Thurmond (both South Carolina Democrats) and James Eastland of Mississippi "not only extreme but rigid" and "so entrenched in the prejudices and racial antagonism that they never show so much as a glimmer of readiness to see the other side of the problem." His legislation provided a chance for "our abler Southern Senators and congressmen to rise to real heights of statesmanship." He hoped that Democrats Spessard Holland of Florida, John Stennis of Mississippi, William Fulbright of Arkansas and Herman Talmadge of Georgia might be flexible enough to promote "the *national* good." At least four others in the southern faction, Eisenhower concluded, were "beyond redemption."

Eisenhower shared two convictions with McGill. "The first of these is that until America has achieved reality in the concept of individual dignity and equality before the law, we will not have become completely worthy of our limitless opportunities. The second thing is that I believe that coercive law is, by itself, powerless to bring about complete compliance on its own terms when in any extensive region the great mass of public opinion is in bitter opposition." But Eisenhower's thinking transcended his usual platitude about the limits of law. "This second fact," he continued, "does not excuse us from using every kind of legitimate influence to bring about enlightenment through education, persuasion, leadership and, indeed, example. Of course, we cannot overlook the need for law, where law is clearly necessary and useful."[13]

The Mack Parker Lynching

In the midst of this legislative struggle, the administration confronted another highly publicized, racially motivated homicide in the South, one comparable to the Emmett Till killing in 1955. Mack Parker, a twenty-three-year-old Negro, had been charged with raping a white woman in Poplarville, Mississippi. On April 24, 1959, forty-eight hours before his trial, a mob of masked men dragged Parker from jail, shot him, and threw his body into a river.

When reporters asked Eisenhower about the case, unlike in 1955 he was not silent. The president deplored Parker's murder and announced that the FBI had found the body. Asked if he thought the lynching indicated the need for federal legislation, since murder was not a federal responsibility, Eisenhower dodged the question: "I know the FBI is on the job and I have every confidence that they and the state authorities will find some way of punishing the guilty, if they can find them."[14]

Because murder was a state crime, the FBI delivered its findings and the identity of the perpetrators to state officials. The Justice Department offered to provide FBI agents to testify before a grand jury, but the agents were never called, nor were witnesses that the

FBI identified summoned to testify. Six months later, the grand jury adjourned without taking action. Attorney General Rogers called this a "travesty on justice" and said that "when the evidence is eventually adduced, I think the nation will be shocked."[15]

Eisenhower and Rogers decided to take an unprecedented step in the face of this injustice. On November 5, the Justice Department announced the convening in Biloxi, Mississippi, of a federal grand jury to inquire into the denial of Parker's federal civil rights, justifying the action by citing laws passed shortly after the Civil War. Eisenhower hoped the grand jury, impaneled on January 4, 1960, would take action that the state had failed to take, and so expressed himself to Congressman John Dingell, Jr. (D-Michigan). On January 14, the grand jury surprisingly announced that it had found no basis for prosecution in the Mack Parker case. A federal grand jury, organized in the Deep South, was still reluctant to act against the perpetrators of a lynching. Rogers called the outcome a "serious injustice" but there was little more that he could legally do.[16]

Eisenhower's Rhetoric

In the face of outrages such as the Mack Parker case, Eisenhower's restrained rhetorical style frustrated civil rights advocates. He constantly preached that law could not change human hearts. While the president believed the maxim, he also expressed it to reassure the white South. Ike had a devious habit of emphasizing the limits of law just when he was seeking new law, as in 1959, or enforcing the law, as he had in Little Rock.

On May 13, a reporter reminded the president that the following Sunday would be the fifth anniversary of the Brown decision and asked for Eisenhower's assessment of the nation's response. Eisenhower once again endorsed the principles of the Supreme Court decision. "I believe," he said, "that the United States as a government, if it is going to be true to its own founding documents, does have the job of working toward that time when there is no discrimination made on such inconsequential reason as race, color, or religion." But then Eisenhower softened his answer by contending that "the real answer here is in the heart of the individual. Just law is not going to do it. We have never stopped sin by passing laws; and in the same way, we are not going to take a great moral ideal and achieve it merely by law. What we must do, all of us, is to try to make a reality in this country the great aspirations voiced by our Founding fathers."[17]

On June 9, Eisenhower addressed the delegates of the National Conference on Civil Rights at the Statler Hotel in Washington. The conference was a gathering of state advisory bodies organized by the Civil Rights Commission, a partial response to the demand of black leaders for a White House conference. In his speech, the president called for "compassion, consideration and justice" and extolled "moral law." "I say moral law rather than statutory law," Eisenhower said, "because I happen to be one of those people who has very little faith in the ability of statutory law to change the human heart, or to eliminate prejudice."[18]

Eisenhower never quite understood the demoralizing effect in the black community of his preachments on the limits of law. He called firmly for obedience to law—as with *Brown* and in Little Rock—yet undermined that demand by asserting how little law could accomplish. Dissatisfaction with Eisenhower's rhetoric abounded, especially in the black press. In response to a *New York Times* survey of black and white clergy in the South, Martin Luther King, Jr., said: "I very definitely feel that the President should state not only that integration is the law of the land but that segregation is morally wrong."

King's comment prompted William Lawrence of the *New York Times* to ask at Eisenhower's July 8 news conference: "Mr. President, have you any opinion as to whether racial segregation is morally wrong?" Eisenhower asked whether the reporter meant segregation due to "local laws." Lawrence replied: "In public facilities." Eisenhower asked whether Lawrence referred to discrimination that would "interfere with the citizens' equality of opportunity in both the economic and political fields?" Lawrence replied, "Yes, sir." Eisenhower replied cautiously: "I think to that extent, that is morally wrong, yes." Eisenhower's careful answer reflected his personal ambivalence with social integration, but he exhibited no comparable discomfort with "the economic and political fields." The *Times* was generous to the president, headlining the page one article about the news conference: "President Condemns Public Segregation."[19]

Hubert Humphrey did not suffer from that kind of rhetorical inhibition. The Minnesota senator knew how to passionately preach what black audiences and white liberals wanted to hear. His fiery speech at the 1948 Democratic convention had led to a walkout of southern delegates. Humphrey's address to the fiftieth anniversary convention of the NAACP in New York City on July 15, 1959, was titled: "Civil Rights: A Moral Issue."

Humphrey was introduced as the "John the Baptist" of the civil rights movement, a "voice in the wilderness." Repeatedly interrupted by applause, Humphrey derided the president's approach: "It is not enough to say that the Supreme Court's desegregation decisions, whether we like them or not, must be obeyed simply because they are the supreme law of the land. More than a question of law enforcement is involved. At stake is a basic moral issue which underlies our very conception of democracy." Humphrey went on to ask: "Do we not have the right then to expect the President and the congress will affirm the great moral principle of human equality and brotherhood by defending the Supreme Court's desegregation decisions on moral grounds?" The senator invoked Franklin Roosevelt, who had said he wanted to be "a *preaching* President." Humphrey roared: "We could use a little *preaching* from the White House right now—preaching the gospel of desegregation because it is right and moral." Without naming the president, Humphrey agreed that "a change of heart" was needed. "But," the senator exclaimed, "it is grievous error to assume that governmental action can do nothing to cause a change of heart." "Keep up the fight," he shouted. "Keep the moral flag of civil rights flying. Together we cannot fail."[20]

The difficulty was not just what Eisenhower said but how he said it. On June 9, Ike had made virtually the same point as Humphrey, espousing the need for "moral law" while Humphrey called segregation "a basic moral issue." At his July 22 news conference, Eisenhower endorsed "equal opportunity, in both the economic and political fields," and extolled his legislative proposals, especially the protection for voting rights, as "the most important of all the legislation proposed." Then he undermined his premise by emphasizing that "progress is not going to be made entirely by law, it's going to be by our own education and understanding and our own regard for moral standards in this world." There was that word—"moral"— yet it did not reverberate for Eisenhower as it did in the oratory of Hubert Humphrey or Martin Luther King, Jr. Humphrey, more than Eisenhower, had "faith in the ability of statutory law to change the human heart." Ironically, the president, despite his words questioning that premise, had introduced legislation designed to do exactly that.[21]

A Small Legislative Victory

By midyear, it was apparent that little of the president's seven-point civil rights legislation could be passed during the 1959 congressional session. In the July 28 Republican legislative leaders meeting, Charles Halleck of Indiana, the House minority leader, noted "a sentiment against any Civil Rights Bill this session and the probability that the House won't stay around for one." Eisenhower continued to fret about lacking options beyond deploying the military to enforce the law. He still wished that "approval could be had of the very moderate provisions suggested by the Administration. Otherwise the Chief Executive would be exposed to such pressures as would make it impossible to maintain a moderate approach."[22]

In the Senate, the Judiciary Committee blocked progress. When the senators constituting the civil rights bloc tried to reprise their 1957 strategy and bypass the committee, the southerners responded by resurrecting the issue they had used to weaken the 1957 bill, demanding a jury trial for any civil rights prosecution. Lyndon Johnson had no intention of revisiting that bone of contention that had so aroused Eisenhower's angry opposition in 1957. LBJ did not want a bill in 1959 and Eisenhower could not pass one without his cooperation. Johnson deserted the civil rights coalition when the southerners, led by Richard Russell, threatened a filibuster that would extend into September when Soviet Premier Nikita Khrushchev was scheduled to visit the United States.[23]

Eisenhower settled for extending the duration of the Civil Rights Commission. He and Johnson agreed to revive the remaining civil rights legislation in 1960. The same day, September 8, that the commission submitted its first report to Eisenhower, the Senate Appropriations Committee voted thirteen to seven to attach a two-year extension of the commission to the foreign aid appropriation bill. In its rush to adjournment, Congress passed the amendment.[24]

The Congress adjourned on September 15. The *New York Times* reported that the session was ending with Eisenhower "in firm control" and that Congress had "either compromised or yielded to a newly aggressive President Eisenhower on a broad range of economic and social issues." The *Times* counted the extension of the Civil Rights Commission as an example of Eisenhower's success.[25]

After Congress adjourned, Eisenhower focused on foreign affairs. The president and Khrushchev met at Camp David September 25–26 and spawned the "spirit of Camp David"—a relationship that bode well for disarmament talks and negotiations over Berlin. Eisenhower was also planning a trip to East Asia to engage in personal diplomacy, but civil rights was still on his mind. At his December 2 news conference, Thomas N. Schroth, from the *Congressional Quarterly*, asked: "Mr. President, do you plan to submit any additional civil rights proposals next year?" Eisenhower, without hesitation, replied: "I do say that I would like to see all the parts of the bill that I submitted last year considered, and if possible, enacted this year." The president wanted a civil rights act in 1960, his final year in office.[26]

The Quest for a Legislative Legacy

Eisenhower could have ended his presidency by focusing on his greatest strength—foreign policy. Instead, he sought to make additional civil rights legislation part of his legacy, confronting an overwhelmingly Democratic Congress in a presidential election year. Despite the frustrations of 1959, some signs were positive. In December, Senate Minority Leader Everett Dirksen of Illinois predicted that "some kind" of civil rights bill would be passed early in the next session. Lyndon Johnson, ready to enhance his presidential credentials, pledged to call civil rights legislation up for debate in mid-February. Senator Estes Kefauver (D-Tennessee) argued for postponing new legislation for two years, the extended life of the Civil Rights Commission, but Eisenhower refused.[27]

Eisenhower's State of the Union address on January 7, 1960, broadly discussed national security, citing diminished tensions with the Soviet Union, American military strength, and a passionate plea for the rich nations to assist the "emerging nations" of the globe. Then the president noted "in certain instances the denial to some of our citizens of equal protection of the laws." "In all our hopes and plans for a better world," Eisenhower stated, "we all recognize that provincial and racial prejudices must be combatted. In the long perspective of history, the right to vote has been one of the strongest pillars of a free society. Our first duty is to protect this right against all encroachment." While there had been some progress, "bias still deprives some persons in this country of equal protection of the laws." Eisenhower cited the legislation he introduced in 1959, and called for those proposals to "be among the matters to be seriously considered in the current session. I trust that Congress will thus signal to the world that our Government is striving for equality under law for all our people." The president had cited equal protection of the laws—the great proviso of the Fourteenth Amendment to the Constitution—three times. "The fissure that divides our political planet is deep and wide," he proclaimed. "We must make clear our peaceful intentions, our aspirations for a better world." "And," the president pointedly added, "we must live by what we say."[28]

Registrars and Referees

The Civil Rights Commission was an independent body, free to investigate and make recommendations without clearing them with the administration. The body's report on September 8, 1959, had included a provocative recommendation—to legally authorize the president to appoint temporary voting registrars in states where there was blatant discrimination against Negro voter registration. In the commission's proposed process, nine or more persons from a county or other subdivision would file affidavits with the president, alleging denial of the right to register due to race, color, religion, or national origin. The president would refer those affidavits to the commission for investigation. If the charges were validated, the president would appoint temporary registrars to enroll voters in that realm. Northern liberals characterized the report as "heartening, constructive, and reasonable." Southern leaders condemned the document even before it was published, labeling the report "shocking, extreme, indefensible, irresponsible, radical, vicious, unconstitutional, and obnoxious."[29]

The commission's proposal to send voter registration complaints directly to the president was problematic; it could flood his office with cases the chief executive could not effectively handle, as well as directly embroil the president in numerous contentious cases. The proposal constituted a clear invasion of states' rights, something with which Eisenhower was uncomfortable.

Yet, Eisenhower and Rogers were forced to recognize the political potency of the proposal for federal registrars. Their original legislative proposal had been weak on specific enforcement provisions for prosecuting voting violations. On Wednesday, January 20, Jacob Javits (R-New York) led a group of senators to visit the president and urged Eisenhower to endorse the registrar proposal. Eisenhower said he "wanted to know more about the Constitutionality of the proposal, but in addition had some real concern about its practicality." Eisenhower warned the senators about trying to pass too many laws and "expressed his belief that if voting rights were protected and exercised a major portion of the task would be accomplished."[30]

Nonetheless, Eisenhower took the senators seriously. After his meeting with them, he asked Rogers to discuss the matter with him. On January 26, a reporter asked the president about the commission's proposal. Eisenhower responded: "The Attorney General has another plan that he thinks, within the framework of existing law, will improve very much the procedures that have been followed."[31]

The key was to work "within the framework of existing law." To Ike and his attorney general, that meant relying on the federal courts. The Supreme Court had prescribed the courts as the proper arena for action in *Brown II*. So Rogers, rather than route complaints of voter intimidation to the president, proposed that charges be filed with a federal district court. If the court found a pattern of discrimination, it could issue an order. The means of enforcing the court's ruling would not be a "registrar" who would replace the duly elected or appointed registrar, but instead a "referee" to investigate whether individuals had been denied voting rights. If the investigation validated the complaints, the referee would ask the federal court to order local election officials to cease the discrimination.[32]

Rogers's solution was politically and legally brilliant. Columnist Roscoe Drummond asserted that the Rogers plan enhanced the possibility of passage: "Those who want to practice voting discrimination against Negroes are not going to thank Mr. Rogers for finding a way to protect voting rights with minimum interference with states' rights." Arthur Krock commended Rogers for devising a plan that "cannot be effectively or long attacked in the courts." Krock wrote that several factions in the Congress might support this provision as part of Eisenhower's larger civil rights bill in an election year because it provided an alternative for Lyndon Johnson, whose southern allies were hostile to the commission's temporary registrar proposal. A *New York Times* editorial suggested that the Rogers plan was stronger than the commission's proposal because its "referees" could ensure that qualified voters were actually permitted to vote, not just register, "on pain of contempt proceedings against recalcitrant officials." The attorney general's plan "would apply not only to voting but also to registration; not only to state but also to national elections. And its enforcement would be through contempt proceedings before a judge, without a jury."[33]

On Tuesday, February 2, Eisenhower asked Republican legislative leaders to support the Rogers plan and repeated "his desire to take a moderate approach in these difficult and sensitive civil rights matters." Rogers asserted that the commission's plan would put the president "in the middle of such situations, especially where there were accompanying problems having to do with State rather than Federal voting." Eisenhower said that his aims were first "to make sure that the Administration is doing whatever might be necessary to carry out the Constitution, and secondly, to have a bill which, while moderate, would be regarded even by the extremists as a definite step forward." Ike assured Republican leaders that, if the matter came up in a press conference, he would express his "full support."[34]

On February 8, Everett Dirksen introduced the civil rights bill in the Senate, including the six sections not passed the previous year, as well as the Rogers proposal for voting referees. Rogers stated that if the southern states acted "in good faith," there would be no need for federal action. The attorney general said that civil rights measures must meet two tests: "Will they stand up under court challenge and will they be effective?" Dirksen was hopeful about passage, although the provisions calling for grants for school desegregation and statutory establishment of the committee on government contracts faced difficulty. Some senators feared that the latter would be "a means of getting an FEPC" (fair employment practices commission), which the southerners had been resisting for decades.[35]

Sit-Ins in the South

As the legislative struggle began, black protestors in the South reminded Eisenhower of the gap between constitutional doctrine and practice in America. On Monday, February 1, four Negro students from North Carolina A&T College had walked into a Woolworth store in Greensboro, North Carolina, sat down at the lunch counter, and waited. An hour later, when the store closed, they had not been served. Frederic Morrow alerted the White House staff that, while there had been sit-ins before, these marked a new trend by focusing on lunch counters in stores, usually a branch of a larger chain that sold other products to Negroes. Given what had happened in the Montgomery bus boycott, the message was clear: provide access to African-Americans or face economic retaliation. Morrow saw three alternatives for the store owners and managers: to maintain segregation that could lead to violence, to eliminate the lunch counters, or to grant equal treatment.[36]

Edward P. Morgan of ABC News asked Eisenhower at his March 16 news conference whether he approved of the "Gandhi-like passive resistance demonstrations of Negroes in the South." Eisenhower responded that "a sweeping judgment" would be difficult. Then he surprised the reporters: "Now, let me make one thing clear. I am deeply sympathetic with the efforts of any group to enjoy the rights of equality that are guaranteed by the Constitution. I do not believe that violence in any form furthers that aspiration, and I deplore any violence that is exercised to prevent them—in having and enjoying those rights." While Eisenhower professed some ignorance about the particular incidents, he concluded "that if a person is expressing such an aspiration as this in a perfectly legal way, then I don't see any reason why he should not do it."

Another reporter asked if Eisenhower perceived any federal role in the lunch counter protests. Eisenhower replied: "So far as I know, this matter of types of segregation in the South has been brought time and again before the Supreme Court." The president continued: "My own understanding is that when an establishment belongs to the public, opened under public charter and so on, equal rights are involved; but I am not sure that this is the case whatsoever. I was talking about demonstrations, of marching in the streets, or any other kind of peaceful assembly that is trying to show what the aspirations and desires of a people are. Those, to my mind, as long as they are in orderly fashion, are not only constitutional, they have been recognized in our country as proper since we have been founded." (These comments contrasted sharply with former president Truman's statement that if any protestor tried to stage a sit-in at a store he ran, "I'd throw him out.") Eisenhower turned to his legislative agenda, distinguishing "a local incident" from the federal government's obligation for "getting the voting rights of a Negro in the South protected and insured." "That is why," he concluded, "we are trying to get a civil rights bill through the Congress."[37]

Ernest Hollings, the Democratic governor of South Carolina, told the president in a telegram that he was "mistaken as to the law" regarding a restaurant owner's obligation to serve any customer, and asserted that Eisenhower's remarks "did great damage to peace and good order in South Carolina." Eisenhower, on advice from Attorney General Rogers, did not respond to Hollings. Brigadier General Benjamin F. Caffey, Eisenhower's army colleague, wrote the president about this "silly lunch counter demonstration business" and concluded: "In my opinion the great bulk of the white people of the South have acted with a great restraint and dignity in this asinine situation." Caffey warned Eisenhower that whites were getting "very restless and the Good Lord only knows what will happen if this business continues."[38]

Martin Luther King, Jr., commended the president in a tele-gram: "Such an affirmation gives new hope to men seeking to move from the long night of oppression into the bright day break of free-dom and human dignity." King assured Eisenhower that the protes-tors were committed to nonviolence, but "non-cooperation with evil is as much a moral obligation as is cooperation with good. And we know that we cannot have self respect or win the respect of others by complacently adjusting to an evil system." Gerald Morgan, Eisen-hower's White House counsel, wrote King on the president's behalf and enclosed quotations from the news conference. On March 30, reporters reminded Eisenhower that Governor LeRoy Collins of Florida had called it morally unjust for store operators to take Ne-groes' money in one part of a store but not serve them at the lunch counter. Eisenhower responded: "I think that eventually the con-science of America is going to give to all of us equal economic and political rights, regardless of inconsequential differences as race."[39]

The Civil Rights Act of 1960

While Lyndon Johnson had been unwilling to confront his southern allies on civil rights legislation in 1959, he still had presidential aspi-rations. As 1960 approached, he and Everett Dirksen, the Republi-can minority leader, had agreed that they would not permit the Judiciary Committee to block civil rights legislation beyond Febru-ary 15. On that date, Johnson bypassed the Judiciary Committee by attaching civil rights amendments to a bill that the House had al-ready passed to permit the Army to lease a barracks as a temporary replacement for a burned-out school in Missouri. In response, the southern bloc, led by Senator Richard Russell of Georgia, launched a filibuster. Johnson and Dirksen agreed to institute around-the-clock sessions starting Monday, February 29, as a strategy for con-fronting the filibustering southerners with what the *New York Times* called "a battle of physical attrition." A full southern filibuster against civil rights legislation had never been broken, although the effort had been made numerous times in the past. Senator Strom Thurmond's filibuster of the civil rights bill in 1957 had been an in-dividual effort, not involving a large group of southern senators.[40]

By early March, the outline of legislation that could be passed was evident. Richard Russell had indicated in debate that the voting rights provisions of the Eisenhower bill were less objectionable to southern senators than the sections addressing school desegregation. The *New York Times* summarized the situation on March 6. Progress in school desegregation had been slow, partly because the Supreme Court had "tried to walk softly on the school issue," but Eisenhower's proposal for federal aid to assist the states in desegregation was in trouble. While the record of the administration was "a matter of sharp dispute," Eisenhower had intervened in Little Rock, desegregated the District of Columbia, and instituted the Civil Rights Commission. The paper hoped that the protection of the right to vote might "be the lever to achieve the general goal of equality for the Negro."[41]

On March 6, Lyndon Johnson declared a Sunday break in debate, saying, "Every man has the right to a Saturday night bath." The Senate had sat 125 hours and thirty-one minutes with one fifteen-minute recess, breaking all previous records. When the debate resumed, a bipartisan coalition of Eisenhower Republicans and northern Democrats, led by Jacob Javits and Paul Douglas, forced Johnson into a vote on ending debate on the bill, which still included most of the original Eisenhower proposals. The motion was defeated 53–42, a clear indication that a voting rights bill was all that could pass the Senate.[42]

At the Tuesday, March 8 meeting of legislative leaders with the president, Senator Thomas Kuchel (R-California) said that "the deadlock will continue as long as the proposed bill contains the provision for grant assistance to certain school districts and the statutory basis for the Government Contracts Committee." Eisenhower responded that he wanted "the essentials that he had originally recommended, and particularly the one big objective of protecting the sanctity of voting," but he would not insist on the grants. Lyndon Johnson wanted to drop the two disputed items, but, the leaders noted, the majority leader "wanted to put the onus for dropping them on someone else since the Northern liberal elements attach so much importance to them." Eisenhower responded that "the Administration proposal was essentially a moderate one," and "if anything at all had to be knocked out, the Administration should not have to be responsible for it."[43]

At their March 15 meeting, the Republican leaders faced reality. The House of Representatives would pass what would become the Civil Rights Act of 1960—a basic protection of voting rights, with Rogers's voting referee plan largely intact—but without the disputed provisions for desegregation grants and legal status for the committee on contracts. Senator Dirksen concluded that if he surrendered on the administration's comprehensive bill and fought for the House version of the bill, they could defeat another southern filibuster.[44]

On March 24, the House of Representatives voted 311–109 to approve a civil rights bill focused on voting, including Rogers's proposal for referees. Lyndon Johnson immediately moved to send the House bill to the Senate Judiciary Committee with instructions to return it to the full Senate within five days. Senator Eastland, the Judiciary Committee chairman, moved to remove the instructions but his motion lost and he was ordered to return the bill to the Senate floor by Tuesday, March 29. On April 1, after angry debate, the Senate voted 69–22 to kill an amendment offered by Senator Kefauver designed to weaken the referee provision.[45]

By April 5, the end was in sight. The weary southerners had ended the filibuster when they learned that the act would be limited to voting rights and the Senate was ready to pass its version of the House bill. Eisenhower cautioned Republican leaders "that any jubilation should be restrained until the bill was finally passed, otherwise premature rejoicing might bring on further filibustering." Northern liberals wrangled over whether the bill was "meaningful." Halleck responded that the discussion about the legislation being "meaningful" was "just so much hogwash." Dirksen agreed that the bill "had plenty of teeth in it."[46]

The Civil Rights Act of 1960 passed the Senate on April 8 by a vote of 71–18. The civil rights coalition, reflecting the Democratic majority from the 1958 election, now numbered forty-two Democrats and twenty-nine Republicans. The eighteen negative votes were cast by die-hard southern segregationists. *New York Times* correspondent Russell Baker credited Senate passage to "the work of

Lyndon Johnson of Texas, the Senate leader whose campaign for the Democratic nomination is expected to benefit from the result." On April 21, the House, although it had passed its version of the bill on March 24, went through the formality of adopting the Senate version by a vote of 288–95.[47]

The act authorized the appointment of voting referees by federal courts in a manner virtually unchanged from the attorney general's original proposal. It required voting officials to retain and protect state voting records for twenty-two months, and make them available to the attorney general to determine if racial discrimination had occurred. District judges could appoint referees in areas where the court found a discriminatory "pattern of practice." If denied registration, a Negro could apply to a referee for registration and, if the applicant was qualified, the referee would certify the black person to vote. A list of certified Negroes would be submitted to the court. Local officials would be notified and given the chance to contest anyone they deemed unqualified. If certification occurred close to an election, the Negro could cast a provisional ballot that would not be counted until the court issue had been decided. With the final decision, the court would notify election officials, and anyone who obstructed a qualified Negro from voting would be subject to contempt of court. The act also guaranteed free public education for the children of members of the armed forces if local public schools were closed, authorized the FBI to investigate "hate" bombings of schools and houses of worship when "there is reason to believe that the perpetrators have fled across state lines," and made it a federal crime for anyone to obstruct a court order by threats or force.[48]

Attorney General Rogers asserted that the legislation demonstrated "that all branches of the federal government firmly support the proposition that the Fourteenth and Fifteenth Amendments of the Constitution are not to be considered mere promises but must become realities for all citizens in all areas of the country." The new law, he said, protected black voting rights at every point in all elections, and empowered the government to "proceed against a state itself, as well as against those state election officials who have violated federal law." Rogers urged citizens to "attempt to exercise those rights" and promised that "the Department of Justice will promptly investigate all complaints of substance, and within the framework of the law, proceed vigorously against those who violate any of its provisions."[49]

At the April 26 legislative meeting, Republican leaders complained that Lyndon Johnson was receiving too much recognition for passage of the bill. The president characterized this as "annoying" but he did not want to make a partisan-sounding statement at a press conference unless the reporters asked a question. "The important thing," he said, "was the actual accomplishment of these things that were needed." Later, Eisenhower asked Jim Hagerty for "a very short statement giving credit to the Republican group regarding the passage of the civil rights bill" to use at his news conference the following day. The question did not arise, as reporters focused on the president's preparation for a summit meeting with Soviet leader Khrushchev in May.[50]

On May 1, the Soviet Union shot down an American U-2 reconnaissance airplane and was holding the pilot, Francis Gary Powers, in Moscow. The White House tried to cover up the espionage by claiming that an unarmed weather-observation plane, piloted by a civilian, had lost its way near the Turkish-Soviet border. A week later, Eisenhower admitted that he had authorized the spy missions. Eisenhower and Khrushchev were scheduled to hold a summit meeting in Paris on May 16. Khrushchev used the U-2 incident to torpedo the summit and cancelled a previous invitation to President Eisenhower to visit the Soviet Union.[51]

In the midst of this international turmoil, Eisenhower signed the last civil rights legislation of his presidency on Friday, May 6. He noted that the act made it "a crime to obstruct rights or duties under federal court orders by force or threat of force." He praised the provisions that dealt with "that key constitutional right of every American, the right to vote without discrimination on account of race or color." While regretting that Congress had eliminated his other recommendations, he called the act "an historic step forward in the field of civil rights" and believed that it would help reach the "goal of equality under law in all areas of our country for all Americans." On May 9, Attorney General Rogers quickly enforced the new act, requesting voting records from one county each in South Carolina, Louisiana, Georgia, and Alabama. If the registrars resisted or the records contained evidence of racial discrimination, the department was prepared to go into court.[52]

The Campaign

The leading candidates for president in 1960 soon became Vice President Richard Nixon and Democratic Senator John F. Kennedy of Massachusetts. At the party conventions, the platforms were battlegrounds for civil rights. The Democratic platform called for every school district to submit a desegregation plan by 1963, authority for the attorney general to file civil injunctions against the denial "of any civil rights on grounds of race, creed, or color" (much like part three of Eisenhower's 1957 proposal, dropped as a result of Lyndon Johnson's pressure), a fair employment practices commission, and permanent standing for the Civil Rights Commission. Nixon pushed the Republican National Convention's platform committee to take an even stronger position. When southern Republican delegates rebelled, Nixon and Governor Nelson Rockefeller of New York reached an agreement that angered party conservatives, especially Senator Barry Goldwater of Arizona, but Eisenhower quietly supported Nixon.[53] The Republican platform called racial discrimination "immoral and unjust." Eisenhower spoke to the Republican convention on July 26 and uttered one sentence on civil rights: "Racial and religious discrimination must be combatted."[54]

Eisenhower still had a card to play on Nixon's behalf. The Congress reconvened on August 8 for a three-week session. The senators—including the new Democratic nominees, John Kennedy for president and Lyndon Johnson for vice president—had barely taken their seats when Eisenhower submitted a special message detailing a twenty-one-point legislative program. Eisenhower, in effect, dared the Democrats to enact much of their own platform. The president called for increased foreign aid, a farm bill, federal aid for school construction, an increase in the minimum wage and medical benefits for older persons, and civil rights.

Eisenhower's civil rights proposal was designed to embarrass the

Democrats. He challenged the Congress to pass the two sections of the administration's proposal that had been deleted in April—the federal grants to states to assist in desegregating schools (effectively endorsing the Supreme Court desegregation decision in *Brown*) and statutory authority for the president's commission on government contracts. The Democrats reacted angrily. Kennedy charged that the president's own party would not support the program. Johnson would not touch a civil rights bill that would expose the schisms in the Democratic Party. He announced he would send the president's civil rights proposals to Senator Eastland's Judiciary Committee, a certain legislative graveyard.[55]

Columnist James Reston described an energetic Eisenhower at his August 10 news conference. Ike was "doing an effective job of commanding the headlines and holding the balance in the debate with the Democratic leaders." A reporter repeated the Democratic charge that the president was using civil rights to make political points. The president responded: "I should like to point out that all this talk about me starting a bunch of new programs is just a little bit silly. Go back and look at what I have been recommending, not only during the months past, but for years in some instances."

Reston, often an Eisenhower critic, was impressed. "The President looked just as brisk as he sounded," the columnist observed. "He was relaxed and ruddy after his recent vacation in Newport, and more combative than usual." "This was not," he wrote, "the non-provocative, programmatic Eisenhower of yore," nor did the president "act like a lame duck who was prepared to hand over the direction of his party and the strategy of the legislative battle to Vice President Nixon."[56]

Lyndon Johnson killed Eisenhower's postconvention civil rights proposal that day. In a straight party-line vote, the Senate voted 54–28 to table the bill. Nixon accused the Democrats of acting irresponsibly, and Johnson responded that the Republicans were attempting to "disrupt" the real agenda of the Senate. Richard Russell led the opposition, arguing that the Republican tactics were a "sure way to kill any legislation in any other area."[57]

On August 16, Eisenhower told Republican legislative leaders that he was ready to end the political games. He believed his administration had "an excellent record on civil rights, that it had made the practical moves that were possible and desirable." The Republicans could carry Texas, Virginia, and North Carolina if "we do not go too far." Senator Thruston Morton of Kentucky, the RNC chairman, asked whether Attorney General Rogers could "desist from making Civil Rights inquiries into southern counties the President had carried in 1956." Eisenhower agreed that this was not the time to do the "spectacular stuff," but some steps could be taken after the election.[58]

Crisis in New Orleans

Ever since 1954, the launching of the school year had precipitated desegregation crises in some southern states. In 1960, in the heat of the presidential campaign, Eisenhower confronted a situation in Louisiana comparable to Little Rock. J. Skelly Wright, a federal judge for the eastern district of Louisiana, had issued an order on May 16 for desegregation to begin in the New Orleans public schools in the fall. The New Orleans school board had planned to integrate kindergarten and first grade beginning September 8, but Democratic Governor Jimmie H. Davis, emulating Orval Faubus, invoked a new state law to take over the Orleans Parish public schools. On Saturday, August 27, a three-judge federal panel of the Fifth Circuit Court of Appeals issued an injunction against the state officials interfering with integration of the New Orleans schools, and the Supreme Court denied the state's appeal. On Wednesday, August 31, Wright, a member of the three-judge panel, granted the school board a delay in implementing integration on the grounds that the turmoil generated by the governor's intervention had prevented the school board from planning for orderly implementation. Although the schools would begin their term on September 8, the school board was authorized to wait until November 14—after the election—to admit Negro students. The Supreme Court denied the NAACP lawyers' request that they overrule Judge Wright's grant of a stay until November 14.[59]

On Saturday, November 12, four days after Kennedy defeated Nixon, Louisiana's superintendent for education, Shelby M. Jackson, announced a school holiday for Monday, November 14, in a desperate attempt to head off desegregation. Attorney General Rogers warned Governor Davis about this action, threatening "to use the full powers of my office to support the orders of the Federal Court." Rogers quoted the president: "The very basis of our individual rights and freedoms rests upon the certainty that the President and the executive branch of government will support and insure the carrying out of the decisions of the Federal courts." The *New York Times* reported that "the president was informed of—and apparently approved" Rogers' warning to Davis. A special Louisiana legislative session approved steps on November 13 to forcibly prevent integration of the New Orleans schools, but Judge Wright issued a restraining order that day prohibiting state interference.[60]

The federal government's manager of this crisis was the assistant attorney general for civil rights, the head of the Civil Rights Division created by the 1957 Civil Rights Act. W. Wilson White, Ike's first appointee, had resigned after a difficult tenure. Eisenhower had replaced White in January 1960 with Harold Russell Tyler, Jr., a liberal New York attorney associated with Governor Nelson Rockefeller and Senator Kenneth B. Keating.[61]

Tyler later recalled that during the crisis, the phone rang, and he heard White House Press Secretary Jim Hagerty's voice. "We're down here in Georgia," Hagerty said, "relaxing and playing some golf." Eisenhower had been reading newspaper accounts of the threats of violence in New Orleans and wanted to talk with the assistant attorney general. Ike took the phone, and Tyler remembered him saying: "Listen, young fellow, I am tired of threats like that and endangering children. If we need to, I will mobilize the eighty-second airborne division troops and send them in." Surprised, Tyler responded that they already had marshals on the scene who could probably handle the situation (the department had created a cadre of seventy-five to eighty riot-trained U. S. marshals as an alternative to using federal troops). Eisenhower continued: "Don't go to General Persons with this kind of thing. He is not in favor of civil rights. Just tell him you need to talk with me about something important. If we have to mobilize the troops, we'll do it. Little Rock was a tragedy and I hoped they learned their lesson. But if they need to learn it again, we'll deal with it."[62]

On November 14, four Negro students attended two New Or-

leans elementary schools for the first time. Two days later, two thousand youths rioted against school desegregation in New Orleans but
police and U.S. marshals handled the situation without federal
troops. After the Thanksgiving holiday, the schools reopened on
November 26 with the four black students still in attendance. Eisenhower's campaign for alternatives to using the army had borne fruit,
embodied in the mobilization of the Justice Department's special
cadre of U.S. marshals. According to Tyler, the president had been
willing to use troops again, as much as he dreaded doing so. Ike
would be able to end his presidency without another military intervention on behalf of school desegregation.[63]

Postelection Assessment

If it had been legally possible, Eisenhower probably would have run
for a third term and won. The Gallup Poll just prior to the election
reported that 58 percent of respondents approved of the way the
president was handling his job. A postelection survey sought to identify the public's "most admired man" in "any part of the world"; the
clear choice was Eisenhower. At the end of his presidency, Ike was
still the most popular politician in America.[64]

Kennedy narrowly won the election. In the final days of the campaign, an incident took place that eventually assumed legendary
proportions. Martin Luther King, Jr., had been arrested in Georgia
on September 23 for driving without a state driver's license, but his
sentence had been suspended as long as he did not violate any
other laws during his one-year probation. Then, King was arrested
after leading sit-in demonstrations at Atlanta eating places on October 19 and 20. Deputy Attorney General Lawrence Walsh suggested
that the White House issue a statement declaring that it was "unjust
that a man who has peacefully attempted to establish his right to
equal treatment free from racial discrimination be imprisoned on
an old, unrelated and relatively insignificant charge, driving without
a license." Walsh proposed that the president could say he had
asked the attorney general "to take all proper steps to join with Dr.
King in an appropriate application to vacate his sentence." Eisenhower, unwilling to even appear to play politics with the situation,

never issued a statement, nor did Nixon. But the Democratic candidate was not so timid. Kennedy phoned Mrs. King to express his concern, and his brother Robert called Judge Oscar Mitchell, with the result that King was released on bail on Thursday, October 27. Eisenhower is alleged to have later blamed Nixon's electoral defeat on "a couple of phone calls" by the Kennedys.[65]

On December 15, Eisenhower met with Nixon, Republican National Committee Chairman Senator Thruston Morton, General Persons, and Bryce Harlow for a postmortem on the election. Eisenhower confessed that he was "nonplussed" by the Republican failure. They would have to "roll with the punches" for now but he thought that they should do something "sort of dramatic" before leaving office to prove that the party was not dead.

Eisenhower sounded unwilling to leave the presidential stage. Until he realized they might not win the election, he said, he had intended "to stand back from public affairs in retirement." Eisenhower viewed with alarm the prospect of the forces of Senator Barry Goldwater of Arizona attempting to take over the party, and so had a reason to stay active in party politics.

Ike turned the discussion to civil rights. He observed that Attorney General Rogers was "somewhat to the left" of himself on civil rights. Nixon groused that a statement during the campaign by his vice-presidential running mate, Henry Cabot Lodge, Jr., about possibly putting a Negro in the cabinet "just killed us in the South." Eisenhower bitterly complained: "We have made civil rights a main part of our effort these past eight years but have lost Negro support instead of increasing it." Negroes, the president said, "just do not give a damn." Nixon remarked that black loyalty to the Democrats was "a bought vote, and it isn't bought by civil rights." Morton agreed with the vice president and said, "the hell with them."

Eisenhower was tempted to agree with Morton, but he pulled the conversation back to a more civil tone. He would not say "the hell with them," although he could not comprehend why his efforts were not more appreciated. No one, he said, was "more sincere" than he was in "bettering opportunities" for African-Americans. He recalled reading about economic reprisals against Negroes in Tennessee and said that such reports still "infuriated him."[66]

The old Eisenhower contradictions were evident in the discussion. He fell back on his mantra "that to rely entirely upon law for remedies of this problem is entirely wrong"—this from the president who had passed two civil rights laws, had insisted on obedience to the law of the land as enunciated by the Supreme Court, had appointed judges to enforce that law, and had even used troops to uphold a court decision. In many respects, he had left a legacy of law. Although he had failed to win the political loyalty of many African-Americans, Eisenhower's deeds as president far surpassed his words.

CHAPTER TWELVE

Leading from Gettysburg

*This pioneering work in civil rights must go on. Not only
because discrimination is morally wrong, but also because its
impact is more than national—it is world-wide.*
—Eisenhower's final State of the Union address,
    January 12, 1961

During World War I, Eisenhower had been stationed at Camp
Colt, on the edge of the Civil War battlefield at Gettysburg,
Pennsylvania. Ike recalled in a 1963 television interview that, as a
young soldier, he had frequently visited the battlefield cemetery: "I
would nearly always stop in front of the spot, which is close to where
he delivered the Address, and just sit there and read it again. It is
just immortal in its effect on people." Eisenhower, who was never as
eloquent as Lincoln, concluded that because Lincoln "had that
great gift, I think the war was won much quicker than [it] otherwise
might have been."[1]

The Civil War haunted Eisenhower's presidency. It was somehow
fitting that, on December 7, 1960—the nineteenth anniversary of
the attack on Pearl Harbor that had changed his life—he issued a
proclamation designating 1961 to 1965 as the centennial observance of War for the Union. A year earlier he had noted the death
of Walter W. Williams, reputed to be the last surviving veteran of
that war, stating that "the wounds of the deep and bitter dispute that
once divided our nation have long since healed." Eisenhower knew
better. The great domestic conflicts of his presidency, especially

school desegregation and the struggle to pass civil rights legislation, had arisen from that war's residue of racial conflict and discrimination; indeed, his sending of troops to Little Rock in 1957 had raised the specter of renewed civil conflict.[2]

That bitter legacy was personified in the situation of Ike's lone black staff member in the White House, E. Frederic Morrow. At Eisenhower's final White House Christmas gathering in 1960, the president pulled Morrow aside and delivered a "difficult" message. He had contacted numerous friends and party members, seeking an executive position for Morrow. "They all admit to your competence and ability," Morrow remembered Eisenhower saying, "but they cannot offer you a job at the level you deserve. Apparently big business is not ready at this time to take a chance on black employment in executive ranks." Eisenhower said he was "truly sorry" and, as they shook hands, Morrow thought he saw tears in the president's eyes. Two days later, Morrow told a *New York Times* reporter that "a jungle of racial barriers" had obstructed his attempt to obtain an executive position and that his only offers were those that "would confine me to working with the Negro community."[3]

Other farewells were less awkward. Eisenhower had taken particular pride in the Justice Department, which had molded and supported his civil rights policies, especially his judicial appointments. Responding to Attorney General William Rogers's final report, the president wrote that he was "particularly gratified by the establishment and functioning of the new Civil Rights Division." The division had processed 4,300 complaints, had 124 cases pending in federal court, and had instituted successful test suits in Georgia, Alabama, and Louisiana, the latter restoring 1,377 Negroes to the voting rolls. The department had invoked the 1960 voting rights legislation to demand voting records in seventeen counties and had filed suits to compel compliance.[4]

On January 12, 1961, Eisenhower delivered a written State of the Union message to Congress, which was read by a House clerk. The document cited Eisenhower's accomplishments in civil rights— the legislation creating the Civil Rights Division and the Civil Rights Commission, the committees combating employment discrimination, and his successful desegregation of the armed forces, veterans' hospitals, and District of Columbia. The president concluded: "This pioneering work in civil rights must go on. Not only because discrimination is morally wrong, but also because its impact is more than national—it is world-wide."[5]

Following John F. Kennedy's inauguration on January 20, the Eisenhowers returned to their home at Gettysburg. Once again, Ike would have time to prowl the battlefield.

Kennedy's Conservatism

In the early 1960s, both political parties regressed from the Eisenhower position on civil rights. Negro leaders such as Martin Luther King, Jr., soon discovered that Kennedy's promises of progress had been campaign rhetoric. During most of his short presidency, Kennedy pandered to the southern wing of his party, resisting the pressure to propose new civil rights legislation until mid-1963.[6]

Kennedy's conservatism on civil rights was reflected in his judicial appointments, the realm of Eisenhower's most vital contribution. Eisenhower had set high standards for judicial appointments. In 1959, Deputy Attorney General Lawrence Walsh had negotiated an arrangement with Senator James Eastland, the Democratic chair of the Senate Judiciary Committee; Eastland would support legislation to create twenty-five new federal judgeships if Walsh pledged to consult Eastland and his southern allies on candidates for the positions. That would open the door to the appointment of judges who were opposed to *Brown*. Suddenly, a letter from Attorney General Rogers to Eastland vetoed the deal. Rogers revealed that, while the president was willing to consider Democrats for nominees, Eisenhower was committed to nominating "the best qualified men to fill these vacancies irrespective of party." "Best qualified" meant, among other things, candidates who did not openly support segregation. In response, Eastland and Majority Leader Lyndon Johnson angrily torpedoed the legislation to create the judgeships.[7] Kennedy had none of Eisenhower's compunctions on such appointments. He and his brother, Attorney General Robert F. Kennedy, proposed an omnibus judiciary bill that, when President Kennedy signed it on May 19, 1961, created seventy-three new judgeships. When added to twenty-two existing vacancies, President Kennedy was poised to appoint ninety-five federal judges.[8]

This time, Eastland got what he wanted. In return for shepherding the bill through Congress, Eastland demanded that the first appointee come from Mississippi. He chose William Harold Cox, who had been previously rejected by the Eisenhower Justice Department for his white supremacist views. Kennedy nominated a parade of judges who were sympathetic to segregation, including candidates who were openly opposed to *Brown*. Taylor Branch concluded that Eisenhower had appointed "the best civil rights judges in the South," but "the most egregious segregationists were Kennedy's." As Nick Bryant, the author of a recent book on Kennedy and civil rights, puts it: "While Eisenhower's appointments had encouraged blacks to believe the federal courts were firmly on their side, Kennedy's candidates had the opposite effect. Throughout the fifties, most blacks believed they could settle their grievances through the courts. By the mid-sixties, the streets replaced the courts."[9]

Kennedy also failed to live up to Eisenhower's standards in handling the first school desegregation crisis of his presidency. When a Negro, James Meredith, attempted to enroll at the University of Mississippi in Oxford in the fall of 1962, riots erupted. If there was ever a time when Kennedy needed to consult Eisenhower, this was it. The government's intervention, unlike Eisenhower's smooth execution in Little Rock in 1957, was badly botched. The Kennedys conducted fruitless negotiations with Mississippi Governor Ross Barnett. After federal marshals were overwhelmed by the violence, Kennedy finally dispatched troops, but two people were killed and dozens of soldiers and U.S. marshals were injured before Meredith was admitted on October 1. Eisenhower, as he watched this debacle, was resentful. In a 1967 interview, he still grumbled about Kennedy's mismanagement and the fact that the Democratic leadership, so critical of his actions in Little Rock, "didn't say a damned word about it."[10]

In October, following the Mississippi crisis, Nathan M. Pusey, the president of Harvard University, gave Eisenhower a rare message of black appreciation. Dr. William Hinton, the first Negro professor at the institution, had provided in his will that his life savings (about $75,000) be used to establish a scholarship in Eisenhower's name in recognition of his leadership in civil rights. Eisenhower wrote in his memoirs that, when notified, he told Pusey that "I could not recall having been given a personal distinction that had touched me more deeply."[11]

In mid-1963, Kennedy confronted another school desegregation crisis at the University of Alabama. In its wake, he decided to submit civil rights legislation. This time, he sought Eisenhower's counsel, although his objective was securing Republican votes rather than seeking substantive advice. Kennedy addressed the nation on June 11. The next day he met with Eisenhower, who wrote to Kennedy on June 14, promising to inform Republican leaders of his support for the legislation and affirming, "I do believe that we must strive in every useful way to assure equality of economic and political rights for all citizens." That same day, Eisenhower kept his promise, writing the Republican minority leader, Senator Everett Dirksen of Illinois. Ike noted that in spite of the Democrats' large majority in the Senate, Kennedy needed more support from Republicans than he could hope for from Democrats; otherwise "his proposal would be defeated."[12]

Goldwater and Civil Rights

Eisenhower was troubled by trends in his own party. By early 1964, Senator Barry Goldwater of Arizona was on his way to capturing the Republican nomination. Goldwater openly opposed the civil rights bill that was making its way through Congress, then being promoted by President Lyndon B. Johnson following Kennedy's assassination in November 1963.

Eisenhower was disturbed over both Goldwater's bellicose approach to foreign affairs and his opposition to civil rights legislation. As the battle over the civil rights bill went forward, Eisenhower took an unusual step: he wrote an article for the *New York Herald Tribune,* published on May 25. In what the *New York Times* editors called "the Eisenhower Manifesto" and CBS newscaster Walter Cronkite called "a bombshell," Eisenhower outlined his criteria for an acceptable presidential candidate for his party—qualifications that clearly did not fit Goldwater. Calling civil rights "the nation's most critical domestic challenge," Ike praised the Republican leadership for supporting the legislation making its way through Congress—a clear affront to Goldwater.[13]

The Civil Rights Act of 1964 was passed by Congress on July 2, with six Republicans in opposition, including Goldwater. Twenty-seven Republican senators honored Eisenhower's request and supported the bill. Amid rumors of "white backlash," Goldwater prepared to implement what later would be called "the southern strategy," an attempt to encourage disillusioned southern Democrats to vote for or join the Republican Party. The Republican convention took place in San Francisco after the act's passage and, in his July 16 acceptance speech, Goldwater further divided his party when he delivered the line, "Extremism in defense of liberty is no vice."[14] That kind of talk did not please Dwight Eisenhower, the apostle of the middle way. Goldwater knew he faced difficulty in unifying the Republican Party.

A week after the convention, the Republican nominee called Ike to discuss a summit meeting of party leaders he had scheduled for August 12 in Hershey, Pennsylvania. After his blunt phone conversation with the candidate, Ike was still worried. He decided to pressure Goldwater by putting out the word that he might publicly withdraw his support. On August 3 and 4, Eisenhower made a series of phone calls. He told James Hagerty that "if the Republicans begin to count on white backlash—we will have a big civil war." He asserted to William S. Paley, chairman of the board at CBS, that he had "no sympathy with the 'white backlash.' I will not encourage it and if it is encouraged I will vote the other side." Ike told Lewis Strauss, the former chairman of the Atomic Energy Commission during the Eisenhower presidency, that he, Ike, had a "very troubled mind," and if the party leaders could not achieve unity on the 12th, "I would rather be alone than thought to be deserting what I believe in." He also shared these sentiments with Cronkite and with Governor William Scranton of Pennsylvania.

The next morning, Ike called his brother Milton and read a draft of a letter that he was contemplating sending to the newspapers. Milton urged him to hold it until they found out if Goldwater would support the party platform "and carry out the Civil Rights

Bill." Later that day, Eisenhower informed Governor George Romney of Michigan that unless things changed, he would not help with the campaign, and Goldwater had to state that "if he is elected he will support the civil rights bill."[15]

Goldwater got the message. Two days later, on August 6, the Republican candidate and his running mate, New York Congressman William E. Miller, traveled to Gettysburg to consult with Eisenhower. In an informal news conference after the meeting, Goldwater repudiated any support from the Ku Klux Klan—reversing the previously stated positions of Miller and his newly chosen Republican National Committee chairman, Dean Burch. He and Eisenhower also agreed to collaborate closely on the content of Goldwater's speech for the gathering on August 12.[16]

Goldwater delivered a reassuring speech to party leaders at the Hershey meeting. He promised to enforce the Civil Rights Act and to "use the great moral influence of the presidency to promote prompt and peaceful observance of civil rights laws." In a news conference after the meeting, Eisenhower said he had sought clarifications and was now "satisfied." Goldwater candidly confessed that the content of the address had grown out of his August 6 meeting with the former president. He and Eisenhower had "made notes" on what should be said, and two Eisenhower aides had assisted in drafting the speech.[17]

On September 22, Eisenhower appeared on television with Goldwater in a program filmed at the Gettysburg farm. While the primary focus of their outdoor discussion was world peace, Eisenhower asserted and Goldwater agreed that a president "has a legal as well as a moral duty to treat his fellow citizens as an equal." "Unless we do this," Eisenhower stated, "we are not living up to the rules laid down by the Founding Fathers."[18]

By then Eisenhower knew that Goldwater could not win the election. Ike had made a grand effort to keep his party progressive on nuclear policy and civil rights, but he had failed to derail Goldwater's disastrous candidacy. In response to the Johnson landslide, Eisenhower lent his presence to a September 4, 1965, meeting of the Republican Coordinating Committee, a group comprised of governors, congressional leaders, and past presidential candidates.

The *New York Times* ran a photo of Ike and Goldwater and reported that the group had issued a statement demonstrating that they "had reached substantial agreement on the one issue—civil rights—that was more divisive among Republicans than any other in 1964."[19]

End of the Eisenhower Era

In July 1967, Raymond Henle, the director of the Herbert Hoover Library's oral history project, interviewed a frail Eisenhower at Gettysburg and expressed his puzzlement that, although Gettysburg had been so important in the freeing of Negro slaves, "I haven't seen any colored people here." Eisenhower responded: "The worst enemies of the civil rights thing have been a great group or section of the Democratic Party and yet most of our Negroes go and vote Democratic. It's a strange thing."[20]

By the time the next presidential election arrived in 1968, Eisenhower's health was in severe decline. Disillusion and protests over Vietnam, race riots in the cities, and the assassinations of Robert Kennedy and Martin Luther King, Jr., created a tense climate that resurrected the political career of Richard Nixon, who won the narrowest of victories over Hubert Humphrey. Nixon had been a faithful ally on civil rights during Ike's presidency; he had managed the legislative strategy for the passage of the Civil Rights Act of 1957 and had frequently served as Eisenhower's political spokesman on civil rights.[21] But amid the tensions of 1968, Nixon adopted more conservative positions, saying he intended to appoint Supreme Court justices who would not legislate from the bench. Earl Warren had submitted his resignation as chief justice to President Johnson in June 1968 and Johnson had nominated Associate Justice Abe Fortas to succeed him, but Fortas failed to win Senate confirmation. As a result, Nixon would nominate the next chief justice.[22]

Eisenhower, although deathly ill at Walter Reed Hospital, pondered the appointment of the next chief justice. Ike remembered how Herbert Brownell and he had discussed civil rights in Paris in 1952 and how the New Yorker had advised him on civil rights policy, legislation, judicial appointments, and the intervention in Little

Rock. This was the man about whom Ike had written in his diary in 1953, "I am devoted to him and am perfectly confident that he would make an outstanding President of the United States."[23]

On December 13, 1968, Eisenhower summoned the strength to make a recommendation to Nixon. "Personally, I believe that a fine man for the post of Chief Justice would be Herb Brownell," Ike wrote, calling his recommendation "a very earnest one." Remarkably, Eisenhower had recommended a man for chief justice whom he knew might be more liberal on civil rights than Earl Warren.[24]

Nixon did not take Ike's recommendation. In mid-1969, he nominated Warren E. Burger, former assistant attorney general appointed by Eisenhower to the Court of Appeals for the District of Columbia in 1956. During the 1960s, Burger had developed a reputation as a "strict constructionist" judge who interpreted the Constitution more narrowly than the Warren Court. The implications of the Supreme Court appointment for civil rights and the enforcement of *Brown* were profound. Burger's nomination was enthusiastically endorsed by segregationist Democrats—John McClellan of Arkansas, Sam Ervin of North Carolina, Strom Thurmond of South Carolina, and James Eastland of Mississippi. Eastland, still the chairman of the Senate Judiciary Committee, called Burger "an outstanding jurist and a very fine man." Those southerners had rarely expressed such sentiments about any Eisenhower judicial appointment.[25]

Dwight D. Eisenhower died on March 28, 1969, two months before that nomination. The Eisenhower era was truly over.

A Matter of Justice

*Now, if there was anything good done, they mostly want to
prove that it was somebody else that did it and that I went
along as a passenger.*
—EISENHOWER ON ASSESSMENTS OF HIS PRESIDENCY,
JULY 13, 1967

Dwight Eisenhower received remarkably little credit for his civil
rights leadership in the decades after he left office. A half century later, that distortion of the record is no longer sustainable. Eisenhower had his weaknesses, but so did every other prominent white
politician of his era. John F. Kennedy and Lyndon Johnson did not
champion strong civil rights legislation until 1963–64. Until then, despite rhetorical flourishes, they and former president Truman were
often more conservative in their policies than Eisenhower.

Eisenhower was a "gradualist," but so were most other politicians of his time. Martin Luther King, Jr., was morally correct to contend that "justice delayed is justice denied" but Eisenhower was
attempting to govern, not score debating points. An immediate and
complete end to segregation was not politically feasible in the 1950s.
Too often, the "gradualist" label is used to close off serious analysis.
The purpose of this book has been to clarify what Eisenhower intended and accomplished. Once that record is corrected, a more
constructive dialogue about his leadership will be possible. To do
that with integrity, the myth that he did nothing must be put to
rest.

The Civil Rights Executive

Eisenhower's first steps on civil rights reflected his executive skills and orientation, honed in his military years. An effective executive's first obligation is to appoint strong people to positions of responsibility. In civil rights, Eisenhower's cornerstone appointment was Herbert Brownell as attorney general. Brownell, in turn, put together the strongest pro–civil rights Justice Department in American history to that time. By modern standards, Ike's appointments of blacks may look like tokenism, but such tokenism was notably lacking in previous administrations. In context, Eisenhower's appointments of J. Ernest Wilkins as assistant secretary of labor and E. Frederic Morrow to the White House executive staff were unprecedented.

Eisenhower's other executive priority was to eliminate segregation and discrimination where he already had authority. His military experience had taught him to do what he could, not belabor what he could not do. In 1953, the federal government had almost no authority to address discrimination, segregation, and racial violence in the states. Eisenhower's critique of his predecessors was that they had made promises they could not keep and submitted legislation they knew would fail, but refused to exercise the authority they already possessed.[1]

In 1953, civil rights was not yet a pressing national issue. The popular war hero could have ignored it, but Eisenhower acted resolutely in three areas. He desegregated the District of Columbia. Then, by means of presidential committees, he tackled the thorny problem of discrimination in employment by firms with federal contracts and by the federal government itself. Eisenhower's role in the third area, the desegregation of the armed forces, is particularly noteworthy. Truman had issued the executive order to end segregation in 1948 but encountered significant resistance in implementing it. By the end of his second year, Eisenhower had eliminated segregation in all combat units. He could have stopped there. Instead, he went on to desegregate schools for military dependents under federal authority and southern naval bases, including the facilities for civilian employees.

By modern standards, these three steps seem small, but in 1953–54, they were not. If desegregating the District of Columbia had been easy, Truman would have done it.[2] If desegregating the armed forces had been uncomplicated, Truman's 1948 executive order would have been fully implemented four years later. When Eisenhower came to office, most of the job remained to be done, and Eisenhower finished it.

At the end of Eisenhower's first term, government decision-makers in Washington, D.C., had begun to experience a new racial social order that nurtured a climate for further progress. The military had become and still is the most racially integrated institution in American life. Eisenhower, by means of his appointments and commitment to enforcing existing law, made an unprecedented impact.

The Civil Rights Legislator

Eisenhower avoided seeking civil rights legislation during his first term, preferring not to confront the southern segregationist barons who controlled Congress. Events eventually forced him to seek broader authority, partly in a search for options other than military intervention for handling racial conflict. Eisenhower proposed and achieved passage of the first civil rights legislation since 1875, in 1957, then repeated the feat in 1960. Limited to two terms by the Twenty-second Amendment, Ike helped his legislative program by shrewdly assuming the posture of a statesman without further political ambitions.[3]

The bills that were passed in 1957 and 1960 were inadequate by modern standards but that was not Eisenhower's fault. He proposed, in context of the time, landmark legislation that the southern Democrats, aided by Majority Leader Lyndon Johnson, diluted beyond recognition. Again, if it had been easy to pass civil rights legislation before 1953, Truman would have done it; his party's civil rights advocates could not muster enough votes to shut off debate in the Senate. Eisenhower's proposals changed all that. He quietly undermined the old anti–civil rights coalition of conservative Republicans and southern Democrats. The new coalition did not come into being until Eisenhower converted enough Republicans to make the difference. That reoriented Republican support for civil rights continued even after Eisenhower left office, with Republicans voting overwhelmingly for the 1964 and 1965 civil rights acts.

By 1957, Eisenhower was a leader, not a "passenger" in civil rights legislation. While his attorneys general produced progressive proposals, they did not do so in a vacuum. Eisenhower had appointed them and had given them their marching orders. The Eisenhower who is revealed in the minutes of the Republican legislative leaders' meetings was active, knowledgeable, and truly in charge of the legislative process.[4]

A major criticism of Eisenhower's legislative leadership revolves around his decision to drop part three of the 1957 civil rights bill—the provision that would have given the attorney general broad authority to file suits to protect all kinds of constitutional rights. We need to place responsibility where it belongs. Lyndon Johnson told the president that he had no choice; if he did not give up on part three, Johnson had the votes to kill the entire bill. To make Eisenhower solely responsible for gutting the bill is inappropriate.

The 1960 Civil Rights Act merits attention because its enforcement provisions protected the right to vote more effectively than the 1957 act. In addition, Eisenhower advocated a program to provide grants to states taking steps to implement desegregation, although that provision did not survive southern opposition. Anthony Lewis of the *New York Times* called the president's 1959 proposals "a broad civil rights program" that "included a declaration of support for the Supreme Court's 1954 decision holding public school segregation unconstitutional."[5]

While Eisenhower brought a narrow view of his duty in civil rights to the White House in 1953, he grew. By 1959–60, he had become an enlightened legislative warrior. Because of the landmark civil rights acts of 1964 and 1965, President Johnson earned the reputation of being a great civil rights legislator. He earned that accolade after 1963, but not before. Johnson played a role, much of it negative, in 1957 and 1960, when the truly important proposals were made by Dwight Eisenhower and his attorneys general. Without them and the Eisenhower coalition, the ground would have been less well prepared for Johnson's later triumphs.

Rhetorical Leadership

Eisenhower's greatest deficiency as a civil rights leader was his disdain for using the "bully pulpit" to denounce segregation. Many writers have accepted, without question, Earl Warren's contention in his memoirs that if Eisenhower had just "said something" about *Brown*, many difficulties would have been avoided. This perception is rooted in Ike's statement after *Brown* was announced: "The Supreme Court has spoken and I am sworn to uphold the constitutional processes in this country; and I will obey."[6] This legalistic response convinced many people that Eisenhower did not support the decision, even though he desegregated the Washington, D.C., schools, appointed pro-*Brown* judges, and sent troops into Little Rock, Arkansas, in 1957 to uphold *Brown*.

Civil rights advocates such as Democratic Senator Hubert Humphrey of Minnesota could not comprehend the president's reluctance to bluntly assert, "I am against segregation. I firmly believe that the Supreme Court decision of 1954 was correct, legally and morally." Although Eisenhower held 193 news conferences, Meena Bose and Fred I. Greenstein note that Ike "was often ambiguous in reply to reporters' questions, sometimes professing ignorance of matters because he believed they were best not discussed." That was especially true of civil rights.[7]

Despite Eisenhower's narrow view of his rhetorical leadership, a burden of proof rests on those who contend that stronger rhetoric would have made the difference. If words would have carried the day, Truman and Kennedy both would have been more successful than they were. Presidential statements are important, but they are no substitute for policy and execution. The segregationists understood that Ike was not on their side, regardless of what he said. Therefore, the primary negative effect of Eisenhower's rhetorical reticence was to confuse and discourage civil rights activists, especially African-Americans, as to his intent.

Despite his reluctance, Eisenhower grew in this regard. He said nothing publicly about the Emmett Till murder in 1955, but publicly deplored a similar crime when Mack Parker was lynched in Mississippi in 1959. While he spoke in measured terms in response to

Brown in 1954 (although he ordered the immediate desegregation of the D.C. schools), in 1958 he spoke out strongly on the continuing Little Rock case in *Cooper v. Aaron,* even while the case was in progress. In 1960, he affirmed the constitutional right of protestors to sit and be served at lunch counters in the South.

No words damaged Ike's reputation so much as his alleged comments to Earl Warren at the February 8, 1954, stag dinner, saying that southerners just wanted to protect their little girls from being "required to sit in school alongside some big overgrown Negroes."[8] Because of Warren's reputation, the story has gone unchallenged, contrary as it was to Ike's normal way of doing business. Warren's personal motivation for telling the story merits closer scrutiny. Whatever its credibility, it is time to relegate the tale to its appropriate place as a minor part of the Eisenhower civil rights legacy.

But journalists and scholars have frequently frozen Eisenhower's reputation in time, in early 1954 with the stag dinner story and his verbal response to *Brown.* They assume that these two statements reveal all we need to know about Eisenhower's attitudes on race, and that the rest of his presidency does not matter. That conclusion is unacceptable. Despite Warren's attempt to paint Eisenhower as a southern-style racist, he was not. He had his racial blind spots; while he believed fully in economic and political equality, he was ambivalent about compulsory integration, especially with children caught in the crossfire.[9] He did not fully understand what it meant to be black in America in the 1950s, but neither did the white politicians who so fiercely criticized him.

If we look at deeds—not just words—the case can be made that Eisenhower was more progressive in the 1950s than Truman, Kennedy, or Johnson. When Kennedy and Johnson finally proposed important legislation in 1963–64, Eisenhower openly supported that legislation and chastised Senator Barry Goldwater of Arizona, the 1964 Republican candidate for president, for voting against it.

Defender of the Courts

While Eisenhower was a disappointing rhetorical advocate for racial equality, we must balance that assessment with his uncompromising defense of the courts. Eisenhower revered the federal judiciary and spoke eloquently about it. To Eisenhower, his duty was not to give *Brown* a passionate, personal endorsement; he believed that personalizing the issue would violate the separation of powers. His call for obeying the law as defined in *Brown* should be taken on its own terms. The law he was insisting that the segregationists obey was *Brown,* not *Plessy v. Ferguson.* There is no credible evidence for Stephen Ambrose's contention that "Eisenhower personally wished that the Court had upheld *Plessy v. Ferguson,*" although Ike frequently expressed frustration with the impact of the decision on his presidency. After sending troops into Little Rock in 1957, Eisenhower emphatically expounded his defense of the courts: "These courts are not here merely to enforce integration," he said. "These courts are our bulwarks, our shield against autocratic government."[10]

Above all, Eisenhower defended the courts with his judicial appointments. His nominees for the Supreme Court—five northerners who firmly supported *Brown*—and his appointment of desegregation advocates to the lower federal courts made the difference in civil rights enforcement for decades. Eisenhower believed that the future of the country depended on honest, progressive judges who were committed to equal protection of the laws. Those who seek to label Eisenhower a racist must confront this record for judicial appointments—a record that Chief Justice Earl Warren, who knew more about it than anyone, chose to ignore in his memoirs.

Most dramatically, Eisenhower defended the federal courts in Little Rock. It is easy to forget that Eisenhower could have chosen not to send troops. If quelling mob violence was the problem, Orval Faubus and his National Guard troops would have kept the peace. The real issue was resistance to a federal court order for school integration. Senator Herman Talmadge, a segregationist Democrat from Georgia, understood that "Eisenhower, after all, was a general." "A professional politician might have backed down," Talmadge wrote in his autobiography, "but not Ike. When he called in federal troops to integrate the school, we knew he meant business."[11]

It is a myth that Eisenhower was indecisive about Little Rock. The crisis began with Faubus's deployment of National Guard troops on September 3, 1957. Eisenhower approved a public warning by Brownell on September 4 that included the possibility of military intervention. Eisenhower himself publicly warned Faubus in a telegram on September 5 and in person on September 14, but the latter ultimatum was not publicized. Faubus's actions, not Eisenhower's, made military action inevitable. To argue that Eisenhower could have changed this situation by some kind of public statement is naïve. No matter what the president said in public, southerners such as the Arkansas governor were committed to "massive resistance" to the ruling of the Supreme Court.[12]

Eisenhower confronted a dangerous situation that required prudent, even-handed management. Could his intervention have escalated into civil war? It is tempting, in retrospect, to minimize the possibilities. A peaceful outcome was not guaranteed in 1957. Eisenhower quizzed Faubus on September 14 as to whether military commanders of southern origin would be loyal to the federal government. The president chose army over National Guard troops because he did not want to pit "brother against brother" in Little Rock, a phrase rooted in Civil War mythology. Eisenhower expressed his fears to Ann Whitman on September 20, and she noted: "The President is loath to use troops—thinks movement might spread—violence would come."[13] When Eisenhower deployed troops in a former Confederate state, it was the first time that had been done in eighty years, an extraordinary action. Without the president's careful management, United States Army soldiers might have confronted National Guard troops on Arkansas soil. Unlike Kennedy's intervention at the University of Mississippi in 1962, Eisenhower's military operation in Little Rock was smoothly executed.

Eisenhower's great contribution to civil rights during his presidency was his bold support for the courts, their judges, and their decisions, with Little Rock the symbol. In 1861, Abraham Lincoln preached preservation of the union, not ending slavery, as a justification for making war on the South. Eisenhower argued for obeying the federal courts, not integration, as justification for intervention in Little Rock, as he addressed the nation "from the house of Lincoln" on September 24, 1957. Neither said what the activists of his day wanted to hear, but both led the nation in a new direction.

Eisenhower's policy in Little Rock reinforced the verdict of the Civil War—the supremacy of federal authority, including federal court orders—over the states. While the gains for civil rights during his administration were limited, a revolution had truly begun.

Ike had stubbornly resisted engaging in partisan demagoguery, adhering to his belief that "the true way" to advance civil rights was with "less oratory, and more action." Although that stance damaged his reputation for civil rights leadership, Eisenhower did not abandon his pledge that he would not "claim political credit for a simple matter of American justice."[14]

Notes

ABBREVIATIONS

ABA: American Bar Association
ACHR: American Council on Human Rights
ACW: Ann C. Whitman
ADA: Americans for Democratic Action
CF: Central Files (Eisenhower Library)
COHP: Columbia Oral History Project
DDE: Dwight D. Eisenhower
DDEP: Papers of Dwight David Eisenhower
DNC: Democratic National Committee
EL: Dwight D. Eisenhower Presidential Library
FBI: Federal Bureau of Investigation
FDR: Franklin Delano Roosevelt
FEPC: Fair Employment Practices Commission
GF: General File (Eisenhower Library)
HHH: Hubert H. Humphrey
JFK: John F. Kennedy
LBJ: Lyndon B. Johnson
LC: Library of Congress
LL: Legislative Leaders file (Eisenhower Library)
MHS: Minnesota Historical Society
NAACP: National Association for the Advancement of Colored People
NATO: North Atlantic Treaty Organization
OF: Official File (Eisenhower Library)
OH: Oral History (Eisenhower Library)
OSAPPM: Office of the Special Assistant to the President for Personnel Management (Eisenhower Library)
PCGC: President's Committee on Government Contracts
PCGE: President's Committee on Government Employment
PPP: Public Papers of the President
RNC: Republican National Committee

SCLC: Southern Christian Leadership Conference
TL: Harry S. Truman Library
UA: University of Arkansas
UPA: University Press of America (microfilm)
VA: Veterans Administration
WHOSS: White House Office, Office of the Staff Secretary (Eisenhower Library)
WHTO: White House Telegraph Office (Eisenhower Library)

INTRODUCTION

1. Stephen E. Ambrose, *Eisenhower: Soldier and President* (New York: Simon &
    Schuster, 1990), p. 542; Chester J. Pach, Jr., & Elmo Richardson, *The Presidency
    of Dwight D. Eisenhower* (Lawrence: University Press of Kansas, 1991), p. 157;
    Arthur M. Schlesinger, Jr., *The Cycles of American History* (Boston: Houghton
    Mifflin, 1986), p. 390; Tom Wicker, *Dwight D. Eisenhower* (New York: Times
    Books, 2002), pp. 53–55; William E. Leuchtenburg, *The White House Looks
    South: Franklin Roosevelt, Harry Truman, Lyndon Johnson* (Baton Rouge: Louisi-
    ana State University, 2005), pp. 415–16, writes that Eisenhower was a "closet
    racist"; Steven Wagner, *Eisenhower Republicanism: Pursuing the Middle Way*
    (DeKalb: Northern Illinois Press, 2006), pp. 64–87, contends that Eisenhow-
    er's policies "solidified the Democrats' hold on the African-American vote";
    Steven A. Shull, *American Civil Rights Policy from Truman to Clinton: The Role of
    Presidential Leadership* (Armonk, NY: M. E. Sharpe, 1999), p. 36, says that Eisen-
    hower "provided little direction on civil rights"; Richard Kluger, in *Simple Jus-
    tice: The History of Brown v. Board of Education and Black America's Struggle for
    Equality* (New York: Random House, 1977), wrote that Eisenhower, "either by
    design or obtuseness, comforted and dignified those who raged against the
    Court," and Kluger concluded that the great general of the war in Europe
    "had proven unwilling to muster a comparable moral effort in his homeland
    when the hour called for it." In a volume dedicated to civil rights, Robert
    Frederick Burk, *The Eisenhower Administration and Black Civil Rights* (Knoxville:
    University of Tennessee Press, 1984), p. 261, concluded that Eisenhower pre-
    ferred not to be active in civil rights leadership beyond a "policy of racial sym-
    bolism." Herbert S. Parmet, *Eisenhower and the American Crusades* (New York:
    Macmillan, 1972), p. 576, wrote that Eisenhower "appeared insensitive and ig-
    norant about the plight of the black man in America."
2. Fred I. Greenstein pointed the way to a major reinterpretation of Eisenhower's
    leadership, focused on deeds, not just words, in *The Hidden-Hand Presidency:
    Eisenhower as Leader* (New York: Basic Books, 1982), although Greenstein did
    not directly address civil rights. Two dissertations during the 1980s pointed the
    way toward a fresh interpretation of Eisenhower and civil rights, Michael S.
    Mayer, "Eisenhower's Conditional Crusade: The Eisenhower Administration
    and Civil Rights" (Princeton University, 1984), University Microfilms Interna-
    tional, and Ronald R. Huggins, "Eisenhower and Civil Rights" (University of
    California, Los Angeles, 1985), University Microfilms International.
3. Richard Neustadt in *Presidential Power, the Politics of Leadership* (New York: John
    Wiley & Sons, 1960), pp. 163–71, assessed Eisenhower as an indecisive leader,
    although he admitted that his knowledge was based primarily on Ike's public
    statements and what men around him said, not his detailed record. In a later

edition, retitled *Presidential Power and the Modern Presidents* (New York: Free Press, 1990), pp. 137–44, Neustadt retained his interpretation of Eisenhower as an indecisive president, reluctant to lead in the Roosevelt style. That perception of Eisenhower's leadership has been perpetuated by numerous other scholars, e.g., James T. Patterson, *Grand Expectations: The United States, 1945–74* (New York: Oxford University Press, 1996), pp. 243–75 and 412–16.

CHAPTER ONE: THE CANDIDATE

1. DDE to Milton Eisenhower, Sept. 12, 1955, Louis Galambos and Daun van Ee, eds., *The Papers of Dwight David Eisenhower* (Baltimore: Johns Hopkins University Press, 1996), vol. 16, p. 1850. The *Papers* are hereinafter referred to as *DDEP*.
2. William B. Pickett, *Eisenhower Decides to Run: Presidential Politics and Cold War Strategy* (Chicago: Ivan R. Dee, 2000), p. 189; Brownell Interview, OH-282, pp. 11–12, 29, EL; Herbert Brownell, *Advising Ike: The Memoirs of Attorney General Herbert Brownell* (Lawrence: University Press of Kansas, 1993), p. 98.
3. The 1890 census listed the population of Abilene as 3,547, with roughly 160 blacks living in Dickinson County; *Report: Population of the United States at the Eleventh Census, 1890* (Washington, D.C.: U.S. Government Printing Office, 1895), part 1, pp. 145, 498.
4. Dwight D. Eisenhower, *At Ease: Stories I Tell to Friends* (New York: Doubleday, 1967), pp. 183–87; Phillip G. Henderson, "Duty, Honor, Country: Parallels in the Leadership of George Washington and Dwight David Eisenhower," in Ethan Fishman, William D. Pederson, and Mark J. Rozell, eds., *George Washington: Foundation of Presidential Leadership and Character* (Westport, Conn.: Praeger, 2001), p. 88. For other details of Eisenhower's early life and influences, see Geoffrey Perret, *Eisenhower* (Holbrook, Mass.: Adams Media, 1999), pp. 1–34, and pp. 87–89 on Conner's influence.
5. Ann Brownell Sloane, Brownell's daughter, recalls that her father's constitutional scholarship was recognized with offers of teaching positions at the law schools at Yale and the University of Chicago when he was in his twenties.
6. E-mail message, Franklin G. Hunt to Ann Brownell Sloane, Feb. 2, 2004; Thomas E. Stephens Interview, Herbert Brownell, Jr., Papers, B 270, EL; Warren Olney III Interview, Brownell Papers, B 36, Criminal (1), EL.
7. Brownell Interview, OH-282, pp. 11–12, 29, EL; Brownell, *Advising Ike*, p. 98; DDE Diary, May 14, 1953, Dwight D. Eisenhower's Papers as President (Ann Whitman File), B 9, DDE Personal 1953–54 (2), EL; Pickett, *Eisenhower Decides to Run*, p. 189.
8. Pickett, *Eisenhower Decides to Run*, pp. 189–93, 199–200; W. H. Lawrence, "Eisenhower Outlines Campaign Issues Based on World Peace and Security; He Blames 'Party in Power' for China," *New York Times*, June 6, 1952.
9. *The People Ask the President*, television broadcast, Oct. 12, 1956, *Public Papers of the Presidents: Dwight D. Eisenhower, 1956* (Washington, D.C.: U.S. Government Printing Office, 1960), pp. 912–13; hereafter referred to as *PPP*.
10. Eisenhower, *At Ease*, p. 323.
11. DDE to Marshall, March 25, 1942, *DDEP*, vol. 1, pp. 208–9; ACW Diary, Nov. 23, 1958, B 10, EL.
12. DDE to Lee, March 1, 1944, National Staff Files, *Papers of the NAACP*, ed. John

H. Bracey Jr. and August Meier, Supplement to Part I, 1951–55 (Ann Arbor: University Publications, 1987), microfilm; Draft for Files, Jan. 4, 1945, *DDEP,* vol. 4, p. 2394; Ulysses Lee, *The Employment of Negro Troops* (Washington, D.C.: Center for Military History, United States Army, 1965), pp. 689–94.

13. DDE to Marshall, Jan. 7, 1945, *DDEP,* vol. 4, pp. 2394, 2409.
14. DDE to Clarke, May 29, 1967, Eisenhower Post-Presidential Papers, Secretary Series, B 20, EL; news conference, Oct. 5, 1956, *PPP,* p. 851.
15. DDE to Milton Eisenhower, March 15, 1946, *DDEP,* vol. 7, pp. 942–43; Interview with Milton Eisenhower, June 21 and Sept. 6, 1967, COHP, 1973, OH-292, EL; Ike's approach to desegregation may have been influenced by his brother's approach at Kansas State University, as explained in Stephen E. Ambrose and Richard H. Immerman, *Milton S. Eisenhower: Educational Statesman* (Baltimore: Johns Hopkins University Press, 1983), pp. 98–104.
16. DDE to Reddick, Feb. 12, 1947, *DDEP,* vol. 8, pp. 1514–15.
17. DDE Diary, March 21, 1956, B 9, DDE Personal 1955–56 (1), EL; DDE to Clarke, May 29, 1967, Post-Presidential Papers, Secretary Series, B 20, EL; *DDEP,* vol. 8, p. 1515.
18. Secretary's Office File, Civil Rights, Truman Papers, TL; The full report is also published in Steven F. Lawson, ed., *To Secure These Rights: The Report of Harry S. Truman's Committee on Civil Rights* (Boston/New York: Bedford/St. Martin's, 2004); Harry S. Truman, *Years of Trial and Hope* (Garden City, N.Y.: Doubleday, 1956), vol. 2, p. 181.
19. Walter White, "Eisenhower and Civil Rights," April 1, 1948, in Eisenhower's Pre-Pres. Papers, Principal File, B 123 (White, Walter), EL.
20. Hearing, April 3, 1948, Armed Services Committee of the United States Senate, Eightieth Congress, Second Session on Universal Military Training (Washington, D.C.: U.S. Government Printing Office, 1948), pp. 995–98; Eisenhower's testimony is summarized in "Truman Asks Speedup on Civil Rights," *Washington Post,* June 14, 1952; Sherie Mershon & Steven Schlossman, *Foxholes & Color Lines: Desegregating the U.S. Armed Forces* (Baltimore: Johns Hopkins University Press, 1998), pp. 266–67.
21. Secretary's Office File, Civil Rights, TL; Truman, *Years of Trial and Hope,* vol. 2, p. 181; Morris J. MacGregor, Jr., *Integration of the Armed Forces 1940–1965* (Washington, D.C.: Center of Military History, United States Army, 1981), pp. 292–93; McCullough, *Truman* (New York: Simon & Schuster, 1992), pp. 635–51; Alonzo L. Hamby, *Beyond the New Deal: Harry S. Truman and American Liberalism* (New York: Columbia University Press, 1973), pp. 242–65; Michael R. Gardner, *Harry Truman and Civil Rights* (Carbondale and Edwardsville: Southern Illinois University Press, 2002), pp. 112–21.
22. DDE to Reddick, Feb. 12, 1947, *DDEP,* vol. 8, pp. 1514–15; Perret, *Eisenhower,* p. 377.
23. Anthony Leviero, "Eisenhower's '11' A Specialist Team," *New York Times,* March 16, 1953; Rabb Interview, May 4, 1971, COHP, OH-309, EL.
24. Hagerty Interview, OH-91, vol. 4, pp. 504–05, EL; Goodpaster interview with the author, Jan. 20, 2004. A detailed analysis of Eisenhower's approach to delegation is found in Fred I. Greenstein, "'Centralization Is the Refuge of Fear': A Policymaker's Use of a Proverb of Administration," in Robert T. Golembiewski and Aaron Wildavsky, eds., *The Costs of Federalism: Essays in Honor of James W. Fesler* (New Brunswick, N.J.: Transaction, 1984), pp. 117–39, with analysis of Eisenhower's delegation to Brownell on pp. 129–30.

25. William Knowland Interview, Nov. 16, 1970, COHP, OH-333, p. 136, EL; William Bragg Ewald, Jr., *Eisenhower the President: Crucial Days, 1951–60* (Englewood Cliffs, N.J.: Prentice-Hall, 1981), pp. 65–73; Goodpaster interview with the author, Jan. 20, 2004; Roemer McPhee interview with the author, Jan. 9, 2004.

26. Dwight D. Eisenhower, *Crusade in Europe* (New York: Doubleday, 1949), p. 231.

27. Off the Record Remarks, interview with General Wilton B. Persons, May 29, 1974, OH-399, EL; Eisenhower, *At Ease,* pp. 51–55; DDE to C. D. Jackson, Oct. 14, 1957, *DDEP,* vol. 18, p. 495.

28. Ewald, *Eisenhower the President,* p. 32; Henderson, "Duty, Honor, Country," provides a detailed comparison of Eisenhower and George Washington in their approaches to the presidency, temperament, and skills; pp. 71–97 in Fishman et al., eds., *George Washington.*

29. Fred I. Greenstein, in *The Hidden-Hand Presidency: Eisenhower as Leader* (Baltimore: Johns Hopkins University Press, 1994), provides a detailed analysis of Eisenhower's personality in a chapter titled, "What Manner of Man," pp. 15–54.

30. Brownell, *Advising Ike,* p. 301; Richard M. Nixon, *Six Crises* (Garden City, N.Y.: Doubleday, 1962), p. 161.

31. DDE to Chynoweth, July 20, 1954, DDE Diary, B 4, Jan.–Nov. 1954, EL.

32. Gerald Morgan Interview, May 7, 1968, no. 3, OH-223, EL.

33. DDE to Phillips, June 5, 1953, DDE Diary, B 3, July 1953 (2), EL.

34. DDE to Lucy M. Eldredge, Jan. 17, 1946, *DDEP,* vol. 7, pp. 764–65.

35. Pickett, *Eisenhower Decides to Run,* pp. 189–93, 199–200; Lawrence, "Eisenhower Outlines Campaign Issues."

36. Review of the 1952 platform, Dec. 8, 1955, LL, B 2, Dec. 1955 (5), EL.

37. On August 1, Eisenhower wrote effusively about his appreciation for Brownell's service, saying that the New Yorker had "paid me a very great honor" and expressing his admiration for "a distinguished American citizen," and "my very good friend"; DDE to Brownell, Aug. 1, 1952, in a letter in the private collection of Ann Brownell Sloane, also found in *DDEP,* vol. 13, pp. 1304–5; Brownell, *Advising Ike,* pp. 130–31.

38. "FEPC Fight Is Predicted By Humphrey," *Washington Post,* April 8, 1952, B 420, HHH Papers, MHS; DDE to Clement, March 19, 1952, *DDEP,* vol. 13, pp. 1087–88; "Eisenhower Stirs Democratic Hopes," *New York Times,* June 6, 1952; Clayton Knowles, "16 G.O.P. Leaders Tie F.E.P.C. to Party," *New York Times,* Aug. 4, 1952.

39. Walter White to DDE, Oct. 6, 1952, Sherman Adams to White, Oct. 7, 1952, Dwight D. Eisenhower's Records as President, CF/OF 142-A, B 731, 1952 Campaign, EL; Russell Porter, "Eisenhower Plans to Stump South In First Such Invasion by the G.O.P.," *New York Times,* July 20, 1952; "Southern Editors Rally to General," *New York Times,* Aug. 2, 1952; Jack Bass, *Unlikely Heroes* (New York: Simon & Schuster, 1981), pp. 29, 121.

40. "Truman Asks Speedup on Civil Rights," *Washington Post,* June 14, 1952.

41. "V. Washington to Lead Negro Drive of GOP," *Washington Post,* July 31, 1952; E. Frederic Morrow, *Forty Years a Guinea Pig* (New York: Pilgrim Press, 1980), p. 74; Val Washington, "The Fourteen Points," Aug. 8, 1955, CF/OF 138-A-6, B 704, Negro Voting, EL. Brownell had recruited Washington, a black executive with the *Chicago Defender,* to the RNC in the 1940s. He became the offi-

cial campaign spokesman for Negro issues for the RNC in July 1952. In August 1952, Washington produced a pamphlet, "The Republican Party and the Negro," articulating fourteen points that included Republican pledges to "win an honorable and just peace," reduce spending abroad, "end segregation in the Nation's Capital," end discrimination in the federal government, appoint Negroes to important policy-making positions, strengthen the civil rights section of the Justice Department, resist the influence of the southern bloc in Congress, "enforce the anti-bias laws already on the books" (including the nondiscriminatory clauses of the Taft-Hartley Act aimed at labor unions), reduce taxes, reverse the trend toward the centralization of government power, and to "not arouse false hopes of Negroes by promising what it never intends to deliver."

42. "Negro Leader Shifts to General," *New York Times,* Nov. 1, 1952; Roy Wilkins, *Standing Fast: The Autobiography of Roy Wilkins* (1982; rept. New York: Da Capo, 1994) p. 212.

43. Morrow, *Guinea Pig,* pp. 81–82.

44. *Morrow, Guinea Pig,* pp. 73–77, 82–83; "End of Segregation in D.C. Favored by Gen. Eisenhower," Washington, D.C., *Evening Star,* Sept. 9, 1952.

45. Brownell, *Advising Ike,* pp. 123–27; Merle Miller, *Plain Speaking: An Oral Biography of Harry S. Truman* (New York: Berkley Publishing Corporation, 1973), pp. 341–42.

46. Oct. 13, 1952 minutes, Board of Directors, NAACP Papers, UPA.

47. Stephen Benedict Interview, Oct. 18, 1968, no. 2, COHP, pp. 82–83, EL.

48. Max Rabb used the "just talk" phrase in an interview, Oct. 6, 1970, OH-265, EL, p. 12; "Texts of Eisenhower's Speeches at Newark and Wilmington Yesterday," *New York Times,* Oct. 18, 1952.

49. "Democrats Can't End Discrimination Here, Eisenhower Repeats," *Evening Star,* Oct. 18, 1952; "Big Progress Made on Segregation Here, President Declares," *Evening Star,* Oct. 21, 1952; "Donohue Sees End of Segregation Here," *Evening Star,* Dec. 7, 1952.

50. *Congressional Quarterly, Guide to Elections,* 1975, p. 37; Arthur Krock, "Personal Victory," *New York Times,* Nov. 6, 1952; George H. Gallup, *The Gallup Poll: Public Opinion, 1935–1971,* vol. 2 (New York: Random House, 1972), p. 1453. Note that these estimates of the black vote were made before scientific exit interviews became common.

51. Brownell, *Advising Ike,* pp. 131–32.

CHAPTER TWO: INVOKING FEDERAL AUTHORITY

1. Hubert Humphrey Interview, Aug. 17, 1971, tape no. 1, LBJ Library, Austin, Texas, online; Herbert Brownell, "Eisenhower's Civil Rights Program," Eisenhower Centennial Program, Austin, Texas, Oct. 27, 1990, B 16 (2), Brownell Additional Papers, EL; "Leader Bars Segregation at Inaugural," *Washington Post,* Nov. 14, 1952; "Inaugural Fair Play Talk Was Meaningless," Washington, D.C., *Afro-American,* Jan. 24, 1953; Truman's minimal efforts at desegregation in D.C., especially swimming pools, is cited in Michael R. Gardner, *Harry Truman and Civil Rights* (Carbondale and Edwardsville: Southern Illinois University Press, 2002), pp. 154–57.

2. "End of Segregation in D.C. Favored by Gen. Eisenhower," *Evening Star,* Sept.

9, 1952; News Conference, Dec. 18, 1952, *The Public Papers of the President, Harry S. Truman, 1952–53* (Washington, D.C.: U.S. Government Printing Office, 1966), p. 1090; David McCullough, *Truman* (New York: Simon & Schuster, 1992), pp. 908–12; "Democrats Can't End Discrimination Here, Eisenhower Repeats," *Evening Star,* Oct. 18, 1952; "Big Progress Made on Segregation Here, President Declares," *Evening Star,* Oct. 21, 1952; "Donohue Sees End of Segregation Here," *Evening Star,* Dec. 7, 1952.

3. Herbert Brownell, *Advising Ike: The Memoirs of Attorney General Herbert Brownell* (Lawrence: University Press of Kansas, 1993), p. 98; William B. Pickett, *Eisenhower Decides to Run: Presidential Politics and Cold War Strategy* (Chicago: Ivan R. Dee, 2000), p. 189; George H. Gallup, *The Gallup Poll: Public Opinion 1935–1971,* vol. 2 (New York: Random House, 1972) p. 1453.

4. Brownell, *Advising Ike,* pp. 132, 143–45, 192; Norman J. Silber, *With All Deliberate Speed: The Life of Philip Elman* (Ann Arbor: University of Michigan Press, 2004), p. 206. Earl Warren was offered the solicitor general position and accepted, but the death of the chief justice and Warren's appointment to the Supreme Court derailed that plan. Rankin assumed the duties of the solicitor general until Simon Sobeloff was appointed in 1954 (see chapter 3).

5. Rabb Interview, Brownell Papers, B 270, p. 34, EL; Ann Brownell Sloane e-mail communication to the author, Dec. 1, 2006; Persons Interview, June 24, 1970, OH-334, Parts 3–4, pp. 122–23, EL; Maxwell M. Rabb contended that Persons tried "to block anything in civil rights," although Persons later claimed his outlook paralleled the president's.

6. Rabb Interviews, May 13, 1975, OH-479, pp. 23–24, and OH-265, no.1, pp. 2–5, 11–12, EL; Michael S. Mayer, "The Eisenhower Administration and the Desegregation of Washington, D.C.," *Journal of Policy History* (Fall 1991): 26.

7. Brownell to Adams, Jan. 3, 1953, High to Rabb, July 16, 1954, and Rabb to Whitman, July 24, 1954, CF/OF 142-A, B 731, EL; Sherman Adams, *First-Hand Report: The Story of the Eisenhower Administration* (New York: Harper & Bros., 1961), p. 333.

8. Michal R. Belknap, ed., *Civil Rights, The White House, and the Justice Department, 1945–1968* (New York: Garland, 1991), vol. 4, pp. 117, 124; "An Excellent Appointment," and "Labor Post Goes to Negro, First of Race in Sub-Cabinet," *New York Times,* March 5, 1954; Rabb to DDE, Aug. 16, 1954, ACW Diary, B 3 (2), EL. J. Ernest Wilkins, no relationship to Roy Wilkins, who later became the executive secretary of the NAACP, was one of the most important black Republicans in the country. Besides his law practice and political involvement, he served on the judicial committee of the Methodist Episcopal Church. In addition to assistant secretary of Labor, Eisenhower appointed Wilkins to the President's Committee on Government Contracts, the President's Committee on Government Employment, and the Civil Rights Commission created by the 1957 Civil Rights Act.

9. Rabb Interview, OH-265, pp. 29–31, EL; Robert Frederick Burk, *The Eisenhower Administration and Black Civil Rights* (Knoxville: University of Tennessee Press, 1984), pp. 77–88; In 1955, this group consisted of J. Ernest Wilkins; Scovel Richardson, a member of the Board of Parole; Val Washington; Joseph Douglas, a staff member at the office of the secretary of Health, Education, and Welfare; E. Frederic Morrow; Samuel Pierce, assistant to the undersecretary of the Department of Labor; and James M. Nabrit, Jr., who was then a member of the President's Committee on Government Contracts,

found in Rabb Civil Rights Papers, Box 27 (7), EL; "Ike's Record on Negro Appointments Hailed," *Pittsburgh Courier*, July 30, 1955, in Maxwell M. Rabb Papers (temporary organization), Box 35 (7), EL; Morrow's swearing-in took place on July 11, 1955, CF/OF 72-A-2, B 288, EL; Morrow's appointment is covered in more detail in chapter 6.

10. Taft to Dulles, May 18, 1953, Byroade to Dulles, March 11 and May 24, 1954, Dulles Papers, Personnel Series, B 1, Evaluation of Chiefs of Mission (1), B 8, Negro Ambassador, Dulles Papers, EL; Michael L. Krenn, *Black Diplomacy: African Americans and the State Department 1945–1969* (Armonk, N.Y.: M. E. Sharpe, 1999), pp. 85–86.

11. The "showpiece" phrase is from Eisenhower's memoir, *The White House Years: Mandate for Change, 1953–56* (New York: Doubleday, 1963), pp. 234–36; C. P. Trussell, "Home-Rule Move For Capital Gains," *New York Times*, July 16, 1959. The *Times* noted that Negroes constituted 36 percent of the district population according to the census of 1950, and were expected to surpass 50 percent by the end of the decade.

12. "While Politicians Talk, Washingtonians Are Working Out Their Own Problems," *Evening Star*, Oct. 19, 1952; details of the district government's organization are reviewed in "Study Indicates Segregation Is Already Enforced by Law," *Evening Star*, Feb. 8, 1953; Ben W. Gilbert, "Sudden Segregation Ban Eyed Dimly," *Washington Post*, Jan. 18, 1953; Marvin Caplan, "Eat Anywhere!" *Washington History* (Spring 1989): 26.

13. News release by Case, Jan. 11, 1953, CF/OF 71-U, B 282, EL; Thomas Winship, "Ike Hints Cautious Approach to Segregation in District," *Washington Post*, Jan. 16, 1953; "Eisenhower Discusses D.C. Problems With Committee Chairmen," *Evening Star*, January 15, 1953.

14. Legislative Leaders Meeting, Jan. 26, 1953, March 31, 1953, LL, B 1 (2-3) EL.

15. Caplan, "Eat Anywhere!" pp. 37–39; Mayer, "Desegregation of Washington, D.C.," p. 28; "Café Decision Is Not the End," *Afro-American*, Jan. 31, 1953.

16. Brownell Address, Oct. 27, 1990, B 16 (2), Brownell Additional Papers, EL; "Ike Redeems Rights Pledge," *Afro-American*, March 3, 1953; "Georgian Blasts U.S. Attempt to End Segregation," *Evening Star*, March 12, 1953.

17. Chalmers M. Roberts, "Suit Called Key to Home Rule Put to High Court," *Washington Post*, March 11, 1953; Joseph Paull, "D.C. Antiracial Laws Operative, High Court Told," *Washington Post*, April 25, 1953; West and Brownell, "Suggestion That Case Be Advanced," William O. Douglas Papers, March 13, 1953, B 733, LC; "Plea to Speed Segregation Ruling Filed," *Washington Post*, March 14, 1953.

18. Winship, "Ike Hints Cautious Approach"; "Gang Around Ike to Battle Civil Rights, White Charges," *Washington Post*, Feb. 2, 1953.

19. State of the Union address, Feb. 2, 1953, Eisenhower, *PPP*, pp. 30–31.

20. "Eisenhower and His Message," *Washington Post*, Feb. 3, 1953; William S. White, "Civil Rights Plans Get Wide Support," *New York Times*, Feb. 3, 1953; "Freedom For All," *Washington Post*, Feb. 3, 1953; Don S. Warren, "President Calls For End of D.C. Segregation," *Evening Star*, Feb. 2, 1953; "Eisenhower's D.C. Reforms Face Hurdles," *Evening Star*, Feb. 3, 1953; "Ellender Criticizes Eisenhower's Plan To End Segregation," *Evening Star*, Feb. 8, 1953; Gilbert C. Fite, *Richard B. Russell, Jr.: Senator from Georgia* (Chapel Hill: University of North Carolina Press, 1991), pp. 329–30.

21. John W. Stepp, "Donohue Offers Resignation At Meeting With Eisenhower,"

Evening Star, Jan. 22, 1953; Richard L. Lyons, "Resignation Handed Ike by Donohue," *Washington Post,* Jan. 23, 1953.

22. "Selection of D.C. Heads May End Segregation, Donohue Says," *Evening Star,* Feb. 10, 1953; "Eisenhower Is Urged To Pick Segregation Foes for D.C. Heads," *Evening Star,* Jan. 26, 1953; Legislative Leaders Meeting, DDE Diary, Feb. 9, 1953, *DDEP,* vol. 14, p. 33; Simeon Booker, "Ike Weighs Board Post for Negro," *Washington Post,* Feb. 13, 1953.

23. Ben W. Gilbert, "Case Bill Reactions Aiding Home Rule," *Washington Post,* Feb. 15, 1953; "Unnecessary Stepping Stones," *Evening Star,* Feb. 3, 1953.

24. "Our Uncertain Commissioners," *Evening Star,* Feb. 28, 1953; "NAACP Fights Commissioner Bid to Fowler," *Washington Post,* March 1, 1953; Thomas Winship, "White House May Appoint D.C. Head(s) in Day or 2," *Washington Post,* March 6, 1953; Davidson to DDE, Jan. 15, 1953, Rabb Papers, B 26 (2), EL.

25. Thomas Winship, "Samuel Spencer Boosted as Commissioner," *Washington Post,* Jan. 28, 1953.

26. Thomas Winship, "Spencer Nominated As Donohue Successor," *Washington Post,* March 26, 1953; "Spencer Nomination," *Washington Post,* March 27, 1953; "Civic Groups Back Spencer," *Afro-American,* April 4, 1953; Thomas Winship, "Senate Confirms Spencer as D.C. Commissioner," *Washington Post,* April 3, 1953.

27. "Spencer Faces Hard Work as New City Head," *Washington Post,* April 5, 1953: "Javits Holds Racial Parley with Spencer," *Washington Post,* May 14, 1953; "City Heads Queried on Segregation Plans," *Evening Star,* May 8, 1953.

28. "Eisenhower and Spencer Get Segregation Ban Plan," *Evening Star,* April 14, 1953; "Orders Go Out to End Segregation at Posts in Military District," *Evening Star,* April 24, 1953; see http://www.globalsecurity.org/military/agency/army/mdw.htm for the history of the military district; Allen to Shanley, April 30, 1953, CF/OF 71-U, B 282, EL; Simeon S. Booker, "Ike Reaffirms Vow to end 'Second-Class Citizenship,'" *Washington Post,* May 20, 1953.

29. *District of Columbia v. John R. Thompson Co., Inc.,* 346 U.S. 100, 97 L.Ed. 1480, 73 S.Ct. 1007 (1953).

30. "Top Court Rules D.C. Cafes Must Serve Negroes," *Evening Star,* June 8, 1953; "Restaurant Integration Ruling Brings Varied Reaction Here," *Evening Star,* June 9, 1953; "D.C. Café Segregation Killed; Decision on Schools Postponed," *Washington Post,* June 9, 1953; "Supreme Court Lifts Negro Ban by Cafes," *New York Times,* June 9, 1953.

31. Edward T. Folliard, "Ike Includes End of D.C. Segregation in 10 'Deeds,'" *Washington Post,* June 12, 1953.

32. Joseph Paull, "High Court's Ruling Aids Battle for Home Rule," *Washington Post,* June 9, 1953; Al Sweeney, "Welcome Signs Out At D.C. Restaurants," *Afro-American,* June 13, 1953.

33. Allen to Shanley, April 30, 1953, Rose to DDE, March 17, 1953, to White House Staff on Human Relations, July 2, 1953, to DDE, July 30, 1953, all in CF/OF 71-U, B 282, EL; Rice to DDE, Sept. 27, 1953, CF/GF 124-A-1, B 910 (Segregation 1952–53) EL.

34. Susan Eisenhower in *Mrs. Ike: Portrait of a Marriage* (Herndon, Va: Capital, 1996), p. 301, gives Mrs. Eisenhower credit for desegregating the Easter egg roll; Adam Clayton Powell, Jr., *Adam by Adam: The Autobiography of Adam Clayton Powell, Jr.* (New York: Citadel, 1994), pp. 97–98; Rabb, OH-165, pp. 32–33, EL; Mayer, "Desegregation of Washington, D.C.," p. 30; Eisenhower's ap-

pointments with the motion picture executives are listed in the volumes, President's Appointments 1953, January–June, and President's Appointments 1953, July–December, EL; "'Go anywhere,' theaters say," *Afro-American,* Oct. 10, 1953.

35. Eisenhower, *PPP,* 1953, pp. 152, 205.
36. Report of the Executive Secretary, May 11, 1953, *NAACP Papers,* UPA; Roy Wilkins to DDE, July 13, 1953, CF/GF 124-A-2, B 922, NAACP (1), EL.
37. "New Bias Curb Reported," *New York Times,* July 3, 1953; "Fighter for Civil Rights," *New York Times,* July 4, 1956; Ira Henry Freeman, "Harlem Perplexed by Powell's Defection to Eisenhower," *New York Times,* Nov. 1, 1956; Charles V. Hamilton, *Adam Clayton Powell, Jr.: The Political Biography of an American Dilemma* (New York: Cooper Square, 1991), pp. 197–98; Powell, *Adam by Adam,* pp. 85–101; Wilton Persons was upset at reading a news story about Powell's comment, and Bryce Harlow, who worked with Persons on congressional relations, assured his colleague that the proposed body was not a "commission" but rather "an interdepartmental committee" and concluded, "It is not an F.E.P.C." Max Rabb, Harlow noted, was "carrying the ball" on organizing the new committee; see Harlow to Persons, July 6, 1953, CF/GF 124-A-1, B 910 (Segregation 1952-53), EL; "Major Accomplishments," CF/OF 142-A, B 731 (2), EL.
38. "Text of Eisenhower's Order on Bias Panel," and "President Sets Up Panel To End Bias in U.S. Contracts," *New York Times,* Aug. 14, 1953; "Nixon Will Direct Panel on Job Bias," *New York Times,* Aug. 16, 1953; Rabb, OH-265, p. 36, EL; Brownell, *Advising Ike,* p. 111; Burk, *The Eisenhower Administration and Black Civil Rights,* pp. 89–108. Eisenhower would eventually appoint Wisdom to the Fifth Circuit Court of Appeals, as noted in chapter 4.
39. "Eisenhower carries out 'little FEPC' promise," *Afro-American,* Aug. 15, 1953.
40. DDE to Nixon, Aug. 15, 1953, B 3 (2), DDE Diary, EL; Damon M. Stetson, "Eisenhower Bids Board Fight Bias," *New York Times,* Aug. 20, 1953.
41. David Robertson, *Sly and Able: A Political Biography of James F. Byrnes* (New York: Norton, 1994), pp. 510–12; Carol Anderson, *Eyes Off the Prize* (Cambridge: Cambridge University Press, 2003), pp. 241–48; Ex. Sec. report, Sept. 14, 1953, *NAACP Papers,* UPA; Byrnes had held numerous positions, including a Senate seat and appointment to the Supreme Court by Franklin Roosevelt, and he served as Truman's secretary of state in 1945–47 before being elected governor in 1951, McCullough, *Truman,* p. 368.
42. DDE to Rabb, Aug. 12, 1953, DDE to Byrnes and drafts, Aug. 14, 1953, Name Series, Byrnes, B 3 (2) EL; Byrnes to DDE, Aug. 27, 1953, DDE to Nixon, Sept. 4, 1953, DDE Diary, B 3 (2), EL. Emmet John Hughes and Max Rabb worked on drafts of the letter.
43. Exec. Sec. Report/Minutes, Sept. 14, 1953, *NAACP Papers,* UPA.
44. Spencer to Nixon, Oct. 26, 1953, James P. Mitchell Papers, Box 125 (1), EL; Sam Zagoria, "New D.C. Policy Ends Racial Bias In Contracts" and "D.C. Contracts End Job Bias," *Washington Post,* Oct. 27, 1953, clipping in John Mitchell Papers, B 125, President's Committee on Government Contracts (1), EL; "District to act against racial bans in employment," *Afro-American,* Oct. 17, 1953; Michael Mayer's "The Eisenhower Administration and the Desegregation of Washington, D.C.," pp. 30–32, provides a detailed account of the negotiations with these firms; Report, President's Committee on Government Contracts, Sept. 9, 1954, B 2, Jacob Seidenberg Papers, EL.

45. Bobovsky to DDE, Dec. 15, 1953, CF/GF 124-A-1, B 910, Segregation 1952–1953, EL; "President's Committee settles 37 of 104 discrimination cases," *Afro-American,* Feb. 12, 1955; Rabb, Civil Rights Papers, Box 27 (18), EL.

46. Spencer to DDE, Nov. 25, 1953, CF/OF 71-U, B 282, EL; the commission's order exempted two industrial home schools, the district training school, the jail division of the corrections department, and the home for aged and infirm, saying only that full integration would take place "as soon as possible"; "D.C. Orders 23 Agencies to Lower Racial Bars," *Washington Post,* Nov. 26, 1953; "FEPC, minus teeth, exempts Fire Dept.," *Afro-American,* Nov. 28, 1953.

47. "Firemen Lose Plea for Delay On Integration," *Evening Star,* Sept. 14, 1954. Only token integration had been achieved by 1957 due to resistance from the firemen's union, according to Mayer, "The Eisenhower Administration and the Desegregation of Washington, D.C.," p. 33.

48. Rabb to Adams, Sept. 20, 1954, CF/OF 103-U, B 472 (1), EL; Young to DDE, Dec. 30, 1954, CF/OF 103-U, B 473 (1), EL. Truman's initiatives in eliminating discrimination in government employment are mentioned in Mc-Cullough, *Truman,* pp. 651, 915; Gardner, *Harry Truman and Civil Rights,* pp. 107–12.

49. Regulations and Procedures, President's Committee on Government Employment Policy, March 31, 1955, CF/OF 103-U, B 474 (6-1), EL; Young to DDE, Dec. 30, 1954, Press Release, Jan. 18, 1955, Willis to Adams, Jan. 14, 1955, McCoy to Rabb, June 27, 1955, CF/OF 103-U, B 473 (1), EL; "Ike strikes at federal job JC," *Afro-American,* Jan. 22, 1955; DDE to Carey, Jan. 6, 1961, CF/OF 103-U, Box 474 (PCGE – 2), EL; Burk, *The Eisenhower Administration and Black Civil Rights,* pp. 71–77.

50. Belknap, ed., *Civil Rights,* vol. 1, pp. 160–61; Eisenhower, 1953, *PPP,* pp. 796–98.

51. Spencer to DDE, Nov. 25, 1953, DDE to Spencer, Nov. 30, 1953, CF/OF 71-U, B 282, EL.

52. Legislature Leaders Meeting, Dec. 17–19, 1953, LL, B 1 (6), EL. A nonvoting delegate to Congress was not approved until 1970. A home rule act in 1973 provided for an elected mayor and thirteen-member council.

53. "Report 'Ike' personally in printers' case," *Afro-American,* Dec. 26, 1953; "Eisenhower Praised In NAACP Report; District Hotels Scored," *Evening Star,* Jan. 1, 1954.

54. "Negro Nominated for Job in Capital," *New York Times,* Feb. 13, 1955.

55. E. Frederic Morrow Interview, April 15, 1968, OH-92, no. 2, p. 164, EL; Report on District of Columbia, Feb. 15, 1957, Gerald Morgan Papers, B 6, Civil Rights, no. 2 (1), EL; Rabb OH-265, 34, EL; Gardner, *Harry Truman and Civil Rights,* pp. 36–37.

56. "NAACP Attacks Integration Lag," *Evening Star,* Dec. 24, 1955, in Rabb Papers, Box 27 (7), EL; Eisenhower, *PPP,* 1954, p. 1095; Davidson to DDE, June 10, 1955, CF/GF 124-A-1, B 911 (2), EL.

57. Samuel Hoskins, "The last time I saw Washington," *Afro-American,* Jan. 22, 1955.

58. Rabb OH-265, p. 34, Report on District of Columbia, Feb. 15, 1957, Morgan Papers, B 6, Civil Rights, no. 2 (1), EL; Eisenhower, *The White House Years: Mandate for Change,* p. 236; Gardner, *Harry Truman and Civil Rights,* pp. 36–37. Mayer, in "The Eisenhower Administration and the Desegregation of

Washington, D.C.," presents a detailed narrative of the desegregation of the capital. Robert Frederick Burk's *The Eisenhower Administration and Black Civil Rights* has been the standard one-volume interpretation of Eisenhower and civil rights, but, on pp. 45–54, it minimizes the significance of the desegregation progress in Washington and Eisenhower's role in it.

59. Morris J. MacGregor, Jr., *Integration of the Armed Forces 1940–1965* (Washington, D.C.: Center of Military History, United States Army, 1981), pp. 313, 317, 322, 331–42; Eric F. Goldman, *The Crucial Decade—And After: America, 1945–1960* (New York: Knopf, 1971), pp. 183–87, gives no credit to Eisenhower's role in completing desegregation of the armed forces.

60. High to Rabb (Powell draft article), July 16, 1954, Rabb to Whitman, July 24, 1954, Rabb to Adams, Dec. 3, 1953, Ragland to DDE on Powell's Feb. 28 speech, March 5, 1954, CF/OF 142-A, B 731 (2), Negro Matters, EL. Powell's article was published in *The Reader's Digest* 65, no. 390 (October 1954), cited in *DDEP,* vol. 15, p. 1342; "VA Hospital Bias Seen," *New York Times,* Feb. 7, 1953; Rabb OH -265, pp. 22–23, EL; Hamilton, *Adam Clayton Powell, Jr.,* pp. 197–208; Powell, *Adam by Adam,* pp. 85–101.

61. "Orders Go Out to End Segregation at Posts in Military District," *Evening Star,* April 24, 1953; Powell's figures are different in his autobiography, saying that "40 percent of the Army's all-Negro units were still intact and 75 percent of the Negroes in the Navy were still serving in the segregated messmen's branch," Powell, *Adam by Adam,* p. 98; "New Bias Curb Reported," *New York Times,* July 3, 1953; MacGregor, *Armed Forces Integration,* p. 485.

62. News conference, March 19, 1953, Eisenhower, *PPP,* p. 108.

63. Powell's draft article, High to Rabb, July 16, 1954, CF/OF 142-A, B 731; Powell to Charles Wilson, Feb. 24, 1954, CF/GF 124-A-1, B 911, 1954 (1) EL; Hamilton, *Adam Clayton Powell, Jr.,* pp. 199–201. "Services Abolish All-Negro Units," *New York Times,* Oct. 31, 1954; MacGregor, *Armed Forces Integration,* p. 73; Sherie Mershon and Steven Schlossman, *Foxholes & Color Lines: Desegregating the U.S. Armed Forces* (Baltimore: Johns Hopkins University Press, 1998), pp. 267–68, contend that Eisenhower rejected Truman's liberalism on civil rights and credit his positive actions primarily to his being an "astute politician."

64. "Army School Policy Hit," *Washington Post,* Jan. 15, 1953; Jeanne Rogers, "Ike Orders Probe of Segregated Schools at Fort Belvoir and Other Posts in South," *Washington Post,* March 20, 1953.

65. MacGregor, *Armed Forces Integration,* p. 487.

66. MacGregor, *Armed Forces Integration,* pp. 489–96; Press Release, March 25, 1953, CF/OF 142-A, B 731, EL; Eisenhower, *PPP,* 1953, p. 127; Wilson to Armed Forces Secretaries, Jan. 12, 1954, Rabb Papers, Box 26 (8), EL; Burk, *The Einsenhower Administration and Black Civil Rights,* pp. 28–34; see chapters 3, 4 and 5 herein for Eisenhower's response to the *Brown* decision.

67. MacGregor, *Armed Forces Integration,* pp. 490–96; Mershon and Schlossman, *Foxholes & Color Lines,* pp. 270–72.

68. Powell to DDE, Feb. 5, 1953, Boone to Persons and Powell, Feb. 17, 1953, Feb. 17, 1953, CF/GF 124-A-1, B 910, Segregation 1952–1955, EL; Gray to Adams, June 5, 1953, Rabb Papers, Box 35 (10, #3), EL.

69. Higley to DDE, Sept. 24, 1954, Rabb Papers, Box 35 (10, #2), EL; DDE to Higley, Oct. 26, 1954, Eisenhower, *PPP,* 1954, p. 959; Burk, *The Eisenhower Administration and Black Civil Rights,* pp. 40–41.

70. Anderson to Persons, May 28, 1953, Rabb Papers, Box 6 (5), EL; MacGregor, *Armed Forces Integration,* pp. 483–85, 492. Anderson was a favorite of Eisenhower's, and later was appointed deputy secretary of defense and Treasury secretary. Some of the early negotiations about naval bases' desegregation before action was taken is found in "Navy Will Modify Job Segregation," *New York Times,* Aug. 10, 1953; "Navy Moves to End Job Segregation," *New York Times,* Aug. 21, 1953.

71. Mitchell to Anderson, March 30, 1953, Mitchell to Rabb, May 28, 1953, Rabb to Mitchell, May 29, 1953, CF/GF 124-A-1, Box 910 (Segregation 1952–53), EL; MacGregor, *Armed Forces Integration,* pp. 484–85; Eisenhower, *Mandate for Change,* pp. 235–36; Burk, *The Eisenhower Administration and Black Civil Rights,* pp. 35–38.

72. DDE to Powell, June 6, 1953, Powell to DDE, June 10, 1953, CF/OF 142-A, B 731, Negro Matters (1), EL; "Ike Restates Antipathy to Segregation," *Washington Post,* June 11, 1953.

73. White to DDE, June 9, 1953, CF/GF 124 A-1, Box 910, Segregation 1952–53, EL; Rabb, OH-265, pp. 25–26; Thomas to DDE, June 23, 1953, Belknap, ed., *Civil Rights,* vol. 3, pp. 433–38; Rabb, OH-265, pp. 16–27; MacGregor, *Armed Forces Integration,* pp. 485–86.

74. "Navy Will Modify Job Segregation," *New York Times,* Aug. 10, 1953; "Navy Policy Criticized," *New York Times,* Aug. 11, 1953; "Navy Moves to End Job Segregation," *New York Times,* Aug. 21, 1953; MacGregor, *Armed Forces Integration,* pp. 486–87.

75. DDE to Byrnes and drafts, Aug. 14, 1953, Byrnes to DDE, Aug. 27, 1953, Name Series, B 3, Byrnes (1-2), EL.

76. Anderson to DDE, Nov. 9, 1953, Belknap, ed., *Civil Rights,* vol. 3, pp 443–44; DDE Statement, Nov. 11, 1953, CF/OF 142-A-4, B 731, (1), EL; Eisenhower, *PPP,* 1953, p. 757; MacGregor, *Armed Forces Integration,* p. 487.

77. "48 Negro Soldiers Fined in Race Issue," *New York Times,* Nov. 28, 1953; C. E. Wilson to DDE, Jan. 27, 1954, CF/OF 142-A, B 731, Negro Matters (2), EL; "Navy Barbers Fired, Won't Serve Negroes," *Washington Post,* Feb. 9, 1954, in Rabb Papers, B 6 (5); Priester to DDE, June 27, 1954, CF/GF 124-A-1, B 911, 1954 (3), EL; MacGregor, *Armed Forces Integration,* pp. 499–500; Mershon and Schlossman, *Foxholes & Color Lines,* pp. 269–70.

78. Morrow to Rabb, Sept. 12, 1955; Rabb to Harlow, Sept. 13, 1953, Rabb Papers, B 27 (4), EL.

79. Radio report, Aug. 6, 1953, Eisenhower, *PPP,* p. 556; "President to Get Award," *New York Times,* Aug. 16, 1953.

80. Powell, draft article, High to Rabb, July 16, 1954, Rabb to Whitman, July 24, 1954, CF/OF 142-A, B 731, EL; Hamilton, *Powell,* pp. 209–10.

81. News conference, Oct. 5, 1956, Eisenhower, *PPP,* pp. 851–52.

82. Edward T. Folliard, "Ike Includes End of D.C. Segregation in 10 'Deeds,'" *Washington Post,* June 12, 1953; Belknap, ed., *Civil Rights,* vol. 1, pp. 160–61; Report of the President's Committee on Equal Opportunity in the Armed Forces, June 13, 1963, Post-Pres. Papers, Principal File 1963, B 67 (Wa-2), EL.

83. Outline of Ex. Sec. Report, Jan. 4, 1954, *NAACP Papers,* UPA; Ragland to DDE, March 5, 1954, quoting Powell's Feb. 28 speech, CF/OF 142-A, B 731 (2), Negro Matters, EL.

CHAPTER THREE: **THE PRESIDENT AND** *BROWN*

1. "Ruling on School Segregation Unlikely Before Next Spring," *Evening Star,* June 9, 1953, p. A4.

2. *Missouri ex rel. Gaines v. Canada,* 305 U.S. 337, 83 L.Ed. 208, 59 S.Ct. 232 (1938); *Sweatt v. Painter,* 339 U.S. 629, 94 L.ED. 1114, 70 S.Ct. 848 (1950); *McLaurin v. Oklahoma State Regents,* 339 U.S. 637, 94 L.Ed. 1161, 68 S.Ct. 851 (1950).

3. "Judicial Soul Searching," *Washington Post,* June 10, 1953; Supreme Court Conference, Dec. 13, 1952, Douglas Papers, B 1150, Segregation Cases, LC.

4. "W. H. Lawrence, "Administration Expected to Fight School Segregation in High Court," *New York Times,* Nov. 9, 1953; "5 Questions Asked by Court on School Issue," *Washington Post,* June 9, 1953.

5. Shivers to DDE, July 16, 1953, Michael R. Belknap, ed. *Civil Rights, the White House, and the Justice Department* (New York: Garland, 1991), vol. 7, p. 17; DDE to Shivers, July 21, 1953, CF/OF 142A-4, B 731 (1), EL.

6. DDE Diary, July 24, 1953, B 9, Copies of DDE Personal 1953–54 (2); Voting Analysis Shared by Jimmy Byrnes with DDE, approx. July 20, 1953; DDE to Byrnes, Aug. 14, 1953, all in Name Series, James F. Byrnes, B 3 (2), EL.

7. Memorandum for the Record, Aug. 19, 1953, DDE Diary, B 3, Aug.–Sept. 1953 (2), EL; *DDEP,* vol. 14, p. 481; Herbert Brownell, *Advising Ike: The Memoirs of Attorney General Herbert Brownell* (Lawrence: University Press of Kansas, 1993), pp. 193–94. The decision at the end of the conversation is not in DDE's diary entry, but the path both men followed in subsequent months validates Brownell's account. However, Eisenhower later, for political reasons during the 1956 presidential campaign, articulated the myth that Brownell was speaking as a lawyer, not representing the administration. See telephone call, Eisenhower to Brownell, Aug. 19, 1956, ACW Diary, Box 8, EL

8. Hugo Black to the President, Sept. 9, 1953, CF/OF 100-A, B 371, Supreme Ct. of the U.S. (1); "Chief Justice Vinson Dies of Heart Attack in Capital," *New York Times,* Sept. 8, 1953; News Conference, Sept. 30, 1953, Eisenhower, *PPP,* pp. 618–19.

9. DDE to Young Berryman Smith, Sept. 14, 1953, *DDEP,* vol. 14, p. 519; DDE to Milton Eisenhower, Sept. 11, 1953, DDE Diaries, B 3, August–September 1953 (2), EL.

10. Lawrence E. Davies, "Warren Bars 4th Term Bid; Favored for Supreme Court," *New York Times,* Sept. 4, 1953; DDE to Swede Hazlett, Oct. 23, 1954, Name Series, B 18, Swede Hazlett, 1954 (1), EL; DDE Diary, Oct. 8, 1953, B 9, Copies of DDE Personal 1953–54 (2), EL.

11. "Californian Won Fame as Crusader," *New York Times,* Oct. 1, 1955, p. 16.

12. Brownell, OH-362, 27–28, EL; "Earl Warren: The Chief Justiceship," interview with Herbert Brownell, Oct. 29, 1974, Earl Warren Oral History Project, Bancroft Library, University of California, Berkeley 1977, p. 70, EL. The oft-repeated story that implies that Eisenhower was ignorant of Warren's views on civil rights is that he allegedly said that the nomination of Warren was the "biggest damn fool mistake" he ever made as president, with scholars and journalists usually connecting that conclusion to the *Brown* decision on school desegregation. The quotation is of doubtful credibility, and anything comparable may have reflected Eisenhower's upset over later Warren Court decisions on criminal law and Communism; for an example, see James T.

Patterson, *Brown v. Board of Education: A Civil Rights Milestone and Its Troubled Legacy* (New York: Oxford University Press, 2001), p. 60.

13. Brownell Interview, Oct. 29, 1974, Warren Project, pp. 58–64, EL; ACW Diary, Oct. 2, B 1, Aug.–Sept.–Oct. 1953 (2), EL; Brownell, *Advising Ike*, p. 166; Eisenhower, *The White House Years: Mandate for Change, 1953–56* (New York: Doubleday, 1963), p. 227.

14. DDE Interview, July 20, 1967, OH-11, EL, 94; William Brass Ewald, Jr., *Eisenhower the President: Crucial Days, 1951–60* (Englewood Cliffs, N.J.: Prentice-Hall, 1981), p. 77; Brownell Interview, Oct. 29, 1974, Warren Project, pp. 64–67; EL; W. H. Lawrence, "Warren Is Slated for Appointment as Chief Justice," *New York Times,* Sept. 29, 1953.

15. News Conference, Sept. 30, 1953, Eisenhower, *PPP,* pp. 615–23; James Reston, "Eisenhower Names Warren to be Chief Justice," *New York Times,* Oct. 1, 1953.

16. Brownell, *Advising Ike,* pp. 170–71; Brownell Interview, Oct. 29, 1974, Warren Project, p. 67, EL.

17. Arthur Krock, "In the Nation," *New York Times,* Oct. 1, 1953; News Release by Walter White, Oct. 8, 1953, Rabb Papers, B 35 (3), EL; Luther A. Huston, "High Court Opens Its Term Monday," *New York Times,* Oct. 1, 1953.

18. Earl Warren, *The Memoirs of Earl Warren* (Garden City, N.Y.: Doubleday, 1977), pp. 278–80.

19. DDE Diary, Oct. 8, 1953, B 9 (2), EL.

20. Monthly Report, May 1954, NAACP Legal Defense and Educational Fund, Inc., NAACP Papers, UPA.

21. W. H. Lawrence, "Administration Expected to Fight School Segregation in High Court," *New York Times,* Nov. 9, 1953; Chalmers M. Roberts, "School Cases Force Brownell Stand," *Washington Post,* Nov. 15, 1953.

22. DDE Diary, Nov. 16, 1953, B 5, Phone Calls July–Dec. 1953 (1), EL; News Conference, Nov. 18, 1953, Eisenhower, *PPP,* p. 791.

23. Kennon to DDE, Nov. 20, 1953; DDE to Kennon and Byrnes, Nov. 30, 1953, Belknap, ed., *Civil Rights,* vol. 7, pp. 23–26; Byrnes to DDE, Nov. 20, 1953, CF/OF 142-A-4, B 731 (1), EL.

24. Luther A. Huston, "High Court Urged to End School Bias," *New York Times,* Nov. 28, 1953; "Transition Period Suggested," *New York Times,* Nov. 28, 1953; William T. Coleman, Jr., a Washington, D.C., attorney who collaborated with Thurgood Marshall on the NAACP brief, insisted in a letter to the author, August 24, 2006, that Rankin and Elman told him that President Eisenhower himself had edited the pages of the *Brown I* brief that stated the government's position on the issue of segregated schools. Elman confirmed that Eisenhower edited the *Brown II* brief in Norman I. Silber, *With All Deliberate Speed: The Life of Philip Elman* (Ann Arbor: University of Michigan Press, 2004), pp. 221–23.

25. DDE to Byrnes, Dec. 1, 1953, DDE Diary, B 4, December 1953 (2), EL.

26. DDE call to Brownell, Dec. 2, 1953, DDE Diary, B 5, Phone Calls July–Dec. 1953 (1), EL.

27. Frank R. Kent, Jr., "Court Is Told It Can Change School Policy," *Washington Post,* Nov. 28, 1953; "D.C. Schools Not Affected by Supreme Court Action," *Afro-American,* June 13, 1954; "Nabrit gives plan to mix D.C. schools," *Afro-American,* Dec. 12, 1953; DDE Diary, Nov. 5, 1953, B 5 (1), EL.

28. Memorandum for the Supreme Court Conference, Dec. 3, 1953, Douglas Papers, B 1149, Segregation Cases, LC.

29. Frank R. Kent, Jr., "High Court Told It Has Duty to End School Segregation," *Washington Post,* Dec. 8, 1953; "Final Fight Opens in Supreme Court on Bias in Schools," *New York Times,* Dec. 8, 1953.

30. Bem Price, "4 Southern States Fight Integration, *Washington Post,* Sept. 26, 1954; "Negro Has Trod a Century-Long Road in His Legislative and Legal Battles for Equality," *New York Times,* May 18, 1954; Kent, "High Court Told It Has Duty"; "Argument in Case Ran a Wide Gamut," *New York Times,* May 18, 1954, p. 23; Leon Friedman, ed., *Argument,* vol. 1 (New York: Chelsea House, 1983), pp. 194–206, 233–40.

31. Supreme Court Conference, Dec. 12, 1953, Douglas Papers, B 1150, Segregation Cases, LC.

32. State of the Union Address, Jan. 7, 1954, Eisenhower, *PPP,* p. 22; DDE-Brownell phone conversation, Jan. 25, 1954, DDE Diary, B 5, Phone Calls, EL.

33. Brownell, *Advising Ike,* pp. 169–70; Jim Newton, in a new biography of Warren, *Justice for All: Earl Warren and the Nation He Made* (New York: Riverhead, 2006), provides a detailed account of what he calls the "smear" by Langer and Warren's enemies, pp. 279–91.

34. "Mr. Warren Is Confirmed," *New York Times,* March 2, 1954; Supreme Court Conference, April 16, 1954, Douglas Papers, B 1150, Segregation Cases, LC.

35. Supreme Court Conference Notes, Jan. 25, 1960, Douglas Papers, B 1149, Segregation Cases, LC.

36. *Brown v. Board of Education of Topeka,* 347 U.S. 483, 98 L.Ed. 873, 74 S.Ct. 686 (1954); *Bolling v. Sharpe,* 347 U.S. 497, 500, 98 L.Ed. 884, 74 S.Ct. 693 (1954); "Brownell and Acheson in Court for Decision," *New York Times,* May 18, 1954; "High Court Voids School Segregation; Upsets 'Separate But Equal' Doctrine," *Evening Star,* May 17, 1954.

37. Judge Charles Metzner, interview with author, Feb. 4, 2004; Roy Wilkins, *Standing Fast: The Autobiography of Roy Wilkins* (1982; rept. New York: Da Capo, 1994), p. 213.

38. "Editorial Excerpts from the Nation's Press on Segregation Ruling," *New York Times,* May 18, 1954; "Equal Education For All," *Washington Post,* May 19, 1954.

39. John N. Popham, "Reaction of South," *New York Times,* May 18, 1954.

40. *DDEP,* vol. 17, p. 2616; "DC to Seek School Integration By September After Parley Decides No Legal Bars Remain," *Evening Star,* May 18, 1954; Hagerty to Everett Hodge, Sept. 12, 1956, CF/GF 124-A-1, B 912 (2), EL; Eisenhower, *The White House Years: Waging Peace, 1956–61* (Garden City, N.Y.: Doubleday, 1965), p. 150; Luther A. Huston, "Eisenhower Spurs Capital's Schools to End Race Bars," *New York Times,* May 19, 1954; Samuel Spencer to DDE, May 26, 1954, CF/OF 71-U, B 282, EL; "Walls Crumbling," *Afro-American,* May 22, 1954.

41. James Hagerty Diary, May 18, 1954, Belknap, ed., *Civil Rights,* vol. 7, pp. 13, 28.

42. News Conference, May 19, 1954, Eisenhower, *PPP,* pp. 491–92.

43. Hobart R. Corning to Board of Education, May 25, 1954, CF/OF 71-U, B 282, EL; "Corning Sets Forth His Program on Abolishing Segregation in Schools," *Evening Star,* June 3, 1954; "17 D.C. Groups Ask Speedy Integration," *Washington Post,* May 20, 1954; "Debate Rages Over School Integration," *Afro-American,* May 29, 1954.

44. Spencer to DDE, June 7, 1954, CF/OF 71-U, B 282, EL; James G. Deane,

"Timetable Is Drawn For 15-Month Shift To School Integration," *Evening Star,* June 3, 1954.

45. "Federation Asks Ban on Integration," *Washington Post,* Sept. 20, 1954; "School suit killed; Ike intervenes," *Afro-American,* Sept. 11, 1954.

46. Spencer to DDE, Sept. 20, 1954, CF/OF 142-A-5, B 731 (1), EL; Bem Price, "4 Southern States Fight Integration," *Washington Post,* Sept. 26, 1954; "Mix 66,020 pupils in District schools," *Afro-American,* Sept. 18, 1954.

47. Jeanne Rogers, "Most of South Stalling on School Ruling," *Washington Post,* Aug. 1, 1954; Paul W. Yost, "Article 1—No Title," *Washington Post,* Oct. 3, 1954; Humphrey to Al Maurer, Jan. 19, 1957, HHH Papers, B 136, MHS.

48. Yost, "Article I—No Title"; Frank R. Kent, Jr., "Court Gets Opposing Opinions on Integration," *Washington Post,* Nov. 16, 1954.

49. Brownell, *Advising Ike,* p. 179; News Conference, November 23, 1954, Eisenhower, *PPP,* pp. 1062–66; both the Harlan nomination and the brief were discussed in the president's November 23 news conference; Michael S. Mayer, "A Kansan Looks at Brown," in John R. Wunder, ed., *Law and the Great Plains: Essays on the Legal History of the Heartland* (Westport, Conn.: Greenwood, 1996), pp. 62–63; "Senate Unit Backs Harlan for Supreme Court," *New York Times,* March 10, 1955; "Senate Confirms Harlan to Bench," *New York Times,* March 17, 1955.

50. DDE to Hazlett, Oct. 23, 1954, Name Series, Swede Hazlett, 1954 (1), B 18, EL.

51. NAACP Brief, November 1954, NAACP Papers, Section II, B 138–39, 143, pp. 16–30, LC.

52. Brownell, *Advising Ike,* pp. 196–98; Brownell Interview, OH-157, no. 3, p. 162, EL; see chapter 4 for the story of DDE's nomination of Soheloff for the Fourth Circuit Court of Appeals; Michael S. Mayer provides significant detail on DDE's editing of the *Brown II* brief in "With Much Deliberation and Some Speed: Eisenhower and the *Brown* Decision," *Journal of Southern History* 52, no. 1 (February 1986): 62–69; According to Daun van Ee, Library of Congress historian, the draft of the brief with DDE's handwritten notes on it once existed but was lost.

53. News Conference, Nov. 23, 1954, Eisenhower, *PPP,* pp. 1065–66.

54. Justice Department Brief, November 1954, Simon E. Soboloff Papers, B 26 (1-2), LC; Frank R. Kent, Jr., "Justice Asks for 90 Days for Integration," *New York Times,* Nov. 24, 1954; Mayer, "With Much Deliberation," pp. 65–69.

55. ACW Diary, Dec. 2, 1954, B 3, December 1954 (5), EL.

56. *Brown v. Board of Education of Topeka,* 349 U.S. 294, 99 L.Ed. 1083, 75 S.Ct. 753 (1955); Charles J. Ogletree, Jr., *All Deliberate Speed: Reflections on the First Half Century of Brown v. Board of Education* (New York: Norton, 2004), pp. 10–11.

57. Brownell call to DDE, May 31, 1955, DDE Diary, B 9, Phone Calls—January–July 1955 (1), EL; Brownell, *Advising Ike,* pp. 196–97. DDE's October 23 prediction to Hazlett was undoubtedly based on conversation with Brownell while they were working on the brief.

58. Warren, *Memoirs,* p. 288.

59. Roy Wilkins, Report of the Executive Secretary, June 13, 1955, NAACP Papers, UPA.

60. Brownell, *Advising Ike,* pp. 196–97; the struggles inside the Supreme Court over *Brown I & II* are ably described in James F. Simon, *The Antagonists: Hugo Black, Felix Frankfurter and Civil Liberties in Modern America* (New York: Simon

& Schuster, 1989), pp. 213–34; a study that is critical of the *Brown* rulings and their legacy is Peter Irons, *Jim Crow's Children: The Broken Promise of the Brown Decision* (New York: Penguin, 2002), pp. 156–87.

CHAPTER FOUR: A JUDICIARY TO ENFORCE *BROWN*

1. Brownell's phrases come from the titles of chapters 10–11 in his memoir, *Advising Ike: The Memoirs of Attorney General Herbert Brownell* (Lawrence: University Press of Kansas, 1993) pp. 176–201.
2. Brownell, *Advising Ike*, p. 176; Eisenhower, *The White House Years Mandate for Change, 1953–56* (New York: Doubleday, 1963), p. 226; DDE Diary, B 9, Copies of DDE Personal, 1955–56 (2) EL.
3. Brownell, *Advising Ike*, p. 176; Warren Olney Interview, Brownell Papers, B 36, Criminal—Warren Olney Interview (3), EL.
4. DDE Diary Entry, Feb. 5, 1957, Administration Series, B 8, Brownell—1957 (4), EL; News Conference, Oct. 27, 1954, Eisenhower, *PPP,* p. 970; Brownell, *Advising Ike*, pp. 176–77; DDE Diary, B 9, Copies of DDE Personal, 1955–56 (2); DDE to Edgar, March 23, 1956, DDE Diary, B 14, March 1956 Misc. (2), EL.
5. Brownell, *Advising Ike*, p. 178; News Conference, Oct. 27, 1954, Eisenhower, *PPP,* p. 970; Henry J. Abraham, *Justices, Presidents, and Senators: A History of the U.S. Supreme Court Appointments from Washington to Clinton* (New York: Rowman & Littlefield, 1999), p. 41.
6. DDE Diary, Feb. 5, 1957, Administration Series, B 8, Brownell—1957 (4), EL.
7. DDE to Rogers, Sept. 17, 1958, Rogers Papers, B 4, Pres. Eisenhower—Correspondence With, May 1958–December 1959, EL; DDE to Nixon, Dec. 13, 1968, B 14, Richard M. Nixon 1968 (2), Post-Presidential Papers, Special Names Series, EL.
8. Michael A. Kahn, "Shattering the Myth About President Eisenhower's Supreme Court Appointments," *Presidential Studies Quarterly* 22, no. 1 (Winter 1992) 47–56. Kahn is a prominent West Coast attorney, active in cases involving the federal courts, and the author of articles on litigation practice and the Supreme Court. Henry J. Abraham in *Justices, Presidents, and Senators,* p. 191, gives Eisenhower a "well-done" for his Supreme Court appointments excepting Charles E. Whittaker. Geoffrey Perret, in *Eisenhower* (Holbrook, Mass.: Adams Media, 1999), p. 553, gives Eisenhower credit for superior judicial appointments, upheld by the "consensus among legal scholars and historians that the Warren Court . . . was the greatest body of American jurists since the early days of the Republic."
9. "Justice Jackson Dead at 62 of Heart Attack in Capital," *New York Times,* Oct. 10, 1954; "'Career Jurist' Favored," *New York Times,* Oct. 14, 1954; "Speculation Rises on Court Nominee," *New York Times,* Oct. 11, 1954.
10. Brownell to DDE, Nov. 5, 1954, CF/OF 100-A, B 371, Supreme Court of the U.S. (1), EL; "Eisenhower Names U.S. Judge Harlan to Supreme Court," *New York Times,* Nov. 9, 1954; Abraham, *Justices, Presidents, and Senators,* pp. 197–98.
11. Michael S. Mayer, "With Much Deliberation and Some Speed: Eisenhower and the *Brown* Decision," *Journal of Southern History* 52, no. 1 (February 1986): 63.

12. "Harlan Name Put to Senate Again," *New York Times,* Jan. 11, 1955; News Conference, Feb. 2, 1955, Eisenhower, *PPP,* pp. 231–32; "Eisenhower Scores Delay on Harlan," *New York Times,* Feb. 3, 1955.

13. "Senate Unit Backs Harlan for Supreme Court," *New York Times,* March 10, 1955; "Senate Confirms Harlan to Bench," *New York Times,* March 17, 1955; Brownell, *Advising Ike,* p.179; Eisenhower expressed regret over the confirmation struggle to Harlan, April 6, 1955, CF/OF 100-A, B 371, Supreme Court of the U.S. (1), EL.

14. ACW Diary, Dec. 2, 1954, B 3, December 1954 (5), EL; DDE to Brownell, March 8, 1955, *DDEP,* vol. 16, p. 1607.

15. Eisenhower, *Mandate for Change,* p. 230; "President Names Jersey Democrat to Supreme Court," *New York Times,* Sept. 30, 1956; Abraham, *Justices, Presidents, and Senators,* pp. 199–200.

16. DDE to Reed, Jan. 28, 1957, and Brownell to DDE, CF/OF 100-A, B 371, Supreme Court (2), EL; Brownell, *Advising Ike,* p. 181; Abraham, *Justices, Presidents, and Senators,* pp. 203–04.

17. Assumptions that Brownell was aggressive on judicial appointments and Eisenhower was passive permeate otherwise excellent studies on the subject, including Jack Bass, *Unlikely Heroes* (New York: Simon & Schuster, 1981), and J. W. Peltason, *58 Lonely Men: Southern Federal Judges and School Desegregation* (New York: Harcourt, Bracc & World, 1961). Scholars have consistently failed to understand how closely Eisenhower and Brownell collaborated in managing the judicial appointment process and that Eisenhower himself was the architect of that process.

18. DDE to Rogers, March 5, 1958, and DDE to Rogers, January 1959, Rogers Papers, B 4, President Eisenhower—Correspondence With, EL; DDE to Rogers, Feb. 10 and 12, 1959, Rogers Papers, B 32, Rogers 1959 (4), EL; ACW Diary, Feb. 12, 1959, B 10, February 1959 (2), EL.

19. Burton to DDE, July 17, 1958, CF/OF 100-A, B 371, Supreme Court (2); DDE to Rogers, Sept. 17, 1958, Rogers Papers, B 4, Pres. Eisenhower—Correspondence With, May 1958–December 1958, EL.

20. Cramer to DDE, Oct. 7, 1958; DDE to Cramer, Oct. 8, 1958; Rogers to DDE, Oct. 7, 1958, all in CF/OF 100-A, B 371, Supreme Court (2), EL; Abraham, *Justices, Presidents, and Senators,* pp. 204–6.

21. Kahn, "Shattering the Myth," p. 54.

22. Brownell, *Advising Ike,* p. 182.

23. Bass, *Unlikely Heroes,* pp. 16–19; Brownell, *Advising Ike,* p. 182; Jack Bass, *Taming the Storm: The Life and Times of Judge Frank Johnson, Jr. and the South's Fight Over Civil Rights* (New York: Doubleday, 1993), pp. 88, 108–17.

24. Cutler to Brownell, May 5, 1954, and Kennon to DDE, Jan. 18, 1957; Wisdom to Adams, Feb. 8, 1955; C. E. Wilson to Brownell, Dec. 20, 1956; George C. Stafford to DDE, March 4, 1955, all in CF/GF 4-C-5, B 80, Endorsements, Kennon and Wisdom, EL; Bass, *Unlikely Heroes,* pp. 16–17.

25. Bass, *Unlikely Heroes,* pp. 84–96; Peltason, *58 Lonely Men,* pp. 26–27.

26. Lawrence E. Walsh, *The Gift of Insecurity: A Lawyer's Life* (Chicago, ABA, 2003), pp. 176–77, confirmed in an interview with the author, Sept. 1, 2006.

27. Included in Rogers to Morgan, Sept. 14, 1959; Rogers to Eastland, Dirksen, Sept. 11, 1959, CF/GF 4, Endorsements, Judicial Branch (The Federal Judiciary), EL.

28. The resignation of Morris A. Soper came in a letter to Eisenhower, April 15,

1955; CF/OF 100-B-4, B 372, Fourth Judicial Circuit, EL; Brownell to DDE, July 12, 1955, CF/OF 100-B-4, B 372, Fourth Judicial Circuit, EL; DDE to Brownell, Dec. 2, 1954, ACW Diary, B 3, December 1954 (5), EL; This communication from Eisenhower to Brownell may indicate that if Eisenhower had been given the opportunity to appoint a sixth justice to the Supreme Court, that person would have been another advocate for *Brown*, possibly Sobeloff. For a detailed account of the congressional fight over Sobeloff's nomination to the Fourth Circuit, see Michael Mayer, "Eisenhower and the Southern Federal Judiciary: The Sobeloff Nomination," in Shirley Anne Warshaw, ed., *Reexamining the Eisenhower Presidency* (Westport, Conn.: Greenwood, 1993), pp. 58–83.

29. Thurmond to DDE, May 24, 1955; Mark W. Clark to DDE, June 24, 1955, CF/GF 4-C-4, B 79, Endorsement, Figg, EL.

30. Dees to DDE, July 18, 1955, Sobeloff, CF/GF 4-C-4, B 80, Endorsement, EL.

31. Address to Annual Convention of the American Bar Association, Aug. 2, 1955, Eisenhower, *PPP*, 1955, p. 804; "Brownell Affirms Choice of Sobeloff, *New York Times*, Nov. 9, 1955; Mayer, "Eisenhower and the Southern Federal Judiciary," p. 64.

32. News Conference, May 23, 1956, Eisenhower, *PPP*, p. 519.

33. Mayer, "Eisenhower and the Southern Federal Judiciary," pp. 64–72; "Washington Proceedings," *New York Times*, June 26, 1956.

34. Byrnes to DDE, Feb. 24, 1956, DDE to Byrnes, Feb. 27, 1956, Rogers to Minnich, n.d., CF/OF 100-B-4, B 372, Fourth Judicial Circuit, EL.

35. Thurmond to DDE, July 17, 1956; Thurmond to Adams, Dec. 8, 1956, CF/GF 4-C-4, B 79, Endorsement, Figg, EL.

36. Brownell to DDE, Feb. 14, 1957, CF/OF 100-B-4, B 372, Fourth Judicial Circuit, EL. Haynsworth was eventually nominated to the Supreme Court in 1969 by Richard Nixon but was not confirmed.

37. Brownell to Adams, CF/GF 4-D, B 86 (Richardson, Scovel), EL; Elliott to Shanley, Oct. 4, 1956, Shanley to Gray, Oct. 6, 1956, Shanley to Elliott, Gray to Rogers, Oct. 18, 1956; handwritten note from Gray to Shanley says "it is almost positive that Richardson is NOT going to get it before election if at all"; all in CF/GF 6F-4-D, Box 86, Richardson, 6F, EL; Harold W. Chase, *Federal Judges: The Appointing Process* (Minneapolis: University of Minnesota Press, 1972), p. 93; Sheldon Goldman, *Picking Federal Judges: Lower Court Selection from Roosevelt Through Reagan* (New Haven: Yale University Press, 1997), pp. 143–46.

38. Brownell, *Advising Ike,* p. 183.

39. Brownell, *Advising Ike,* p. 183. Chase, *Federal Judges,* generally affirms the high quality of Eisenhower's judicial appointments, pp. 89–119; Michael S. Mayer, "With Much Deliberation," p. 75, contends: "Eisenhower's appointments to federal judgeships, especially to the fourth and fifth circuits, constituted his greatest contribution to the cause of civil rights."

40. Peltason, *58 Lonely Men,* p. 217; Taylor Branch, *Parting the Waters: America in the King Years, 1954–63* (New York: Simon & Schuster, 1988), pp. 633–72, and *At Canaan's Edge: America in the King Years, 1965–68* (New York: Simon & Schuster, 2006), pp. 68–75; Bass, *Unlikely Heroes,* pp. 259–62, and *Taming the Storm,* pp. 249–53; David L. Lewis, *King: A Biography* (Urbana: University of Illinois Press, 1978) pp. 264–96.

41. The "unlikely heroes" phrase comes from the title of Jack Bass's book that fo-

cuses on the four courageous judges in the Fifth Circuit: Elbert Tuttle, John Brown, John Minor Wisdom, and Richard Taylor Rives, the first three of whom were Eisenhower appointees.

CHAPTER FIVE: THE PRESIDENT AND THE CHIEF JUSTICE

1. Earl Warren, *The Memoirs of Earl Warren* (Garden City, N.Y.: Doubleday, 1977), p. 291.
2. Brownell Interview, OH-362, EL, p. 26; Herbert Brownell, *Advising Ike: The Memoirs of Attorney General Herbert Brownell* (Lawrence: University Press of Kansas, 1993), pp. 173–74; Adams Interview, OH-162, EL, p. 243. Beyond Brownell's explanation, it is difficult to find a source for this particular quotation. However, it is ubiquitous in news reports and on the Internet, almost always without attribution.
3. Milton Eisenhower Interview, OH-292, EL, pp. 91–92; William Bragg Ewald, Jr., *Eisenhower the President: Crucial Days, 1951–60* (Englewood Cliffs, N.J.: Prentice-Hall, 1981), p. 85. Stephen E. Ambrose, "The Eisenhower Revival," in Thomas E. Cronin, ed., *Rethinking the Presidency* (Boston: Little, Brown, 1982), p. 107.
4. Brownell, *Advising Ike*, pp. 173–74; Adams Interview, OH-162, EL, p. 243.
5. The California delegation, led by Warren, assisted the Eisenhower forces in winning a contest over the seating of a delegation pledged to the general. Some scholars make this the source of the alleged political debt; see Mark V. Tushnet, *Making Civil Rights Law: Thurgood Marshall and the Supreme Court, 1936–1961* (New York: Oxford University Press, 1994), p. 202; DDE Diary, Oct. 8, 1953, B 9, EL; G. Edward White, *Earl Warren: A Public Life* (New York: Oxford University Press, 1982), pp. 138–41; Brownell, *Advising Ike*, p. 119; Hagerty Interview, Nov. 5, 1973, Earl Warren Oral History Project, Bancroft Library, University of California, Berkeley, 1977, p. 5, EL.
6. Brownell, OH-362, pp. 27–28; "Earl Warren: The Chief Justiceship," interview with Herbert Brownell, Oct. 29, 1974, Earl Warren Oral History Project, p. 70, EL; James Reston, "Court and Civil Rights," *New York Times*, Sept. 30, 1953, p. 21.
7. Adams Interview, June 19, 1970, No. 4, OH-162, EL, pp. 241–43.
8. Diary Entry, June 16, 1954, Robert H. Ferrell, ed., *The Diary of James C. Hagerty* (Bloomington: Indiana University Press, 1973), p. 67; Eisenhower, *The White House Years: Mandate for Change, 1953–56* (New York: Doubleday, 1963) p. 27.
9. Milton Eisenhower to DDE, Sept. 15, 1953, Name Series, Milton Eisenhower, 1952–53 (3), EL.
10. DDE to Brownell, Aug. 5, 1953, *DDEP*, vol. 14, p. 461; Brownell, *Advising Ike*, p. 165; Brownell Interview, Warren Oral History Project, p. 56, EL; *Warren, Memoirs*, pp. 268–69.
11. Eisenhower, *Mandate for Change*, p. 228; Lawrence E. Davies, "Warren Bars 4th Term Bid; Favored for Supreme Court," *New York Times*, Sept. 4, 1953.
12. "Offers to Warren of a Supreme Court Justiceship," Interview with Herbert Brownell, Oct. 29, 1974, Earl Warren Oral History Project, p. 53, EL; Warren, *Memoirs*, p. 260; Jack Bass, in *Taming the Storm: The Life and Times of Judge Frank M. Johnson, Jr.* (New York: Doubleday, 1993), pp. 85–86, cites a 1989

interview in which Brownell says he first suggested Warren for the court.

13. Warren, *Memoirs,* p. 260, Eisenhower, *Mandate for Change,* p. 228.

14. A version of the appointment process reflecting Warren's family and staff perspectives is found in Jim Newton, *Justice for All: Earl Warren and the Nation He Made,* (New York: Riverhead, 2006), pp. 1–11.

15. Hazlett to DDE, Oct. 14, 1954, DDE to Hazlett, Oct. 23, 1954, Name Series, B 17-18, Swede Hazlett, 1954 (1), EL; DDE interview, July 20, 1967, OH-11, p. 94, EL.

16. Brownell, *Advising Ike,* pp. 173–74; I am indebted to Daun van Ee, editor of the *DDEP,* for ideas related to the theory that an Eisenhower motivation for the Warren appointment related to 1956.

17. ACW Diary, Oct. 2, 1953, B 1, Aug-Sept-Oct 1953 (2), EL; Brownell, *Advising Ike,* p. 167.

18. David Lawrence, "Warren Appointment Disappoints," in CF/OF 100-A, B 371, Supreme Court of the U.S. (1), EL; Minnich to DDE, Oct. 13, 1953, CF/OF 100-A, B 371, Supreme Court of the U.S. (1), EL.

19. DDE to Edgar Eisenhower, Oct. 1, 1953, Name Series, B 11; EL; DDE to Milton Eisenhower, Oct. 9, 1953, *DDEP,* vol. 14, p. 576.

20. Warren to DDE, March 19, 1954, and DDE to Warren, March 23, 1954, Warren Papers, B 104, President-Correspondence, LC; also in *DDEP,* vol. 15, p. 977.

21. Brownell Interview, Warren Oral History Project, pp. 65–66, 71, EL.

22. News Conference, May 19, 1954, Eisenhower, *PPP,* pp. 491–92; Warren, *Memoirs,* p. 289.

23. Brownell, *Advising Ike,* pp. 168, 173–74; DDE to Charles B. Shuman, Jan. 13, 1959, *DDEP,* vol. 19, pp. 1290–91.

24. News Conference, Sept. 3, 1957, Eisenhower, *PPP,* p. 640; Warren, *Memoirs,* p. 289.

25. Rabb Papers, Civil Rights, B 6 (5) EL; Taylor Branch provides background on the preaching tradition in southern black churches, especially in chapter 1 of *Parting the Waters: America in the King Years, 1954–63* (New York: Simon & Schuster, 1988), pp. 1–26.

26. Warren, *Memoirs,* p. 291.

27. Brownell, *Advising Ike,* pp. 174–75.

28. News Conferences, March 16, 1955, Eisenhower, *PPP,* pp. 333–34, and March 23, 1955, p. 350.

29. DDE to Warren, June 21, 1957, Warren Papers, B 104, President's Correspondence, LC; Warren to DDE, July 15, 1957, Administration Series, B 38, Earl Warren, EL; Newton, *Justice for All,* pp. 354–55.

30. News Conference, Jan. 28, 1959, Eisenhower, *PPP,* pp. 133–34; Warren Papers, B 104, President's Correspondence, LC. Eisenhower's 1959 civil rights legislative proposals are examined in chapter 11.

31. *Gallup Poll,* April 13, 1955, "Republican Presidential Candidates," vol. 2 (New York: Random House, 1972), p. 1325; William H. Stringer, "Warren 'No' Ups Pressure on President," *Christian Science Monitor,* and Warren Statement, both on Apr. 15, 1955, found in Warren Papers, B 1104, Presidential Ambition, LC.

32. News Conference, Jan. 25, 1956, Eisenhower, *PPP,* pp. 194–95. Martin Agronsky, the ABC correspondent, interviewed Supreme Court justices and Chief Justice Warren in late 1955 and early 1956 regarding the possibility of Warren running

for president. Warren insisted that his decision to stay out of politics was still "irrevocable" and commented on "how satisfying" his work was, Reporter's Notes, 1955–56, Agronsky Papers, B 68 (9-US Supreme Court), LC.

33. Warren, *Memoirs,* pp. 291–92.

34. DDE Diary, July 24, 1953, B 9, Diary—Copies of DDE Personal, 1953–54 (2), EL. See chapter 3 for more about this conversation with Byrnes.

35. Ewald, *Eisenhower the President,* pp. 81–82; Brownell, *Advising Ike,* p. 174. Warren's account of the stag dinner episode continues to appear in studies related to Eisenhower and civil rights. See any of the following; Robert Caro, *The Years of Lyndon Johnson: Master of the Senate* (New York: Knopf, 2002), p. 778; Robert Frederick Burk, *The Eisenhower Administration and Black Civil Rights* (Knoxville: University of Tennessee Press, 1984), p. 142; James T. Patterson, *Brown v. Board of Education: A Civil Rights Milestone and Its Troubled Legacy* (Oxford: Oxford University Press, 2001), p. 81; Charles J. Ogletree, Jr., begins his book with the story, in *All Deliberate Speed: Reflections on the First Half Century of Brown v. Board of Education* (New York: Norton, 2004), p. 3, and concludes that the story proves that Eisenhower's heart "seemed to be with the opponents of segregation." Among Warren's biographers, Ed Cray, *Chief Justice: A Biography of Earl Warren* (New York: Simon & Schuster, 1997), cites the story on p. 292, and Jim Newton, in his new biography of Warren, *Justice for All,* p. 314, uses the anecdote as evidence to conclude that "Eisenhower was a dunce on matters of race."

36. Interview with Eisenhower by Ed Edwin, July 20, 1967, OH-11, 95, EL; Eisenhower, *Mandate for Change,* p. 230.

37. Sherman Adams, *First-Hand Report: The Story of the Eisenhower Administration* (New York: Harper & Brothers, 1961), pp. 331–32.

38. Interview with the President, July 20, 1956, Larson Papers, B 22, EL; also in Arthur Larson, *Eisenhower: The President Nobody Knew* (New York: Scribner's Sons, 1968), pp. 124–25, 127.

39. Emmet John Hughes Diary, Sept. 9 or 10, Hughes Papers, Seeley G. Mudd Manuscript Library, Princeton University. The same account, modified slightly, appears in Hughes's book, *The Ordeal of Power: A Political Memoir of the Eisenhower Years* (New York: Atheneum, 1963), p. 201.

40. Meeting with the President, Oct. 1, 1957, Larson Papers, B 22, EL; Larson makes the account more dramatic in his book than his notes on the meeting, *Eisenhower: The President Nobody Knew,* pp. 124–125, 127, although the content is consistent. See chapter 9 to find out what Ike said to the southern governors on October 1, 1957—comments radically different from Larson's account. Eisenhower's notes in preparation for that meeting are found in "Notes on the legal principles," B 6 (1), Notes for DDE, Oct. 1, 1957, B 6 (4), Hagerty Papers, EL.

41. David L. Stebenne, *Modern Republicanism: Arthur Larson and the Eisenhower Years* (Bloomington: Indiana University Press, 2006), pp. 213–16, concludes that Larson, in his later years, came to believe that Eisenhower's critique of *Brown* was more substantial than he had originally thought. "Eisenhower's views on the subject of segregation," Stebenne writes, "were more complex and thoughtful than many observers, including Arthur Larson, realized at the time."

42. Brownell, *Advising Ike,* pp. 173–74; ACW Diary, Aug. 14, 1956, B 8, Aug. '56 Diary (1), EL; Mayer, "With Much Deliberation and Some Speed: Eisen-

hower and the *Brown* Decision," Journal of Southern History 52, no. 1 (February 1986): 59–61, 76.

43. DDE to Hazlett, July 22, 1957, *DDEP,* vol. 18, pp. 321–23; Robert Caro, *Master of the Senate,* p. 925, says that the segregationist cited in the letter was Senator Richard Russell. Given that Eisenhower's meeting with Russell was on July 10, that assumption is reasonable.

44. DDE to Hazlett, Oct. 23, 1954, Name Series, B 17-18, Swede Hazlett, 1954 (1), EL.

45. See chapter 9 for a detailed account of Eisenhower's sending of troops into Little Rock.

46. Interview with Gerald D. Morgan, May 7, 1968, no. 3, OH-223, EL.

47. Warren, *Memoirs,* p. 301.

48. See chapters 6 and 7 for the passage of the civil rights legislation, chapters 8 and 9 for the Little Rock crisis. Eisenhower's decision to send troops to Little Rock is noted only in the editor's notes in Warren, *Memoirs,* p. 290. Newton, in *Justice for All,* p. 359, notes Warren's failure to comment publicly on Little Rock at the time of the event.

49. Eisenhower, *Mandate for Change,* p. 229.

50. Ewald, *Eisenhower the President,* p. 85; Michael S. Mayer, "A Kansan Looks at Brown," in John W. Wunder, ed., *Law and the Great Plains: Essays on the Legal History of the Heartland* (Westport, Conn.: Greenwood, 1996), p. 66, writes that, "Eisenhower could agree in principle with the decision's intent, but he had qualms about the exercise of judicial power it represented and even more serious doubts about the extension of federal power it implied." Mayer concludes that Ike's discomfort "remained with the Court's methods, not its intent."

CHAPTER SIX: **CONFRONTING SOUTHERN RESISTANCE**

1. "President Pushes Fight on Job Bias," *New York Times,* Jan. 19, 1955; Hagerty Diary, Jan. 19, 1955, Hagerty Papers, B 1a, A 71-79, EL; News Conference, Jan. 19, 1955, Eisenhower, *PPP,* p. 198.

2. Report by the Attorney General on the Administration's Efforts in the Field of Racial Segregation and Discrimination, Jan. 26, 1955, Cabinet Series, B 4, EL; Cabinet Meeting, Jan. 28, 1955, Cabinet Series, B 4, EL; Michal R. Belknap, ed., *Civil Rights, the White House and the Justice Department 1945–1968* (New York: Garland, 1991), vol. 6, p. 38.

3. "The year of the Great Decision," Report of the Executive Secretary, NAACP Annual Report, 1954, CF/GF 124-A-2, B 922, NAACP (1), EL; Wilkins Speech to the NAACP Annual Convention, Feb. 3, 1955, CF/OF 142-A, B 731, Negro Matters (1), Integration Program for Public Schools, Colleges and Universities, EL; Report to the Board of Directors, Roy Wilkins, April 11, 1955, NAACP Papers, UPA Microfilm; "54 Gains Hailed by Negro Group," *New York Times,* June 21, 1955.

4. Max Rabb to DDE, attaching two editorials, April 29, 1955, ACW Diary Series, B 5, EL.

5. Kevin McCann to Gallagher, May 11, 1955, Gallagher to Maxwell Rabb, May 12, 1955, CF/OF 142-A, B 731, Segregation-Integration (3), EL; "'54 Gains Hailed by Negro Group," *New York Times,* June 21, 1955.

6. Val Peterson to Max Rabb, Feb. 3, 1954, Cabinet Series, B 4, EL; Peterson's

memorandum was provided for the January 28, 1955, cabinet meeting that featured Herbert Brownell's report on civil rights.

7. State of the Union Address, Jan. 6, 1955, Eisenhower, *PPP,* pp. 24–25; Special Message to the Congress Concerning Federal Assistance in School Construction, Feb. 8,1955, Eisenhower, *PPP,* pp. 243–50; News Conference, Feb. 9, 1955, Eisenhower, *PPP,* pp. 252–53.

8. "Progress and Reaction, 1955," NAACP Annual report, p. 38, CF/OF 123-A-2, B 922, NAACP (2), EL; "Arguments Against Powell Amendment," n.d. 1956, Harlow Records, 1953–61, B 28, School Construction (1), EL.

9. News Conference, June 8, 1955, Eisenhower, *PPP,* p. 584; E. Frederic Morrow, *Black Man in the White House* (New York: Mcfadden, 1969), p. 24; News Conference, July 6, 1955, Eisenhower, *PPP,* p. 678.

10. DDE to Powell, June 21, 1955, *DDEP,* vol. 16, pp. 1752–53, with summaries of Powell's communications. This letter also addressed a similar amendment attached to the legislation for funding the military reserves, including the National Guard.

11. Legislative Leaders Meeting, May 1, 1957, Supplementary Notes, DDE Diary, B 24, May '57 Miscellaneous (5), EL.

12. Brownell Interview, Jan. 31, 1968, by Ed Edwin, OH-157, no. 4, p. 225, EL.

13. Morrow, *Black Man,* p. 10; *Forty Years a Guinea Pig* (New York: Pilgrim, 1980), pp. 92–93. When no White House position materialized in 1953, Washington had secured a position for Morrow in the Department of Commerce. Morrow believed Alabama-born General Wilton J. ("Jerry") Persons had allegedly "taken umbrage at my proposed appointment and had indicated to colleagues that he would walk out of the White House taking the white secretaries with him if I appeared." Max Rabb doubted this account, describing Persons as quietly reluctant, not openly hostile. Once he was assigned to the White House, Morrow's duties were not clearly "executive." As "Administrative Officer, Special Projects Group," he initially performed fairly menial tasks, reflecting some degree of tokenism. Morrow encountered difficulty immediately in obtaining approval for a secretary, and then suffered further ignominy trying to identify a secretary who was willing to work with him.

14. Washington to DDE, July 28, 1955, CF/OF 142-A, B 731, Negro Matters (3), EL; see chapter 1, note 40 for a summary of the fourteen points.

15. *Gallup Poll,* Aug. 8, 1955, "President Eisenhower," vol. 2, (New York: Random House, 1972), pp. 1351–52; Rabb to Pyle, Aug. 8, 1955, "The Gallup Poll," Aug. 7, 1953, *Washington Post,* found in CF/OF 142-A-4, B 731, Negro Matters (3), EL.

16. Press Release, Republican National Committee, Aug. 9, 1955; DDE to Washington, Aug. 1, 1955, CF/OF 142-A-4, B 731, Negro Matters (3); "Ike Cites Far Advances in Field of Civil Rights," *Washington Post,* Aug. 9, 1955.

17. Hoover to Anderson, Sept. 6, 1955, Sept. 13, 1955, Oct. 11, 1955, White House Office, Office of the Special Assistant for National Security Affairs: Records, FBI Series, FBI T-Z (1), EL; Mamie E. Bradley to DDE, Sept. 2, 1955, Rabb to Jim Hagerty, Oct. 23, 1956, CF/Alpha, B 3113, Till, Emmett Louis, EL.

18. Morrow, *Forty Years a Guinea Pig,* pp. 100–1; Washington to Sherman Adams, Sept. 29, 1955, CF/GF 124-A, B 909 (1955), EL.

19. John N. Popham, "Trial Tomorrow in Boy's Murder," *New York Times,* Sept. 18, 1955; Report of the Secretary to the NAACP Board of Directors, Dec. 12, 1955, NAACP Papers, UPA Microfilm; Editor's Note on Eisenhower's Heart

Attack, Eisenhower, President's Remarks on Leaving Denver, Colorado, Nov. 11, 1955, Eisenhower, *PPP*, pp. 822, 840–41; Rabb to Goodpaster, Jan. 6, 1956, Rabb Papers, B 28 (1), EL; "NAACP Attacks Integration Lag," *Evening Star*, Dec. 24, 1955, in Rabb Papers, B 27 (7), EL; Eisenhower's illnesses are reviewed in Robert E. Gilbert, *The Mortal Presidency: Illness and Anguish in the White House* (New York: Basic Books, 1992), pp. 74–141.

20. Brownell Interview, Jan. 31, 1968, OH-157, no. 4, pp. 230–31, EL; Olney Interview, Brownell Papers, B 36, Criminal—Warren (4), EL; Nov. 29, 1955, memorandum, Morrow Papers, B 10, Civil Rights Memo '55–56, EL; Morrow, *Forty Years a Guinea Pig*, p. 103.

21. "Buses Boycotted Over Race Issue," *New York Times*, Dec. 6, 1955; Roy Wilkins, *Standing Fast: The Autobiography of Roy Wilkins* (1982; rept. New York: Da Capo, 1994), pp. 225–26; a particularly thorough study of the racial conflicts in Alabama, including the bus boycott, is Diane McWhorter's *Carry Me Home: Birmingham, Alabama; The Climactic Battle of the Civil Rights Movement* (New York: Simon & Schuster, 2001), pp. 84–145.

22. Murray Snyder to Goodpaster, Feb. 23, 1956, Belknap, ed., *Civil Rights*, vol. 10, p. 44; Adam Fairclough, *Better Day Coming: Blacks and Equality* (New York: Viking, 2001), pp. 227–47.

23. NAACP Annual Report, 1955, pp. 7–10, CF/OF 123-A-2, B 922, NAACP (2), EL.

24. James Reston, "Move Grows for a Draft of Eisenhower or Warren," *New York Times*, Nov. 10, 1955.

25. Hagerty Diary, Dec. 15, 1955, Hagerty Papers, B 1a, December 10–14, 1955, EL; Adams Interview, June 19, 1970, OH-162, no. 3, EL.

26. *Gallup Poll*, Dec. 4, 1955, "Party Strength," vol. 2, pp. 1381–82; Gallup Poll newspaper clippings, Dec. 4, 1955, in Rabb Papers, B 27 (10), EL; Dec. 19, 1955, Diary Entry, Morrow, *Black Man*, pp. 19–20; Morrow to Adams, Dec. 16, 1955, Washington to Adams, Jan. 4, 1956, CF/OF 138-A-6, B 704, Negro Voting, EL; Diggs to DDE, March 9, 1956, CF/OF 102-B-3, B 430, Civil Rights—Civil Liberties (1) EL; Douglas to Rabb, Dec. 22, 1955, Administrative Officer—Special Projects (Morrow Files), B 11, Inter-Racial Affairs—Correspondence and Materials, 1956–54, EL.

27. Paul J. Scheips, *The Role of Federal Military Forces in Domestic Disorders, 1945–1992* (Washington, D.C.: Center of Military History, U.S. Army, 2005), p. 12.

28. Wilkins, *Standing Fast*, p. 234; William S. White, "No Push Expected for Civil Rights, *New York Times*, Dec. 4, 1955.

29. Cabinet Paper, Nov. 30, 1955, Belknap, ed., *Civil Rights*, vol. 1, p. 197; Cabinet Meeting, Dec. 2, 1955, Belknap, ed., *Civil Rights*, vol. 15, pp. 7–9; Brownell, *Advising Ike*, pp. 218–19; Brownell Interview by Ed Edwin, OH-157, no. 4, pp. 203–4, EL.

30. Brownell Interview by Ed Edwin, p. 204.

31. State of the Union Address, Jan. 5, 1956, Eisenhower, *PPP*, p. 25.

32. "Probe Terror in Dixie, Ike Asks," *Chicago Defender*, Jan. n.d., 1956, in Rabb Papers, B 30 (3), EL; Anthony Lewis, "Eisenhower Asks Civil Rights Study," *New York Times*, Jan. 6, 1956.

33. DDE to Milton Eisenhower, Sept. 12, 1955, *DDEP*, vol. 16, p. 1850; News Conference, Jan. 8, 1956, *PPP*, pp. 33–37.

34. News Conference, Jan. 25, 1956, Eisenhower, *PPP*, pp. 194–95.

35. DDE Diary, Jan. 30, 1956, B 9, Copies of DDE Personal, 1955–56 (2), EL.

36. News Conference, Feb. 8, 1956, Eisenhower, *PPP*, p. 231.

37. "Alabama U. Rally Protests a Negro," *New York Times*, Feb. 5, 1956, p. 60; Wayne Phillips, "Tuscaloosa: A Tense Drama Unfolds," *New York Times*, Feb. 26, 1956; News Conference, Feb. 8, 1956, Eisenhower, *PPP*, pp. 233–34; Jack Bass, *Unlikely Heroes* (New York: Simon & Schuster, 1981), pp. 64, 180–81.

38. J. Edgar Hoover, Report to the Cabinet, March 9, 1956, Cabinet Series, B 6, pp. 2, 8–10, EL; "The Nation," *New York Times*, Feb. 26, 1956; Morrow to Adams, Feb. 27, 1956, CF/OF 142-A, B 731, EL.

39. "Powell Hails Eisenhower," *New York Times*, Feb. 14, 1956, p. 16.

40. Pre–Press Conference Briefing, Feb. 29, 1956, Belknap, ed., *Civil Rights*, vol. 7, pp. 70–71.

41. News Conference, Feb. 29, 1956, Eisenhower, *PPP*, p. 271.

42. Brownell to Murray Snyder, March 6, 1956, Belknap, ed., *Civil Rights*, vol. 7, pp. 75–76.

43. Rabb to Anderson, White House Office, Office of the Special Assistant for National Security, FBI Series, FBI L-N (3), EL.

44. Hoover Report, Cabinet Series, B 6, pp.10, 14–16, 19, 24, EL; Handwritten Notes on Cabinet Meeting, March 9, 1956, White House Office, Office of the Staff Secretary (WHOSS): Records 1952–61, Cabinet Series, B 4, EL.

45. Proposed Statement by the Attorney General, March 7, 1956, for the March 9 Cabinet Meeting, Cabinet Series, B 6, EL.

46. Rabb to Brownell, Minutes of Cabinet Meeting, March 9, 1956, Cabinet Series, B 6, EL; Handwritten Minutes, Cabinet Meeting, March 9, 1956, WHOSS, B 4, EL.

47. Rabb to Brownell, March 9, 1956; Handwritten Minutes, March 9, 1956.

48. "The Southern Manifesto," 84th Congress, 2nd sess. *Congressional Record* 102, part 4 (March 12, 1956).

49. News Conference, March 14, 1956, Eisenhower, *PPP*, pp. 303–5, 312–13.

50. Legislative Leaders Meeting, March 20, 1956, LL, B 2, EL.

51. William Martin, *A Prophet with Honor: The Billy Graham Story* (New York: William Morrow, 1991), pp. 170–72, 201–3; *DDEP* footnotes, vol. 16, p. 2087; Rosenfeld to Lang For Suydam, sent to James Hagerty, Sept. 18, 1956, CF/GF 124-A, B 909, EL; DDE Diary, March 21, 1956, B 9, Copies of DDE Personal 1955–56 (1), EL.

52. DDE to Graham, March 22, 1956, DDE to Graham, March 30, 1956, DDE Diary, B 14, March 1956 Miscellaneous (1-2), EL; ACW Diary, March 29, 1956, B 8; Graham to DDE, March 27, 1956, Name Series, B 16, Rev. Billy Graham, EL; DDE to Graham, June 21, 1956, *DDEP*, vol. 17, pp. 2189–90.

53. Cabinet Meeting, March 23, 1956, Handwritten Notes in WHOSS, B 4, EL; Summary Minutes in Cabinet Series, B 7, Cabinet Meeting, March 23, 1956, EL.

54. President's Schedule, March 23, 1956, ACW Diary, March 23, 1956, B 8 (1), EL; Morgan to Whitman, March 24, 1956; DDE Diary, B 14, March 1956 Misc. (2), EL; Taylor Branch, in *Parting the Waters: America in the King Years, 1954–63,* (New York: Simon & Schuster, 1988), pp. 181–83, contends that the primary opposition to the civil rights proposals came from Sherman Adams.

55. Brownell to Whitman, April 8, 1956, Administration Series, B 8, EL.

56. Statement before the House Judiciary Committee, April 10, 1956, Cabinet Series, B 7, March 23, 1956, Meeting File, EL.

57. Civil Rights Hearings before the House Judiciary Committee, Executive Sessions, April 10, 1956, 84th Congress, Serial No. 11 (Washington, D.C.: U.S. Government Printing Office, 1956), pp. 557–88.

58. Brownell, *Advising Ike,* p. 301; Herbert Brownell, "The First Civil Rights Act in the 20th Century," Harry J. Sievers Memorial Lecture, Fordham University Law School, Sept. 26, 1990, Brownell Additional Papers, B 16, Eisenhower (3), EL.

59. Marshall to Rabb, April 13, 1956, Statement to *Pittsburgh Courier,* April 21, 1956, Rabb Papers, B 12 (5), EL.

60. Legislative Leadership Meeting, April 17, 1956, Supplementary Notes, LL, B 2, 1956, March–April (2), EL.

61. Humphrey to Wilkins, May 5, 1956, HHH Papers, B 127 (1) MHS.

62. "Rights Bill Gain Seen," *New York Times,* June 16, 1956; Legislative Leaders Meeting, July 10, 1956, Belknap, ed., *Civil Rights,* vol. 12, p. 4.

63. "Civil Rights Action Expected," *New York Times,* May 8, 1956, p. 8. The May 3 letter is discussed in Harlow to Persons, July 18, 1956, SJS to Harlow, July 17, 1956, DDE to Keating, undated, all in Harlow Records 1953–61, B 10, Civil Rights (1), EL.

64. C. P. Trussell, "Civil Rights Bill Passed In House by 279–126 Vote," *New York Times,* July 24, 1956; "Rights Bill Dead, Eisenhower Told," *New York Times,* July 26, 1956.

65. ACW Diary, Aug. 6, 1956, B 8 (2), EL.

66. Pre–Press Conference Briefing, Aug. 8, 1956, ACW Diary, B 8, Aug '56 (2), EL; News Conference, Aug. 8, 1956, Eisenhower, *PPP,* p. 665; Anthony Lewis, "President Wary on Rights Plan, Conciliatory on South's Problems," *New York Times,* Aug. 9, 1956; Memorandum for Record by Wilton B. Persons, Aug. 1, 1956, DDE Diary, B 17, August 1956, Diary—Staff Memos, EL.

67. Allen Drury, "Southerners Gaining Headway on Rights," *New York Times,* Aug. 20, 1956; Warren Olney Interview, Brownell Papers, B 36, Criminal (4), EL; Telephone Call, DDE to Brownell, Aug. 19, 1956, ACW Diary, B 8, EL; "Text of the Republican Platform as Adopted by the Party's National Convention," *New York Times,* Aug. 22, 1956.

68. Wilkins, *Standing Fast,* p. 241; John N. Popham, "Democratic Leaders Move to Keep the South in Line," *New York Times,* Sept. 2, 1956.

69. Powell Speech, "Why This Democrat Is for President Eisenhower," Aug. 12, 1956, Rabb Papers, B 21 (7, no. 5), EL.

70. Morrow, *Black Man,* pp. 61–62; Address Accepting Nomination, Aug. 23, 1956, Eisenhower, *PPP,* p. 710.

71. J. W. Peltason, *58 Lonely Men: Southern Federal Judges and School Desegregation* (New York: Harcourt, Brace & World, 1951), pp. 143–48; Bass, *Unlikely Heroes,* pp. 121–22; Robyn Duff Ladino, *Desegregating Texas Schools: Eisenhower, Shivers, and the Crisis at Mansfield High* (Austin: University of Texas Press, 1996); News Conference, Sept. 5, 1956, Eisenhower, *PPP,* p. 736; Marshall to DDE, Sept. 5, 1956, CF/GF 124-A-1, B 916, School Decision (1), EL.

72. News Conference, Sept. 11, 1956, Eisenhower, *PPP,* pp. 758–59, 765; Justice Tom Clark was born in Texas; News Release, Sept. 19, 1956, John M. Budinger to DDE, Sept. 28, 1956, both in CF/OF 100-A, B 371, Supreme Court of the U.S. (1 EL); DDE to Marcellus Dodge, Oct. 4, 1956, *DDEP,* vol. 17, p. 2305.

73. News Release, Sept. 19, 1956, Rabb Papers, B 22 (8), EL.

74. Morrow, *Black Man,* pp. 69–70; ACW Diary, Oct. 23, 1956, B 8 (2), EL.

75. "Text of Stevenson's Address in Harlem Promising Social Progress," *New York Times*, Oct. 5, 1956; News Conference, Oct. 5, 1956, Eisenhower, *PPP*, pp. 850–52.

76. Morrow, *Black Man*, pp. 67–68; "G.O.P. Appeal in Harlem," *New York Times*, Oct. 18, 1956; Hagerty OH-91, vol. 2, pp. 249–52, EL; Memorandum by Bernard M. Shanley on Appointment of Powell with the President, Oct. 11, 1956, DDE Diary, B 19, Oct '56, Diary-Staff Memos, EL; "Powell's Switch Laid to Pressure," *New York Times*, Oct. 13, 1956; "Powell Sees G.O.P. Winning Negroes," *New York Times*, Oct. 19, 1956.

77. Television Broadcast, "The People Ask the President," Oct. 12, 1956, *PPP*, pp. 912–13.

78. Address in Seattle, Oct. 17, 1956, Eisenhower, *PPP*, p. 946; Address at Madison Square Garden, Oct. 25, 1956, Eisenhower, *PPP*, p. 1022.

79. Statement Released by the White House, Oct. 23, 1956, CF/OF 142-A, B 731, EL; "Powell Retracts Report on Talks," *New York Times*, Oct. 24, 1956, p. 37. Drafts of the statement in the Rabb Papers suggest that Rabb drafted the statement; Rabb Papers, B 21 (7, no.4), EL.

80. "Byrnes Rejects Both Candidates," *New York Times*, Oct. 27, 1956; Ira Henry Freeman, "Harlem Perplexed by Powell's Defection to Eisenhower," *New York Times*, Nov. 1, 1956.

81. DDE Diary, Oct. 28, 1956, Belknap, ed., *Civil Rights*, vol. 1, p. 244.

82. *Gallup Poll*, vol. 2, Nov. 4, 1956, p. 1453.

83. Radio and Television Remarks, Nov. 7, 1956, Eisenhower, *PPP*, p. 1090; "Negro Vote Shift Heaviest in South," *New York Times*, Nov. 11, 1956; Morrow, *Black Man*, p. 75.

84. John D. Morris, "Democrats Edge in House Growing," *New York Times*, Nov. 11, 1956. The press exaggerated the size and impact of the black vote for Eisenhower. The Republican National Committee studied the data following the election, assuming approximately 3.5 million Negroes had voted—a number probably too high—including 900,000 in the eleven southern states. In a time before scientific exit polls, the Michigan Survey Research Center calculated that 36 percent of African-American voters had supported Eisenhower, and the Gallup Poll estimated 39 percent, with the shift most pronounced among southern blacks. The percentages looked better than the electoral reality. The gain was minimal if Congressman Powell's district in New York City and the city of Baltimore were excluded. The data offered little hope for the future; the largest increases in estimated black voting percentages occurred in states and localities where the Republican Party had little chance to make long-term electoral inroads; see William B. Prendergast to Maxwell Rabb, Aug. 19, 1957, "The Negro Vote," Study by the Research Division, Republican National Committee, CF/GF 124-A, B 909,1957 (2), EL.

85. Report of the Secretary to the NAACP Board of Directors, Dec. 10, 1956, NAACP Papers, UPA Microfilm.

86. Luther A. Huston, "High Court Rules Bus Segregation Unconstitutional," *New York Times*, Nov. 14, 1956; ACW Diary, Nov. 14, 1956, B 8, Nov '56, EL; News Conference, Nov. 14, 1956, Eisenhower, *PPP*, pp. 1095–1108.

87. W. H. Lawrence, "Eisenhower Will Push Ahead with Program," *New York Times*, Nov. 18, 1956.

88. White House Statement by Republican Leaders, Dec. 31, 1956, Eisenhower, *PPP*, p. 1131.

CHAPTER SEVEN: **THE CIVIL RIGHTS ACT OF 1957**

1. Legislative Meeting, Dec. 31, 1956, LL, B 2, (3), EL; William S. White, "President Pushes Civil Rights Plan at G.O.P. Parley," *New York Times,* Jan.1, 1957.

2. State of the Union Address, Jan. 10, 1957, Eisenhower, *PPP,* p. 23.

3. Wilkins to DDE, Jan. 10, 1957, CF/GF 124-A-1, B 912, 1957 (1), EL; HHH to Drew Pearson, Dec. 31, 1956, HHH to Stewart Alsop, July 20, 1957, B 136, Humphrey Papers, MHS.

4. ACW Diary, June 15, 1954, B 2, June 1954 (2), EL; News Conference, May 22, 1957, Eisenhower, *PPP,* p. 400; HHH to Olin Swenson, Jan. 25, 1957, B 136, Humphrey Papers, MHS.

5. Reuther to HHH, Jan. 14, 1957, HHH to Reuther, Jan. 22, 1957, HHH to Paul Ziffren, Jan. 28, 1957, Humphrey Papers, B 136, MHS.

6. Before 1949, cloture had required the approval of two-thirds of the senators actually voting. From 1949 to 1959, the rule was more stringent, requiring two-thirds of the Senate's membership, regardless of how many voted. In 1959, the former rule was reinstated. In 1975, the Senate reduced the requirement to three-fifths (sixty), where it still stands in 2007.

7. John D. Morris, "Democrats Agree to Senate Test for Civil Rights," *New York Times,* Jan. 12, 1957; three books that confirm the relationship of LBJ's presidential ambition to his collaboration with civil rights legislation include Robert A. Caro, *The Years of Lyndon Johnson: Master of the Senate* (New York: Knopf, 2002), pp. 849–1012; Robert Dalleck, *Lone Star Rising: Lyndon Johnson and His Times, 1908–1960* (New York: Oxford University Press, 1991), pp. 517–26; Randall B. Woods, *LBJ: Architect of American Ambition* (New York: Free Press, 2006), pp. 325–31. George Reedy, Johnson's press secretary, writes that the Eisenhower-Brownell proposal was "so perfectly tailored to the Johnson strategy that I suspected collusion the first time I read it" and it "could not have fitted LBJ's purposes better if he had written it himself." Reed believed that part three was the ideal item to trade off for southern support of a voting rights act; George Reedy, *Lyndon B. Johnson: A Memoir* (New York: Andrews and McMeel, 1982), p. 115; Wilkins, *Standing Fast: The Autobiography of Roy Wilkins* (1982; rept. New York: Da Capo, 1994), p. 243.

8. DDE to Edgar Newton Eisenhower, Jan. 21, 1957, *DDEP,* vol. 18, p. 6; ACW Diary, Jan. 21, 1957, B 8, EL; President's Appointments, Jan. 20, 1957, DDE Diary, B 21, Jan '57 Miscellaneous (2), EL; Second Inaugural Address, Jan. 21, 1957, Eisenhower, *PPP,* pp. 60–65.

9. "Brownell Defines Civil Rights Policy," *New York Times,* Jan. 25, 1957; News Conference, Feb. 6, 1957, Eisenhower, *PPP,* pp. 123–24, 127–28. "Southerners See Rights 'Gestapo,'" *New York Times,* Feb. 8, 1957.

10. "Brownell Vexed By Rights Inquiry," *New York Times,* Feb. 17, 1957.

11. For a more detailed account of this effort by the Johnson forces, see Caro, *Master of the Senate,* pp. 870–71, 891, 921–22.

12. John D. Morris, "Civil Rights Bill Gains in Congress," *New York Times,* Feb. 28, 1957; "Southerners Delay Civil Rights Action," *New York Times,* March 26, 1957; Legislative Leadership Meeting, April 9, 1957, Supplementary Notes, Michal R. Belknap, ed., *Civil Rights, the White House, and the Justice Department* (New York: Garland, 1991), vol. 12, p. 217.

13. King et al. to DDE, Jan. 11, 1957, Rabb to King, Jan. 11, 1957, Adams to King, Jan. 18, 1957, all in CF/GF 124-A-1, B 912, 1957 (1), EL; King to Nixon, Feb.

14, 1957, Clayborne Carson, ed., *The Papers of Martin Luther King, Jr.,* vol. 4 (Berkeley: University of California Press, 2000), pp. 98–101, 133–35.

14. News Conference, Feb. 6, 1957, Eisenhower, *PPP,* p. 131; King et al. to DDE, Feb. 14, 1957, CF/GF 124-A-1, B 912, 1957, (2), EL.

15. "Negroes to Mass in Capital May 17," *New York Times,* April 6, 1957, found in CF/GF 124-A-1, 1957 (2), EL; J. Edgar Hoover to Robert Cutler, April 26, 1957, Staff Files, White House Office: Office of the Special Assistant for National Security Affairs, FBI Series, B 2, FBI L-N (2), EL; Rabb to Adams, April 17, 1957; Wilkins to Rabb, April 24, 1957, Rabb to Adams, May 8, 1957, Rabb to Toner, May 16, 1957, all in CF/GF 124-A-1, B 912, 1957 (2), EL.

16. King to Shanley, May 16, 1957, Shanley to Rabb, May 17, 1957, Rabb to Shanley, May 23, 1957, Memorandum for Files by Rabb, May 23, 1957, all in CF/GF 124-A-1, B 912, 1957 (2), EL.

17. Sherman Adams to King, March 13, 1957, and King to Nixon, May 15, 1957, Carson, ed., *King Papers,* vol. 4, p. 204; King Press Conference, June 13, 1957, Carson, ed., *King Papers,* vol. 4, p. 222; Rabb to Adams, June 24, 1957, CF/GF 124-A-1, B 912, 1957 (2) EL.

18. Unnamed Memorandum (probably Adams) to Morrow, June 25, 1957, CF/GF 124-A-1, B 912, 1957 (2), EL.

19. HHH to Eileen Handlik, May 28, 1957, Humphrey Papers, B 136, MHS; Morrow to Mrs. Zelma George, May 17, 1957, Morrow Files, B 10, Interracial Affairs, EL.

20. James Reston, "Douglas Takes On South," *New York Times,* June 12, 1957; "Rights Plan Assailed," *New York Times,* April 13, 1957.

21. Reston, "Douglas Takes On South"; Speech and Brief by Paul H. Douglas, April 18, 1957, *Congressional Record,* pp. 1–11, found in Humphrey Papers, B 711 (1), MHS.

22. News Conference, May 15, 1957, Eisenhower, *PPP,* pp. 354–57.

23. Legislative Leaders Meeting, June 4, 1957, LL, B 2, EL.

24. Brownell Interview, April 12, 1968, COHP, OH-157, no. 5, EL.

25. William S. White, "Eisenhower Lauds Civil Rights Plan," *New York Times,* June 20, 1957; Wilkins, *Standing Fast,* p. 243.

26. Telephone Call, DDE to Johnson, June 15, 1957, DDE Diary, B 25, July 1957 Phone Calls, EL.

27. Pre–Press Conference Briefing, June 19, 1957, Belknap, ed., *Civil Rights,* vol. 12, pp. 235–36; News Conference, June 19, 1957, Eisenhower, *PPP,* pp. 472–73.

28. White, "Eisenhower Lauds Civil Rights Plan."

29. Both Caro, *Master of the Senate,* p. 904, and Woods, *LBJ,* p. 328, contend that western liberal Democrats voted against placing the House civil rights bill directly on the Senate calendar because of Johnson's promise of southern votes for construction of the Hell's Canyon dam on the Snake River in Idaho. Caro devotes an entire chapter to the Hell's Canyon deal, pp. 895–909; William S. White, "Congress Finds President Takes a Stronger Role," *New York Times,* June 24, 1957.

30. Address to the Governors' Conference, Williamsburg, Virginia, June 24, 1957, Eisenhower, *PPP,* pp. 490, 494.

31. "The President's Williamsburg Speech and the Administration Civil Rights Program," Belknap, ed., *Civil Rights,* vol. 1, pp. 228–30.

32. News Conference, June 26, 1957, Eisenhower, *PPP,* pp. 502–6.

33. "Leader of a Lost Cause," *New York Times,* July 3, 1957.

34. Speech on Senate Floor by Richard B. Russell, July 2, 1957, *Congressional Record—Senate,* pp. 10771–75; Warren Olney to Gerald Morgan, Memorandum on the Authority of the President to Use the Armed Forces to Enforce Civil Rights Decrees, CF/OF 102-B-3, B 430, Civil Rights—Civil Liberties (3), EL.

35. Pre–Press Conference Notes, July 3, 1957, Belknap, ed., *Civil Rights,* vol. 12, p. 241.

36. News Conference, July 3, 1957, Eisenhower, *PPP,* pp. 515, 520–21; William S. White, "President Bars Ballot on Rights; Would Hear Foes," *New York Times,* July 4, 1957.

37. Phone Call, DDE to Brownell, July 3, 1957, B 25, DDE Diary, EL; ACW Diary, July 3, 1957, B 9 (1) EL.

38. Legislative Leaders Meeting, July 9, 1957, LL, B 25, July 1957 Miscellaneous, DDE Diary, EL.

39. ACW Diary, July 10, 1957, B 9, July 1957 (2), EL; Caro, *Master of the Senate,* p. 925, gives Johnson credit for arranging the meeting between Eisenhower and Russell. In a letter to Swede Hazlett, July 22, 1957, *DDEP,* vol. 18, pp. 321–23, Ike described his recent visit with a "violent exponent of the segregation doctrine," who had insisted on the sanctity of the 1896 Supreme Court decision, and Eisenhower had asked him, "Then why is the 1954 decision not equally sacrosanct?" The visitor was probably Senator Richard Russell and the exchange took place on July 10.

40. Legislative Leaders Meeting, July 16, 1957, LL, B 2, July–August, (4), EL.

41. William S. White, "Senate, By 71–18, Votes to Take Up Civil Rights Bill," *New York Times,* July 17, 1957; "The President's Statement," July 17, 1957, *New York Times;* also in Eisenhower, *PPP,* p. 545.

42. News Conference, July 17, 1957, Eisenhower, *PPP,* pp. 546–47; "Compromise?" *New York Times,* July 21, 1957.

43. Morrow to Adams, July 12, 1957, B 9, Civil Rights Bill, Morrow Files, EL; Washington to Rabb, July 16, 1957, Rabb Papers, B 17 (4), EL; Washington to Adams, July 17, 1957, Rabb to Janet Simpson, July 18, 1957, Belknap, ed., *Civil Rights,* vol. 12, pp. 273–74; Washington to DDE, July 18,1957, Morrow Files, B 9, Civil Rights Bill, EL.

44. Brownell, *Advising Ike,* pp. 224–25.

45. Legislative Leaders Meeting, July 23, 1957, LL, B 2, May–June '57 (4), EL. Johnson's political manipulations on the jury trial issue, once title three was defeated, is explained in detail in Caro, *Master of the Senate,* pp. 944–89.

46. Handwritten Notes on Legislative Leaders Meeting, July 30, 1957, WHOSS, B 4, EL.

47. News Conference, July 31, 1957, Eisenhower, *PPP,* p. 573.

48. William S. White, "Eisenhower Backs Civil Rights Bloc Opposing Juries," *New York Times,* Aug. 1, 1957; William S. White, "Senate, 51 to 42, Attaches Jury Trials to Rights Bill in Defeat for President," *New York Times,* Aug. 2, 1957.

49. White, "Eisenhower Backs Civil Rights Bloc"; White, "Senate, 51 to 42."

50. William S. White, "Senate, 51 to 42"; ACW Diary, Aug. 2, 1957, B 9 (2), EL; Handwritten Notes of Cabinet Meeting, Aug. 2, 1957, WHOSS, B 4, EL; Caro, *Master of the Senate,* p. 987.

51. Statement by the President, Aug. 2, 1957, Morrow Files, Official Memoranda, B 10, EL.

52. W. H. Lawrence, "Eisenhower Irate," *New York Times,* Aug. 3, 1957; DDE to Woodruff, Aug. 6, 1957, *DDEP,* vol. 18, pp. 354–55.

53. Humphrey Phoned Release, Aug. 5, 1957, Humphrey Papers, B 711 (2), MHS.

54. Washington to Johnson, Aug. 6, 1957, Morrow Files, Official Memoranda, Republican National Committee, Civil Rights Act of 1957, B 10, EL.

55. Legislative Leaders Meeting, Aug. 6, 1957, WHOSS, B 4, EL; Summary Minutes in Belknap, ed., *Civil Rights,* vol. 12, p. 301.

56. Diary Entry, Aug. 7, 1957, Morrow, *Black Man,* p. 121; Caro, *Master of the Senate,* pp. 992–95.

57. ACW Diary, Aug. 7, 1957, B 9, August 1957 (2), EL.

58. HHH to J. S. Smith, Aug. 7, 1957, HHH to James A. Quinn, Aug. 13, 1957, Humphrey Papers, B 136, MHS; Roger Biles, *Crusading Liberal: Paul H. Douglas of Illinois* (DeKalb: Northern Illinois University Press, 2002), p. 124.

59. Handwritten Notes on Legislative Leaders Meeting, Aug. 13, 1957, WHOSS, B 4, EL; Summary Notes in Belknap, ed., *Civil Rights,* vol. 12, pp. 317–18.

60. James Reston, "Gamble on Civil Rights," *New York Times,* Aug. 15, 1957; Robert Caro, in *Master of the Senate,* pp. 992–93, notes that Johnson feared that the weakened bill would be killed in the congressional conference.

61. Gerald Morgan to DDE, Aug. 16, 1957, Morgan Papers, B 6, Civil Rights no. 3 (1), EL; "The Half Loaf," *New York Times,* Aug. 17, 1957; the three-hundred-dollar fine would be equivalent to $2,150 in 2006 dollars; Caro, *Master of the Senate,* p. 930, and George Reedy, *Lyndon B. Johnson,* p. 118, credit an article by Professor Carl Auerbach for drawing the distinction between civil and criminal prosecutions that laid the foundation for compromise proposal. Reedy also gives credit to former secretary of state Dean Acheson and his legal staff. In fact, that distinction had been integral to Herbert Brownell's proposals ever since 1956 and it is inaccurate to contend, as Caro paraphrases Auerbach, that the administration "bill contemplated only criminal proceedings"; that was the demagogic argument used by the southerners. A detailed examination of the process leading to the passage of the Civil Rights Act of 1957 is found in Steven F. Lawson, *Black Ballots: Voting Rights in the South, 1944–1969* (New York: Columbia University Press, 1976), pp. 140–202. On p. 197, Lawson gives credit for the compromise proposal to Deputy Attorney General William Rogers, a reasonable conclusion since Brownell was preparing to leave the government.

62. Legislative Leaders Meeting, Aug. 20, 1957, Belknap, ed., *Civil Rights,* vol. 12, p. 329; News Conference, Aug. 21, 1957, Eisenhower, *PPP,* pp. 618–26.

63. LBJ Call to DDE, Aug. 23, 1957, Belknap, ed., *Civil Rights,* vol. 12, p. 330; Caro, in *Master of the Senate,* p. 995, gives full credit for the final compromise to Johnson, without mentioning Eisenhower.

64. Memorandum of Appointment, Lyndon Johnson and DDE, Aug. 26, 1957, DDE Diary, B 26, August 1957 Memo on Appts. (1), EL.

65. William S. White, "Senate Votes Rights Bill and Sends It to the President; Thurmond Talks 24 Hours," *New York Times,* Aug. 30, 1957.

66. Press Release by Adam Clayton Powell, Aug. 30, 1957, Morrow Files, B 9, Civil Rights, EL.

67. King to Nixon, Aug. 30, 1957, Rogers Papers, B 50, Nixon—Vice President (Correspondence) (7), EL.

68. William S. White, "Senate Votes Rights Bill and Sends It to the President; Thurmond Talks 24 Hours," *New York Times,* Aug. 30, 1957; Washington to Johnson, Aug. 6, 1957, Morrow Files, Official Memoranda, B 10, Civil Rights Bill, EL; Woods, *LBJ,* pp. 325–31.

69. Phone Call, Johnson to DDE, Aug. 30, 1957, Belknap, ed., *Civil Rights,* vol. 12, p. 332.

70. Wilkins, *Standing Fast,* p. 221; LBJ's biographers—Dalleck, *Lone Star Rising,* Caro, *Master of the Senate,* and Woods, *LBJ*—understandably tend to give him credit for the passage of the Civil Rights Act of 1957, but even the studies less focused on the legislation tend to assume that Eisenhower was not a leader. Michael J. Klarman's volume, *From Jim Crow to Civil Rights* (New York: Oxford University Press, 2004), p. 366, characterizes Eisenhower's involvement by his July 3, 1957, statement that he "didn't completely understand" the legislation. Taylor Branch, in *Parting the Waters,* pp. 220–21, is more balanced but still makes Johnson, rather than Eisenhower, the prime mover. Richard Kluger, in *Simple Justice: The History of Brown v. Board of Education and Black America's Struggle for Equality* (New York: Random House, 1977), p. 754, concludes that the Civil Rights Act of 1957 "owed its existence not to the President, whose ineptness nearly submarined it, but to his attorney general, Herbert Brownell, one of the very few pro–civil rights people in the Eisenhower high command."

CHAPTER EIGHT: **THE LITTLE ROCK CRISIS**

1. Speech by Faubus, Sept. 2, 1957, Orval Faubus Papers, MS F27, 301, Series 14, B 498 (3), UA; Chronology, B 5 (1), Caldwell to Olney, Sept. 1957, Arthur Caldwell Papers, B 5 (2), UA; James C. Duram, *A Moderate Among Extremists: Dwight D. Eisenhower and the School Desegregation Crisis* (Chicago: Nelson-Hall, 1981), p. 145.

2. Duram, *A Moderate Among Extremists,* p. 165; Sherman Adams, *First-Hand Report: The Story of the Eisenhower Administration* (New York: Harper & Bros., 1961), p. 345.

3. Report and Chronology, B 5 (1-2), Caldwell to Olney, Sept. 1957, Caldwell Papers, B 5 (2), UA.

4. Caldwell Report on Aug. 28, 1957 Meeting, Michal R. Belknap, ed., *Civil Rights, The White House, and the Justice Department, 1945–1968* (New York: Garland, 1991), vol. 7, pp. 122-25; Caldwell labeled Faubus's subsequent actions "criminal" in Caldwell to Brooks Hays, Oct. 4, 1957, Caldwell Papers, Little Rock, B 5 (6), UA; Numan V. Bartley, *The Rise of Massive Resistance: Race and Politics in the South During the 1950's* (Baton Rouge: Louisiana State University Press, 1969), pp. 263–64; Robert Frederick Burk, *The Eisenhower Administration and Black Civil Rights* (Knoxville: University of Tennessee Press, 1984), pp. 176–77. Elizabeth Jacoway, in *Turn Away Thy Son: Little Rock, the Crisis That Shocked the Nation* (New York: Free Press, 2007), pp. 93–95, 134–36, 145–46, maintains that Faubus had more serious foundation for his fear of violence than the Justice Department accepted. In addition to Jacoway, John A. Kirk provides a detailed study of the evolu-

tion of the school desegregation crisis in Little Rock in *Redefining the Color Line: Black Activism in Little Rock, Arkansas, 1940–1970* (Gainesville: University Press of Florida, 2002), pp. 106–38.

5. Chronology, B 5 (1), Caldwell to Olney, Sept. 1957, Caldwell Papers, B 5 (2), UA.; Eldon C. Williams, FBI Report, Sept. 9, 1957, Central High Integration Crisis, Serial 933, B 1, UA; Burk, *The Eisenhower Administration and Black Civil Rights,* p. 178.

6. Pre–News Conference Meeting, Sept. 3, 1957, Press Conference Series, B 6, EL; Anthony Lewis, "Washington Studies Little Rock Dispute," *New York Times,* Sept. 4, 1957.

7. News Conference, Sept. 3, 1957, Press Conference Series, B 6, EL; Benjamin Fine, "Little Rock Told to Integrate Now Despite Militia," *New York Times,* Sept. 4, 1957; Roy Reed, *Faubus: The Life and Times of an American Prodigal* (Fayetteville: University of Arkansas Press, 1997), pp. 208–12.

8. "Arkansas Troops Bar Negro Pupils; Governor Defiant," *New York Times,* Sept. 5, 1957; Paul J. Scheips, *The Role of Federal Military Forces in Domestic Disorders, 1945–1992* (Washington, D.C.: Center of Military History, U.S. Army, 2005), pp. 34–35, 40; Robert W. Coakley, *Operation Arkansas* (Washington, D.C.: Histories Division, Department of the Army, 1967), pp. 20–25. Historians have frequently assumed that Eisenhower made no decision linked to military intervention in Little Rock until September 23–24. While he made no final decision until then, the plan that was eventually implemented was essentially in place on a contingency basis on September 4, based on contingency planning in previous years.

9. "Arkansas Troops Bar Negro Pupils; Governor Defiant," *New York Times,* Sept. 5, 1957; Melba Pattillo Beals, *Warriors Don't Cry* (New York: Pocket, 1994), pp. 49–51; Michael Mayer, ed., *President Dwight D. Eisenhower and Civil Rights: Eyewitness Accounts by Terrence J. Roberts and Rocco C. Siciliano* (Washington, D.C.: Eisenhower Institute, 2000), pp. 14–15.

10. "Newport All Bedecked for Eisenhower Visit," *New York Times,* Sept. 4, 1957.

11. Faubus to DDE, Sept. 5, 1957, DDE to Faubus, Sept. 5, 1957, CF/OF 147-A, B 732 (1), EL; Faubus to DDE, Sept. 5, 1957, James Hagerty Papers, B 6 (2), EL; Reed, *Faubus,* p. 213; Scheips, *The Role of Federal Military Forces,* p. 36.

12. Benjamin Fine, "Little Rock Told to Integrate Now Despite Militia," *New York Times,* Sept. 4, 1957; Wilkins to DDE, Sept. 5, 1957, Records of WHTO, B 181, Newport (1) EL; Martin Luther King, Jr., to DDE, Sept. 9, 1957, CF/OF 142-A-5-A, B 732 (6), EL.

13. Adams, *First-Hand Report,* pp. 346, 351.

14. The president gave one of six pens he used to E. Frederic Morrow, the African-American who joined the White House staff in 1955; W. H. Lawrence, "President Backs U.S. Court Order," *New York Times,* September 10, 1957; "President Hails Plea for Caution," *New York Times,* Sept. 16, 1957. A recent study of the slave trade is Charles Rappleye's *Sons of Providence: The Brown Brothers, the Slave Trade, and the American Revolution* (New York: Simon & Schuster, 2006).

15. Eisenhower, *The White House Years: Waging Peace 1956–61* (Garden City, N.Y.: Doubleday, 1965), p. 165; Williams FBI Report, Sept. 9, 1957, Central High Integration Crisis, Serial 933, B 1, UA; W. H. Lawrence, "President Backs U.S. Court Order," *New York Times,* Sept. 10, 1957.

16. "Notes on the legal principles," n.d., Hagerty Papers, B 6 (1), EL. The docu-

ment is not dated, nor is an author indicated, but it is consistent with other documents produced by the Justice Department during this period, most notably Brownell's summary of legal principles presented as he prepared to leave office, Nov. 11, 1957, found in the Administration Series, Box 8, EL. Brownell was the primary author of the principles although Warren Olney and William Rogers were often collaborators.

17. News Conference, Sept. 11, 1956, Eisenhower, *PPP,* pp. 758–59, 766–67.
18. Sept. 8, 1957, Article, HHH Papers, B 136, MHS; Felstiner to DDE, Sept. 10, 1957, CF/GF 124-A-1, B 920, School—Arkansas Initial (2) EL; Lawrence, "President Backs U.S. Court Order."
19. DDE Diary, Sept. 11, 1957, B 27, Sept. 1957 Telephone Calls, EL; Hays's detailed account of the negotiations leading to the meeting is found in his autobiography, *A Southern Moderate Speaks* (Chapel Hill: University of North Carolina Press, 1959), pp. 136–45.
20. DDE Phone Call to Brownell, Sept. 11, 1957, DDE Diary, Sept. 1957 Toner Notes, B 27, EL.
21. Adams, *First-Hand Report,* pp. 346–49; Interview with Brooks Hays, n.d., Brooks Hays Papers, MS H334, Series 3:1, B 44 (20), p. 34, UA; Duram, *A Moderate Among Extremists,* pp. 146–48.
22. Press Release, Sept. 11, 1957, Hagerty Papers, B 6 (3), EL; Adams, *First-Hand Report,* pp. 348–49; W. H. Lawrence, "President Agrees to Bid by Faubus for School Talks," *New York Times,* Sept. 12, 1957; W. H. Lawrence, "President's Talk with Faubus Set for Tomorrow," *New York Times,* Sept. 13, 1957; Scheips, *The Role of Federal Military Forces,* p. 36.
23. Lawrence, "President Backs U.S. Court Order"; Williams FBI Report, Sept. 9, 1957, Central High Integration Crisis, Serial 933, B 1, UA; Burk, *The Eisenhower Administration and Black Civil Rights,* pp. 179–81; Jacoway, *Turn Away Thy Son,* p. 146, contends that the FBI report was "a travesty of justice" reflecting "a culture of arrogance and secrecy" in the Eisenhower administration.
24. News Conference, Sept. 12, 1957, Hagerty Papers, B 6 (3), EL.
25. Lawrence, "President's Talk with Faubus Set for Tomorrow."
26. DDE Diary, Sept. 12, 1957, B 27, Sept. 1957 Toner Notes, EL; Ike expressed his "feeling of nakedness" at the Cabinet Meeting, Oct. 11, 1957, WHOSS, Cabinet Series, B 4, EL; Mary L. Dudziak, *Cold War Civil Rights: Race and the Image of American Democracy* (Princeton: Princeton University Press, 2000), pp. 115–25.
27. ACW Diary, Sept. 13, 1957, B 9, EL.
28. Williams FBI Report, Sept. 12, 1957, Central High Integration Crisis, Serial 937, B 1, UA; Brownell met with J. Edgar Hoover four times on Sept. 13; see Brownell Additional Papers, B 24, Civil Rights Book, Brownell Schedule, EL. Fred I. Greenstein, *The Hidden-Hand Presidency: Eisenhower as Leader* (Baltimore: Johns Hopkins University Press, 1994), argues that Eisenhower often purposely acted ignorant or confused in public when he was privately taking strong action.
29. DDE Phone Call to Brownell, Sept. 20, 1957, DDE Diary, B 27, EL. In 1956, Brownell had urged Eisenhower to avoid any public comment on their discussions about using troops; Brownell to Murray Snyder, March 6, 1956, Belknap, ed., *Civil Rights,* vol. 7, pp. 75–76.
30. Hays Interview, Hays Papers, B 44 (20), p. 40, UA; W. H. Lawrence, "President Ready for Critical Talk," *New York Times,* Sept. 14, 1957.

31. ACW Diary, Sept. 14, 1957, B 9, EL; News Conference, Sept. 14, 1957, Hagerty Papers, Box 6 (3), EL; W. H. Lawrence, "2 Talk in Newport," *New York Times,* Sept. 15, 1957.

32. News Conference, Sept. 14, 1957, Hagerty Papers, Box 6 (3), EL; Adams, *First-Hand Report,* p. 350; DDE Notes Dictated Oct. 8, 1957, Concerning the Sept. 14 Meeting, ACW Diary, B 9, Sept. 1957, EL.

33. Faubus Interview, Aug. 18, 1971, OH-181, pp. 41, 43, 49, EL; Interview with Faubus and Hays, n.d., Hays Papers, B 45,(25), p. 4, UA.

34. Adams, *First-Hand Report,* p. 351; Faubus OH-181, p. 44, EL; DDE Notes Dictated Oct. 8, 1957, Concerning the Sept. 14 Meeting, ACW Diary, B 9, Sept. 1957, EL.

35. Eisenhower, *Waging Peace,* p. 166; details of the meeting setting were provided by Hagerty to the press at the 11:22 A.M. news conference just following the meeting, Hagerty Papers, B 6 (3), EL; Hays Interview, Hays Papers, B 44 (20), p. 41, UA; Adams, *First-Hand Report,* pp. 350–51; Faubus OH-181, p. 50, EL.

36. Faubus OH-181, pp. 45–46; Adams, *First-Hand Report,* p. 351.

37. Faubus OH-181, p. 47, EL; Faubus and Hays Interview, n.d., Hays Papers, B 45 (25), p. 8, UA.

38. DDE Notes Dictated Oct. 8, 1957, Concerning the Sept. 14 Meeting, ACW Diary, B 9, Sept. 1957, EL.

39. News Conference, Sept. 14, 1957, Hagerty Papers, B 6 (3), EL; ACW Diary, Sept. 14, 1957, B 9, Sept. 1957, EL; Duram, *A Moderate Among Extremists,* pp. 148–51; Reed, *Faubus,* pp. 217–18; Stephen E. Ambrose, *Eisenhower, The President,* vol. 2 (New York: Simon & Schuster, 1984), pp. 414–15; Hays, *A Southern Moderate Speaks,* pp. 146–52.

40. Adams, *First-Hand Report,* p. 352; Faubus, OH-181, p. 54, EL.

41. Faubus Statement, Sept. 14, 1957, ACW Diary, B 9, EL.

42. DDE Statement, Sept. 14, 1957, ACW Diary, B 9, EL.

43. Adams, *First-Hand Report,* p. 353; Taylor Branch, *Parting the Waters: America in the King Years, 1954–63* (New York: Simon & Schuster, 1988), p. 223.

44. Lawrence, "2 Talk in Newport."

45. Brownell, Eisenhower Centennial Celebration, 1991, Brownell Additional Papers, B 16 (3), EL; Herbert Brownell, *Advising Ike: The Memoirs of Attorney General Herbert Brownell* (Lawrence: University Press of Kansas, 1993), p. 210.

46. Caldwell to Hays, Oct. 4, 1957, Caldwell Papers, B 5 (6), UA.

47. Democratic Advisory Council, Sept. 15, 1957, Faubus Papers, B 498, UA; HHH to Todd, Sept. 17, 1957, HHH Papers, B 136, MHS.

48. Bush to Adams, National Republican Club Press Release, Sept. 16, 1957, CF/GF 124-A-1, B 920, School—Arkansas Initial (2), EL. Prescott Bush was the father of President George H. W. Bush and the grandfather of President George W. Bush.

49. Wilkins to Rabb, Sept. 17, 1957, CF/GF 124-A-1, B 910 (2), EL; Bryce Harlow Records, 1953–61, B 14, Integration—Little Rock, Football Games, A. C. Powell (1, 3) EL; DDE to Powell, Sept. 18, 1957, Hagerty Papers, B 6 (3), EL.

50. DDE to Howard W. Jackson, Sept. 19, 1957, CF/OF 147-A, B 732, Little Rock (2), EL. Jackson was an executive with the Baltimore, Maryland Chamber of Commerce.

51. DDE Diary, Sept. 19, 1957, B 27, EL; Brownell was in constant communica-

tion with J. Edgar Hoover, Brownell Additional Papers, B 24, Civil Rights Book, Brownell Schedule, EL.

52. Goodpaster to Hagerty, Sept. 19, 1957, DDE Diary, B 27, Sept. 1957 Telephone Calls, EL.

53. Scheips, *The Role of Federal Military Forces*, p. 37.

54. DDE Phone Call to Brownell, Sept. 20, 1957, DDE Diary, B 27, EL. Months later, Arkansas' Democratic Senator John L. McClellan charged that Major General Edwin Walker, the chief of the military district of Arkansas, had "cased" Central High School as early as September 19—an allegation that was undoubtedly accurate; see "M'Clellan Raises Little Rock Issue," *New York Times,* July 23, 1958.

55. News Conference, Sept. 20, 1957, Hagerty Papers, B 6 (4), EL.

56. "Faubus Yields," *New York Times,* Sept. 22, 1957; Adams, *First-Hand Report,* p. 353; Faubus OH-181, pp. 55–56, EL; News Conference/Release, Sept. 21, 1957, Hagerty Papers, B 6 (4), EL; Hays, *A Southern Moderate Speaks,* pp. 165–73; Bartley, *The Rise of Massive Resistance,* pp. 265–67; Jacoway, *Turn Away Thy Son,* p. 160.

57. DDE Diary, Sept. 22, 1957, B 27, Sept. 1957 Schedules, EL.

CHAPTER NINE: MILITARY INTERVENTION IN LITTLE ROCK

1. DDE Diary, Sept. 23, 1957, B 27; CF/President's Personal File (PPF), B 644, EL.

2. An important new study of the role of the press in race relations in America is by Gene Roberts and Hank Klibanoff, *The Race Beat: The Press, the Civil Rights Struggle, and the Awakening of a Nation* (New York: Knopf, 2006), with particular analysis of the Little Rock crisis, pp. 143–83.

3. Sherman Adams, *First-Hand Report: The Story of the Eisenhower Administration* (New York: Harper & Bros., 1961), p. 353; Robert E. Baker, "Mob Had Job and Leaders Saw It Done," *Washington Post,* Sept. 24, 1957, draft article Central High Integration Crisis, B2, pp. 108–13, UA; Newswire Reports, WHOSS, Subject Series, Alpha Subseries, B 17, Little Rock, vol. 2, Misc. (1), EL; Caldwell to Warren Olney III, Sept. 23, 1957, B 5 (2), Caldwell Papers, UA; Eisenhower, *The White House Years: Waging Peace, 1956–61* (Garden City, N.Y.: Doubleday, 1965), p. 168; Robert Frederick Burk, *The Eisenhower Administration and Black Civil Rights* (Knoxville: University of Kentucky Press, 1984), pp. 185–86; Reed, *Faubus: The Life and Times of an American Prodigal* (Fayetteville: University of Arkansas Press, 1997), pp. 224–27.

4. The new civil rights division provided for in the 1957 Civil Rights Act had not yet been implemented. News Conference, Sept. 23, 1957, Hagerty Papers, B 48, EL; Adams, *First-Hand Report,* p. 354.

5. Burnham to Rabb, Dec. 30, 1986, Centennial Conference File, Brownell Additional Papers, EL.

6. Mann to DDE, Sept. 23, 1957, Hagerty Papers, B 6 (4), EL. Elizabeth Jacoway, in *Turn Away Thy Son: Little Rock, the Crisis That Shocked the Nation* (New York: Free Press, 2007), pp. 176–78, contends that the violence was in decline and that Mann's reaction was out of proportion to the real situation. Therefore, she assumes that Eisenhower believed incorrectly that the situation was out of control; another study from a Southern perspective is Pete

Daniel, *Lost Revolutions: The South in the 1950s* (Chapel Hill: University of North Carolina, 2000), pp. 260–83.

7. Eisenhower, *Waging Peace,* pp. 168–69.
8. Goodpaster to Hagerty, Sept. 19, 1957, DDE Diary, B 27, Sept. 1957 Telephone Calls, EL.
9. Brownell Diary, Sept. 23, 1957, B 24, Civil Rights Book, Brownell Schedule, Brownell Additional Papers, EL; Mary L. Dudziak, *Cold War Civil Rights: Race and the Image of American Democracy* (Princeton: Princeton University Press, 2000), pp. 126–30; News Conference, Sept. 23, 1957, Hagerty Papers, B 6 (4), EL.
10. News Conference, Sept. 23, 1957, B 6 (1), EL.
11. "Troop Precedent Goes Back to 1792," *New York Times,* Sept. 25, 1957.
12. News Conference, Sept. 23, 1957, Hagerty Papers, B 6 (4), EL.
13. Phone Conversation, Sept. 24, 1957, DDE Diary, B 27, EL; William Martin, *A Prophet with Honor: The Billy Graham Story* (New York: Morrow, 1991), p. 248; News Conference, Sept. 24, 1957, Hagerty Papers, B 48, EL; Scheips, *The Role of Federal Military Forces in Domestic Disorders, 1945–1992* (Washington, D.C.: Center of Military History, U.S. Army, 2005), pp. 44–48.
14. DDE to Gruenther, Sept. 24, 1957, DDE Diary, B 26, Sept. 1957, DDE Dictation, EL.
15. News Conference, Sept. 24, 1957, Hagerty Papers, B 48, EL.
16. Mann to DDE, Sept. 24, 1957, DDE Diary, B 26, Sept. 1957 DDE Dictation, EL.
17. Brownell Diary, B 24, Civil Rights Book, Brownell Schedule, Brownell Additional Papers, DDE Diary, Sept. 24 (mislabeled 25th) 1957, B 27, Sept. 1957, ACW Diary, Sept. 24, 1957, B 9, EL; Taylor Branch, *Parting the Waters: America in the King Years* (New York: Simon & Schuster, 1988), p. 224.
18. DDE Diary, Sept. 24, 1957 (mislabeled 25th), B 27, EL; Benjamin Fine, "Troops on Guard at School; Negroes Ready to Return," *New York Times,* Sept. 25, 1957; Jack Raymond, "Soldiers Fly In," *New York Times,* Sept. 25, 1957.
19. ACW Diary, Sept. 24, 1957, B 9; DDE Diary, Sept. 24, 1957 (mislabeled 25th), B 27, EL.
20. News Conference, Sept. 24, 1957, Hagerty Papers, B 48, EL; James C. Duram, *A Moderate Among Extremists: Dwight D. Eisenhower and the School Desegregation Crisis* (Chicago: Nelson-Hall, 1981), pp. 153–56; Stephen E. Ambrose, *Eisenhower, The President,* vol. 2 (New York: Simon & Schuster, 1984), pp. 418–19.
21. WHOSS, B 17, Little Rock II Misc. (3), United Press Bulletin, Hagerty Papers, B 6 (4), EL.
22. DDE Diary, Sept. 24, 1957, EL; Benjamin Fine, "Troops on Guard at School; Negroes Ready to Return," *New York Times,* Sept. 24, 1957; Melba Pattillo Beals, *Warriors Don't Cry* (New York: Pocket, 1994), p. 130.
23. Pyle to DDE, Sept. 24, 1957, Hagerty Papers, B 6 (4), EL.
24. Drafts—Address to the Nation, Sept. 24, 1957, Speech Series, B 22, Integration Little Rock, DDE Diary, Sept. 24, 1957 (mislabeled 25th), B 27, Phone Call, Dulles to DDE, Sept, 24, 1957, B 12, John Foster Dulles Papers, EL; Dudziak, *Cold War Civil Rights,* pp. 131–36.
25. Jack Gould, "TV: President Speaks," and Anthony Lewis, "Eisenhower on Air," *New York Times,* Sept. 25, 1957.
26. Randall Bennett Woods, *Fulbright: A Biography* (New York: Cambridge University Press, 1995), pp. 226–43.

27. Speech as Delivered, Hagerty Papers, B 6 (1), Speech Series, B 22, EL; DDE Diary, Sept. 24, 1957, B 27, EL; Duram, *A Moderate Among Extremists,* pp. 157–59; Eisenhower's rhetoric on Little Rock is examined in Garth E. Pauley, *The Modern Presidency & Civil Rights: Rhetoric on Race from Roosevelt to Nixon* (College Station: Texas A & M University, 2001), pp. 58–104 and Martin J. Medhurst, ed., *Eisenhower's War of Words: Rhetoric and Leadership* (East Lansing: Michigan State University Press, 1994), pp. 195–215.

28. Beals, *Warriors Don't Cry,* pp. 128–29.

29. Farnworth Fowle, "Bayonets of Troops Bring School Order," Benjamin Fine, "Students Accept Negroes Calmly," Homer Bigart, "School Is Ringed," *New York Times,* Sept. 26, 1957, and "Little Rock Calm," Sept. 27, 1957, *New York Times;* WHOSS, B 17, Little Rock, vol. 1, Reports (1), EL; Reed, *Faubus,* pp. 229–32.

30. ACW Diary, Sept. 14–30, 1957, B 9, Poll, Sept. 25, 1957, Hagerty Papers, B 6 (5), EL; "President Fails to Put 'Under God' in Pledge," *New York Times,* Sept. 25, 1957; *Gallup Poll,* Oct. 4, 1957, School Integration, vol. 2, p. 1517. "Under God" was signed into law as part of the Pledge of Allegiance by Eisenhower in 1954.

31. Andrew Tully, "Speech Shows the Real Ike," *New York World-Telegram,* Sept. 25, 1957, Hagerty Papers, B 6 (5), EL.

32. Walter Lippmann, "Today and Tomorrow: The President's Address," probably Sept. 25, 1957, found in HHH Papers, B 136, MHS.

33. DDE Diary, Sept. 25, 1957, B 27, Sept. 1957 Schedules, EL; DDE to Collins, Sept. 25, 1957, News Conference, Sept. 25, 1957, Hagerty Papers, B 6 (5), EL.

34. *Arkansas Gazette,* Sept. 27, 1957, Central High Integration Crisis, MC 1027, Serial 990, B 2, pp. 26–32, UA; "Text of Faubus Address on Little Rock Controversy," *New York Times,* Sept. 27, 1957.

35. Bulletins, Sept. 26, 1957, Hagerty Papers, B 6 (5), EL; Scheips, *The Role of Federal Military Forces,* p. 54; Scheips, p. 49, has Faubus returning to Arkansas on Sept. 24 instead of the 25th; Robert W. Coakley, *Operation Arkansas* (Washington, D.C.: Histories Division, Department of the Army, 1967), pp. 88–89.

36. Pre–News Conference, Oct. 9, 1957, Press Conference Series, B 6, Bulletins, Sept. 26, 1957, Hagerty Papers, B 6 (5), EL; "Text of Faubus Address on Little Rock Controversy," *New York Times,* Sept. 27, 1957.

37. Bulletin, Sept. 26, 1957, Hogarty Papers, B6 (5), EL; Jack Raymond, "Army Bars Alert of Units in South," *New York Times,* Sept. 27, 1957.

38. Brucker to Russell, n.d. WHOSS, B 17, Little Rock, vol. 11, Misc. (2), EL.

39. "Excerpts from Byrnes' Talk on Crisis in Little Rock," *New York Times,* Sept. 27, 1957; Elliott to DDE, Oct. 2, 1057, CF/GF 124-A-1, B 920, School—Arkansas, Initial (3), EL.

40. Russell to DDE, Sept. 26, 1957, Hagerty Papers, B 6 (4), EL; Adams, *First-Hand Report,* p. 356; DDE to Russell, Sept. 27, 1957, Hagerty Papers, B 6 (1), EL; Gilbert C. Fite, *Richard B. Russell, Jr.: Senator from Georgia* (Chapel Hill: University of North Carolina Press, 1991), pp. 343–44; Robert Mann, *The Walls of Jericho: Lyndon Johnson, Hubert Humphrey, Richard Russell, and the Struggle for Civil Rights* (New York: Harcourt, Brace, 1996), pp. 227–28; Duram, *A Moderate Among Extremists,* pp. 159–61; Burk, *The Eisenhower Administration and Black Civil Rights,* p. 188; Ambrose, *Eisenhower, The President,* vol. 2, pp. 421–22. Russell's comparison of the members of the 101st Airborne Division to Nazi storm troopers particularly offended Army Secretary Wilber Brucker, who re-

minded the senator that "a large number of these men are from the South and many are from your own state of Georgia," Brucker to Russell, approx. Sept. 30, 1957, B 14, Integration—Little Rock (1), Harlow Records, EL.

41. Remmel to DDE, Sept. 24, 1957, Tex/Jinx to DDE, DDE's response, Sept. 24, 1957, CF/OF 142-A-5-A, B 733 (11), Little Rock, EL.

42. Daily Report, Radio Broadcasts Supplement, Sept. 27, 1957, Harlow Records, B 14, Integration—Little Rock (3), EL; Michael L. Krenn, *Black Diplomacy: African Americans and the State Department 1945–1969* (Armonk, N.Y.: M.E. Sharpe, 1999), pp. 100–5; Carol Anderson, *Eyes Off the Prize: The United Nations and the African American Struggle for Human Rights, 1944–1955* (New York: Cambridge University Press, 2003), p. 251; Thomas Borstelmann, *The Cold War and the Color Line: American Race Relations in the Global Arena* (Cambridge: Harvard University Press, 2001), pp. 102–3.

43. Lightfoot to DDE, Sept. 25, 1957, Nathan to DDE, Sept. 25, 1957, Yerger Telegram to Eisenhower, *Jackson (Mississippi) Daily News,* Sept. 25, 1957, in CF/GF 124-A-1, B 920, School—Arkansas Initial (1), Calvin Birch to DDE, Carter to DDE, Sept. 25, 1957, WHTO, B 181, Newport (2), Turner to DDE, Sept. 30, 1957, CF/GF 124-A-1, B 920 (2), EL.

44. John W. Finney, "Congress Is Split on Use of Troops," *New York Times,* Sept. 25, 1957; "Arrest of Troops Urged," *New York Times,* Sept. 27, 1957; "Johnson Disturbed," *New York Times,* Sept. 25, 1957.

45. Parents of Little Rock Nine to DDE, Sept. 30, 1957, Online, EL.

46. King to DDE, Sept. 25, 1957, CF/OF 142-A-5-A, B 732 (6), EL; DDE to King, Oct. 7, 1957, *DDEP,* vol. 18, p. 479.

47. King to Smith and Bates, Sept. 26, 1957, *Papers of Martin Luther King, Jr.* vol. 4, ed. Clayborne Carson (Berkeley: University of California Press, 2000), p. 279.

48. Armstrong to DDE, Sept. 24, 1957, CF/GF 124-A-1, B 920, School—Arkansas Initial (2), EL.

49. ACW Diary, Notes Sept. 14 to Sept. 30, 1957, B 9, EL.

50. ACW Diary, Notes Sept. 14 to Sept. 30, 1957, B 9, EL; Duram, *A Moderate Among Extremists,* pp. 161–63; Burk, *The Eisenhower Administration and Black Civil Rights,* p. 189. John Howard Pyle was the former Republican governor of Arizona who joined Eisenhower's staff in 1955 as a director of federal-state relations. He transmitted the southern governors' resolution and request for a meeting to Eisenhower.

51. Meeting with President, Oct. 1, 1957, B 22, Memorandum Book, Oct. 1957 (1), Arthur Larson Papers, EL. In his book *Eisenhower: The President Nobody Knew* (New York: Charles Scribner's Sons, 1968), pp. 124–125, 127, Larson makes this a quotation, unlike in his diary notes, and makes a stronger case for Eisenhower's opposition to *Brown.*

52. "Notes on the legal principles," B 6 (1), Notes for DDE, Oct. 1, 1957, Hagerty papers, B 6 (4), EL.

53. Adams, *First-Hand Report,* pp. 357–58; Faubus OH-181, p. 59, Press Release, Oct. 1, 1957, Hagerty Papers, B 6 (5), EL.

54. President's Statement, Oct. 1, 1957, "Faubus Monkey Wrench," *New York Herald Tribune,* Oct. 3, 1957, Hagerty Papers, B 6 (5-6), EL; Adams, *First-Hand Report,* p. 358; Eisenhower, *Waging Peace,* p. 174.

55. Preparation and News Conference, Oct. 3, 1957, Press Conference Series. B 6, EL; Ambrose, *Eisenhower,* vol. 2, p. 422; Eisenhower, 1957, *PPP,* pp. 704–10.

56. Pre–News Conference and News Conference, Oct. 9, 1957, Press Conference Series, B 6, EL.

57. "Stevenson Sees Disaster," *New York Times*, Sept. 25, 1957.

58. HHH to Stuart, Oct. 14, 1957, HHH Papers, Box 136, MHS; W. H. Lawrence, "President Chided for Little Rock," *New York Times*, Oct. 22, 1957.

59. DDE Interview, July 20, 1967, OH-11, pp. 82–83, EL. President Kennedy sent in federal troops when riots broke out at the University of Mississippi in September 1962, when James Meredith attempted to enroll as the first black student.

60. "Eastland Gives Warning," *New York Times*, Sept. 27, 1957.

61. DDE to Brownell, Oct. 14, 1957, DDE Diary, Oct. 14, 1957, B 27, EL; Goodpaster Memorandum, Nov. 18, 1957, WHOSS, B 17, Little Rock, vol. 2, Miscellaneous (4), EL; Eisenhower, *Waging Peace*, p. 175.

62. President's Statement on Equal Opportunity Day, Nov. 18, 1957, Eisenhower, *PPP*, p. 823, released the day prior to the observance.

63. *DDEP*, vol. 18, p. 599; Ambrose, *Eisenhower*, vol. 2, p. 236; Eisenhower, *Waging Peace*, pp. 227–28.

CHAPTER TEN: **RISING EXPECTATIONS**

1. W. H. Lawrence, "Eisenhower Suffers Chill; Ordered to Bed; Speech Off," *New York Times*, Nov. 26, 1957; Lawrence, "Tension Mounts at White House," *New York Times*, Nov. 27, 1957; E. Frederic Morrow, *Forty Years a Guinea Pig* (New York: Pilgrim, 1980), p. 150; Brownell to DDE, Oct. 23, 1957, B 8, Administration Series, Brownell 1957 (1), EL; DDE to Brownell, Oct. 23, 1957, Eisenhower, *PPP*, pp. 763–64; Anthony Lewis, "Brownell Quits; Rogers Is Chosen as His Successor," *New York Times*, Oct. 24, 1957.

2. Pre–Press Conference Notes, Oct. 30, 1957, Michal R. Belknap, ed., *Civil Rights, The White House and the Justice Department* (New York: Garland, 1991), vol. 10, p. 84; Anthony Lewis, "Eisenhower Picks Civil Rights Unit; Reed Is Chairman," and "Sketches of Civil Rights Appointees," *New York Times*, Nov. 8, 1957; "Six on Civil Rights" and "Thurmond Scores Civil Rights Unit," *New York Times*, Nov. 9, 1957; Diary Entry Oct. 7, 1957, Morrow, *Black Man*, pp. 125–26. Besides Wilkins, the president appointed Governor John S. Battle of Virginia; the Reverend Dr. Theodore M. Hesburgh, president of Notre Dame University; Robert G. Storey, dean of the Southern Methodist Law School; and John Hannah, president of the University of Michigan. When former justice Stanley F. Reed resigned, the vacant seat was filled by a Democrat, former Florida governor Doyle Elam Carlton.

3. Reed to DDE, Dec. 2, 1957, DDE to Reed, Dec. 3, 1957, Eisenhower, *PPP*, p. 829; Anthony Lewis, "Reed Turns Down Civil Rights Post," *New York Times*, Dec. 4, 1957; Anthony Lewis, "Dr. Hannah Is Appointed To Head Civil Rights Unit," and "No Time for Bias," *New York Times*, Dec. 24, 1957.

4. Anthony Lewis, "U.S. Aide Will Get Civil Rights Post," *New York Times*, Nov. 22, 1957; "Senate Unit Delays On Civil Rights Job," *New York Times*, Feb. 26, 1958; "Hearing on White Set," *New York Times*, July 15, 1958; Anthony Lewis, "White Is Backed for Rights Post," *New York Times*, Aug. 12, 1958; "White Confirmed for Rights Post," *New York Times*, Aug. 19, 1958.

5. DDE to Butcher, Nov. 12, 1957, *DDEP*, vol. 18, p. 562; DDE to Arthur Eisenhower, Nov. 8, 1957, *DDEP*, vol. 18, p. 551.

6. DDE to Hazlett, Nov. 18, 1957, *DDEP,* vol. 18, pp. 577–78.
7. Pyle to Rogers, Jan. 14, 1958, "Highlights of Administration Civil Rights Policy," Rogers Papers, B 59, White House Correspondence, vol. 2, EL; State of the Union Address, Jan. 9, 1958, Eisenhower, *PPP,* pp. 2–15; News Conference, Jan. 15, 1958, Eisenhower, *PPP,* pp. 92–93, 98–99.
8. Morrow, *Forty Years a Guinea Pig,* pp. 160–61.
9. Statement by the President, May 8, 1958, CF/OF 142-A-5-A, B 733, Little Rock (14), EL.
10. Melba Pattillo Beals, *Warriors Don't Cry* (New York: Pocket, 1994), pp. 304–5; "Little Rock 40th Anniversary: The 1957–58 School Year," http://www .centralhigh57.org/1957-58.htm.
11. News Conference, May 14, 1858, Eisenhower, *PPP,* p. 397; Anthony Lewis, "President Is Firm on Use of Troops in a School Crisis," *New York Times,* May 15, 1958.
12. Rabb to Stephens, March 25, 1958, CF/OF 142-A, B 731, Negro Matters (6), EL; Diary Entry, May 13, 1958, Morrow, *Black Man,* p. 158, and *Forty Years a Guinea Pig,* pp. 163–64.
13. Remarks at a Meeting of Negro Leaders, May 12, 1958, Eisenhower, *PPP,* pp. 391–94; Felix Belair, Jr., "Eisenhower Bids Negroes Be Patient About Rights," *New York Times,* May 13, 1958; "Another Negro Dissents," and Anthony Lewis, "Negroes Criticize 'Patience' Advice," *New York Times,* May 14, 1958.
14. Robinson to DDE, May 13, 1958, DDE to Robinson, June 4, 1958, Robinson to DDE, June 10, 1958, all in CF/OF 142-A, B 731, Negro Matters (6), EL.
15. Rabb to Morrow, July 13, 1957, Morrow Files, B 10, Official Memoranda, EL; Powell to DDE, Sept. 17, 1957, United Press Bulletin, Sept. 17, 1957, both in CF/OF 142-A-5-A, B 733, Little Rock (10), EL; Wilkins to DDE, Sept. 19, 1957, CF/OF 142-A, B 731, Negro Matters (5), EL; "Nixon's Role in Parley," *New York Herald Tribune,* Sept. 19, 1957, clipping in CF/OF 142-A-5-A, B 733, Little Rock (12), EL; DDE to Powell, Sept. 18, 1957, Hagerty Papers, B 6 (1, 3), EL.
16. Durham to Rabb, Sept. 24, 1957, Robinson to Rabb, Oct. 28, 1957, both in CF/OF 142-A, B 731, Negro Matters (5), EL; Rabb to Adams, Oct. 11, 1957, SW to Rabb, n.d., Powell to DDE, Oct. 17, 1957, Adams to Powell, Oct. 31, 1957, BKN to BH, Oct. 28, 1957, all in CF/OF 142-A-5-A, B 733, Little Rock (10), EL; King to DDE, Nov. 5, 1957, Carson, ed., *King Papers,* vol. 4, pp. 308–9; King also urged the president to appoint two Negroes to the Civil Rights Commission, one from the South and one from the North, but Eisenhower appointed only J. Ernest Wilkins.
17. King to DDE, May 29, 1958, CF/OF 142-A, B 731, Negro Matters (6), EL.
18. Memorandum for Files by Siciliano, June 9, 1958, Siciliano to Adams, June 10, 1958, Memorandum for Files by Lavery, June 13, 1958, Powell to DDE, June 20, 1958, Morrow to Powell, June 24, 1958, all in White House Office. OSAPPM, B 42, Civil Rights—Meeting of Negro Leaders with President, June 23, 1958; Siciliano to Hagerty, June 16, 1958, CF/OF 142-A, B 731, Negro Matters (6), EL; Edward Ranzal, "Powell Indicted in U.S. Tax Inquiry: Tammany to Act," *New York Times,* May 9, 1958.
19. Statement to President Eisenhower by Negro Leaders, June 23, 1958, Memorandum for the Files by Siciliano, June 24, 1958, both in DDE Diary, B 33, June 1958 Staff Notes (2), EL. Siciliano's story of this meeting is reprised in his autobiography with Drew M. Ross, *Walking on Sand: The Story of an Immi-*

grant Son and the Forgotten Art of Public Service (Salt Lake City: University of Utah Press, 2004), pp. 156–67.

20. Joseph A. Loftus, "Negro Leaders Confer with President and Rogers at White House," *New York Times,* June 24, 1958; Siciliano to DDE, June 25, 1958, DDE Diary, B 33, June 1958 Staff Notes (2), EL.

21. "Iraqi Coup Announcement," *New York Times,* July 15, 1958; Felix Belair, Jr., "Eisenhower Sends Marines Into Lebanon," *New York Times,* July 16, 1958; "Message From President," *New York Times,* July 20, 1958; Dana Adams Schmidt, "U.S. Troops to Go if Regime Asks; Dulles Outlines Summit Talk Aim," *New York Times,* Aug. 1, 1958.

22. ACW Diary, Aug. 5, 1958, B 10, (2), EL; Eisenhower, *PPP,* 1958, p. 627, and 1959, p. 113; Rocko Siciliano, in a March 28, 2007, interview with the author, says he knew both secretary Mitchell and Wilkins and did not believe Wilkins was forced to resign for racial reasons.

23. News Conference, Aug. 6, 1958, Eisenhower, *PPP,* p. 588.

24. Arkansas Anti-Integration Acts of 1958, Sept. 1958, Orval Faubus Papers, B 497, UA; Anthony Lewis, "U.S. Officials See Integration Hurt," *New York Times,* June 22, 1958; J. W. Peltason, *58 Lonely Men: Southern Federal Judges and School Desegregation* (New York: Harcourt, Brace & World, 1961), pp. 183–86.

25. "Troop Use Weighed as Integration Step," *New York Times,* July 19, 1958; Cabell Phillips, "Faubus Vote Clouds Integration Outlook," *New York Times,* Aug. 3, 1958.

26. Rogers to DDE, Aug. 18, 1957, Administration Series, B 32, William P. Rogers 1958 (4), EL.

27. "Little Rock Integration Is Reinstated on Appeal: Circuit Court Vote is 6–1" *New York Times,* Aug. 19, 1958; Peltason, *58 Lonely Men,* pp. 186–87.

28. Statement by the president, Aug. 20, 1958, CF/OF 142-A-5, B 732, Little Rock (4), EL; also in Eisenhower, *PPP,* pp. 631–32; James Reston, "President Asks Obedience to Integration Decisions; Faubus Reply Is Defiant," *New York Times,* Aug. 21, 1958.

29. News Conference, Aug. 20, 1958, Eisenhower, *PPP,* pp. 626, 631.

30. "No Equivocation," *New York Times,* Aug. 21, 1958.

31. "Faubus Asks Bills to Close Schools If U.S. Intervenes," *New York Times,* Aug. 27, 1958.

32. News Conference, Aug. 27, 1958, Eisenhower, *PPP,* pp. 639, 647; AP News Release of Statement by President Eisenhower, Aug. 27, 1958, Faubus Papers, B 496, UA.

33. Felix Belair, Jr., "President to Take Newport Vacation," *New York Times,* Aug. 26, 1958; DDE to Robert Cutler, Aug. 27, 1958, *DDEP,* vol. 19, pp. 1077–78.

34. Claude Sitton, "U.S. Opposes Delay in Integration," *New York Times,* August 29, 1958; "Text of the N.A.A.C.P. Brief in High Court on School Dispute," "Text of Brief filed by Justice Department in Supreme Court on Little Rock Case," "Excerpts from Oral Arguments Before Supreme Court on Question of Integration," *New York Times,* Aug. 29, 1958.

35. Anthony Lewis, "Supreme Court Postpones Action on Little Rock Case till Sept. 11," *New York Times,* Aug. 29, 1958.

36. Rogers to Dean Dauley, Sept. 7, 1958, Rogers to Wayne Upton, Sept. 7, 1958, Upton to Rogers, Sept. 9, 1958, Rogers to Upton (Press Release), Sept. 11 and 12, 1958, all in Rogers Papers, B 54, School (5) EL; "Judge Lemley's Re-

quest to Retire Is Received," *New York Times*, Sept. 9, 1958, p. 24; "Judge Miller Gets East Arkansas Post," *New York Times*, Sept. 10, 1958.

37. Anthony Lewis, "High Court Hears Little Rock Plea," *New York Times*, Sept. 12, 1958.

38. Anthony Lewis, "Court Bars Little Rock Delay," "Text of the High Court Ruling," *New York Times*, Sept. 13, 1958; "High Court Opinion That Denied Little Rock Integration Stay," *New York Times*, Sept. 30, 1958.

39. Statement by the President (plus draft), Sept. 12, 1958, Rogers Papers, B 54, School (5), EL; also in Eisenhower, *PPP*, p. 701.

40. "Southerners Vehement," "Reaction Mixed on Court Ruling," "The Court's Decision," all in *New York Times*, Sept. 13, 1958.

41. Felix Belair, Jr., "President Calls for Support," *New York Times*, Sept. 13, 1958; DDE to Khrushchev, Sept. 13, 1958, Eisenhower, *PPP*, pp. 701–3.

42. Statement by the Attorney General, Sept. 16, 1958, OSAPPM, B 42, Civil Rights—School Desegregation (1), EL; "Rogers Says U.S. Will Defer Move to Open Schools," *New York Times*, Sept. 17, 1958, in Rogers Papers, B 54, School (4), EL. Virginia, in addition to Arkansas, was in crisis because the Virginia legislature had authorized the governor to close desegregated schools. In fall 1958, Governor J. Lindsay Almond, Jr., closed schools in cities under federal court order to desegregate. The Virginia Supreme Court of Appeals and a federal district court both declared the school closing laws unconstitutional in January 1959. Eventually massive resistance to desegregation declined and numerous Virginia schools were desegregated, see Peltason, *58 Lonely Men*, pp. 207–220.

43. DDE to Adams, Sept. 22, 1958, Eisenhower, *PPP*, pp. 704–5; "Adams Completes White House Task," *New York Times*, Oct. 26, 1958; Felix Belair, Jr., "Persons Is Sworn for Adams Post," *New York Times*, Oct. 8, 1958; Morrow, *Forty Years a Guinea Pig*, p. 193. Adams had been forced to resign due to a scandal over gifts that he had received from industrialist Bernard Goldfine, including a vicuna coat.

44. DDE to Rolston (released to the press), Sept. 24, 1958, OSAPPM, B 42, Civil Rights—School Desegregation (1), EL; Anthony Lewis, "President Calls School Closings a Peril to Youth," *New York Times*, Sept. 26, 1958.

45. Rogers to DDE, Sept. 25, 1958, Administration, B 31, William P. Rogers, 1958 (1), EL; Memorandum of Law, Sept. 25, 1958, Rogers Papers, B 54, School (1), EL.

46. Bill Becker, "Judge Won't Stop Lease of Schools," *New York Times*, Sept. 26, 1958.

47. "N.A.A.C.P. Appeal Is Expected Next," *New York Times*, Sept. 26, 1958; Supreme Court Opinion, Sept. 29, 1958, *Cooper v. Aaron*, 358 U.S. 1, 3 L.ed. 2d 5, 78 S. CT. 1401 (1958); Peltason, *58 Lonely Men*, p. 199; White southerners' response to the Little Rock intervention and its aftermath is described in Jason Sokol, *There Goes My Everything: White Southerners in the Age of Civil Rights, 1945–1975* (New York: Knopf, 2006), pp. 116–24.

48. Rogers to DDE, Sept. 29, 1958, Administration, B 3, William P. Rogers 1958 (1), EL; Full Decision in Rogers Papers, B 54, School (3), EL.

49. Eisenhower, *Mandate for Change*, p. 230; Kahn, "Shattering the Myth," p. 54; Rogers to DDE, Oct. 7, 1958, CF/OF 100-A, B 371, Supreme Court (2), EL; Henry J. Abraham, *Justices, Presidents, and Senators* (Lanham, Md.: Rowan & Littlefield, 1999), pp. 204–06.

50. Statement by the President, Oct. 1, 1958, CF/OF 142-A-5, B 732, Little Rock (4), EL; also in Eisenhower, *PPP*, p. 722.

51. McGill to Hagerty, Sept. 16, 1958, CF/OF 142-A-5, B 732, Little Rock (4), EL; DDE to McGill, Oct. 3, 1958, *DDEP*, vol. 19, p. 1134.

52. Layhmond Robinson, "Survey Shows Negro Voter Displeased by Both Parties," *New York Times*, Oct. 17, 1958.

53. Radio and Newsreel Panel Discussion, Oct. 22, 1958, both in Eisenhower, *PPP*, pp. 781–82; Allen Drury, "Truman Declares G.O.P. Leads Nation Into Depression," *New York Times*, Feb. 23, 1958; "Truman Is Called Reckless by G.O.P.," *New York Times*, Oct. 26, 1958.

54. James Reston, "Democrats Gain 13 Senate Seats," *New York Times*, Nov. 6, 1958, p. 1; *Gallup Poll*, Nov. 3, 1958, "Congressional Election, Final Poll," vol. 2, p. 1577. The 283 to 153 total (plus one independent) added up to 437 House seats temporarily, due to the admission of Hawaii and Alaska to the Union. It returned to 435 when reappointment was completed after 1960.

55. Legislative Leaders Meeting, Aug. 6, 1957, WHOSS, B 4, EL.

CHAPTER ELEVEN: THE FINAL ACT

1. Anthony Lewis, "Election Brightens Prospects for Civil Rights Action," *New York Times*, Nov. 9, 1958.

2. News Conference, Dec. 10, 1958, Eisenhower, *PPP*, pp. 854–60; Anthony Lewis, "President Scores Alabama Secrecy on Voting Rolls," *New York Times*, Dec. 11, 1958; Legislative Leadership Meeting, Dec. 15, 1958, Michal R. Belknap, ed., *Civil Rights, the White House, and the Justice Department, 1945–1968* (New York: Garland, 1991) vol. 12, p. 348; DDE to Philip Young, Jan. 7, 1959, *DDEP*, vol. 19, p. 1282.

3. State of the Union Address, Jan. 9, 1959, Eisenhower, *PPP*, pp. 17–18.

4. Remarks at the National Press Club, Jan. 14, 1959, Eisenhower, *PPP*, pp. 22–23.

5. "President's Course," *New York Times*, Jan. 25, 1959; Anthony Lewis, "President Urges Civil Rights Code to Halt Violence," *New York Times*, Feb. 6, 1959; Allen Drury, "Johnson Presses His Bill on Rights," *New York Times*, Feb. 9, 1959.

6. Draft Civil Rights Legislative Proposals, Jan. 28, 1959, Persons Papers, B 1, 1955–60, Civil Rights 1958–60, EL.

7. ACW Diary, Feb. 2, 1959, B 10, February 1959 (2), EL.

8. Legislative Leaders Meeting, Feb. 3, 1959, Belknap, ed., *Civil Rights*, vol. 12, pp. 350–56; Anthony Lewis, "President Gives Civil Rights Plan," *New York Times*, Feb. 4, 1959.

9. ACW Diary, Feb. 3, 1959 (but includes notes on LBJ-DDE Meeting on Feb. 4), B 10, February 1959 (2), EL; Dulles Papers, Phone Calls, John Foster Dulles Phone Call to Anderson, J. William Fulbright to Dulles, both Feb. 3, 1959, Dulles Papers, B 9, Telephone Series, EL.

10. Message from the President of the United States, McPhee Papers, Civil Rights, Feb. 5, 1959, B 3, Civil Rights—Legislation for 1959, EL; also in Eisenhower, *PPP*, 1959, pp. 164–67.

11. Lewis, "President Urges Civil Rights Code."

12. "A Compromise on Civil Rights?" *New York Times*, Feb. 6, 1959.

13. McGill to DDE, Feb. 23, 1959, DDE to McGill, Feb. 26, 1959, Name Series, B 23, Ralph McGill, EL.

14. Roy Wilkins, *Standing Fast: The Autobiography of Roy Wilkins* (1982; rept. New York: Da Capo, 1994), pp. 264–65, News Conference, May 5, 1959, Eisenhower, *PPP*, p. 364; Morgan to Herman C. Gray, Morgan Papers, B 43, Chronological, May 1, 1959, to May 29, 1959, EL.

15. Anthony Lewis, "Rogers Assails Mississippi Role in Lynching Case," *New York Times,* Nov. 18, 1959; Senator Sam J. Ervin to Rogers, Nov. 20 and Dec. 9, 1959, Rogers to Ervin, Dec. 1, 1959, Rogers Papers, B 4, Eme–Eze (misc.), EL.

16. Anthony Lewis, "U.S. Jury to Sift Parker Lynching," *New York Times,* Nov. 6, 1959; Claude Sitton, "U.S. Jury to Study Negro's Lynching," *New York Times,* Jan. 4, 1960; DDE to John D. Dingell, Jan. 7, 1960, Belknap, ed., *Civil Rights,* vol. 10, p. 94; Claude Sitton, "U.S. Jury Refuses Lynch Indictment," *New York Times,* Jan. 15, 1960; "Lynch Inaction Decried," *New York Times,* Jan. 27, 1960.

17. News Conference, May 13, 1959, Eisenhower, *PPP*, p. 388.

18. News Release, Jan. 20, 1959, OSAPPM, B 42, Civil Rights—Civil Rights Commission (2), EL; President's Remarks at the National Conference on Civil Rights, June 9, 1959, Eisenhower, *PPP*, pp. 447–49; "Civil Rights Aides Hear Eisenhower," *New York Times,* June 10, 1959.

19. News Conference, July 8, 1959, Eisenhower, *PPP*, p. 509; Joseph A. Loftus, "President Condemns Public Segregation," *New York Times,* July 9, 1959.

20. Hubert H. Humphrey, "Civil Rights: A Moral Issue," Remarks for 50th Anniversary Convention of the NAACP, July 15, 1959, HHH Papers, B 420, MHS; Farnsworth Fowle, "Humphrey Backs N.A.A.C.P. Anew," *New York Times,* July 16, 1959.

21. News Conference, July 22, 1959, Eisenhower, *PPP*, pp. 538–39.

22. Legislative Leaders Meetings, July 28, 1959 and Aug. 11, 1959, Belknap, ed., *Civil Rights,* vol. 12, pp. 379, 384.

23. "Senators Shift Rights Strategy," *New York Times,* Aug. 15, 1959; "Rights Deadlock Broken in Senate," *New York Times,* Aug. 18, 1959.

24. Commission on Civil Rights Report, Sept. 8, 1959, White House Office, Cabinet Secretariat Records, 1953–1960, B 2, EL; Anthony Lewis, "Senate Unit Asks 2-Year Extension for Rights Panel," *New York Times,* Sept. 9, 1959.

25. John D. Morris, "Congress Ending with Eisenhower in Firm Control," *New York Times,* Sept. 14, 1959.

26. Minutes of Cabinet Meeting, Nov. 6, 1959, Cabinet Series, B 14 (1), EL; News Conference, Dec. 2, 1959, Eisenhower, *PPP*, p. 793.

27. "Civil-Rights Action Is Seen by Dirksen," *New York Times,* Dec. 1, 1959; Anthony Lewis, "Eisenhower Wary on Plan to Widen Civil Rights Law," *New York Times,* Jan. 3, 1960.

28. State of the Union Address, Jan. 7, 1960, Eisenhower, *PPP*, pp. 14, 17.

29. Press Release, Sept. 8, 1959, Commission on Civil Rights, Cabinet Secretariat, Records 1953–60, B 2, EL; Lewis, "Senate Unit Asks 2-Year Extension."

30. DDE Diary, Jan. 20, 1960, B 47, Staff Notes—January 1960 (1), EL.

31. McCabe to Whitman, Jan. 20, 1960, DDE Diary, B 47, Staff Notes—January 1960 (1), EL; Anthony Lewis, "Civil-Rights Bill Pushed In Senate," *New York Times,* Jan. 25, 1960; News Conference, Jan. 26, 1960, Eisenhower, *PPP*, pp. 125–26.

32. Legislative Leaders Meeting, Feb. 2, 1960, LL, B 3, 1960 January–February (1), EL.

33. Roscoe Drummond, "Rogers' Negro Vote Plan Called Aid to Rights Bill," *New York Herald Tribune,* Jan. 28, 1960, Arthur Krock, "In the Nation: The Law and Politics of Rogers' Plan," *New York Times,* Jan. 28, 1960, both in Administration Series, B 32, William Rogers 1960–61 (2), EL; "New Move on Civil Rights," *New York Times,* Jan. 28, 1960.

34. Legislative Leaders Meeting, Feb. 2, 1960, LL, B 3, 1960, January–February (1), EL.

35. J. A. O'Leary, "Dirksen to Introduce Rights Bill in Senate," Morrow Files, B 9, article in Civil Rights Clippings and Data, EL; Legislative Leaders Meetings, Feb. 9 and 16, 1960, LL, B 3, Feb. 1960, EL.

36. Memorandum by E. Frederic Morrow, March 7, 1960, CF/OF 142-A-4. B 731, EL.

37. News Conference, March 16, 1960, Eisenhower, *PPP,* pp. 294–96, 301–2. "Dr. King Sees Gain By Negro Sit-Ins," *New York Times,* April 18, 1960.

38. Hollings to DDE, March 17, 1960, Memorandum for the Record by Robert Merriam, March 21, 1960, Leander H. Perez to David W. Kendall, March 31, 1960, all in CF/GF 124-A-1, B 914, 1960 (3), EL; Brigadier General Benjamin F. Caffey to DDE, March 21, 1960, CF/OF 142-A-4, B 731, Segregation–Integration (5), EL.

39. King to DDE, March 17, 1960, Morgan to King, March 17, 1960, both in CF/GF 124-A-1, B 913, 1960 (1), EL; News Conference, March 30, 1960, Eisenhower, *PPP,* p. 320.

40. Russell Baker, "Johnson Assures Civil Rights Test," *New York Times,* February 16, 1960; Russell Baker, "24-Hour Sessions," *New York Times,* March 1, 1960.

41. Anthony Lewis, "Desegregation and Negro Voting Move Slowly and Search Continues for New Federal Sanctions," *New York Times,* March 6, 1960.

42. Russell Baker, "Senate Recesses, Filibuster Is Off Until Tomorrow," *New York Times,* March 6, 1960; Russell Baker, "Senate Calls Off 24-Hour Sessions in Move for Vote," *New York Times,* March 9, 1960.

43. Legislative Leaders Meeting, March 8, 1960, Belknap, ed., *Civil Rights,* vol. 12, pp. 430–31.

44. Legislative Leaders Meetings, March 15 and March 22, 1960, LL, B 3, March-April (2), EL.

45. Russell Baker, "House Approves Voting Referees Asked by Rogers," *New York Times,* March 23, 1960; Russell Baker, "Civil Rights Bill Passed by House; Gains in Senate," *New York Times,* March 25, 1960; Russell Baker, "Senate Rejects A Referee Curb," *New York Times,* April 2, 1960.

46. Legislative Meeting, April 5, 1960, LL Series, B 3, 1960, March–April (2), EL; Anthony Lewis, "Senate Seeking Vote This Week for Rights Bill," *New York Times,* April 4, 1960; Russell Baker, "President Called 'Happy' Over Civil Rights Measure," *New York Times,* April 6, 1960.

47. "Senate Roll-Call Vote on the Civil Rights Bill," *New York Times,* April 9, 1960; Russell Baker, "Johnson Praised," *New York Times,* April 9, 1960; Anthony Lewis, "Long Fight Ends," *New York Times,* April 22, 1960; Wilkins, *Standing Fast,* p. 269. Arthur Caldwell's detailed legislative history of the Civil Rights Act of 1960 is found in Belknap, ed., *Civil Rights,* vol. 16, pp. 360–430.

48. Phillip S. Hughes to DDE, April 28, 1960, Records of the White House Office, B 165, May 13, 1960–May 14, 1960, Reports to the President on Pend-

ing Legislation, EL; "Text of Civil Rights Bill Approved by Congress and Sent to President Eisenhower," *New York Times*, April 22, 1960; Baker, "House Approves Voting Referees."

49. Press Release by the Department of Justice, April 21, 1960, attached to pending legislation report, Hughes to DDE, April 28, Records of the White House Office, B 165, May 13, 1960–May 14, 1960, EL.

50. Legislative Leaders Meeting, April 26, 1960, LL Series, B 3, 1960 March–April (2), EL; DDE to Hagerty, April 26, 1960, *DDEP*, vol. 20, p. 1924; News Conference, April 27, 1960, Eisenhower, *PPP*, pp. 360–70.

51. DDE to Lyndon Johnson, May 10, 1960, *DDEP*, vol. 20, p. 1943; Osgood Caruthers, "Premier Is Bitter," *New York Times*, May 6, 1960; Drew Middleton, "Harsh Exchange," *New York Times*, May 17, 1960.

52. Statement by the President Upon Signing the Civil Rights Act of 1960, May 6, 1960, Eisenhower, *PPP*, p. 398; "Eisenhower Signs Civil Rights Bill," *New York Times*, May 7, 1960; Special Staff Note from the Justice Department, May 9, 1960, DDE Diary, B 49, Toner Notes, May 1960, EL.

53. William M. Blair, "Strongest Plank on Rights Voted Over Threat of Fight," *New York Times*, July 12, 1960; W. H. Lawrence, "Pact Opens Way for Party Amity," *New York Times*, July 24, 1960; Felix Belair, Jr., "President Shuns Goldwater View," *New York Times*, July 25, 1960; William M. Blair, "Leaders Reject Plank on Rights," *New York Times*, July 26, 1960.

54. "Texts of Republican Planks on Civil Rights, Defense and Education and Conclusion to the Platform," *New York Times*, July 27, 1960; Eisenhower's Address at the Republican National Convention in Chicago, July 26, 1960, Eisenhower, *PPP*, p. 593.

55. Felix Belair, Jr., "Plea to Congress," *New York Times*, Aug. 9, 1960; Legislative Leaders Meeting, Aug. 16, 1960, LL, B 3, 1960 (4), EL; "Kennedy Assails G.O.P. on Message," *New York Times*, Aug. 9, 1960.

56. News Conference, Aug. 10, 1960, Eisenhower, *PPP*, pp. 622, 627; James Reston, "Eisenhower Bids Democrats Act or Accept Blame," *New York Times*, Aug. 11, 1960.

57. Peter Braestrup, "Nixon, Johnson Clash on Rights," *New York Times*, Aug. 11, 1960.

58. Legislative Leaders Meeting, Aug. 16, 1960, LL, B 3, 1960 (4), EL.

59. "U.S. and Louisiana Clash on Schools," *New York Times*, Aug. 14, 1960; "Governor Takes Control of New Orleans Schools," *New York Times*, Aug. 21, 1960; Foster Hailey, "3 Judges Forbid Louisiana to Bar Pupil Integration," *New York Times*, Aug. 28, 1960; Foster Hailey, "School Stay Won By New Orleans," *New York Times*, Aug. 31, 1960; "Pleas for Integration Stay Denied by Supreme Court," *New York Times*, Sept. 2, 1960; Jack Bass, *Unlikely Heroes* (New York: Simon & Schuster, 1981), pp. 114–16, 126–29.

60. Claude Sitton, "Louisiana Calls School Holiday in Racial Dispute," *New York Times*, Nov. 13, 1960; "President Given Reports," *New York Times*, Nov. 15, 1960; Claude Sitton, "U.S. Court Bars Louisiana's Move to Seize Schools," *New York Times*, Nov. 14, 1960; Claude Sitton, "2 White Schools in New Orleans Are Integrated," *New York Times*, Nov. 15, 1960.

61. Anthony Lewis, "New Yorker Gets Civil Rights Post," *New York Times*, Jan. 26, 1960.

62. Interview by Author with Harold Tyler, June 4, 2004. Lawrence Walsh, who was deputy attorney general at the time, does not recall ever knowing about this

call from the president. Attorney General William Rogers had been deeply involved with the Nixon campaign, so he was not overseeing the situation in New Orleans; Jason Sokol, *There Goes My Everything: White Southerners in the Age of Civil Rights, 1945–1975* (New York: Knopf, 2006), pp. 124–48.

63. Sitton, "2 White Schools in New Orleans Are Integrated"; Claude Sitton, "2,000 Youths Riot in New Orleans," *New York Times,* Nov. 17, 1960; "New Orleans Is Calm," *New York Times,* Nov. 21, 1960; "New Orleans Reopening," *New York Times,* Nov. 27, 1960.

64. *Gallup Polls,* "President Eisenhower's Popularity," Nov. 16, 1960, and "Most Admired Man," Dec. 25, 1960. George H. Gallup, *The Gallup Poll: Public Opinion 1935–1971* (New York: Random House, 1972), vol. 3, pp. 1690, 1696.

65. "The Nation," *New York Times,* Oct. 30, 1960; suggested statement for the White House by Deputy Attorney General Lawrence Walsh, Oct. 31, 1960, CF/OF 142-A-4, B 731, EL; Taylor Branch, *Parting the Waters: America in the King Years, 1954–63* (New York: Simon & Schuster, 1988), pp. 363–76. Irwin F. Gellman, author of *The Contender: Richard Nixon: The Congress Years, 1946–1952* (New York: Free Press, 1999), the first volume of a multivolume biography of Richard Nixon, says his research indicates that the impact of the King incident on the outcome of the election was exaggerated in the years after 1960.

66. DDE Diary, Memo dated Dec. 28, 1960, B 55, EL.

CHAPTER TWELVE: LEADING FROM GETTYSBURG

1. Eisenhower Interview by Bruce Catton, NBC Television, Feb. 11, 1963, Post-Pres. Papers, Signature File 1962–63, B 22, Public Relations, Appointments, Engagements, and Interviews (PR-3, L, M), EL.

2. Statement, Dec. 21, 1959, Eisenhower, *PPP,* pp. 864–65; Proclamation, Dec. 7, 1960, Eisenhower, *PPP,* pp. 873–74.

3. Morrow, *Forty Years a Guinea Pig,* pp. 214–17; Felix Belair, Jr., "President's Aide Faces Race Bars," *New York Times,* Dec. 23, 1960. An example of Eisenhower's efforts on Morrow's behalf is found in Frank Stanton (CBS) to DDE, Nov. 18, 1960, CF/OF 72 A-2, B 288, Morrow, EL.

4. Rogers to DDE, Jan. 10, 1961, DDE to Rogers, Jan. 11, 1961, Administration, B 32, Rogers, 1960–61 (1), EL.

5. State of the Union Address, Jan. 12, 1961, Eisenhower, *PPP,* pp. 926–27.

6. "Dr. King Denounces President on Civil Rights," *New York Times,* June 10, 1963; Michael Beschloss, *Presidential Courage: Brave Leaders and How They Changed America, 1789–1989* (New York: Simon & Schuster, 2007), pp. 259–68.

7. Rogers to Eastland, Dirksen, Sept. 11, 1959, CF/GF 4, Endorsements, Judicial Branch (The Federal Judiciary), EL.

8. Anthony Lewis, "Kennedy Pledges Able U.S. Judges," *New York Times,* May 20, 1961.

9. Branch, *Parting the Waters,* p. 700; Nick Bryant, *The Bystander: John F. Kennedy and the Struggle for Black Equality* (New York: Basic, 2006), pp. 286–88.

10. Bryant, *The Bystander,* pp. 331–56; Beschloss, *Presidential Courage,* pp. 250–57; DDE Interview, July 20, 1967, OH-11, pp. 82–83, EL.

11. Eisenhower, *The White House Years: Mandate for Change, 1953–56* (New York: Doubleday, 1963), p. 236.

12. Kennedy to DDE, June 10, 1963, DDE to Kennedy, June 14, 1963, B 2, Augusta—Walter Reed (2), EL; DDE to Dirksen, June 14, 1963, Post-Pres. Papers, Principal File 1965, B 26, EL.

13. "The Eisenhower Manifesto," *New York Times*, May 25, 1964; Earl Mazo, "Statement by the General Appears to Fit All in the Race but Goldwater," *New York Times*, May 25, 1964; Cronkite, *Dimension* broadcast transcript, and drafts of the article, May 25, 1964, in Post-Pres. Papers, Principal File 1964, B 22 (ST-2 Statement), EL.

14. Tom Wicker, "Convention Ends: Extremism in Defense of Liberty 'No Vice,' Arizonan Asserts," *New York Times*, July 17, 1964.

15. Phone calls on July 29, Aug. 3–4, Post-Pres. Papers, Appointment Book Series, B 2, Calls and Appointments 1964 (5), EL.

16. Charles Mohr, "Goldwater Bars Klan Aid; Confers with Eisenhower," *New York Times*, Aug. 7, 1964.

17. Eisenhower Statement, Aug. 11 (released Aug. 12), 1964, Republican National Committee Release, Goldwater Remarks, Aug. 12, 1964, Post-Pres. Papers, Principal File 1964, St-1-2, Statement—Goldwater and Statement—Goldwater Remarks, EL; Charles Mohr, "Goldwater, in a Unity Bid, Rejects Extremists' Aid; Eisenhower Is 'Satisfied,'" *New York Times*, Aug. 13, 1964.

18. "Eisenhower on TV with Goldwater," *New York Times*, Sept. 23, 1964.

19. "Republicans Seek a United Front," *New York Times*, Sept. 5, 1965.

20. Interview with DDE, July 13, 1967, Herbert Hoover Oral History Program, OH-106, EL.

21. Max Frankel, "Elector Vote 287," *New York Times*, Nov. 7, 1968.

22. Anthony Lewis, "Warren Firm on Retiring: Leaves Date Up to Nixon," *New York Times*, Nov. 15, 1968.

23. Brownell Interview, OH-282, pp. 11–12, 29, EL; Herbert Brownell, *Advising Ike: The Memoirs of Attorney General Herbert Brownell* (Lawrence: University Press of Kansas, 1993), p. 98; DDE Diary, May 14, 1953, B 9, DDE Personal 1953-54 (2).

24. DDE to Nixon, Dec. 13, 1968, Post-Pres. Papers, Special Names, B 14, Nixon, Richard M. 1968 (2), EL.

25. E. W. Kenworthy, "Burger Nomination Is Lauded by Conservative Members of Senate Judiciary Panel," *New York Times*, May 22, 1969.

CONCLUSION: A MATTER OF JUSTICE

1. In a response to questions by *Ebony* magazine, Dec. 12, 1963, Eisenhower accused the Democrats of "over-promising, under-performing, impracticable solutions, creating disappointment and disillusionment for the Negro race"; Post-Pres. Papers, Principal File 1964, B 26 (Bo-2), p. 6, EL.

2. Truman insisted in a December 1952 news conference that "if I thought I had the power" to desegregate the district, "it would have been done a long time ago"; News Conference, Dec. 18, 1952, Truman, *PPP*, p. 1090.

3. James Hagerty explains Eisenhower's strategy in his interview, OH-91, part 4, p. 438, EL.

4. The quotation at the beginning of this chapter is from Raymond Henle's interview with Eisenhower, July 13, 1967, Hoover Project, OH-106, EL.

5.   Anthony Lewis, "President Urges Civil Rights Code to Halt Violence," *New York Times,* Feb. 6, 1959.

6.   Warren, *The Memoirs of Earl Warren* (Garden City, N.Y.: Doubleday, 1977), p. 291; News Conference, May 19, 1954, Eisenhower, *PPP,* pp. 491–92.

7.   HHH to Eileen Handlik, May 28, 1957, Humphrey Papers, B 136, MHS; Meena Bose and Fred I. Greenstein provide a cogent analysis of Eisenhower's private and public rhetoric on national security issues in "The Hidden Hand vs. the Bully Pulpit: The Layered Political Rhetoric of President Eisenhower," in Leroy G. Dorsey, ed., *The Presidency and Rhetorical Leadership* (College Station: Texas A & M Press, 2002), pp. 184–99.

8.   Warren, *Memoirs,* pp. 291–92.

9.   Eisenhower expressed this ambivalence in a letter to his son John, March 28, 1963, Post-Pres. Papers, Secretary's File, Box 10, EL.

10. Ambrose, *Eisenhower: Soldier and President* (New York: Simon & Schuster, 1990), p. 367; News Conference, Oct. 3, 1957, Eisenhower, *PPP,* pp. 704–10.

11. Herman E. Talmadge, *Talmadge: A Political Legacy, A Politician's Life* (Atlanta: Peachtree, 1987), p. 187; Numan V. Bartley, *The Rise of Massive Resistance: Race and Politics in the South During the 1950's* (Baton Rouge: Louisiana State University Press, 1969), pp. 268–92; Geoffrey Perret, *Eisenhower* (Holbrook, Mass.: Adams Media, 1999), pp. 550–53.

12. The term "massive resistance" was widely used and associated with the Southern Manifesto in 1956; Bartley, *The Rise of Massive Resistance,* pp. 116–17.

13. Faubus OH-181, p. 47, EL; DDE to Brownell, Sept. 20, 1957, and DDE to Brownell, Sept. 24, 1957, DDE Diary, B 27, Sept. 1957 Phone Calls, EL.

14. Address at Madison Square Garden, Oct. 25, 1956, Eisenhower, *PPP,* p. 1022.

Acknowledgments

It is impossible to mention all the people who contribute, in one way or another, to a book like this. I stand on the shoulders of scholars who have gone before me, most of whom I have never met. I will confine my acknowledgments to those who most actively and repeatedly assisted my research and writing efforts.

Fred I. Greenstein, of Princeton University, whose scholarship paved the way for my reinterpretation of Eisenhower and civil rights, connected me with other scholars and repeatedly encouraged me to "push on." Irwin F. Gellman validated my conclusions with his own research, improved my writing, caught my mistakes, and provided wise counsel. The Eisenhower Presidential Library staff, particularly Director Dan Holt, encouraged the project at every juncture, and Archivist David Haight's encyclopedic knowledge and uncanny ability to find obscure documents made all the difference. Ann Brownell Sloane of Sloane & Hinshaw in New York City encouraged me, read manuscript drafts, and provided knowledge of her father, Attorney General Herbert Brownell, that was crucial in understanding his role. Daun van Ee at the Library of Congress, also editor of the published Eisenhower papers, always found time to answer obscure questions and provide provocative interpretations. William T. Coleman, Jr., of Washington, D.C., a member of President Gerald Ford's cabinet and a civil rights leader who worked with Thurgood Marshall on *Brown*, was enthusiastic about the project and he convinced me that correcting the Eisenhower record was an honorable pursuit. Roger Labrie of Simon & Schuster provided skillful and thoughtful editing that made this a better book. Will Lippincott of Lippincott Massie McQuilkin recognized the project's potential and convinced a publisher to embrace it. General Carl W. Reddel, executive director of the Eisenhower Memorial Commission, provided important support and assistance. Michael S. Mayer at the University of Montana wrote insightful articles on Eisenhower and civil rights that pointed the way. The staffs and resources at the University of Arkansas libraries, the Library of Congress, the Minnesota Historical Society, and the Princeton University, Drew University, and Wichita State University libraries were helpful. I especially thank the staff at Memorial Library at Southwestern College in Kansas, my alma mater and where I served as academic dean, for granting me special access to library holdings and interlibrary loan services that were essential to completing a complex project in rural Kansas. And thanks to all my friends, family, and colleagues who have supported my work, even when I have neglected them.

Index

ABOUT THE AUTHOR

David A. Nichols is the leading authority on Eisenhower and civil rights. His previous book, *Lincoln and the Indians: Civil War Policy and Politics,* is the definitive study of Abraham Lincoln's leadership in Indian affairs. He is a veteran of thirty-five years in higher education as a professor and administrator, including eleven years as an academic dean at Southwestern College in Kansas. Nichols lives in Winfield, Kansas.